BOLLINGEN SERIES XCVIII

D1572242

Louis Massignon

THE PASSION OF AL-HALLAJ

MYSTIC AND MARTYR OF ISLAM

ABRIDGED EDITION

Translated and edited by
Herbert Mason

BOLLINGEN SERIES XCVIII

PRINCETON UNIVERSITY PRESS   PRINCETON, NEW JERSEY

Published by Princeton University Press, 41 William Street,
Princeton, New Jersey   08540
In the United Kingdom: Princeton University Press, Chichester, West Sussex
Copyright © 1982 by Princeton University Press; abridgment, with a new
foreword by Herbert Mason, © 1994 by Princeton University Press
All Rights Reserved

Library of Congress Cataloging-in-Publication Data
Massignon, Louis, 1883–1962.
    [Passion de Husayn Ibn Mansûr Hallâj. English]
    The passion of Al-Hallaj: mystic and martyr of Islam / Louis
Massignon.—Abridged ed. / translated and edited by Herbert Mason.
       p. cm.—(Bollingen series; 98)
    Abridgment of the English translation, © 1982.
    Includes bibliographical references.
    ISBN 0–691–01919–3 (pbk.: alk. paper)
    1. Hallāj, al-Husayn ibn Mansūr, 858 or 9–922.   2. Sufis—
Biography.   I. Mason, Herbert, 1932–   II. Title.   III. Series.
BP80.H27M3713   1994
297′.4′092—dc20
[B]   93-11410

This edition is an abridgment of the four-volume translation of *La Passion
de Husayn Ibn Mansūr Hallāj; martyr mystique de l'Islam exécuté à
Baghdad le mars 26 922; étude d'histoire religieuse (nouvelle édition),* by
Louis Massignon (Paris: Gallimard, 1973), the English-language translation
of which appeared as the ninety-eighth volume in a series of works
sponsored by Bollingen Foundation (Princeton, 1982)

First Princeton Paperback printing of the abridged edition, for the
Mythos Series, 1994

1 3 5 7 9 10 8 6 4 2

Printed in the United States of America

Table of Contents

List of Illustrations

1. Hallāj's itineraries
2. Map of Baghdad in the fourth/tenth century, from a sketch by Louis Massignon
3. Vision of the burning lamp. Sixteenth-century Persian miniature
4. Hallāj on the gibbet. Eighteenth-century Indo-Persian miniature. Ms. Coll. Luzac, London. Photo by Lemare
5. Hallaj led to execution. Sixteenth-century Persian miniature. Ms. Oxford, Ouseley add. 24 f. 34b. Reproduced by permission of the Curators of the Bodleian Library
6. The Intercision of Hallāj according to Bīrūnī. Arabo-Persian miniature, dated 707/1307. Ms. Edinburgh. University Library no. 161 f. 113a, communicated by Sir T. W. Arnold
7. The intercision of Hallāj according to Bīrūnī. Seventeenth-century Persian miniature. Ms. Paris, Bibliothèque Nationale, Arabic collection 1489 f. 113a
8. Lapidation of Hallāj. Ms. Indian Office 1318, f. 40b (Ethé).
9. Hallāj on the gibbet. Ms. Bibliothèque Nationale Paris, Pers. Suppl. 1559, f. 53. Reproduced by permission
10. Burning of the body of Hallāj before Caliph Muqtadir and his retinue. Ms. Chester Beatty 60 f. 3
11. "Tomb" of Hallāj in Karkh (1957). Photo by Frère Robert de la Vierge
12. Interior of the "tomb" of Hallāj in Karkh. Sketch by Dr. Suhayl Unver

HALLAJ was indeed a historical person, condemned to death in 922 of our era following a political trial, a *cause célèbre*, of which there survive fragments of hostile accounts that are, by the very fact of their hostility, testaments of his historical authenticity. He has survived also as a hero of legend. Even now in Islamic countries people remember him and represent him as an itinerant worker of miracles, sometimes as a man madly in love with God, sometimes as a charlatan. In Iran, Turkey and Pakistan, where the wide diffusion of great Persian poems took place, poetry has stylized the character of this saint, the deified ecstatic, whom they call "Mansur Hallaj". It was he who, from the height of the gibbet, uttered the apocalyptic cry that announces the Judge of the Last Judgment: *Ana'l-Haqq*, I am the Truth.

So writes Louis Massignon in the preface to the 1922 edition of his magisterial study *The Passion of al-Hallaj.*

Critical study of the authentic sources of this more poetic than literary theme has enabled me to establish that Hallaj had actually found his vocation as the "mystic pillar," the "spiritual martyr" of Islam, while going on the hajj; that he had subsequently wished to "substitute" himself for the legal offering of victims that is consecrated at ʿArafat for the annual general pardon of the community; that afterwards he had publicly proclaimed in Baghdad his vow to seek death in the holy war of divine love—thirteen years, at least, prior to his execution.

This study, undertaken in Cairo in 1907, on the verge of my apprenticeship in spoken and written Arabic, and stimulated by exposure to poignant and wise maxims . . . ended up by convincing me of the veracity of this pure witness, who was strangely a friend of God unto the very sacrifice of himself, Khalil Allah, like Abraham.

So begins the author's preface to the new edition of his *Passion*, published posthumously in its greatly enlarged form in 1975, and translated in its Bollingen Series English edition of 1983. The present volume is an abridgement of volume 1 (*The Life of al-Hallaj*) with inclusions from volume 3 (*The Teaching of al-Hallaj*). This abridgement, stripped of its thorough and at times awesome scholarly apparatus (its transliteration diacritical marks, its footnotes, and exhaustive bibliography), is intended simply to render more accessible to the nonspecialist reader the dramatic life and radical thought of this extraordinary tenth-century Muslim mystic. It is not intended to replace the four-volume text, but rather to point the interested reader back to the larger, fully documented work of its author. Massignon himself foresaw the possibility and indeed need of an eventual abridgement designed for this purpose, and considered especially chapters five (The Indictments), six (The Trials), and seven (The Martyr-dom) to be "the heart and center" of his study. Though large sections of volume 2 (*The Survival of al-Hallaj*), representing his legacy up to the present day in Islamic literature and mystical tradition, are regarded by many scholars of Islam as "original and fundamental" for understanding the thought of Hallaj and of the many Muslim theological schools and sects and their internal corre-spondences with Judaic and Christian traditions, publishing aims and limits re-quired severe cutting and concentration on the primary drama of his life. To this end virtually the whole of volumes 2, 3, and 4 (*Bibliography, Technical Terms, and Index*) was omitted, along with the other aforementioned apparatus materials, all statistical lists and tables, and wherever possible the author's lengthy authentications of primary and corroborative texts that are essential to the larger presentation.

Also absent from this abridgement is an extended biographical introduction to Massignon himself, which appears as part of the translator's foreword to volume 1. Massignon himself would not have objected to this omission in def-erence to concentration solely on Hallaj.

By focusing for the general reader on Hallaj's life and times, and especially on Baghdad the site of his martyrdom and a city then of great prominence on the world stage, there may be temptations to draw parallels with the contempo-rary history of this great surviving city. Above both dramatic epochs, however, soars the figure of Hallaj himself, whose outcry for justice arose from his love of his God as the Eternal Truth. It is a piercing story that Massignon worked throughout his life to make known to the world-at-large.

While the reader is urged to examine firsthand the four-volume work itself, in-cluding the extensive bibliographical listing of Islamic sources and both Muslim and non-Muslim studies of the sources not possible to include here, brief mention should be made of selected contemporary studies available in English of particular relevance to Islamic mysticism, Hallaj, and Louis Massignon:

William Chittick, *The Sufi Path of Love*. Albany, 1983.
Benjamin Clark, ed. and tr. of Louis Massignon's *Essay on the Technical Lan-guage of Muslim Mysticism*. Notre Dame, 1994.
Carl Ernst, *Words of Ecstasy in Sufism*. Albany, 1985.
Martin Lings, *What is Sufism?* London, 1983.
H. Mason, *The Death of al-Hallaj*. Notre Dame, 1979.
H. Mason, *Memoir of a Friend: Louis Massignon*. Notre Dame, 1988.
H. Mason, *Testimonies and Reflections: Essays of Louis Massignon*. Notre Dame, 1990.
Annemarie Schimmel, *As Through a Veil: Mystical Poetry in Islam*. New York, 1982.
Annemarie Schimmel, *Mystical Dimensions of Islam*. Chapel Hill, 1975.
Annemarie Schimmel, *The Triumphal Sun*. London & The Hague, 1980.

K. I. Semaan, *Murder in Baghdad,* a translation of the Egyptian poet Salah ʿAbd al-Sabbur's 1965 play *Maʿsat al-Hallaj.* Leiden, 1972.

For general works of introduction to Islam the following are a few of the many possible suggestions:

John Esposito, *Islam the Straight Path.* Oxford, 1991.
Fazlur Rahman, *Islam.* Chicago, 1979.
Malise Ruthven, *Islam and the World.* Oxford, 1984.
and the older but still valuable *Mohammedanism* by H. A. R. Gibb (Penguin Classics), and, among the many penetrating studies of S. N. Nasr, *Ideals and Realities of Islam.* Boston, 1966.

Herbert Mason

*Preface**

HALLAJ was indeed a historical person, condemned to death in Baghdad in 922 of our era following a political trial, a *cause célèbre* of which there survive fragments of hostile accounts that are, by the very fact of their hostility, not without importance. He has survived also as a hero of legend. Even now in Arab countries people remember him and represent him as an itinerant worker of miracles, sometimes as a man madly in love with God, sometimes as a charlatan. In other Muslim countries the wide diffusion of great Persian poems has stylized magnificently the character of the saint, the deified ecstatic, whom they call "Mansur Hallaj." It was he who, from the height of the gibbet, uttered the apocalyptic cry that announces the Judge of the Last Judgment: *Ana'l-Haqq*, "I am the Truth."

Critical study of the authentic sources of this more poetic than literary theme has enabled me to establish that Hallaj had actually found his vocation as the "mystic pillar," the "spiritual martyr" of Islam, while going on the hajj; that he had subsequently wished to "substitute" himself for the legal offering of victims that is consecrated at ʿArafat for the annual general pardon of the community; that after that he had publicly proclaimed in Baghdad his vow to seek death in the holy war of divine love—thirteen years, at least, prior to his execution.

This study, undertaken in Cairo in 1907, on the verge of my apprenticeship in spoken and written Arabic, and stimulated by exposure to poignant and wise Hallajian maxims (such as *rakʿatani fi'l-ʿishq* . . .) ended up by convincing me of the veracity of this pure witness, who was strangely a friend of God unto the very sacrifice of himself, Khalil Allah, like Abraham. This was in May of 1908 between Kut al-ʿAmara and Baghdad. Afterwards, on rare occasions, a few opportunities were given me to stop in the "composition" of the "site" of his meditations and of his prayer, at Jidda, at Bayda, his birthplace, at Jerusalem, at Nishapur, in the great pines of Gazegah in Herat, on the roads of Qashmir, Bamiyan, and Kandahar.

The first edition of my work, completed in 1914, was published in 1922, and has been out of print since 1936. It has been, with regard to both texts and notes, entirely recast in the present edition.

Section I [Volumes 1 and 2] presents the stages of Hallaj's life. It situates their links of time and place in their "singularity": his family and school education, from Bayda (Aramaian clients of Belharith Yemenites) to Wasit and Basra (in the ascetic school of Hasan); his "departure," going over to the

*From *Passion of al-Hallaj,* vol. 1, liv - lxix and 572–73

"worldly classes" (*abna' al-dunya*), becoming initiated in the classicism of the learned scholars, retaining on the stages of his travels the "common touch" with the *abna' al-sabil,* the humble and the poor, as much on the eastern front of the holy war (Turkestan, India) as at the center of Islamic pilgrimage, in Mecca, which he visited three times; the evolution of his apologetical and apostolic compassion into the ultimate desire of dying anathematized for his brothers; his trial; his punishment, in the lofty theater of Baghdad, the capital of the civilized world at that time. Thereafter, the survival of this "excommunicated saint" through thirty Muslim generations by means of "chains of witnesses," *asanid,* furthering his memory as a lifeline of hope, up to this very day.

These "chains" prepare his official reincorporation in the Islamic Community on earth, rediscovering through him, fulfilling with him, in the full sacrificial sense of the atoning *talbiya* of the hajj at ʿArafat, the mystic union beyond the forgiveness and thanksgiving. A slow, difficult work, taking many a century, it is carried out quietly in meditation by solitary spirits and chosen souls, while popular devotion, here and there, persists in associating his name with afflictions of newborn children, children's games, songs of beggars, and predictions about the end of time.

And, since each new link in these "chains" is a victory over death, chance, and oblivion, and a reinforcement of transmitted grace, these "chains" also prepare the way for the final integration of the masses of the Islamic Community in the ecumenicity of the Elect, at the consummation of the Sacrifice of Abraham "*bi-dhibhin ʿazimin*" (Qur'an 37:107).

Section II [Volume 3] places Hallajian mysticism, according to texts, in the general development of Muslim theological thought; it sets forth the points of philosophical interference and metaphysical penetration implied in the notion of "the essential desire."

Hallaj appeared in the suqs of Baghdad, preaching God as the Only Desire and the Only Truth, at the end of the ninth century of our era, an epoch for Islam of the flowering of its "Renaissance," as Adam Mez called it. At the confluence of two cultures, the Aramaic and the Greek, Baghdad, having become the intellectual center of civilization, received within its walls the true masters of Arabic thought: theologians (from Nazzam to Ibn al-Rawandi), philosophers (Jahiz, Tawhidi), poets (Abu Nuwas, Ibn al-Rumi, Mutanabbi), grammarians (Mubarrad, Sirafi), the physician Razi, the astronomer Battani; Chapter IV of Section I inserts Hallaj biographically among them. At this point is presented an analysis of the complex and subtle forms of technical language that Hallaj employed: daring to express himself, which no mystic had had the idea of doing, in the dogmatic vocabulary of his adversaries, the Muʿtazilites. He did so in order to give an account, in a reasoned manner, of the theopathic experience in which his rule of life (derived from the "science of hearts" of Muhasibi) and his vow of asceticism of mind had, by a *via negativa,* engaged him.

We have accordingly followed the procedure, classic at that time, of the five Mu'tazilite bases for the presentation of the Hallajian solutions in which some gaucheries, here and there, bear witness to his "self-taught" sincerity as a mystic. His theology, which is not static but the interiorizing experience of a denudation of images, rather similar to that of Eckhart, leads him to argue rationally and to go beyond the dualist antimony that the mystics had come up against (A is contrary to non-A; *qidam* to *hadath*), by means of a *tertium quid* (a "becoming" in potential: *haqiqa*). I had at first identified this "tri-phased" mode of meditation with the Aristotelian syllogism in three parts (1922 ed. p. XIII), then with the gnostic triad of the extremist Imamites ('Ayn, Mim, Sin; *Akhbar*, No. 46).

Now I see the origin of Hallaj's method going back further, to the very first Arab grammarians of Basra—to Khalil, especially, and to the tripartite principle of the *I'rab*, "morphologizing" vocabulary and syntax by means of the functional triplicity of final vocalic assonances (*a, i, u : nasb, khafd, raf*). The Hallajian method leads to an involution of reason in its object, which is the pure essence, and not the contingent: God, entirely alone. If the pluralism of the discursive statement thus disappears, it is not into a pantheistic "existential monism" (*wahdat al-wujud*), but into a "testimonial monism" (*wahdat al-shuhud*). Hallaj teaches that one must unite with a thing not in us, but in the thing itself (*Stf.*, No. 84); the world, for example, by means of a transfiguring compassion with the suffering of the world. *An 'i ilayka.* "my cry of mourning is for you (= from me, pitying you, at the time when I am going to die)"; in the shock of a sacred visitation, which places Desire between "you" and "me," by the chaste veil of tears; thus bearing witness to this divine Tertium Quid. *As-raruna bikrun,* "our hearts, in their deepest recesses, are a single Virgin," who conceives thus, in the eternal present, the assumption in God of all the predestined (or rather, who gives God birth in them all).

After theoretical presentation of the theological teaching comes analysis, still theoretical, of the Hallajian juridical principles (*usul*), which borrow the vocabulary of the adversary, the revolutionary Imamism of the Qarmathians, in order to annex it for their own use.

Finally, the works of Hallaj, in a complete annotated translation, with careful examination of their authenticity, their style, their influence through the centuries (already dealt with in Section I, the "survival"), and of the works of art that they have inspired.

It was possible to undertake an internal criticism and interpretation of these only after having done an external criticism, having established the texts and determined their origin.

To begin with, the direct traces left by the personality of this excommunicated mystic become clear a little belatedly. Though the first three "independent" evaluations of his public teaching appear as early as 932 (A. Z. Balkhi), 950 (Maqdisi), and 990 (Daylami), the three earliest dated manuscripts in which his name appears are from 1073 (Sajazi), 1153 (Sarraj), and 1158 (Ibn Bakuya). None of his cenotaphs erected in Baghdad, Mosul, Lalish, Damascus, and Muhammad Bandar is earlier than 1045 (Vizir Ibn al-Muslima); and all seem to have been reconstructed. Finally, his iconography begins only in 1307, and the series of Hallaj miniatures by the celebrated Behzadh has disappeared.

Nevertheless, thanks to thirty-seven testimonial chains, which we shall discuss, and in spite of the official ban, maintained from 922 to 1258, on copying or selling any work by this condemned man, numerous fragmentary pieces by Hallaj (sometimes named simply "Husayn") have been preserved for us by the doxographers of mysticism, which guarantees their semantic value (350 maxims in Khurasan, in the collections of Sulami, and in Fars, in the collections of Baqli). We have six *letters* by him written with the greatest personal sincerity (one to Shakir, turned over at the trial, of great importance; two to Ibn Ata': two of his friends who later gave their lives for him.) There were also false letters produced at the trial, not kept, and denied by him. We have sixty-nine *public discourses* (which compose the *Akhbar al-Hallaj*), unidentified as far as external sources are concerned, and whose semantic value, (undeniable) personal sincerity, and objective accuracy (because of the charisms mentioned), we shall discuss in detail. We have eighty pieces of verse, his *Diwan* (a collection redone several times, some imitations having slipped in, which are not all from his school). Finally, in prose, three fragments of exceptional authenticity (ed. Daylami, Ibn Kahmis), dating from his first appearances; and two self-contained collections: the *Riwayat,* from before the year 902 (Twenty-seven *hadith qudsi,* in a singular style and an almost popular language); and the eleven *Tawasin* (a compilation of the *novissima verba* of Hallaj, the philosophical technicality of which is "signed," for division into chapters, later than the eleventh century). All of the other works in prose, apart from a preface (*Kitab Sayhur*), must have been burned. And as in the cases of Eckhart and Marie des Vallées, the most significant texts have been preserved for us thanks to a mine of hostile commentaries.

Section III [Volume 4] gives an exhaustive study of the "Hallajian bibliography," comprising more than 1415 works by 953 authors; with a foreword extricating from this enormous mine grains of precious metal, significant details, and carefully considered evaluations. There follows the enumeration in schematic form of 37 basic testimonial chains, *asanid,* constituting the "hadith", the Hallajian Islamic tradition. Thirty-seven continuous chains, going back to 15 of the 117 names of contemporaries, direct witnesses of the life and sayings of Hallaj (91 favorable, of whom two are women; 26 hostile); his sons Mansur and Hamd, Ibn 'Ata', Shakir, Ibn Fatik, Shibli, Qannad, Ibn Khafif, Ibn Surayj; with 2 apostates (Dabbas and Awariji) and 4 enemies (Abu 'Umar, Ibn Ayyash, Ibn Rawh, Suli). This proportion of 15/37/117 is remarkably high for a person

officially proscribed, especially if one considers what Shaykh Daba' (dean of
Qur'an reciters in Cairo) pointed out to me in 1945: he noted that, as a matter
of fact, the 15 earliest witnesses of the recitation of the Qur'an (of whom two
were women: cf. Jeffrey [Arthur Jeffrey, *Materials for the Study of the Qur'an*,
Leiden, 1937 (?)]) were known to him through 1060 continuous 'Uthmanian
chains. This proportion is much weaker than the proportion of 15/37/117 (*Sahaba
Hallajiya*); namely, barely 1/1000, instead of 1/10—or 15/1,060/12,314, as
compared with the mass of 12,314 known Companions of the Prophet (of
whom 1552 were women) and some heretics (Harqus) and known apostates
(Rabi' Jumahi, his muezzin at 'Arafat).

One can legitimately infer from these figures that a durable spiritual reverberation of the words of this excommunicate spread them among the believing
masses of the cities, shaken by the news of his being put to death. In Juzjan a
revolt broke out. In Baghdad itself, Mas'udi, an eyewitness, referred to this day
as "solemn," because of the ideas that Hallaj held. Ideas "that brought over to
him a great number of (post-humous) disciples," independent spirits enamored
with philosophy, as one of them, Daylami, heir of Tawhidi, tells us apropos of
the novel position of Hallaj in metaphysics of identifying Desire, *'ishq*, with
the Divine Essence. This, at a time when, in imitation of the "first" Hellenic
philosophers, the Muslim *falasifa* were identifying Love only with a Demiurge.
Let us note, in passing, the already "intercultural" and "interregional" significance, as early as 990, of this "comparativist" remark by a Hallajian on his
master.

Thus, it was undoubtedly through this intellectual affinity by friendship of the
spirit, entirely disinterested and supraracial, that Hallaj's thought reached me
personally. It was less through the "initiatory" and formalistic continuity of the
four Sufi "chains" that I connected in 1908 (Muhammad Yamani, Baghdad),
1909 (Badi Sannari, Cairo), 1911 (Bursali Muhammad Tahir, Çengelkoy),
1928 (Hasan Fehmi Beg, Ankara), than it was because of this sudden reappearance of clear evidence on behalf of a just cause that had been misrepresented:
evidence that "restores" an honest adversary. It could be observed at the home
of my two Baghdad hosts in 1907–1908, the Alussy family: Hajj 'Ali Alussy,
who rediscovered Khatib for me, when he uncovered the favorable opinion of
Amin al-Wa'iz, one of the Hanafite masters of [Hallaj's] father, and began to
help me so tirelessly; and especially Mahmud Shukri Alussy, when his fierce
independence as a *salafi* made me realize that he was rebelling against the retraction extorted in 1073 from Ibn 'Aqil (for his Hallajian treatise) by some
narrow-minded politicians of his Hanbalite rite. Other reappearances of a similar sympathy have arisen over the centuries, even among Shi'ite scholars; and,
more important from a social standpoint, there have been revivals of collective
compassion for Hallaj, envisioned as an eschatological intercessor, among the
masses of persecuted peoples, artisans, and confreres of the *futuwwa* (this per-

haps dating back to the time of Hallaj's death), Yazidis, Druzes, and even Nusayris.

In this sense, I must single out, from the long list of Orientalist and philosopher friends who so graciously aided me in my research on Hallaj from 1907 to 1922 (cited in P., p. 942), the names of Ignaz Goldziher and Joseph Maréchal. With them then, as now with Farhadi, J. M. ʿAbd al-Jalil and Louis Gardet, the feeling of intellectual affinity with Hallaj was direct, quite apart from our friendship. In Islam itself, after 1922, I found a true understanding of Hallajian thought in Muhammad Iqbal, at Lahore; Muhammad Fassi and M. Bennani, at Fez; B. Tuprak, M. A. Yücel, Süheyl Ünver, N. Topçu, S. Z. Aktay, in Turkey; Z. Mubarak, ʿAR Badawi, in Cairo; and M. L. Gumʿa, who "carried" the Hallajian *talbiya* back to ʿArafat. I do not forget the *novissima verba* of Tor Andrae in his *i myrtenträdgarden*. I link them here with the treasured fraternal communications of V. Ivanov, J. Deny, H. Ritter, H. Corbin, S. Pines, R. Chatterjee, and the very spontaneous contributions of Sheref Yaltkaya in Ankara, Servèr Gouya in Kabul, Hamidullah in Hyderabad, T. Ragragi in Rabat, AH Sarraf in Karbala, and especially those of the learned historian of Baghdad, Mustafa Jawad.

"Hallajians," in the broad sense, are to be found even in Israel. They exist among those who yield "priority" to Arabic vis-à-vis the other Semitic languages as explaining grammar and reasoning, sifting their art, condensing their wise maxims. This is the same intellectual attraction for the essentially Semitic rhythm of the Hallajian sentence that prompted mediaeval Caraïtes to transcribe Hallajian poems and prose into Hebrew letters; that led Ignaz Goldziher in 1912 to bend over the proofs of *Tawasin,* revising my efforts at translation; and that determined Paul Kraus, before his death, to reprint in Aleppo in 1943, as a farewell addressed to our friendship, the sections of our *Akhbar al-Hallaj* in which the Essential Desire burns.

My 1922 preface did not specify the working hypotheses actually underlying the initial plan; the present clarification sets them forth in the manner of a methodology of the history of religion.

Section I, for purposes of describing a life, had followed the anecdotal atomism of primitive Arabic historiography, as found in the "Ayam al-ʿArab" and the hadith; and, for its closeness of examination, it drew its inspiration from Trousseau's *La Clinique médicale de l'Hôtel-Dieu de Paris,* which was recommended by a psychologist friend, Jean Dagnan.

Section II had chosen the systematic framework of Muʿtazilite *kalam,* following in that the choice of Hallaj himself, who was borrowing its doctrinal vocabulary in order to "sublimate" it. This section also followed the example of *The Mystical Element of Religion Studied in Saint Catherine of Genoa and Her Friends* by F. von Hügel, which was recommended as a model by the author's spiritual director, Henri Huvelin, to whom Charles de Foucauld had introduced me.

There remained the preparation of a body of explicative annotation for the entire work, which was indispensable for rendering it intelligible to the non-Muslim reader. The responsibility for this annotation was mine: it had to be given a clearly defined orientation; for the study of this life, which aimed passionately toward a supreme certitude, could be neither "an apology, nor a rehabilitation." Hallaj himself, following the Hanbalites and certain Sufis, had worked out a conception of history going beyond the occasionalistic atomism of the hadith and the cyclic theory of astrological fatalism transmitted to the Imamite fiscal scribes of the ʿAbbasid empire by their Aramaean predecessors. For him, historical time was a progression of pulsations of grace, *karrat*, oscillating like the swing of a pendulum, but ascending, an accumulation of recapitulative testimonies preparing the way for the actualization of the Last Judgment.

The following are some of the working hypotheses used:

a) Since the duration in which we live has a direction, one can conceive a human "history" only by postulating a structural continuity that is finalistic (as opposed to the discontinuous that is accidental); and one can write it only by explaining the linguistic facts phonologically (and not phonetically) and the psychic facts by a "psychology of form" (as opposed to the approach of associationist empiricism). Historical finality must become intelligible "interiorly," for it concerns the person who alone extracts from it the meaning of the common ordeal (and not the individual, the differentiated element dependent on the social group that remains its natural end).

b) One can schematize the life of a social group by constructing the individual *life curves* of each of its distinct members according to their relations in the external environment (travels, illnesses, marriages), but it is useless to make it out to be the aggregation of these without having noted in it certain unusual individual curves, blessed with unique points (and even "knots") corresponding to the "interior experiences" of certainties (and even of anguish) by which they have "found" some "psychic resolvents" in their adventures in this environment. Having first become intelligible "dramatic situations" for those, they become unraveled for others afterwards.

c) For the convenience of the schema, one can argue that there are only a limited number of possible "dramatic situations" and themes in a social environment (Aristotle, Gozzi, Goethe; cf. Polti, Aarne-Thompson). But they are rarely resolved, for the resolvents of their peripeteia are strictly personal godsends, or better, are recapitulative realizations of the person in a heroic act (usually "once in a lifetime"). These "testimonial" realizations of divine grace in us are superhuman reactions, not reducible to environmental pressures, juxtapositions of anecdotal atoms (*nawadir*, [i.e., phenomena]), chance patterns of statistics, roles of institutional organisms and folkloric functions (G. Dumézil) expressing themselves in the form of wise proverbs and philosophical maxims (Westermarck) and assent to archetypes (Jung), or other arbitrary and combinational schemas whereby a society deceives itself by believing it can formulate for itself in such things a representation that explains its past and preforms its future.

d) The isolated heroic act, whose formal object is divine, has a pivotal value that is "transsocial." One can represent it as a *projection* outside the world of the life trajectory of its author: not only on an "imaginary" ideal cycle (compassion of Antigone for the enemy of the city), but on a liturgical cycle that is communitarian and real (hospitality of Abraham toward the stranger, intercession of virginal friendship on behalf of the criminal). For this act is not only a solitary reaching beyond, but a sublimation not discontinuous with the masses of the by no means disinterested gamut of mercenary virtues, calculated actions, mediocre desires, sins, and crimes: the wretched masses from whom the most recent conscientious biographers, out of disgust with hypocritical and "orthodox" conventional hagiographies, draw their sweeping conclusions of contempt for all human behaviour.

e) This finalistic "internal" and "personalist'" conception of human history sees in this history a real and efficacious *solidarity* of the afflictions of the mass with the redemptive, saving, and holy suffering of a few heroic souls, "apotropaic substitutes" (Huysmans' thesis; the *abdal* theory held by the Hanbalites and the early Sufis in Islam).

f) The transhistoric continuity of this finalism embodies, in the "substitute saints", the crisis of collective suffering—famines, epidemics, wars, persecutions—suffered by the masses of unfortunate people. Crises of "parturition" (*odinès*) whose true significance, with a few superhuman outcries for apocalyptic vengeance, pierces through the reserved conformism of official chronologists and the insincere perversity of dishonest memorialists (Tanukhi, smearing Ibn Khafif; Suli, "sidestepping" the Shalmaghani affair and the anti-Hanbalite *fatwa*); these two complementary aspects of all historiography originate in the bourgeois class of bureaucratic scribes. It has been said, summarizing [Léon] Bloy: "The deciphering of history is reserved to certain grieving beings" (Béguin): those who have the intuitive compassion of saints.

g) They disclose, in the perishable world, the incorruptible presence of a sacred Truth; they see it appear each time the premonition of the intersign is fulfilled by the unforeseeable miracle of a prayer being granted. They see it guiding the saints in their penetration to the silent divine Source from which their destiny once arose and into which their inward aspiration will be absorbed; in contempt of every premeditated strategy.

h) And the saint's supreme witness is fulfilled, overcoming equivocations and ambivalences, by breaking through the front lines of fear, danger, doubt, and the worst temptation (as Foucauld wrote in his October 30, 1909 letter), for it is only through the mortal suffering of the desired trial that he can reach

Union with the One, with the Divine Essence that is disarmed, abandoned, naked.

i) When the substitute saint, the "witness of the instant," joins in this way the "Witness of the Eternal," this Union in solitude is an intercession for an immense number of souls who have remained behind somewhere along the way. Contrary to the missiological theories of expanding proselytism, recent investigations of religious statistics have established certain *constants*, approximately the same for all environments and periods: a fixed percentage of ritual practices within the confessional group, of good acts and of sins, of fervent vocations and of unbridled outlaws: with the added note that a small, avowedly sinning, minority is set over against the immense array of its "respectable" contemporaries, secret sinners, as eventual *abdal*, the always possible ransom of penitents for a mass in a state of evil. This recognition of the inanity of every official propagandistic apostolate underlines rather clearly the fact that the religious life of believer groups is protected against rotting from hypocrisy by an intermittent treatment, in infinitesimal homeopathic doses, of "substitute" sanctity. Hallaj used to teach (*Riw.,* No. 27) that with one saint God purifies every minute 70,000 just men. One of his predecessors, 'Ali b. Muwaffaq, used to declare that on the day of 'Arafat God found it sufficient for pardoning the 600,000 assembled pilgrims to find six just ones among them. This recalls the prayer of intercession of the first of the *abdal*, Abraham, on behalf of Sodom, the City of Perdition.

A study brought to bear on a heroic life of this sort could not end with his death, for the posthumous "survival" of Hallaj on earth through chains of suffering and sacrificed witnesses involves us and draws us away from earth toward "temples" (*hayakil*) of the eternal City of souls raised up from the transfigured holocaust of their earthly bodies.

Centered spiritually on the pilgrimage to Mecca by way of the Feast of Sacrifices, the thrust of Hallaj's prayer expanded actually to the reaches of the Muslim world of that period, and beyond the frontiers of the jihad to the front rank of militant souls who defended, in a fierce spiritual "hand-to-hand" combat, the Islamic Community threatened in its heart and in its *ikhlas* by mysterious, tempting, and schismatic forces of disintegration and perversion. Among the latter was the spirit of hypocrisy that handed over the Holy Site of the great pilgrimage on holiday to the panderers of the Court, of trade, of banking, and of poetry, thereby exposing it here and there to atheistic cynicism, covetousness, and the dagger of the wretched poor, the Qarmathian revolutionaries.

The Muslim world was intersected by two opposing currents, one aspiring to the *qibla* of sacrifice, the other disavowing it. An immense flow of mercenary prayers and perfidious works, foamed forth against the pure prayer of a few solitaries and against the spirit of poverty, fasting, and sacrifice that cried out to God *aslih,* "reform" Islam by Justice, "as You promised Abraham," even though we die of it. That this voice prevailed is proven by the malevolent forces' almost immediate change of camp, their desertion from the imperial cause, which brought on the collapse of the old political and social structure of the 'Abbasids, and their rallying to the Qarmathian cause, thereby contaminating by luxury and riches the latter's revolutionary "purity" acquired by the 'Alid "legitimist" messianism through two centuries of persecution. While this handful of heroic militants perished, delivering up the "temples" of their bodies in expiation (such as Jurayri accepting death in the Qarmathian ambush at Habir, the same Jurayri who regretted having deserted Hallaj), the Qarmathians, after having thought that they had destroyed the spirit of the Pilgrimage by stealing the Black Stone, resigned themselves to giving it back to the temple of the Ka'ba (in the presence of the grand qadi of Cairo, Ibn al-Haddad, a Hallajian).

It is not only a question of affirming the spiritual progress of disembodied souls after death (Ibn 'Arabi), virtually in the sense of their predestinations as "ideas." Hallaj affirmed that the ultimate finality of a human person's history is not the mere return to his intelligible form that God previsioned, but "the coming of His realization." And this "realization" implies that souls will "resuscitate" their glorified bodies, in an order of hierarchical apotheosis, preserving from their confessional observances only the degree of "theopathy" (ikhlas) that was put into them on earth.

The substitute saints (abdal) are neither mahatmas (whose ascetic effort is intransmissible and "miraculously" struck with sterility), nor great men (whose social creations perish with the cities of this world), nor even inventors and discoverers (saints of the positivist calendar), whose succession is discontinuous and fortuitous. Certainly the sum total of scientific experimentation across the centuries continues to grow, but it serves only to accelerate the process of disintegration by superdifferentiation (and "fission") of the cities of this world. Experimental science can "desensitize" and even increasingly eliminate bodily sufferings, but bodies will die regardless; whereas "substitute" sainthood is "sensitized" by God in order to sympathize with broken and "carded" hearts, whose wound it transfigures through consolation, the source of immortal cures.

We have considered Hallaj here as one of these given souls, substitutes for the Muslim Community, or, put more Biblically, for all men, among Believers in the God of Abraham's sacrifice and among the expatriated pilgrims, the gerim, who desire to find their way again upon dying back to the "bosom of Abraham," where this God will bring about their immortal spiritual promotion. That raises us above the level of Carlyle and Gundolf and their "cult of heroes," totems of race, nation, or class. And above the academic biographers who "canonize" religious or laity as "benefactors of humanity." We are propounding here the absolute transcendence of the humblest of heroic acts as sole cornerstone of the eternal City. The history of religions thus conceived envisages it as the axis and the apex of the world in motion toward the next life, even if the author of this act forgets it, or himself remains misunderstood or unknown to the end.

One can consider the whole history of humanity up to the Judgment as a spherical fabric whose three-dimensional spatial chain of "dramatic situations," unconsciously suffered by the masses, is crossed, "drawn" by a weft, which the irreversible shuttle of succeeding moments weaves with the creative life curves of fellow-suffering and restorative "royal" souls, famous or hidden, who "realize" the divine plan.

Such a soul was that of Hallaj. Not that the study of his life, which was full and strong, upright and whole, rising and given, yielded to me the secret of his heart. Rather it is he who fathomed mine and who probes it still. A brief allusion to him on the margin of Khayyam's "quatrains" set down by an uncertain hand, a simple sentence by him in Arabic seen in the Persian "memorial" of 'Attar, and the meaning of sin was returned to me, then the heart-rending desire for purity read at the start of a cruel Egyptian spring. It is with lowered eyes, *markhiya 'aynayya* , that I hail from afar this lofty figure, always veiled for me, even in his tortured nakedness: then snatched up from the ground, borne away, covered with blood, torn completely to pieces with fatal wounds, carried by the jealousy of the most ineffable Love.

Murta'ish declared (ten years after his martyrdom and a hundred years before A. I. Kazaruni's vision): "If Hallaj's fate exposed him publicly to everyone, his soul keeps his secret even from the most intimate friends of God." Why did this ascetic, to begin his career, break with his first teacher? Why did he marry and why, going forth to preach God, did he renounce his frock? Why did this ecstatic, outside a state of ecstasy, speak of himself as being "one with God"—a scandalous longing claim to a charismatic and judiciary divine power and an insolence which, as even Ghazali admitted, is tolerable only in the mouth of the Messiah and as a simple theopathic expression? Why did this pilgrim from 'Arafat, who had shouted out in a provocative manner in the suqs of Baghdad his desire for sacrificial immolation, run away disguised under a false name at the time of the first actions against him? And why did he protest upon hearing himself treacherously condemned to death? Finally, why, during his last vigil in prison, did he doubt for such a long time, before understanding and crying out, that the fire in which his remains were going to be burned foretold the future glory of his resurrection? God knows.

But what I have understood very well, now, is that it is useless to apply to such a case the normalizing rules of prudence of hagiographical criticism sanctioned by Father Delehaye (in whose hands they have already proven so unsuccessful in the cases of Pokrov and La Salette). To proceed with the proper *toilette* of the "acta martyrum," to expurgate them of their "enormities," "unduly argumentative" repartees with the judges, sessions of "excessive" tortures, charisms manifested "needlessly," is to refuse to understand that true sanctity is necessarily excessive, eccentric, abnormal, and shocking; it is to prohibit the soul in search of God from escaping the prison of "common courtesies," "accepted manners," and "respectable habits": by its breakthrough. A breakthrough certainly unusual and disconcerting. But is it reasonable to treat an existential affirmation as unacceptable because it has no precedent and because it presents a fact as being outside the norm? We have given up the "logical" representation of history by the pre-existence (Plato) or the evolution (Hegel) of ideas; and we have proposed for it a "paralogical" representation by the pre-existence of archetypes (Jung) or the evolution of functions and situations, extending up to the cycles of reincarnation in persons (Imamite, Druze, and Nusayri theories). But the final, liberating unification of the individual soul, personalized through adoration of the One God, is brought about during a single lifetime (Suhrawardi Halabi). Is there mediation, an attraction exercised on the consciousness by certain premonitional archetypal oneiric themes? And are these themes "illusions" resulting from the artificial "tensions" of our fable-making fantasy (G. Dumas), or from "the introduction of the subjective element into reality" (Delehaye)? Are they not often, especially among Semites, anagogical modalities of grace acting upon phantoms of the infrarational imagination to prepare us for a pure conception of the mental word? To them, virtue is not a Greek balance, a medium "méson," between two extremes, but a "supremely noble moral behavior" (*makarim al-akhlaq*), a heroic tension, at its peak, without either counterpoises or counterslopes (Eckhart).

It is undeniable that the lives of mystics contain strange images and involve peculiar apparitions: unknowable mental forms, as much inevitable as uninventable, that they themselves do not explain immediately. These are nevertheless, often realities of a certain order, in a state of "becoming," potential finalities that will objectify themselves, indefinitely "open" in the sense of quest and theologal hope. Through the process of dramatic "recognition" (anagnorisis), our retrospection nourishes our expectation, our dream opens up to us the sense of a series of events, insofar as our prayer blends with its source, which is grace. We realize how futile it would be to "normalize" these entirely personal sequences and these independent series after the manner of mathematicians' "random functions" and statisticians' contingent probabilities. I see in them rather a whole musicality of predictive intersigns of election, dissociating the privileged soul from the "others," delivering it as a hostage to their lack of understanding and their resentment.

I have no intention, therefore, of expurgating the "acta sincera" relating the agony of Hallaj to the beginnings of his future legend; for the legend pre-exists in them, latent, like the spark in the flint. I forgo dissociating his miracles from his maxims, in spite of their *décalage* (P. Kraus). I refuse to separate his prayers and discourses from their assonanced presentation; for the latter reveals, not a superimposed stylization nor an outline tracing, but the abrupt scansion, the inspired rhythm, of the Semitic seer. I decline, finally, to disarticulate my French translation of Hallaj's maxims and poems by minimizing his sentence's ordered structure, by taking each of his words in the literal sense, without their "germinal burial" (*tadmin*), without their anagogical and disruptive sublimation. I annex even to historical facts the further meditations that they have suggested. He spoke and repeated his sentences, for his true listeners, as recapitulative and prophetic intersigns; their inspiriting and fulfilling value must be respected; their orchestration is inseparable from the melody they evoke. No doubt these statements shock probabilists and statisticians; their method, when confronted by exceptional cases, is elimination, for it has not been outfitted for detection. But it so happens, scandalously, that Hallaj is a spiritual being, an exceptional case, a *gharib* ("a species" unto himself, like an archangel who faces struggles from on high); his destiny was so strange that he "recognized" it only *in extremis*, at the moment when grace nailed him to the summit of his vow. But what soul of good will would not be prepared to reach that point, at the end? And doesn't that soul arrive there actually, therefore, if it accepts the fact that the end fulfilling its life reencloses it in the divine origin of its potentialities, forever, through a kind of spiritual "upward curve" of time?

It is at the end of the ascension, from the height of the conquered peak, that we can embrace the entire traveled itinerary and elucidate the ambiguous contours of the first gropings. The personality is unified in the face of danger, the harbinger of death and of the Judge:

> When grief befalls us, rise to it with desire (*'ishq*):
> We must climb to the top of Rabwe (with Maryam),
>   in order to gaze upon Damascus.
>   Rumi, *Mathnawi*, 3:3753: on the Annunciation.

The execution of Hallaj, described in several independent sources, throws light on the mentality of his adversaries:

—to the *tribunal*, vizir and qadis, it is the application of capital punishment to a transgression of the law, which he deliberately committed by teaching that hajj rites performed outside of Mecca were allowed;

—to the *imperial palace*, Caliph and high officials, the sentence is carried out for the sake of public safety, with the sovereign exercising his role as defender of the threatened order;

—the petty officials among the *salaried witnesses* upholding the religious life of the masses, the *shuhud* (legal notaries) and *qurra'* (Qur'an reciters), applaud the tortures suffered by the criminal as their own revenge, the ransom paid for the outrage inflicted on their formalistic piety by a direct vocation of intimacy with God on earth.

For understanding the psychology of Hallaj himself, the basic document is still the so-called "prayer of the last vigil," collected and edited barely two years after the execution by a Surayjian, the leader of the Cairo *shuhud*, a future interim grand qadi, Ibn al-Haddad.

Isnad of AB ibn al-Haddad; Ibrahim ibn Fatik, according to Shakir:

When night fell on the place where he was to be taken, at dawn, from his cell, Hallaj stood up for the prayer and performed one that consisted of two *rak'a*. Then, when this prayer was finished, he continued to repeat himself, saying "illusion, illusion": until the night was almost over. Then, he was silent for a long time; and then he cried out "truth, truth." And he stood up again, put on his head veil and wrapped himself in his coat, stretched out his hands toward the *qibla* (= in the direction of Mecca) and entered into ecstatic prayer (*munajat*):

"We are here, we, Your witnesses (*shawahid*). We are seeking refuge in the (pre-eternal) splendor of Your glory, in order that You show (finally) what You wanted to fashion and achieve, O You who are God in heaven and God on earth. It is You Who shine forth when You desire just as You shone forth (in the pre-eternal heaven before the Angels and Satan) Your decree under "the most beautiful form" (=the human form, in Adam): the form in which the enunciating Spirit resides, present in it through knowledge and speech, free will and evidence of [being].

"You then bestowed on this present witness (= myself, Hallaj) Your "I," Your essential Ipseity.

"How is it that You, . . . You Who were present in my self, after they had stripped me, Who used me "to proclaim Myself to me," revealing the truth of my knowledge and my miracles, going back in My ascensions to the Thrones of My pre-eternities to utter there the Word itself which creates me.

"(You now wish) me to be seized, imprisoned, judged, executed, hung on the gibbet, my ashes to be thrown to the sand storms which will scatter them, to the waves which will play with them.

"If only because their smallest particle (of my ashes), a grain of aloes (burned in this way to Your glory), assures to the glorious body (literally: "temple") of my transfigurations a more imposing foundation than that of immovable mountains."

Then he recited the following verses:

I cry to You for the Souls whose (present) witness (= I myself) now goes—beyond the "where" to meet the very Witness of Eternity.

I cry to You for hearts so long refreshed (in vain)—by clouds of revelation, which once filled up with seas of Wisdom:

I cry to You for the Word of God, which since it perished,—has faded into nothing in our memory;

I cry to You for the (inspired) Discourse before which ceases— all speaking by the eloquent and wise orator.

I cry to You for Signs that have been gathered up by intellects;—nothing at all remains of them (in books) except debris.

I cry to You, I swear it by Your love,—for the self-controls of those whose
mastered mount was the discipline of silence;

All have crossed (the desert), leaving neither well nor trace behind;—vanished
like the 'Ad tribe and their lost city of Iram;

And after them the abandoned crowd is muddled on their trails,—blinder than
beasts, blinder even than she-camels.

In this highly significant text, one which is as mysterious as it is admirable,
Hallaj becomes aware of the seal of sanctity that the terrifying denouement of
his life is going to imprint upon so many premonitional intersigns; he perceives
his predestination as a Witness, delivered beforehand to his Only One "completely alone"; he senses his future resurrection, he sees it in the last incensing
that will shoot forth from the naptha in which his corpse is going to burn. Conveyed beforehand onto the esplanade of his forthcoming punishment, to weep
there over that ignorant, awed, onlooking crowd, as insensitive tomorrow to his
tortures as it was indifferent yesterday to hearing his ecstatic calls. Put as a
flaming target before the fratricidal faces of the high officials, abettors of crises
and riots, to which his fire points, and which he probes. Struck down on their
behalf by the just verdict of the Sovereign Judge. In vain had he cried out ecstatically, long before: "O Muslims, save me from God, *aghithuni 'an Allah*"
(*Akhbar* , No. 10). "No, no one will save him from God . . ." (Qur'an,
72:22) ". . . nor will I find any refuge except Him" (Qur'an 72:23).

Louis Massignon
(d. October 31, 1962)

Biographical Outline

I. PROLOGUE*

A religious group commemorates an event only if such retrospection strengthens its hope in the future and contributes to building the ultimate City that faith promises to it beyond its individual deaths.

There are religious personalities who are sentenced to death and excommunicated, yet who end by inserting themselves, with real spiritual import, long after their death, into history such as their original community itself conceives it. If Christ is not yet linked again to the historic tradition proper to his maternal race, Joan of Arc has been incorporated after four centuries into the history of France as a social factor of survival and a leaven of immortality.

In the case of Hallaj, judged and sentenced in Baghdad in 309/922, the fact of his death only took on a sense of historicity in Islam more than a century later: in 437/1046, when a Baghdadian vizir, ʿAli ibn al-Muslima, ex-professional witness at the canonical Court, attested to the innocence of this condemned man, still excommunicated, by pausing for a short prayer at the site where Hallaj was tortured—which he called "blessed site"—on the very day of his investiture, when the official cortege was leading him from the Caliphal Palace to the cathedral mosque of al-Mansur.

In fact, after the tragic death of this vizir, it was one of his friends, the historian Abu Bakr ibn Thabit Khatib (d. 463/1071), who, while compiling the 7831 biographical notices of his *History of Baghdad, Taʾrikh Baghdad*, dared to publish among them a notice on Hallaj, which ranks third in size after those on Abu Hanifa and Bukhari. This "History," according to Sunnite Muslim practice, arranges all of the names of the *muhaddithun* of Baghdad in a continuous chronological series going back to the Prophet. The names are of those first transmitters of the sayings of the Prophet who lived and taught in the Caliphal capital, and who thereby attested in an Islamic manner to the city's living historical continuity. The unexpected presence among them of Hallaj, who transmitted no hadith, indicates that Khatib, like Ibn al-Muslima, memorialized Hallaj as an exemplary Sunnite Muslim, and that his aim was to persuade his Sunnite readers of this view.

Already in 445, Khatib had prayed on the hajj for permission to read his

*From *Passion of Al-Hallaj*, vol. 1, 3–18 and 21–52

Ta'rikh in public in Baghdad; and he was able to do it in 463, with Shaykh Nasr ibn Ibrahim Maqdisi at his right side.

Far from being banned, Khatib's "History" was transmitted from *rawi* to *rawi*, in Baghdad and beyond, making Hallaj finally emerge out of the flux of outdated events and obsolete portraits as a reference point and a cornerstone.

We shall extract from this notice by a historian, the only notice that may have come down to us collating official and private sources, two characteristic documentary references to earlier authors: to Qannad, and this is a portrait of Hallaj, a brief literary evocation, restored here according to the *recensio plenior* of Habbal; to Ibn Bakuya, and this is the only chronological canvas of the life, presented under the name *Hamd*, the youngest son of Hallaj. These, by way of a prologue.

Translation of the "Portrait" (Qannad)

The first sketch that was attempted of the physiognomy of Hallaj appears in the "literary anecdotes" (*hikayat*) of Qannad, who died around 330/941, twenty years after Hallaj. It is thanks to these early "anecdotes," with the picturesque silhouettes that they drew, not without sympathy, of eccentric mystics like Hallaj and Bistami, that the names of these Sufis found their way into profane literature. Qannad himself, in fact, was a literary critic, highly regarded for his studies of the poetry of Abu Tammam, before becoming, under the influence of Nuri, a frequent visitor to mystic circles.

The following is his "portrait" of Hallaj, in which, according to the rules of the literary genre of the anecdote in Arabic, a prose narrative framework acts as commentary on the verse part, which expresses the state of the hero's soul. Three recensions of this "portrait" are extant. We present here the one by Ibrahim Habbal (A.H. 392–482), via AH 'Ali ibn Muwaffaq:

> One day I came upon Hallaj in wondrous attire; by that I mean, he was dressed pitifully. I said to our companions, "Go quickly and get one of your old cast-off robes to give him," which they did. But he came up to me and said: "Abu'l-Hasan! Have you really nothing more for me than this commiseration?" He then recited the following verses:
>
> > If you have met me tonight in clothing
> >   which is doubly that of poverty,
> > Be assured that by being threadbare on my back
> >   this clothing has bestowed on me
> >   the most generous Freedom;
> > Do not be misled, therefore, if you see me
> >   in this state,
> > So different from my former condition,

Because I have a soul, and indeed it must
either perish or rise up,
Yes, I swear to you, in carrying me away
to the highest destiny.

Then, AH Qannad added, time passed with its vicissitudes, and when I asked for news of him, I was told: "Abu'l-Hasan, this man has just been deservedly hung on the gibbet in the 'Abbasiya square." And he was really there, dead, on the gibbet. But it so happened that I met Abu Bakr Shibli there at the same time, and I told him of my previous meeting with Hallaj and recited his verses to him. Abu Bakr, struck by the ending of the last line, exclaimed: "It is true! there he is, raised now to the highest destiny." I asked then: "O Abu Bakr, what is your opinion of him therefore?" He replied: "He had received knowledge of one of the Names of God and realized its power truly through miracles; afterwards, he relied on his own personality; then God took back from him control over it and killed him." Then I asked: "O Abu Bakr, have you retained something of his to this effect?" "Yes," he told me, and he recited for me the following couplet:

I have looked all over the world for a place
to settle,
But I find no place on the earth to settle.
I have obeyed my desires, and they have
enslaved me.
Oh! if only I were contented with my fate,
I would still be free.

Translation of the "Life According to His Son Hamd" (Ibn Bakuya)

The only chronological sketch of Hallaj's life that Khatib was able to obtain was dictated to him by Mas'ud Sijzi, who got it from Ibn Bakuya. This was the "narrative account by Hamd," an essential document that permitted him to give to his biographical notice on Hallaj a critical solidity that was lacking in all of the other notices of his "History." Though younger than Khatib, Mas'ud Sijzi was already recognized as a critic in the study of hadith by men of the caliber of Nizam al-Mulk, the future Saljuq Sultanate vizir. Among the witnesses whom Khatib cites as authorities on Hallaj, he is surely the determining one. Mas'ud Sijzi was the only authorized "editor" of the Hallajian monograph composed by Ibn Bakuya (d. 428), who had given him the *ijaza* to transmit it in 426: the *ijaza* that Sijzi in turn gave to Khatib. Ibn Bakuya Shirazi, to whom Sulami bequeathed at the time of his death (in 412) the directorship of his convent-library in Nishapur, was, like him, a traditionist historian, whose perspectives, however, were narrower and method less solid, but whose inquisitiveness with regard to the behavioral eccentricities of mystics was sharp. As to his Ash'arite theological leanings, these were derived from his master, Ibn Khafif. In the course of long and tireless journeys, he had collected 30,000 anecdotes about pious men (*salihin*), which were recorded in separate sections (*ajza'*) without sufficient specification as to the circumstances of their transmission (*sama'at*). This latter failure earned him the judgment of "unreliable" as a transmitter. Excepted from that judgment were those anecdotes in which he was the master recognized by Qushayri and his sons, by Ibn Abi Sadiq Hiri, Ibn Zinjawayh, Farmadhi, Harawi, Shirawi, and Khadija Shajahaniya. He himself seems to have singled out two monographs from his large collection, the one on Bistami (entrusted in 419 to Sahlaji, based on his *Kitab al-nur*) and the one on Hallaj (entrusted in 426 to Mas'ud Sijzi).

The latter is the *Bidayat hal al-Hallaj wa nihayatuhu*, "The Beginnings and the End of the Mystic Career of Hallaj." In this prudent and artful treatise on a ticklish subject, Ibn Bakuya wants to appear to recount the way in which Hallaj, after having "begun well," "ended badly." Its plan is reassuring to easily disturbed readers, who actually find, among the work's twenty-one texts, nine that call this excommunicate a heretic, and six that call him an ambitious and unscrupulous man, a charlatan or a sorcerer. Two texts (numbers twelve and eighteen), however, point out how prompt Ibn Khafif, the saint of Shiraz, was to defend the memory of Hallaj; and Ibn Bakuya, his disciple in mysticism and in Ash'arism, admitted to Harawi that he too believed Hallaj innocent. This is why the treatise begins, using the "narrative account by Hamd" as text number one, with the presentation, under the sole *isnad* of Hamd, of a kind of grand introductory mosaic. This mosaic, to give them more documentary force, brings together at least seven favorable testimonies, which in the earlier sources had been scattered under separate *isnad*.

We shall number its separate paragraphs progressively. This account is both a guideline and an eloquent résumé of the entire life of Hallaj; and it is under this title that, not only Khatib, but also Dhahabi in his masterly *History of Islam*, gave it a prominent place. Also, we retranscribe just before the text the special annotations, found at the beginning and at the end of the manuscript in the Zahiriya library in Damascus, which attest to the authenticity of the canonical transmission of this Hallajian memorial. This is the only memorial of Hallaj that was excluded from the transmission ban decreed in 309/922 and ruthlessly enforced up to the end of the 'Abbasid Caliphate.

(Incipit): "memorial . . . collected by A 'AA M-b-'AA-b-'UA-b-Ahmad, called Ibn Bakuya Shirazi Sufi (may God be pleased with him)—transmitted by Abu Sa'id Mas'ud-b-Nasir-b-Abi Zayd-b-A-b-M-b-Isma'il Sijistani, as coming from him—transmitted by A Hy Mubarak-b-'Abd al-Jabbar-b-A Tuyuri, as coming from him—it was read to us, as coming from him, by Shaykh Imam Salah al-Din

AB Ahmad-b-Muqarrab-b-Husayn Sufi Karkhi (may God bestow on him a long life), through personal dictation, to Shaykh and illustrious Imam, *hafiz*, wise man, ascetic, and superior critic Abu'l-Mahasin ʿUmar-b-ʿAli-b-Khadir Qurashi Dimishqi: to M-b-ʿA Rahman-b-M Masʿudi Fanjdihi; to Shaykh Mahmud-b-M Abiwardi; to ʿAli-b-M-b-A Tahir Tarqi; to Shaykh AQ ʿAA-b-M-b-A Mansur Tusi Sufi; on the 13th day of *Hijja* 553, in the Haram of Mecca (may God protect it). (Addendum: Abu'l-MaʿAli-b-ʿAA Badhi participated with them in this audition.)"

The following is the text itself of this narrative account:

In the name of God the Merciful and the Compassionate. This text was taught to us by Imam Salah al-Din AB Ahmad-b-Muqarrab-b-H-b-Husayn Karkhi Sufi, to whom we read it back on the 13th of *Hijja* 553, in the Holy Mosque (may God confirm it in honor and glory), repeating to him: this was taught you by AHy Mubarak-b-ʿAbd al-Jabbar-b-A Sayrafi, to whom you read it back on Saturday, 29 *Qaʿda* 493, after the transmission of what was just said (*baʿd naql ma marra*), that which follows (*ma nassuhu*):

This was related to us orally by Abu Saʿid Masʿud ibn Nasir Sijistani, in these terms: A ʿAA M-b-ʿAA-b-AA-b-Ah ibn Bakwa Shirazi, Sufi, related to us in Nishapur in the year 426:

This was related to me orally by Hamd ibn Husayn Ibn Mansur at Tustar. He told me the following:

1. My father, Husayn ibn Mansur, was born in Bayda, in a place called al-Tur. He was brought up in Tustar, and for a period of two years he became the disciple of Sahl ibn ʿAbdullah Tustari, after which he went to Baghdad.

2. He walked around sometimes dressed in hair shirts, other times in two coats of dyed material, other times in a woolen robe with a turban, or in a greatcoat with sleeves, like a soldier.

3. He left Tustar first for Basra and was eighteen years old at the time. Next he left (for Basra? for Baghdad?), dressed in two coats, to go to see ʿAmr ibn ʿUthman Makki and Junayd ibn Muhammad; and he lived near ʿAmr for eighteen months. After that he married (in Basra) my mother Umm al-Husayn, daughter of Abu Yaʿqub Aqtaʾ, but ʿAmr ibn ʿUthman was unhappy about this marriage and a great quarrel flared up between Abu Yaʿqub and ʿAmr over this subject. My father went at that time alone to Junayd ibn Muhammad and told him how unbearable the crisis between Abu Yaʿqub and ʿAmr was making his situation in Baghdad. Junayd advised him to keep calm and to show them respect, which he did patiently for some time.

4. Next he left for Mecca and remained there a year, on a pious visit. Afterwards he returned to Baghdad with a group of Sufi *fuqaraʾ*. He went to Junayd ibn Muhammad to pose a question, which the latter, however, did not answer, judging it to be motivated by the desire for a personal mission (*muddaʿi*). My father, hurt

by this, returned, together with my mother, to Tustar, where he remained for nearly two years.

5. And there he received such a warm general welcome that all of his (Sufi) contemporaries hated him, particularly ʿAmr ibn ʿUthman, who persisted in sending letters about him to eminent persons of Khuzistan in which he accused him of very grave errors (ʿaza'im).

6. To such a degree and so effectively that my father put aside the religious garb of the Sufis, rejected it and put on the sleeved coat, frequenting the company of worldly society (abna' al-dunya).

7. He left (Tustar) after that and we saw no more of him for five years. During this time he traveled through Khurasan and Mawaralnahr; from there, he went into Sijistan and Kirman, and afterwards returned to Fars. He began to speak in public, to hold meetings (majlis, pl. majalis), to preach God to the people. In Fars, people knew him as Abu ʿAbdallah the *zahid* (the ascetic) and he wrote several works for them. Then he went from Fars back to Ahwaz, and called for her who brought me into the world to come to him.

8. He spoke in public and everyone, great or small, approved of him. He spoke to his listeners of their consciences, of what was in their hearts, which he unveiled for them. They called him "the carder of consciences" (hallaj al-asrar); and the name Hallaj, for short, stayed with him.

9. Next he left for Basra; he stayed there only a little while, leaving me in Ahwaz with his disciples. He went a second time to Mecca, dressed this time in a coat of rags and patches (muraqqaʿa) and an Indian cloak (futa). Many people accompanied him on this journey, during which Abu Yaʿqub Nahrajuri, out of hatred, spread the charge against him with which people are familiar.

10. Then he returned to Basra, where he stayed for a month and returned to Ahwaz. This time he took my mother with him, also my (future) father-in-law (hama) and a number of eminent persons of Ahwaz, and installed himself with them in Baghdad, remaining there a year. Then he said to one of his disciples: "Take care of my son Hamd until I return; for I must go into the land of idolatry (balad al-shirk; variant: balad al-Turk) to call its inhabitants to God, may He be praised and exalted."

11. He left and I knew what he had done: he had gone to India, then to Khurasan for the second time; he had entered the regions of Mawaralnahr and Turkestan and gone as far as Ma Sin, calling those people to God and writing works for them which have not reached me.

12. I know only that after his return, the letters that came to him from India referred to him as "*al-Mughith*" ("the intercessor"), from Turkestan and Ma Sin as "*al-Muqit*" ("the nourisher"), from Khurasan as "*al-Mumayyiz*" ("the discerning"), from Fars as "*Abu ʿAbdallah al-zahid* " ("Abu ʿAbdallah the ascetic"), and from Khuzistan as "*Hallaj al-asrar*" ("the carder of consciences"). Also, there was a group in Baghdad that called him "*al-Mustalim*" ("the enraptured"), and a group in

Basra that called him *"al-Muhayyar"* ("the dazed"). And the gossip about him increased after his return from this journey.

13. He departed again after that and made a third pilgrimage, including a two-year spiritual retreat (in Mecca). He returned this time very changed from what he had been before. He purchased property in Baghdad and built himself a house (for receiving people). He began to preach in public a doctrine only half of which I understood.

14. In the end, Muhammad ibn Dawud rose against him, together with a whole group of *'ulama'* (learned men); and they took their accusations against his views to [Caliph] al-Mu'tadid.

15. Some arguments took place after that between him and 'Ali ibn 'Isa because of Nasr Qushuri; then between him and Shibli and other Sufi shaykhs.

16. Some people said: he is a sorcerer. Others: he is a madman. Still others: he performs miracles and his prayer is granted (by God).

17. And tongues wagged over his case up to the moment when the government arrested and imprisoned him.

18. At that time Nasr Qushuri went to the Caliph, who authorized him to build (my father) a separate cell in the prison. Then a little house was constructed for him adjoining the prison; the outside door to the building was walled up, the building itself was surrounded by a wall, and a door was made opening into the interior of the prison. For about a year he received visits from people there. Then that was forbidden him, and he went for five months without anyone being able to see him—except for one time when he saw Abu'l-'Abbas ibn 'Ata' Adami, who tricked his way in; and another time I saw Abu 'Abdallah ibn Khafif (there). At that time I was spending my nights with my mother within my maternal family outside, and staying during the day near my father. They then imprisoned me with him for a period of two months. At the time I was eighteen years old.

19. And when the night came in which my father was to be taken, at dawn, from his cell, he stood up for the prayer, of which he performed one of two *rak'a*. Then, with this prayer completed, he continued repeating over and over again the word "illusion . . . illusion," until the night was almost over. Then for a long time he was silent, when suddenly he cried out "truth . . . truth." He stood up again, put on his head cloak and wrapped himself in his coat, extended his hands, turned toward the *qibla* (the direction of Mecca), and went into ecstatic prayer (*munajat*).

20. His servant Ahmad ibn Fatik was present, and we have preserved a portion of this ecstatic prayer, which follows now:

21. 'We are here, we, Your witnesses. We are seeking refuge in the (pre-eternal) splendor of Your glory, in order that You show (finally) of Yourself what You desire;

22. 'O You who are God in heaven and God on earth,

23. 'It is You who shine forth when You desire, just as You shone forth (in the pre-eternal heaven, before the Angels and Satan) Your divine decree under "the most beautiful form" (= the human form, in Adam): the form in which the enunciating Spirit resides, present in it through knowledge and speech, free will and evidence [of being].

24. 'You then bestowed on this present witness (= myself, Hallaj) Your "I," Your essential Ipseity.

25. 'How is it that *you*, . . . *you*, who were present in my self after they had stripped me, *who* used Myself to proclaim Me Myself, revealing the truth of my knowledge and my miracles, going back in My ascensions to the Thrones of My pre-eternities to utter there the Word itself which creates Me,

26. '(You now wish) me to be seized, imprisoned, judged, executed, hung on the gibbet, my ashes to be thrown to the sand storms that will scatter them, to the waves that will play with them,

27. 'If only because their smallest particle (of my ashes), a grain of aloes (burned in this way to Your glory), assures to the (glorious) body of my transfigurations a more imposing foundation than that of immovable mountains!"

28. Then he recited the following verses:

'I cry to You for the Souls whose (present = I myself) witness now goes beyond the "where" to meet the Witness of Eternity.

'I cry to You for hearts so long refreshed—(in vain) by clouds of revelation, which once filled up with seas of wisdom.

'I cry to You for the Word of God, which since it perished—has faded into nothing in our memory.

'I cry to You for Your (inspired) Discourse before which ceases—all speaking by the wise and eloquent orator.

'I cry to You for Signs that have been gathered up by intellects—nothing at all remains of them (in books) except debris.

'I cry to You, I swear it by Your love—for the Virtues of those people whose only mount was to keep silent;

'All have crossed (the desert), leaving neither well nor trace behind— vanished like the 'Ad tribe and their lost city of Iram:

'And after them the abandoned crowd is muddled on their trails— blinder than beasts, blinder even than she-camels.'

Then he was quiet.

29. After that, his servant, Ahmad ibn Fatik, said to him: 'Master, bequeath me a maxim.' [My father said:] 'Your carnal soul! If you do not subdue it, it will subdue you.'

30. When the morning came, they led him from the prison, and I saw [him] walking proudly in his chains, reciting: 'My companion, so as not to appear to wrong me, made me drink from his own cup, as a host treats his guest; but as soon as the cup had passed from hand to hand, He made the (leather) execution mat be brought and the sword; thus it falls to him who drinks Wine with the Lion (*Tinnin*) in the height of summer.'

31. They led him then (to the esplanade) where they cut off his hands and feet, after having flogged him with 500 lashes of the whip.

32. Then he was hoisted up onto the cross (*suliba*), and I heard him on the gibbet talking ecstatically with God: 'O my God, here am I (this morning) in the dwelling place of my desires, where I contemplate Your marvels. O my God, since You witness friendship even to whoever does You wrong, how is it You do not witness it to this one (= myself, Hallaj) to whom wrong is done because of You.'

33. Afterwards, I saw Abu Bakr Shibli, who approached the gibbet, crying out very loudly, the following verse: 'have we not forbidden you to receive any guest, man or angel?'

34. Then he said to him: 'What is Sufism?' He answered: 'the lowest degree one needs for attaining it is the one that you behold.' Shibli asked further: 'What is the highest degree?' Hallaj responded: 'It is out of reach for you; but tomorrow you will see; for it is part of the (divine) mystery that I have seen it and that it remains hidden to you.'

35. At the time of the evening prayer (*'isha''*), the authorization by the Caliph to decapitate Hallaj came. But it was declared: 'It is too late; we shall put it off until tomorrow.'

36. When morning came, they took him down from the gibbet and dragged him forth to behead him. I heard him cry out then, saying in a very high voice: 'All that matters for the ecstatic is that his Only One bring him to His Oneness!'

37. Then he recited this verse: 'Those who do not believe in the (Final) Hour call (ironically) for its coming; but those who believe in it await it with loving shyness, knowing that this will be (the coming of) God.' These were his last words.

38. His head was cut off, then his trunk was rolled up in a straw mat, doused with fuel, and burned.

39. Later, they carried his ashes to Ra's al-Manara, to disperse them to the wind.

"I took this account from Hamd ibn Huysayn ibn Mansur. He told me:

> Ahmad ibn Fatik Baghdadi, a disciple of my father, reported to me the following three days after my father's death: 'I have seen the Lord of Glory (= God) in a dream, as if I were standing right before Him. I asked Him: "Lord, what did Husayn ibn Mansur do to You? He told me: "I revealed to him one of the divine attributes (*ma'na*), but he adapted it to himself, preaching for his own esteem; thus I inflicted him with the punishment that you have seen."

II. CHRONOLOGICAL TABLEAU OF HALLAJ'S LIFE AND POSTHUMOUS SURVIVAL

This tableau is not a mere tracing of the "account of Hamd." The account must be corrected in accordance with the contributions of isolated, independent, and older testimonies.

Résumé of Hallaj's Life

He is born around A.H. 244 in Tur in the district of Bayda (Fars), a particularly Arabicized south Iranian center that was an entrenched subcamp of the *jund* of Basra, and later a military depot (with a shop for minting coinage) for the troops going out from Shiraz into Khurasan to fight the Turks. Bayda was colonized by the Harithiya, clients of an Arab Yemenite tribe (Balharith: descendents of Madhij, a legendary family of Turks and Islamicized Kurds), and became a relay station for propaganda agents of the ʿAbbasid dynasty. Later, people were to make Hallaj out to be an Ansarian (thus a Yemenite); but his grandfather was an Iranian—moreover, a Zoroastrian.

(Years 253–262) His father, a "cotton-wool carder" (*hallaj*), emigrates with him, moving about the textile centers of Ahwaz and Tustar (whose imperial Dar al-Tiraz, an outgrowth of the Harithiya of Najran, weaves the annual *kiswa* for the Kaʿba), Nahr Tira, Qurqub, and right into the middle of Arab country, to Wasit (Harithiya were there, at Nahr al-Mubarak); the infant Hallaj becomes profoundly Arabicized in this great Sunnite Hanbalite city, which was endowed with a famous school of "Qurʾan reciters."

Thus he "uproots" himself from his native Iranian soil and, as he did not have maternal Arab parentage, he enters culturally the "*mawali*" grouping, of those "Arabicized" converts who were the best craftsmen of urban Muslim civilization, and who provided Islam from its beginnings with the majority of its "pillars," its *abdal*, its Intercessors, from the time of Salman and Bilal.

(260) At sixteen years old, with his education completed (grammar, Qurʾanic reading, and commentary), he sets out again for Tustar, [where he] enters the service of a fervent Sunnite Shaykh, a bold and independent mystic, named Sahl. One foresees in this decisive step, which sets in motion his entire life, the need of a method for "interiorizing" his practice of worship through spiritual poverty, in order to relish in the Qurʾanic text a substantial word; Sahl is a withdrawn ascetic and also the first author of a symbolic and anagogical *tafsir*.

(262) He leaves him, rather suddenly, to go to Basra to make formal profession of Sufism and to receive the Sufi habit (*khirqa*). To become a Sufi is to affiliate oneself with a genealogy of masters going back to the Prophet, and to come to know thus the full Islam, through a common rule of life that imitates Abraham, Moses, and Jesus as well as Muhammad; which takes its inspiration also from Idris (= Enoch, Hermes) and Khidr (= Elias); and which perfects that true monastic life (*ruhbaniya*), of which the Christian monks, in "desiring to please God," had been the imperfect precursors. The Sufi life is the spiritual "exile" of the "exiles" (*ghurbat al-ghuraba'*), who, according to a hadith of Ibn Hanbal, "will be huddled close to Jesus at the Judgment." Basra is the center of diffusion of the movement, which was born among the disciples of Hasan Basri, together with the monastery of ʿAbd al-Wahid ibn Zayd in ʿAbbadan,

where so many well-known traditionists came to make retreat. But Sufis of Basra, like the preacher Ghulam Khalil, so vehemently against the luxury of the Yemenites of his native town, were outclassed from that time onward in doctrinal development by the young group that Muhasibi, who came from Basra, had organized in Baghdad and that Junayd began to direct. It is probably in Basra that Hallaj serves his apprenticeship with ʿAmr Makki, but ʿAmr Makki came under the influence of Junayd.

(264) He marries in Basra the daughter of A Yq Aqtaʿ Basri, a Sufi and colleague of ʿAmr Makki, who, out of spiritual jealousy, quarrels with Aqtaʿ. Hallaj, in an anxious state, goes to Baghdad to consult Junayd, at the Shunizi, and following his advice "to be patient," he returns to live in Basra with his father-in-law—probably in the Tamim quarter, if, as we think, we must identify the Hallajian Karnabaʾi with Hallaj's brother-in-law, Karnabaʾ being, together with Nahr Tira, a center of weaving of the Banuʾl-ʿAmm, clients and, later, members of the Tamimite Banu Musjashi.

Basra was not only the old Arab literary center where in poetry Hallaj came under the influence of the school of Bashashar; this town was shaken by an unparalleled social crisis of an apocalyptic Shiʿite coloration, namely, the insurrection of black slaves, the Zanj, who were diggers in the natron mines. It was led by a Zaydi ʿAlid pretender, two supporters of whom, at least—M b. Saʿid Karnabaʾi, *katib* of the Zanj vizir ʿAli b. Aban Muhallabi Azdi (having among others the Karnabaʾ appanage), and Muʿalla ibn Asad ʿAmmi, personal secretary (and future historian) of the pretender—were members of the Banuʾl-ʿAmm of Karnabaʾ. We believe that through his brother-in-law (= Karnabaʾi), Hallaj lived in the milieu of the Zanj pretender, a Zaydi Shiʿite milieu permeated with gnostic propaganda, with the Ghurabiya sect of Ibn Jumhur ʿAmmi, master of the Karkhi and of the Shalmaghani, who preached belief in a theophany in the Five of the Mantle (= Muhammad and his own family = Al). In good Sunnite fashion, Hallaj is obliged to react against the Shiʿite idea of the carnal transmission of the divine emanation, and to affirm that the only true *Al Muhammad* are the *ghuraba*ʾ, the "exiles." But his grammatical and theological (*jafr*) lexicon will remain marked throughout his life by this reaction against extremist Shiʿite tribal members.

(270) The Zanj revolt collapses; the regent Muwaffaq reestablishes order in Basra; the hard fiscal screws are tightened up again. Hallaj leaves for Mecca, not on a simple, canonically prescribed (*sarura*) hajj, but, following the counsel of Shafiʿi, on the *ʿumra* [minor pilgrimage performable at any time of year and with fewer ceremonies], for a year-long retreat. He makes the retreat in the court itself of the Kaʿba (between the *Rukn* and the *Maqam*, where the Mahdi is supposed to appear [on the Last Day], and where "the pure soul" (*Nafs Zakiya*) is supposed to be sacrificed). This is the fulfillment of a vow to fast for twelve months, the youthful impulse of an ascetic calling as annunciator, or rather, of a combatant for the holy war, calling upon God in dialogue, summoning Him.

He searches for the secret of the "fiat" (*kun*), which is not an emanation like the *kuni* (*qabda ma'luma* = Muhammad) of the Qarmathians. He seeks the way to surrender his heart to the *Nutq*, to the vital utterance of the inmost divine creative liberty. Sanctity is a "*clairaudience*" that expresses itself. He feels he will reach it only by the strictest discipline in his observance of prescribed religious duties and the most stringent purification of his heart. And when his speech becomes only a pure, divine, inspired utterance, he will and must speak, in order to oppose with it, not only the Shi'ites, who reserve to the Imams the *hadith qudsi*, but also the Sufis, who fear that public use of theopathic utterances would set in motion legal repression. But Love cannot keep quiet: "I am the Truth" means "God is wholly within me."

(271) Returning from the hajj, where he had surely made contact with some Khurasani and Turkish (Shaybani) amirs, he states incisively his personal position, and his experience with regard to inspiration (*ilham*), vis-à-vis other Sufis, in three memorable debates: in Mecca with 'Amr Makki; in Kufa at the home of an 'Alid [282] with Ibrahim Khawwas; (in Baghdad—did it actually take place?—with Junayd). Then he returns to his wife in Basra. There he gains some prominent disciples, one such being a Hashimite, Abu Bakr Rab'i, who is the son-in-law of a rich Ahwazi *shahid*, Ibn Janbakhsh, and an ally of the Hashimites Zaynabi and Sulaymani of Basra.

(272–273) Disowned by his father-in-law, he settles in Tustar with his brother-in-law and his wife; for two years he preaches, and his sermons, heard by popular audiences with a sufficient smattering of Arabic, have a great success.

Harassed by 'Amr Makki, his patience overtaxed by accusing letters that the latter dispatches against him (from Basra), Hallaj gives up the wearing of wool—a symbolic gesture of breaking with the Sufi group (which will not prevent his going back to this garb again later, while on his travels and in prison). He mingles deliberately with "high society people" (*abna' al-dunya*), which is to say, with those who consider any profit legal: with "publicans," with that old cast of fiscal bureaucrats, going back to the Sassanid *dibheran*, cultured scribes, only partly Islamized, of Nestorian, Jewish, or Zoroastrian origin, who are enamored of stylized Arabic prose, science, philosophy, alchemy, and medicine, and are blasé and lax in their morals. Through contact with them, Hallaj changes his style as a popular preacher (*wa'iz*); the familiar phrases and ascetic counsels of his *Riwayat* give way to a vocabulary of abstract ideas and nuances, polemical [in nature] (for "intellect," he cut out the word "*'aql*" and used instead "*fahm*"); the vital feeling of nature gives way to the dialectical schema then currently in use among the Mu'tazilites and Shi'ites of Ahwaz.

At this time he is arrested briefly (and flagellated) in Nahiyat al-Jabal (= Diri, between Sus and Wasit); due to the fact that he is mistaken for a political agent, either Zaydi (Zanj) or Qarmathian, on behalf of an 'Alid Mahdi; at a time when the only Mahdi whose return and reign he had preached was Jesus:

the Jesus who would promulgate in Islam the final Law, the spriritual consummation of the canonical rites and their literal meanings.

(274–279) Hallaj departs alone, on his first great apostolic journey, through the Arabicized centers of the Iranian plateau; in Khurasan he reaches Talaqan (from Juzjan, not Daylam), a city prophesied for two centuries as the chosen seal of the enthronement of the Mahdi; [he lives] among local amirs (in Quhistan, Juzjan, Marrudh, Balkh) and Turkish nomads (Khalaj, Islamized already by the Muqanna'iya Rawandites). He goes from *ribat* to *ribat,* [originally Muslim military outposts, later Sufi retreat houses], as far as Mawaralnahr, returning to Sijistan and Kirman. He is stranded in Isfahan (center of Karramiya Sufis) and in Qumm (Imamites). He stops in Fars (probably at Bayda), where he composes his first books, without being disturbed by the Saffarid administration.

(280) Return to Ahwaz, and to his wife (birth of his third son Hamd); his preaching, in which he "cards hearts" (from whence his name: *hallaj* = carder), resumes in a resounding fashion; people tell tales of his public miracles, of the evangelical sort; two well-known Mu'tazilite theologians, the Sunnite Jubba'i and the Shi'ite A Sahl Nawbakhti become aroused and accuse him of charlatanism.

(281) Hallaj has become famous; he makes a second hajj to Mecca, coming and going via Basra (via Yamama and Bahrayn, where he would have come to know the Qarmathian Jannabi). Coming to Mecca with four hundred disciples, dressed in *muraqqu'a* (patchwork coats; the outward signs of the *futuwwa* (brotherhood), a mysticism that frees itself from worldliness), he stays with the Abu Qubays; not only tolerated but favored by the Meccan authorities, both local (*shaykh al-haram* = the Khurasani Mundhiri), and delegates sent by Baghdad (Caliph Mu'tadid at that time was having repairs made on the Ka'ba, a fragment of which he had encased in the *dihliz* [corridor] of Bab Nubi, the entrance to the new palace); for it is in vain that local Sufis (his father-in-law Aqta', together with Fuwati) and his former disciple Nahrajuri (close to the Karnaba') erupt against him, accusing him of a magical "pact" with the *jinn.*

(282) The *wali* of Ahwaz, Mansur Balkhi, having died, Hallaj returns, via Kufa, to Tustar, only to leave it again for good; he emigrates with his wife, his brother-in-law (who remained faithful to him) and a whole group of Ahwazi notables (*kibar*), to settle together in Baghdad, in the Tustari quarter (west bank). This emigration could take place only with official support: the support of collaborators of the new vizir, 'UA-b.-Sul. ibn Wahb, thus in the milieu of the Harithiya *mawali*, the recently Islamized scribes, formed in the Nestorian schools of Dayr Qunna'; the support, in particular, of Hamd Qunna'i, later an avowed Hallajian. Tustar being the city for luxury textiles, this emigration of notables must be connected with the organization of a Baghdadian branch of the imperial Dar al-Tiraz of Tustar.

(283) Hallaj stays one year in Baghdad, where he sees again two indepen-

dent Sufis, the aging Nuri (connected with the vizir, and master of Qannad) and AB Shibli, a Turkish amir-deputy *hajib* of Muwaffaq, who held onto his important connections in the palace: he became a very dear friend. Then he departs, by sea route, for India (with a diplomatic envoy of Mu'tadid).

(284–289) Second great apostolic journey, with the conversion of the infidels, the Turks, as his avowed goal, this being the apocalyptic sign of the end of time; he travels only through western India (principalities of Mansura and Multan, where Isma'ilis from Qashmir, which was in the process of Islamization, preached); then he goes back through Khurasan (Balkh, Talaqan) and Mawaralnahr, in order to reach Turkestan (Isfijab, Balasaghun) and Ma Sin (= Qocho, near Turfan), the capital of the Uyghur Turks, who were Manicheans by religion. To reach there, he had to join one of the caravans of his *bazzazin* friends from Tustar, which was carrying there expensive Iraqi brocades and bringing back Chinese paper (*sini*, from Shacheou), under the protection of the Samanid amirs who enlisted the Mutawwi'a "volunteers" for the jihad and the Muslim apostolate. If he preached, he did so through Soghdian interpreters and Nestorian or Manichean scribes, in order to confront in the Manichean *zandaqa*, the dualist heresy, the rebellion of evil against good, at the farthest frontier of Islam (as he had done in Mu'tazilite Ahwaz); in order to safeguard the spiritual balance of the world by means of the apotropaic saints, the Intercessors, the *abdal*, who keep watch at the believers' frontier (*ahl al-thughur wa'l-ribatat*); and in order to bring about love of God alone, against the temptation of Evil.

Hallaj returns by way of Khurasan (Nishapur, probably where his eldest son, Sulayman, is settled; in the friendly atmosphere of some Mutawwi'a, such as A 'U Hiri and Abu 'Amr Khaffaf, founder of a Shafi'ite *waqf* that the Surayjiyan Dariki will direct; Hallaj must also have seen Amir Akh Su'luk, the future Samanid *wali* of Rayy, by whom Nasr Qushuri, as a prisoner of war, was treated in a friendly manner; it is there also that he would have known the great doctor AB M b. Zak. Razi), also by way of Nihawand (where he stayed the month of *Nayruz* 288/April 21, 900) and Dinawar.

The notable persons for whom he had written treatises at that time keep in close correspondence with him, as with a spiritual director. He returns to Baghdad, where his rising influence leads M ibn Dawud, leader of the Zahirite canonists, and theorist of a pure Uranistic love, to denounce him to Caliph Mu'tadid himself; without success, for the Shafi'ite canonist Ibn Surayj maintains that such a mystic inspiration is outside the jurisdiction of canon law.

(290–291) Third hajj and '*umra* of two years, ending with his farewell address at 'Arafat, where the denouement of his final crisis of conscience manifests itself. Continual meditation on the Qur'an, strict discipline of observance in worship, severe purification of heart, all have brought about in Hallaj the sign of the sanctifying Spirit in an interior voice obtaining in himself the divine intimacy of theopathic conversation (*shath*), in which he is able to greet his

God through the *talbiya* of the pilgrim, in utter truth. This is the Spirit of God who speaks the *talbiya* through his lips, which makes him the "present (immediate) witness" (*shahid ani*) of this eternal love, this Spirit who has sworn him to the Covenant and will speak to him again at the Judgment; under a human form; not that of Husayn, "the great victim," nor that of Salman, but that of a Muslim Jesus. And, in order that there be maintained a historical continuity of religious witnessing, in order that a single spiritual radiation might pass into humanity, through and through, from Covenant to Judgment, traversing the continuous chain of apotropaic saints, the *abdal* (and not the discontinuous cyclic reappearances of Shiʿite Imams), Hallaj, like his precursor saints, must express the victimal desire of becoming absolutely poor, transparent, annihilated, so that God may expose him under the appearance of powerlessness (*ʿajz*), death, condemnation, guilt, pointing in advance thereby to His Hour, the hour of Judgment (as with Jesus; Qurʾan 43:61; cf. Qurʾan 42:17). Exceeding the Shiʿites, who offer themselves through love to be cursed by the Imam to better mask their plotting on his behalf, and who await this year 290, in order to rise in revolt (the Fatimid revolt of Sahib al-Khal: announced by Abu Saʿid [Ghiyath Shaʿrani])—Hallaj, at the approach of this date, whose numerical value (in *jafr*) is prophetic (290 = Maryam = Fatir), contemplates asking God to let him die anathematized for the Muslim Community (and even for all mankind). At ʿArafat, the sacred site where God "descends" for the annual collective Grand Pardon, where those who have gone astray are put back on the straight path, *huda*, of the mahdi (Qurʾan 2:196), Hallaj asks Him to let him "be even more lost" and to let him become *kafir* [an infidel], in order to be struck down. In actual fact, by a startling inversion of the *Mubahala*, the ordeal that the Prophet had only sketched out vis-à-vis the Harithiya Christians of Najran, and for which he surrenders himself as hostage in his place, Hallaj is going to return to Baghdad, to ask "to die there in the confession of the Cross."

(292) Hallaj leaves Mecca for the last time and wends his way back, saying farewell to Medina, by way of Jerusalem (where he rekindles, ahead of time, on the evening of Holy Saturday A.D. 905, the sacred flame, and from which city he brings back, perhaps, Ibrahim ibn Fatik), to Baghdad. It is there, in the capital, that he wants to transfer (outside the Hijaz), by a complete intercessory sacrifice, the privilege of the hajj, the grace of the annual liturgical *nuzul*, the Grand Pardon. And, returning to his own people, the Tustariyin (in Qatiʿat al-Rabiʿ, on the west bank), he builds there an enclosure, containing a Kaʿba in miniature (AB Madhara'yi will imitate him, before 303, at the Qarafa in Cairo; Muʿtasim had erected in Samarra a Kaʿba for his Turkish officers much earlier than Muʿtadid encased a fragment of the Meccan Kaʿba at Bab Nubi); in it he celebrates in private the Taʿrif, the ʿId al-Qurban, and the whole of the annual hajj.

(292–295) This liturgical initiative to be connected with generosities of the Court for the *Taʿrif* in Baghdad (at the time of the coronation of Muqtadir) rests on a doctrinal teaching dictated to copyists (supported by patrons, probably the Qunna'iya), and is accompanied by solitary nocturnal prayers in cemeteries (Shuhada' Hanifiya, the tomb of Ibn Hanbal) and ecstatic discourse before the crowd, in the markets and mosques of Baghdad; all of which intensely stirs both the people and the Court. Possessed with divine love, Hallaj cries out, "Save me from God, O Muslims. . . . God has given you my lawful blood, quick, kill me: then you will be soldiers in the Holy War, and I a martyr. . . . Kill this accursed one (pointing to himself)." He says to God: "Pardon everyone, but do not pardon me . . . do with me what you will." He speaks not to incite them thereby to murder, but to ask that they uphold, by striking him, the sanctions of the Law, for the common good.

The paradoxical vehemence of this loving preaching revives in many hearts the desire for a reform of the Community, both in its Leader and in its members, for the sake of its spiritual (hajj) and temporal (jihad) defense. It awakens the conflict between Zahirite (Ibn Dawud) and Shafi'ite (Ibn Surayj) canonists, but it convinces many believers of the social efficacy of the prayers and counsels of the saints, of the *abdal* and of their immediate invisible leader (*Shahid ani, Mughith* of Hallajians, *Mustakhlif* of Hanbalites, *Muta'* = *Ghawth*: precursor of the Seal of the saints). There are at that time, according to Istakhri, a number of important figures who see Hallaj as this invisible and inspired leader; among them secretaries of state, relatives and collaborators of Ibn 'Isa and of Hamd Qunna'i (such as Abu'l-Mundhir Nu'man, his friend Ibn Abi'l-Baghl, M ibn 'Abd al-Hamid), amirs (Hy ibn Hamdan, Nasr Qushuri and his family), *walis* of the *amsar* ('Abbasids such as AB Madhara'yi, Nujh Tuluni, and Samanids, such as Akh Su'luk, Simjur, Hy Marrudhi, Bal'ami, Qaratikin), *muluk* (= *dahaqin*: Sawi, Mada'ini, perhaps Rasibi) and Hashimite *ashraf* (AB Rab'i, Haykal, Ahmad b. 'Abbas Zaynabi). They kept up a correspondence with Hallaj for spiritual guidance, getting him into difficulty on the general political plane; it is then that Hallaj must have dedicated to Hy ibn Hamdan, Nasr, and Ibn 'Isa his works on political theory and the duties of viziers. There was at that time, even among the *'ulama'*, a general desire to purify the administrative machinery: they demanded a government that was sincerely Muslim; a vizirate that rendered justice, especially in fiscal matters (against the wicked abuses of the anti-dynastic Shi'ite tax farmers; and a Caliphate that was conscious of the responsibilities of its office before God, one that upholds on God's behalf the liturgical duties of the Muhammadan Community (prayer, hajj; jihad). They hoped that Hallaj would concern himself with those things; but a *fata* (a spiritual brother) does not aim at temporal success. Hallaj had a presentiment that either friends or enemies would take away his liberty, and he wished to retire to his native country, so Istakhri tells us.

(296) The reform plot of the orthodox Sunnites breaks out, with the effort lasting one day, of the "Barbaharite Hanbalite" Caliphate of Ibn al-Mu'tazz. It

fails, not having been able to become financially supported by the Jewish bankers of the Court, who were accomplices of the Shi'ite party; Muqtadir, the infant Caliph, is reinstated, with a new vizir, Ibn al-Furat, a Shi'ite. The military chief of the insurgents, Hy ibn Hamdan, has to flee (he will reappear on the scene twice, in 297 near Baghdad and in 298 near Bayda); which leaves Hallaj, his personal adviser, vulnerable; the vizir puts him under surveillance.

(297–298) A second plan of the "pious" Sunnite vizirate (of M-b-'Abd al-Hamid) supported by one of the Qunna'iya, Sul b. H-b-Makhlad, miscarries. Ibn al-Furat, warned in time, stops it; the police apprehend, at Bab Muhawwal, the leading disciples of Hallaj: he escapes with Karnaba'i and goes into hiding, while waiting to be able to return to Bayda, in Ahwaz; he waits at Sus, a *hasbiya* Hanbalite city and place of refuge of the mystic Subayhi; it is in the fiefdom of Amir Rasibi, who must have looked conveniently the other way.

(299–301) The investigations by the police, and by the ex-Hallajian Dabbas Basri, are spurred on by the strong hatred of an enemy of Hallaj, Hamid, the tax farmer of Wasit and one of the trusted bankers of the palace (he furnished in cash, at the beginning of each month, two-thirds of the pay of the foot archers of the Baghdad garrison). Hamid was a Sunnite, but he had for a son-in-law A Hy ibn Bistam, a Mukhammisi extremist Shi'ite, thus disposed to go with him after Hallaj, who was considered not only a social agitator already watched closely in Ahwaz (Diri), but also a man possessed by demons. A "lucky break" leads to the arrest of Hallaj and Hamid hastens there, to have Hallaj delivered into his hands: at Dur al-Rasibi, outside his jurisdiction.

(301) But, at the moment when Hallaj was led into Baghdad, a coup on the political stage had given the power to a new vizir, a Qunna'i, Ibn 'Isa, at least one of whose secretaries of state, Hamd Qunna'i, his cousin, is a declared Hallajian. Ibn 'Isa causes the failure of the trial, which implies that this vizir, the Queen Mother, and Grand Chamberlain Nasr are in agreement to shield Hallaj and his case from the jurisdiction of the qadi, in accordance with the Shafi'ite *fatwa* of Ibn Surayj. His disciples who were arrested in 298 (Samarri, Shakir) are released; and the only satisfaction that the enemies of Hallaj get is three days' public exposure in the pillory, under an ignominious inscription on a placard reading "Agent of the Qarmathians" (dreamed up by the military commander, Mu'nis Fahl, to oppose the vizir).

(301–308) For nearly nine years, Hallaj will remain confined in the palace, caught between the crossfire of his friends and enemies; as early as *Hijja* 303, he cures the Caliph (and his mother) of a fever attack: the "resurrection" of the parrot of the heir-apparent, Prince Radi, would occur in the year 305 (if this is the Omanian, reported by Filfil); from whence comes the Mu'tazilite pamphlet by Awariji, a friend of Tabari, on his "charlatanism."

(304–306) Second vizirate of Ibn al-Furat, who doesn't dare touch Hallaj; having to provide for Umm Musa and Hy ibn Hamdan, two of his backers, and so Hallaj can write, in prison, his last works.

One of these writings, saved by Ibn ʿAta' in 309, is the *Ta' Sin al-Azal*, in which Hallaj put together an account of the history of Creation, correcting those made by previous Shiʿite gnostics. Two beings have been predestined to witness that the unity of God is inaccessible, Iblis [Satan] before the angels in Heaven, Muhammad before the men on earth; and both stopped half way: through love of the simple idea of the Deity, which veiled God to them; and through abuse of the *shahada*. At the covenant, Iblis did not want to endure the thought that a God to be adored would assume the form of Adam (a prefigure, then, of the Judge). At the *Miʿraj*, Muhammad did not dare enter the consuming fire of divine sanctity, did not intercede for all of the great sinners. In so stopping, the one provoked the sins of men, the other retarded the hour of their Judgment, which it was his mission to announce. And yet the one, in his damnation, incites us to go beyond this threshold of the supreme dereliction of Love, and the other, by his delay, measures out the time for the molding of saints (*ahl al-kahf*). The one and the other defend, like two boundary marks of pure nature, the threshold that the divine Spirit makes cross the sanctified beings whom He introduces into Union through an unforeseeable and transnatural stratagem of love.

(306–308) New coup on the Baghdad political stage, leading to a coalition Sunnite vizirate; in which Hamid is associated with Ibn ʿIsa. In the beginning, Hamid's hatred contains itself, Nasr builds Hallaj a private cell right within the palace; AB Rabʿi and some Qunna'iya circulate his books.

(*Qaʿda* 308) The inevitable conflict breaks out, over fiscal policy, between the virtuous physiocrat, Ibn ʿIsa, and the cynical tax collector, Hamid. Ibn ʿIsa, having set up an inventory, which will become famous, of the budgetary resources of the empire, is winner at the outset; but Hamid baits the Caliph with an odious speculation on the stocks of monopolized corn; Ibn ʿIsa counters by fomenting a popular uprising against this "famine pact" (in which Nasr allows the Hanbalites to play a role). The trade guilds, such as in Basra, Mecca, and Mosul, attack the wholesalers, throwing open the prisons (Hallaj would have refused to escape); Hamid, removed from power, stays out of it. But according to the remark of a witness, Hamza Isfahani, this riot is the first of a deadly series in which the crowd vilifies the ʿAbbasid Caliphate, accuses it of failing in its canonical role, and of leading Islam into dishonor and ruin.

(309) Hamid takes advantage of the return of the military commander-in-chief, Muʿnis, in order to return to Baghdad. Muʿnis, who has just saved the empire in Egypt from the Fatimids of the West, must defend it in Iran against the menace of the Daylamites of the East, who are dividing up the feudal lands and have entered Rayy; Layli, Daylamite prince of Ishkavir, has taken Rayy after Nishapur in Hijja 308/Rabiʿ I 309, thanks to the treason of the wali, Akh Suluk, ex-aid to Muʿnis in 307, who was always under the protection of Nasr and Ibn ʿIsa. Hamid explains to Muʿnis that they must ruin Akh Suʿluk, and, because the latter is a Samanid amir, must break with the Samanid vizir,

Bal'ami, a pro-Hallajian Shafi'ite (who delivers the head of Layli in 309, at the same time that he will refuse to extradite the Hallajians in 309). Such a shift in policy demands a fiscal hardening; the Caliph will agree to it only if he loses confidence in Ibn 'Isa and in Nasr.

In order to ruin them both and to attain his goal, Hamid decided to have the trial of Hallaj, their protégé, reopened; he succeeds, thanks to a third person, AB ibn Mujahid, the respected leader of the corps of Qur'an reciters, and, though anti-Hallajian, a friend of the Sufis Ibn Salim and Shibli. Ibn 'Isa is removed from Hallaj's case, and Nasr from the custody of his person: both to the advantage of Hamid.

Imprudently, the Hanbalites demonstrate against Hamid; they "pray against" this vizir in the streets of Baghdad, as much to protest against his fiscal policy as to save Hallaj (at the instigation of one of their own, the Hallajian Ibn 'Ata'). Then, when Ibn 'Isa and his friend, the aging historian Tabari, disapprove of the recourse to violence, the Hanbalites attack Tabari and besiege his house.

Vizir Hamid has gained control of the game; appointed to maintain order, he is given free reign to make Ibn 'Ata' appear before the court, to kill him and to work out together with a Malikite qadi, Abu 'Umar Hammadi, known for his accommodations to those presently in power, the scenario for Hallaj's death sentence. They will draw their argument from his doctrine on the hajj in order to liken him to the Qarmathian insurgents who wanted to destroy the temple of Mecca. A Hanafite qadi, A Hy Ushnani, agrees to put his name to that.

(19 Qa'da 309) In and out of the court session, in spite of notorious abstentions (Ibn Buhlul and the Shafi'ites), Qadi 'AA ibn Mukram, official leader of the professional witnesses (*wajh al-shuhud*), finds among them an impressive number of counter signatories to the capital sentence delivered by Abu 'Umar; eighty-four, it is said, by adding canonists and *qurra'*; 'AA ibn Mukram will win for that the rich judgeship *in partibus* of Cairo.

(20–21 Qa'da) Nasr and the Queen Mother react to the Caliph; down with an attack of fever, he countermands the execution; Hamid then evokes before Muqtadir the specter of a Hallajian social revolution, and conspires with General Mu'nis to do away with the two protégés of his old friend Nasr: Akh Su'luk and Hallaj.

(22 Qa'da) On coming out of a great banquet offered to his guests in honor of Mu'nis and Nasr, Caliph Muqtadir signs both Hallaj's death warrant and the pardon of Amir Yf ibn Abi'l-Saj, designated (to succeed the dismissed Akh Su'luk) as *wali* of Rayy. This was at the request of Mu'nis, who thereby performs for Ibn Abi'l-Saj the same debt of military honor that kept Nasr busy performing since 291 for Akh Su'luk; both, like magnanimous victors, had freed them after having taken them captive. Mu'nis also obtains the pardon of two (or three) Saffarid amirs destined one day to threaten the Samanids' flank. And the promotion of Ibn Abi'l-Saj will lead to control of the finances of Rayy by Niramani, the brother-in-law of Ibn al-Hawari, paymaster general of

Mu'nis' army, who passes thus from the Nasr faction to that of Ibn Abi'l-Saj; like Amir M-b-'Abd al-Samad, who is going to relinquish the police department of Baghdad to Nazuk, friend of Mu'nis. With Akh Su'luk conquered and killed on 8 Hijja 311, Ibn Abi'l-Saj will send his head to the Caliph; via the good offices of Muflih and without the knowledge of Nasr; "in order not to depress him."

(23 Qaʿda) Trumpet calls (tanfir) announce that vizir Hamid entrusts the execution of Hallaj, after having cruelly worsened its terms (probably under a Shiʿite influence), to the police chief, Ibn ʿAbd al-Samad; measures are concerted for warding off a riot. That evening, in his cell, Hallaj exhorts himself to martyrdom and foresees his glorious resurrection (prayer recorded by Ibr ibn Fatik).

(24 Qaʿda–25 Qaʿda) At Bab Khurasan, on the threshold of the west bank police headquarters, "before an enormous crowd," Hallaj is flogged, hands and feet cut off, exhibited on a gibbet: still living. Friends and enemies call upon him to answer for himself there, rioters set fire to some shops. The coup de grâce (decapitation) is postponed to the next morning, to permit the vizir to be present at the reading of the death sentence. Hamid, to shore up the Caliph's resolve for the execution, had indeed said to Muqtadir "if you find it wrong, afterwards, kill me"; but some amazing accounts had already spread during this dramatic night; and it may very well be that Hamid had judged it prudent to disavow his responsibility (with that of the Caliph) and had loudly urged the shuhud, consignatory witnesses, grouped around Ibn Mukram, as qualified representatives of the Muslim Community, to cry out: "This is for the salvation of Islam. Let his blood fall on our necks." And the head fell, the trunk was soaked with oil and set fire to, the ashes were thrown, from the top of a minaret, into the Tigris.

This execution casts all around this final flame a penetrating light on the movements of various actors in the trial, underlined by some incidents that reveal their inner states of mind.

Within the group of enemies: at its head, the old vizir Hamid; his long career as tax farmer had accustomed him to considering the payment of the tax to the Treasury as a simple return levied in advance by the Court on his own tax farm, of which he spent a large part, with a bantering and earthy cunning, for a retinue adorned with freedmen and not very refined festivities; also his tough-fisted bureaucratic Sunnite faith had fixed him for a long time against Hallaj, his spirituality, his asceticism, his sermons on the hereafter and his charisma; to him, this man was just a hideous sorcerer whom he had to destroy, and he was pushed precisely to that end by a confidant whom his son-in-law A Hy M ibn Bistam respected: Shalmaghani, a strange and somber Shiʿite gnostic, dissembling and cruel, whose turn will come, thirteen years later, for having dared to summon a dangerous rival to a judgment of God. But once Hallaj was beaten, his sorcery could still prove harmful, and Hamid, ever distrustful, intended only to undertake the death sentence of a rebel, leaving to the *qadis* sole responsibility with the *shuhud* for the canonical condemnation for heresy.

Next, the military commander Mu'nis, a Greek eunuch, not much younger; he did not declare himself until then against Hallaj, who was a protégé of his friend, Grand Chamberlain Nasr; but this man was, above all, a leader of mercenary soldiers, and, increasingly, the oath of allegiance which bound him personally to Mu'tadid and to his sons, thus to Caliph Muqtadir, was interpreted by him as a prior right, a privilege qualifying him to carry out his military job; in agreement with the vizir, against the policy of Ibn 'Isa whom he had supported up to then in his financial and diplomatic management. Since it was necessary, against Nasr, to replace, as military amir of Rayy, Ibn Abi'l-Saj for Akh Su'luk, Mu'nis, connected furthermore by his word to Ibn Abi'l-Saj, demonstrates his power strongly to Nasr and to the Queen Mother by abandoning their friend Hallaj to the hatred of the vizir; this is the beginning of the break with the Queen Mother, which will culminate in the pretorian coup d'état of 317/930.

Next, Qadi Abu 'Umar, ambitious, patient and subtle, who at the time of this coup d'état will get the post of grand qadi; accomplished courtier, possessed of a magnificent grace in manners that will remain legendary, and curiously addicted to perfumes, he was in the habit of reversing his decisions with the most disconcerting cynicism; he compensated for the imperfect tools provided by the Malikite rite in hadith and in *qiyas* by a refined concern for formal elegance in legal casuistry, and was very proud of having succeeded, for "the common good," in bringing to a successful conclusion a trial as difficult in solution as it was specious, in which he was serving, one more time, the vengeance of a vizir.

Finally, the weak and fickle sovereign, Muqtadir, tired of hearing himself summoned to live up to his Caliphal responsibilities to God, turns away from Ibn 'Isa and from Hallaj; disposed by some Shi'ite legitimist agents, such as Ibn Rawh, to doubt his own legitimacy, recaptured and won over by gold pieces that his Shi'ite ex-vizir, Ibn al-Furat, has glittering before him in veritable seances of hypnotism, Muqtadir prefers to yield to the entreaties of a corrupt black mercenary, the head eunuch Muflih, an accomplice paid expressly by Muhassin, son of Ibn al-Furat, working in the third vizirate of his father, and to reject the supplications of the Queen Mother, who was beseeching him to save Hallaj.

In the group of friends: the vice-vizir Ibn 'Isa, honorable, but a prudent opportunist, looks to his personal position when ceasing to protect the life of Hallaj; but he apparently keeps his sympathy for him, since he preserves one of his works in a little case, extends welcome in 310 to a Hallajian, the head of the *shuhud* of Cairo, Ibn al-Haddad, and in 312 breaks the career of Ibn Mukram, the qadi of Cairo hostile to Ibn al-Haddad, and former head of the *shuhud* who sentenced Hallaj.

Then, certain persons on a secondary level, spectators more or less moved to pity by phases of his punishment: 'Isa Dinawari (perhaps the father of the

Hallajian Faris), Abu'l-'Abbas-b-'Abd al-'Aziz, the Qur'an reciter 'Atufi, Qalanisi, the Mu'tazilite Qannad and especially Ibrahim ibn Fatik, who appears indeed to have been imprisoned with Hallaj, but is presented in the oldest Sufi tradition as a sort of impersonal reporter of the martyrdom.

One Hashimite, Haykal, about whom we know only that he was supposed to be executed alongside Hallaj.

Finally, four distinguished witnesses testifying to the religious sincerity of Hallaj, each of whose historical influence will be major; at first, two close friends, Ibn 'Ata' and Shibli, then two last-minute disciples, Shakir and Ibn Khafif.

As for Ibn 'Ata', whose desire to be tested, like the prophets, in the crucible of suffering, had been previously granted, we know that he musters courage to share the fate of his friend: (letter and clandestine visit to his prison), accepting in his keeping some manuscripts (which he will entrust to his own heir, 'Ali Anmati), endeavoring himself to stir up on [Hallaj's] behalf the Hanbalite common people, witnessing boldly before their communal court faith in direct mystic union with God; the source of all charism brutalized then by guards of the vizir, who are irritated by his upbraidings, Ibn 'Ata' dies as a result of beatings received, two weeks before Hallaj, having thereby hastened and perhaps worsened the conditions of the latter's punishment.

As for Shibli, Turkish nobleman, ex-chamberlain under Muwaffaq, we know that his conversion to the Sufi rule of life had led him to renounce not only his fief at Dimawand, but also his studies in Malikite law begun during his youth in Alexandria, when Hallaj appeared to him, in the great mosque of Baghdad, in the "poets' corner," as the chosen witness of that divine splendor that transfigures the human face. He was from that time on attached to him, not without indulging in some public acts of behavior that were intentionally eccentric (a shrewd, but chronic, "madness," whereas the madness of Ibn 'Ata', that was momentary in character, had been unconscious) which kept him from being found guilty with Hallaj; while half denying him at the trial, he came to assist him, with his anguish, and to repent at his execution; and there, before his gibbet (where he was supposed to have hurled a rose at him), he meditated and understood in part the mystery of sainthood; he transmits henceforward to Sufi novices, in secret, the worship of Hallaj's memory: as a jewel of forbidden beauty, not as a sacrament of immortality to be distributed to everyone.

As for Ibn Khafif, another convert, from a rich family in Shiraz, we know that he saw Hallaj only once, at the very end, in his prison, in such a complete state of attachment to the divine will that he came away convinced forever of having seen there a "man of God" (*rabbani*).

In the palace: the *hajib* Nasr, a Greek convert, turned Hanbalite, who will dare to go into mourning for his executed friend, will get his son and daughter and his disciples released from prison. Elsewhere, in the depths of the imperial harem, with daylight settling on the colonnades of date palms, their trunks inlaid with teakwood and copper, and over the solid pewter pool within its closed garden, the silence of the Queen Mother Shaghab, she too of Greek origin; to her would fall the preservation of certain relics (of Hallaj's head in the palace) and the pilgrimage to the *maslib*.

And in the center, raised above and out of himself, there was Hallaj himself, manifesting to all on the gibbet, that particular night, in a prolonged ecstasy of the body triumphant over death, the immortal personality of the Qur'anic Christ, the soulful effigy of the Spirit of God, "The one whom they have not killed, whom they have not crucified . . ." (Qur'an 4:157): according to the answer countering the sarcasms of the Mu'tazilite AH Balkhi, and taken up with force by Abu Hamid Ghazali.

CHAPTER TWO

The Years of Apprenticeship: His Teachers and Friends

I. NATIVE MILIEU*

His Birthplace: Bayda

Hallaj was probably of Iranian, not Arab, stock, despite what people said to the contrary later. He was born in one of the eastern provinces of the 'Abbasid Caliphate, in Fars. This region, at that time still profoundly Iranian in language and Zoroastrian in culture, with its fire altars set in the mountains and its archives in fortified castles, was beginning, however, to become Arabicized at its trading centers and all along its strategic routes. And the birthplace of Hallaj, Bayda, the second stop, after Juwaym (Guyum), on the Shiraz-Isfahan route, became the very first center of Arabicization in the region. It had been the camp of the Muslim *muqatila* sent to lay siege to Istakhr by the *wali* of Basra, 'AA-b-'Amir-b-Kurayz 'Abshami in A.H. 29; the favorite residence of the famous Ziyad, when he was *wali* of Fars in A.H. 38–42; and the birthplace of the greatest Arab grammarian, Sibawayh. It was known as "Madinat al-Bayda, the White City," and equalled Istakhr in importance in the ninth century of our era. It was also the place from which the first *shaykh al-shuyukh* (d. 473) of Fars came.

Its name "The White," quite unusually, became Arabicized immediately, because "Bayda" is a translation of an original Iranian toponym containing the element "Isfid," which in fact exists as a place eighty kilometers farther to the west, at Qal'a Isfid. It seems to have come about in the following way: the Arab conquest, emphasizing the importance of the Shiraz-Isfahan route, attracted the capital of the district away from the old citadel built by Gushtasp on the western slope of a ridge overhanging the narrow pass through which the route from Sus to Persepolis twisted southward toward Juwaym; and it moved it eastward beyond the eastern slope, to the edge of the plain of Kur, at the military base camp that the besieging armies of Istakhr set up adjacent to a smaller castle, Diz Nishnak (known also as Dar-i Isfid, which became Bayda). This castle had been built there to guard the entrance to the mountain that gave access to the old citadel, Isfid Diz (which became Qal'a Isfid), "The White Castle."

The geographer Istakhri informs us that this new command post, Bayda, not only had a castle, but also a *rabad* or "suburb" outside the Iranian city proper (the *shahristan*), obviously born out of a way-station for Arab caravans, inhab-

*From *Passion of Al-Hallaj*, vol. 1, 53–59, 60–84, 85–89, 90–95, 98, 107–10, 111–34

ited both by Arabs, camel drivers, and merchants, and by artisans of the region, Arabicized and Islamized. Hallaj's father must have belonged in this last category, and it was in this milieu that the son was raised. As to his exact place of birth, it was al-Tur, another Arabic toponym, a simple stopover for caravans four parasangs to the east of Bayda toward the Kur plain, which this route crosses and extends the length of as it rises toward Sumayram and Isfahan.

To determine the extent of Islamization of Bayda in this era, we note that a qadi court (shar'i) was located there, that a ribat (convent) of ascetics was founded there, on the Mayin route, less than twenty years after the death of Hallaj, and, finally, that in the hundred years that followed, there were among the Baydawi, the "natives of Bayda" named in the collections of biographies, four jurisconsults (including two future Shafi'ite qadis of Karkh (in Baghdad), three ascetics, and a muqri'.

Administratively, Bayda was at that time one of five territorial districts or kura of Istakhr, together with Mayin, Nayriz, Abarquh, and Yezd. Several of these districts have now been separated or combined: Bayda split off from Kamfiruz, Mayin split off from Ramjird. There was also in Fars, outside the five districts, a subdivision made up of pasturage lands for the Kurd transhumants, the five zumum: Bayda belonged to zumm Bazanjan of the Jilawayh as early as A.H. 144.

Bayda was at that time, and still is, a district (buluk) of "cold lands" and healthy climate; populated now by Lur peasants, scattered throughout fifty-four ghariya or areas far from administrative centers. In the north to northwest some oaks (ballut) survive still on the side of the mountain; in the east to southeast, poppy and cotton fields, intersected by ditches, grazing lands where the Qashgha'is (Bayat) live in summer as nomads, still speaking a Turkish dialect—then some rice fields, toward the Kur River, running past the Karela, whose spacious valley, in the direction east to southeast, stretches out toward Persepolis.

I visited Bayda, now called "Tell Bayda," November 28, 1930, with Gaston Maugras, our ambassador to Tehran. In a light car, through barren trails frequently intersected by irrigation ditches, then afterwards on foot, we reached, six parasangs from Shiraz, Tell Bayda: an insignificant group of shanties gathering together no more than sixty inhabitants in the headquarters of a district of 864 square kilometres containing in 1913, according to Demorgny, 20,000 souls; and at that time paying in taxes 2,821 tumans in cash and 2,000 kharvars of cereals in kind. In Tell Bayda, the land belonged to four capitalists from Shiraz, all identified as "hajji": Zaynal, Taliat Saltana, I'timad Saltana, and Mustapha Ghuli Khan. About two parasangs further east, the Malliyan knoll holds together, with shanties, some ruins that some believe to be an ancient site of Bayda.

What was said previously about the high degree of Arabization of Bayda in the ninth century makes plausible the curious remark by Daylami, a disciple of Ibn Khafif, "that Hallaj did not understand Persian." In contrast with his great precursor in mysticism, (Bayezid) Bistami (d. A.D. 874), who knew only Persian and whose prayers and meditations were thought out in the Iranian language, Hallaj always thought and prayed only in Arabic: even in Bayda. It is not certain that he left Bayda before the age of 16; he kept some friends there (four of his *rawi* are Baydawi, as opposed to three Wasiti and four Baghdadi, in the collection of *Akhbar al-Hallaj*); he returned there to stay on two occasions. In the thirteenth century, an Arab family established in Bayda claimed descendence from him; also the Hallajian *isnad* of a Sunnite congregation's affiliation still transmitted in our day was authenticated.

His Awakening to the Moral Life (Anecdote of the Woman)

We have only one account of the sojourns of Hallaj in his birthplace, and it is very impressionistic in character; it is not very sound, for it does not fit either of the two periods when Hallaj was known to have actually resided in Bayda: during his early infancy and his period of preaching in 280. By Musa ibn Abi Dharr Baydawi, it runs as follows: "I was walking behind Hallaj through the alleyways of Bayda, when the shadow of a figure was cast on him from the roof of a terrace; Hallaj, looking up, saw a beautiful woman; then he turned toward me and said: 'You will see one day what calamity will befall me, because of this (imprudent) glance, even though you have to wait a long time.' Then, on the day when they put him on the pillory, I was in the crowd weeping; his glance fell on me, from high on the pillory, and he said to me: 'Musa, whosoever raises his head, as you have seen me do, and stretches his neck (*ashrafa*) towards a forbidden sight, deserves to have his neck stretched in public like this . . .' and he pointed toward the pillory."

How was the religious problem settled for the infant Hallaj? Later legend will claim that his mother made a vow, when pregnant, offering him in advance to the divine service of the *fuqara'*, a vow of which God was supposed to have given him a premonition, and which she was supposed to have fulfilled as soon as he had reached the age of seven (cf. the vow of Gandhi's mother). His mother must have been an Arab: of the Harithiya. We know, from Khatib, that his grandfather, Mahamma, was a Zoroastrian, but his father, Mansur, was a convert to Islam. The majority of the family seems to have gone over to Islam, with a sizable minority remaining Zoroastrians, plus a few Christians and Jews. There were no Sabaeans or Manicheans in Fars; Hallaj could have met Sabaeans in Tustar and in Wasit.

Istakhri and Muqaddasi give us information about the distribution of Muslim sects in Fars in the tenth century, the great majority of which were Sunnite. The lands of the coast to the south, like Ahwaz to the west, were Hanafite in law, Qadarite in dogma, under Basra's influence. The "cold lands," including Bayda, belonged to the *ahl al-hadith*, which is to say, Malikites, rather than

Hanbalites, in law, and *Hashwiya* in dogma; their qadis were of loose morals. Among the qadis of Shiraz, Ibn Surayj (296–301, d. 305) was the first to become interested in the mystics, probably because of Hallaj, whom he had known in Baghdad; then came the Shafi'ite *muhaddith*, Hy Muhamili (301–318), then AM 'AA-b-A-b-Sul-b-Ibr ibn Abi Burda Fazari (324), whose descendents were office holders for two centuries, with two interruptions imposed by the Buwayhid power in favor of two pro-Shi'ite Zahirid qadis, A Sa'd Bishr-b-Hasan (around 340, d. 381) and A Faraj Fami (around 365, d. 390). But prior to that, there were Shi'ites only in Khurra (near Kazarun), and it is not known if the tomb attributed to a son of the Eighth Imam in Mayin near Bayda already existed. Nevertheless, Hallaj must have heard Shi'ism discussed by administrative scribes originally from Fars, whom he will meet again in Baghdad. Among his early friends, from Bayda, we call attention to three significant names, of which two were definitely Shi'ite, Musa-b-Abi Dharr and Jundab-b-Zadhan, and the third a doubly Zoroastrian name, Khurrazad-b-Firuz.

The Sojourn in Wasit

"He was raised (= *nasha'a*) in Wasit and in Iraq," affirms Khatib, following Sulami (*Tabaqat*) concerning this point in preference to Ibn Bakuya (the account of Hamd), who says that "he was raised in Tustar," and has Hallaj saying to Jurayri (the account of Hadrami): "I was educated (= *rabbayt*) in Khuzistan and in Basra." But, while editing the account of Hamd in which he has given him his nickname of *hallaj* or "carder (of consciences)" in Ahwaz (= Khuzistan = Tustar), Ibn Bakuya reproduces (number 3) the account by a father of a well-known *muqri'* of Wasit, 'Ali-b-A Ibn Bardhanaqa: in which Hallaj receives this nickname in Wasit for having miraculously come to the aid of a cotton carder in his shop there. Sulami (in his *Ta'rikh*) even puts this Wasiti etymology before the Ahwazi, and adds that Hallaj's father was, in fact, a carder: in Wasit, A YF Qazwini specifies. 'Attar says also: "He was reared (= *perwerdeh*) in Wasit."

We can place this sojourn in Wasit from about 249 (or 253) to 258: from his fifth (or ninth) to his fourteenth year. The awakening of intellects is early in these times and regions; some memorized hadith as early as age four and became *shahid* affiliated with a qadi at fifteen; the cycle of elementary studies, often concluded in the tenth year, comprised, at the maximum: learning the Qur'an by heart; then a grammar manual and several hadith by heart; drilling in the art of reciting the Qur'an (*tajwid*); and, between times, hearing and memorizing certain formulas of prayer (*awrad*) instructed by *muhaddith*, and certain secular stories in rhymed prose or in verse, transmitted by blind persons or by women in the family. The rest was learned, either in the Qur'anic school, or in a corner of the mosque, or around the qadi court; that is, if the town was a center of Arabic culture.

This was the case of Wasit, an Arab colony on Aramaen land, founded in 85/704 by the Umayyad governor Hajjaj: located "midway" (whence its name) a parasang to the west of Dayr Hizqal (convent of the "resurrection" of Eze-kial), equidistant (= forty parasangs) from Mada'in, Kufa, Basra, and Suq al-Ahwaz; on the right bank of the Tigris, opposite ancient Kashkar, chief town of an extremely fertile flooded district, Shadhsabur (divided into four fiscal *tussuj*: Kashkar, Zandaward, Badhbun, Jawazir): comprising, in the north to-ward Baghdad, the small market towns of Fam al-Silh, Nahr Sabus, and Madharaya; in the east toward Ahwaz, al-Tib and Qurqub; in the west, toward Kufa (via Junbula-Tallfakhkhar), Nahraban (= Najraniya, colony of Harithi Christians, successors of the Hamra Daylam Iranians); in the south, toward Basra, Faruth. In the countryside, alongside the Aramaean peasantry, there were some Arab tribes, of Bakr (B. Dhuhl-b-Shayban) and of Qays ('Abs, B. Rifa'a), stirred up in the period by some Shi'ite revolutionary movements (es-pecially in Junbula). In the town itself, the Arab majority (with some clients of the Azd tribe and some Turks brought from Bukhara) was violently Sunnite, pro-Umayyad, and Hanbalite; and its Jami' mosque was the center of a *qurra'* school (= reciters of the Qur'an) and of a hadith school.

Owing to the presence there of princes in exile (Musta'in, in 252; Muwaffaq, in 264), then to the Court of Muwaffaq after 257, Wasit took on some of the aspects of an intellectual capital (theological contests between the Mu'tazilite Abu Mujahid (d. 269) and the Zahirite Ibn Dawud held before Muwaffaq, while remaining, in fact, essentially a pietistic Hanbalite center. Leading fiscal agent families had their estates there, in Madharaya, particularly the Shalmaghani family, who held extremist Shi'ite views at the time of the viz-irate of Ibn Bulbul. This family will found the 'Azaqiriya sect, cursed in the *diwan* of another extremist, Hy Khasibi (born in Junbula, d. 357), second founder of the Nusayris: at the same time as the Hallajiya sect and the Basliya, an Isma'ili vegetarian sect located around Wasit, directed by Abu Hatim Burani (295), then (later) by a nephew of the famous 'Abdan, 'Isa-b-Musa (316).

Many Christian converts of the Wasit region, particularly in Sarqarmaqa (homeland of the vizirial family of the Banu Wahb), had remained clients of the Balharith-b-Ka'b tribe, whose industry was weaving (= Nahraban), also in Qurqub and Tustar; and they were surely in close contact with the Balharith of Mada'in and Dayr Qunna, the cradle of Caliphal scribes in Baghdad; it is among these that Hallaj will find disciples. Junbula, on the other hand, was not only the homeland of extremist Shi'ites like 'Isa-b-Mahdi and Khasibi, but of a celebrated Sabaean writer, Ibn Wahshiya (d. 291, born in Qussayn), who Ibn al-Zayyat says was interested in Hallaj as an experimenter in magic. We add that some Imamites will accuse Hallaj of having learned magic from 'AA-b-Hilal Kufi, teacher of the extremist Shi'ite Abu Khalid Kabili; but, as this Ibn Hilal was sent for by Hallaj (as the astrologer Nawbakht was sent for by Caliph

Mansur for the building of Baghdad), specifically to arrange the augural theme
at the time of Wasit's founding, one realizes why scholars have been tempted
to explain the very strange presence of extremist Shi'ite terms in the Hallajian
mystical lexicon by the heterodox associations that Hallaj might have had in
Wasit. But he was too young then, and it is in Basra and Tustar, where the
people of Wasit came continually, that Hallaj later could have known the heretical sects cited above.

We should keep in mind that it is in Wasit, in a purely Arabic milieu, that
Hallaj received his first religious formation, a strictly Sunnite formation,
among Hanbalite traditionists. It is Wasit that explains Hallaj's curious lack of
familiarity with discussion in a Persian dialect, as is evident later from an incident in Isfahan.

It is also in Wasit that Hallaj, expressly characterized as a *hafiz* by his disciples, learned the Qur'an by heart: probably according to the *qira'a* of 'Asim,
which was the one followed in the local school. And, even though in that era,
the dictation classes of the *muhaddith* had fifty times as many students as the
courses for *tajwid* (reciting) (in Wasit, 30,000 *rawis* passed through the *halqa*
of 'Ali-b-'Asim Wasiti [d. 201]; and in Baghdad, 70,000 in that of Yahya-b-
Harun Wasiti [d. 206]), it is not certain that Hallaj had attended them assiduously, for, if he refers occasionally to hadith, it is never accompanied by an *isnad*,
but is presented in a very strange and eccentric way. It is perhaps only in Tustar
with Sahl, and not in Wasit, that he will study hadith—and in his own way.

The Departure for Tustar: Sahl Tustari

In 260, at the age of sixteen, Hallaj leaves Wasit and goes to Tustar to study
with a master, Sahl; he will remain there for two years (260–262) in "his service" (*khadim* = famulus), according to the custom followed by those whom a
master accepts as disciples. For Hallaj this does not yet involve putting on the
woolen robe and entering the Sufi community, to which Sahl himself did not
adhere. But his decision to leave, made and carried out on his own (his father is
no longer mentioned, having died, no doubt in Wasit; and the role of his
mother, pledging him to the service of Junayd, occurred only in legend), does
show that Hallaj, at the end of his early intellectual training, enters the critical
period of the mystic vocation.

First of all, we believe his leaving is due to an inner dissatisfactioin. Most
often the first awakening of the personality is experienced as a painful conflict
of opinion, a failure of understanding that one feels is faulty without being able
to correct it.

We have several attempts at representation of the initial Hallajian crisis,
sketched out in the form of premonitions (Musa Baydawi: the sin of an unpre-
meditated glance, in Bayda, or of threatening prophesies (Junayd: for an indis-

creet question, or a swallowed amulet; Makki, for disrespect to the Qur'an, or theft of its esoteric *Ganjnama*); but all of them supposing Hallaj to have already entered the mystic life; however, it is the passing of the threshold that interests us.

Hallaj could have heard people speak of Sahl in Wasit at the home of Qadi Sarifini (former qadi of Jundisabur): as an eminent Sunnite (Sufyanite, through his maternal uncle Ibn Sawwar: *rawi* of Abu ʿAmr, head of the Basrian *qurra'* school), and as an imitator, trying, not only to transmit to his disciples a correct text of the Qur'an, but also to make them understand it and to penetrate its spirit (*fahm al-Qur'an*): surely a bold attitude of mind: Sahl is, before Ibn ʿAta', the first mystic to have drafted an outline of *tafsir*.

On the other hand, Hallaj could not have remained indifferent to the political crisis, to the threat of social subversion that the proletarian insurrection of the Zanj around Basra represented (since 255; black slaves and impoverished, starving Bedouins), along with the raids into Ahwaz by Kurds coming, with Ibn Wasil, from his native land. What became of the unity and the legitimacy of the ʿAbbasid Caliphate (the Hanbalites of Wasit were faithful to the memory of [the Umayyad Caliph] Muʿawiya)? On that, Sahl could also enlighten. He was staunchly for the ʿAbbasids as providential guardians of order and unity in the Community. He prayed for them, however great their private faults may have been, and in spite of all the apocalyptic forebodings peddled around (son of Ghulam Khalil), concerning the ruin of Basra and the fateful year of 260, by the Shiʿites.

Hallaj remained with Sahl for two years. He was not supervised "privately" by a spiritual director, but was simply one pupil of a head of a school, the founder of the future Salimiya, assisting him in his numerous receptions together with such co-disciples as Jurayri, Barbahari, ʿUmar-b-Wasil Anbari, following day by day the flow of discussions and events that revolved in Tustar, as in all Ahwaz, around a traditional capital: Basra; traffic was continual between the towns of Ahwaz and Basra. Did Sahl go there, with Hallaj, between 260 and 262? We do not think so, since he saw Yq-b-Layth during his invasion of Ahwaz (262–265), before being exiled to Basra, and before the Zanj were driven out of it (in 267).

Hallaj retained throughout his life the stamp of Sahl's practices and ideas: *wudu'* (ritual purification) before every prayer, sustained effort in penitential asceticism, continual renunciations of self, united to the attention of a direct divine counsel, illuminating (*tajalli*) the soul positively, and the notion of the pre-eternal Nur Muhammadi; also the Salimiya will be pro-Hallajian. But Hallaj will split away from Sahl over several points: he will repeat the hajj.

At the end of two years, in 262, Hallaj left Sahl; a sudden departure for Basra, which two (hostile) sources interpret as a lack of respect shown toward his old teacher; the motive for it is not given.

Local history may give us a clue. From 260 to 262, Ahwaz and especially

Tustar, administered by 'Abbasid military governors ('AR-b-Muflih, Abu Saj, Ibr-b-Sima, A-b-Laythuya), lived under the constant and double threat of the insurgent Zanj and the allied Kurdish highlanders. After *Rajab* 262, M-b-'UA ibn Azarmard, a Kurd given authority over Ahwaz by the Saffarid rebel Yq-b-Layth before his defeat of Dayr al-'Aqul, succeeds in penetrating briefly into Tustar; he then promises his ally, the Zanj leader in Ahwaz, 'Ali Muhallabi, to have the *khutba* pronounced there for the 'Alid rebel of Basra (the whole affair collapsed; Tustar, evacuated, was retaken only in 263, for two years, by Yq-b-Layth). The negotiator, on the Zanj side, was the *katib* and *khalifa* (secretary and successor) of Muhallabi, M-b-Yahya-b-Sa'id Karnaba'i, one of the most important *mawla* ('*ilj*) notables of Basra, who had rallied to the rebel. He was a member of a leading Ahwazian family established for more than a century in Basra, in which city the family debated as equals with that of the Al Sulayman Hashimites, and in which it was satirized by the 'Abdite poet Ibn al-Mu'adhdhal. Another Karnaba'i, 'AA-b-M-b-Hisham, who will be captured in Tahitha (in 267), had accepted from the Zanj the post of qadi (of Tahitha: his father, Abut Wathila M Karnaba'i, must have been the Zanj qadi of Basra, for he is described in the *Akhbar al-Zanj* of Shaylama as a *rawi* on the same level as the Maliki qadi, M-b-Hammad) (if the Kirmani correction is authentic). And one other Karnaba'i was one of the leading Ahwazian disciples of Hallaj, the one who was able to hide him there from 298 to 301. We believe that he should even be identified as Hallaj's own brother-in-law (*khal waladihi*:), the one who had led the emigration to Baghdad of the people of Tustar (thus an eminent person: with a financial interest in the weaving of brocades), the one who was brought back with him from Sus to Baghdad in 301.

Hallaj must have been connected intimately in 262 in Tustar with some member of the Karnaba'i family, who may have enticed him to leave for Basra; where he was married some months later.

The Arrival in Basra

In 262, upon his arrival in Basra, Hallaj found himself for the first time in one of the intellectual capitals of Islam. After the massacres of 257 and a short-lived 'Abbasid reoccupation (by Ishaq-b-Kurdaj, 258–260), the Sunnite religious life had resumed there; the mystic community of 'Abbadan had not been disturbed, the hajj caravans were getting through as usual. It was with one of the teachers of mysticism, a Hijazian who continued to organize those caravans, 'Amr Makki, that Hallaj came to live. 'Amr was clearly a Sufi; he persuaded Hallaj to make his profession with him; and it was he who must have performed the ritual of trimming his moustaches. According to the testimony of Khurrazadh, Hallaj was leading at that time a profoundly mortified life, one of an already advanced asceticism. But he was not a recluse. He probably resided in Mirbad (the quarter for caravans and noble Hashimites), with 'Amr or the Banu Mujashi or the Azd (Balharith). He used to pray, we know from the sources, in the Jami' mosque; probably also in the *Masjid al-Amir* (the one preferred by early ascetic Hasan Basri, d. A.D. 728) in the *khums* of Khurayba, where he rediscovered, in the quarter of the Ziyadiyin (clients of the viceroy, Ziyad), some comrades from his native village; in the proximity of the populous and rich *khums* of the Azd, chosen (because of the rallying to the Zanj of the Yemenite faction of the Bilaliya and of 'Ali Muhallabi, who had become the vizir of the pretender) as residence of the Zanj governor (A-b-Sa'id Qalus 257–267, and afterwards his nephew Malik 267–268: in the Sayhan quarter).

It is certainly there that the Karnaba'i director of the vizir's cabinet resided, and there that Hallaj must have become close friends with his future father-in-law, Abu Ya'qub Aqta' (= "the one-hand amputee") Basri. If, as we suppose, Aqta' was not only acquainted, but allied with the Karnaba'i family, why is this *nisba* (family ascription) not given to him? Was it perhaps to conceal, after the defeat of the Zanj, the brief rallying of the Karnaba'i to a rebellion (none of the Karbaba'i appear to have been executed; people were satisfied with demolishing their country seat). Aqta' is called *katib*, secretary of Junayd, which implies a scholarly training (relatively rare among the Sufis of that time), and among the disciples of Junayd a reputation dating necessarily from the period subsequent to 270. Aqta', in the period of 262–264, was surely in Basra (which he will leave again later for a prolonged stay in Mecca). It is in Basra that Hallaj married his daughter, Umm al-Husayn ('Attar affirms this; and the "account of Hamd," in spite of an obscure *thumma kharaja*, suggests it); Aqta' gave her in marriage to him, out of admiration for his rigorous asceticism.

Then a strange incident took place: Hallaj seems to have contracted this marriage without having consulted 'Amr Makki about it, with whom Aqta' was also on close terms. 'Amr Makki, taken by surprise, was angry at him ("began to hate him," account of Hamd): and, without reproaching him either for lack of respect or for violation of the rules (novices could marry), he broke with Aqta', which put Hallaj in a difficult position. One can imagine, as the course of 'Amr's life suggests, that it is not through the jealous zeal of the director, but through the rancor of an ambitious man who had been deceived, that 'Amr conceived this hatred: against a disciple who, though still very young, appeared already, among the notables of Basra, to be somehow predestined to the sanctity for which Aqta' might have coveted him for his son-in-law.

It was after eighteen months of close association with 'Amr, ending in 263, that Hallaj made this marriage. It was the following year, in 264, that he went alone to Baghdad to consult Junayd on the quarrel between Aqta' and Makki; and, as Junayd arbitrated by advising him to be patient, that is to say, to continue to live together with his wife in the family home of Abu Ya'qub Aqta' Basri, then in Basra, I think now that the long novitiate ascribed by legend to Hallaj with Junayd, in the Baghdad convent of Shuniz, cannot be taken literally. it is only through letters (together perhaps with infrequent visits) that Hallaj, remaining in Basra, received for a few years (*muddatan*) from Junayd the formation that ʿAmr was no longer willing to give him. That Junayd, from that time onward, exercised an acknowledged influence over the Sufis, even outside of Shuniz and Baghdad—this is what this arbitration verifies. However, there is a genuine Basrian period in Hallaj's life, from 262 to 272, before he settles his family in Tustar (272–281), and afterwards in Baghdad (281–309).

It is from Basra that he was to leave for his first two hajj (270–271, 280; his wife will even return there in 279); it is in Basra that he became attached to his first disciples, an Ahwazi *mawla*, Karnaba'i, a Hashimite "*rabʿi*" nobleman (that is to say, a "descendent of Rabiʿa-b-Harith-b-A Muttalib"); Basra where Ibn Hazm says there were some *zindiq*, which means in this instance people "belonging to the party opposed to the Saʿdi party, meaning of the Bilali party" (= of the *wali* Qadi Bilal-b-Abi Burda Ashʿari, d. 120 A.H.), party of the Azd and Rabiʿa, opposed, by pre-Islamic *hilf* [tribal federation], in Basra as in Khurasan, to the Tamim party (= B. Saʿd and Qays); and a Bakri Arab of the Banu Salul-b-Dhuhl-b-Shayban, ʿUbayd-b-A Saluli.

II. THE CULTURAL MILIEU OF BASRA

The Muslim Community's Crises of Growth: Sunnism

At the moment when Hallaj, having entered Tustar, becomes a disciple of Sahl, a master in tradition and asceticism—and enters through him into one of the milieus already clearly differentiated from Islamic thought—the Muslim Community, then in the third century of its history, had already suffered three crises of growth.

The first, twenty-five years after the death of Muhammad, occurred at Siffin, when Qur'ans—fixed to the points of lances to stop a fratricidal battle—stood silent on the issue of what kind of political regime was indicated for the Community of people of one and the same book and one and the same *qibla*; the most fervent members split into legitimists (Shiʿites) and egalitarians (Kharijites), while the majority proceeded very slowly to form a little elite, in Basra, *ahl al-sunna waʾl-jamaʿa*, which was to grow into Sunnism: holding the view that one must not risk breaking the unity of the Community by trying to punish certain of its leaders for their shortcomings.

The second, a hundred years later, was a reaction of this little Sunnite elite, who were convinced of the possibility of unifying the practice of canonical regulations in the daily life of each Muslim around the examples given privately by the Prophet to the most scrupulous of his Companions—examples that it worked assiduously to find and to coordinate, thanks to chains of witnesses. These *ahl al-hadith*, or traditionists, nearly all supporters at the outset of a political movement, Zaydism, which aimed at reconciling Shi'ites and Sunnites on the juridical plain, and which collapsed in 145/762 (the revolt of Nafs Zakiya), broke up into the rival canonical schools of Sufyan Thawri (97, d. 161), 'AR. Awza'i (80, d. 157), Layth Fahmi (94, d. 175), Malik (93, d. 179), which forced at least the official Hanafite jurisconsults to pay more serious attention to hadith; then came M-b-Idris Shafi'i (150, d. 204), to whom is owed the first general definition of consensus, and the dissident Shafi'ite leaders of schools, Ahmad-b-Hanbal (164, d. 241), Abu Thawr Ibr Kalbi (d. 246), Dawud Zahiri (200, d. 270), and M-b-Jarir Tabari ([224], d. 310); of these ten schools only the four classical rites survive today: Malikites, Hanafites, Shafi'ites and Hanbalites; which the Wahhabite reformers (late 18th century onward in Arabia) will wish particularly to reduce to one, on a foundation of Hanbalite hadith.

The third crisis was born among these *ahl al-hadith* at the end of the second century of the Hijra, out of a need for moral purification; wounded deeply by political dissensions and disagreements over juridical interpretation between believers, several, as Muhasibi recounts it, in order to recover for the Community its early unity, joined together in a voluntary exile (*hadith al-ghurba*), with groups of pious and chaste solitaries or even resolute ascetics, whom their journeys to collect traditions, for nearly all are of the *ahl al-hadith*, had finally settled in more or less threatened regions. These were frontier regions (*thughur*) where they fought against the infidels, outlying areas where they preached to the uneducated, isolated places where they worshipped God in patience, sacrifice, and thanksgiving, recalling His blessings given to His faithful, in order to love Him more deeply for these gifts. The name *sufi* begins to describe, in this era, these little groups, which wore the robe of wool (*suf*), either black or white, as a sign of their identity. Convinced, moreover, of the providential importance of their vocation, they possess in common a very old *hadith al-ghibta*, designating them as this predestined elite of privileged people, of saints, who, constantly renewed, intercede on behalf of the Muslim Community. The Basra group appears first, with Farqad Sabakhi (d. 131) and 'Utba, disciples of Hasan Basri, and established the monastic community of 'Abbadan. After that comes the Kufa group, with Kulayb, Abu Hashim 'Uthman-b-Sharik (d. 160); we find in this group such Zaydites as Sufyan Thawri and Abu'l-'Atahiya (and the Zaydite *mahdi* of Talaqan, M-b-Qasim, d. 219), even some Shi'ites, such as 'Abdak; to this group the Syrian ascetic foundations of Ramlah (Abu Hashim) and of Lukkam (Ibrahim-b-Adham, who came there from Khurasan by way of Kufa) attached themselves, for nothing could be established in Kufa itself. Finally, after a puritan outbreak of *sufiya* in Alexandria in 199, an Egyptian Sufi appears, Dhu'l-Nun Misri (d. 245), deported at an opportune moment to Baghdad, when, in combined imitation of the foundations of 'Abbadan, Ramlah, Lukkam, and of the more recent convents founded by Ibn Karram

(d. 225) in Khurasan as well as in Jerusalem, the first ascetic foundation of the capital was built by the disciples of Ma'ruf Karkhi (d. 200), Bishr Hafi (d. 225), and Muhasibi (d. 243) on the west bank in Shuniz.

Also around 250, in Baghdad and elsewhere, the doctrine of these groups tends to become defined in the form of questions (*masa'il*) of psychology publicly debated in conferences. Dhu'l-Nun, then Yahya-b-Mu'adh Razi (d. 258; at first with the Karramiya of Nishapur, afterwards in Baghdad), Abu Hamza (d. 269; in Baghdad), and Sahl Tustari (after 245; d. 283) are the first to speak of it in these terms and in an incisive manner. They follow in this the systematic and critical tendency highly esteemed in Basra, whereas the poignantly anecdotal sermons delivered by Mansur-b-'Ammar can be associated with the poetic and idealistic Yemenite tendency of the Kufa school.

Sahl Tustari

Sahl-b-'Abdallah Tustari (born 203, d. 273 or 283), who lived principally in Ahwaz, but also in Arrajan, and must have left his own province to die in Basra, is connected with the ascetic school of Basra; however, his intellectual horizon is much wider than that of the disciples of 'Abd al-Wahid-b-Zayd and of his nephew Bakr. After his pilgrimage to Mecca at age sixteen (in 219) escorted by the *muhaddith* M-b-Sawwar, Sahl lived for a period under the direction of Dhu'l-Nun Misri, the first specialist in Muslim mysticism, who had traveled extensively, listened well to masters, and proved, during the course of prosecutions before the courts, his hostility towards the Mu'tazilite heresy. Sahl has neither the introspective fineness nor the imaginative richness of this master; he is before all an ascetic of intense faith and a vigorous dialectician, determined to harmonize mystical experiences with a systematic account of Sunnite orthodoxy.

The following are the characteristic distinctions of the school that he founds (which will become the Salimiya *madhhab*): submission to the state; recourse to verses of the Qur'an as the principal source: Sahl is the first to have written a mystical *tafsir* on the Qur'an, one which will be criticized by Shatibi in his *Muwafaqat*; veneration of the Prophet, about whom, by an unexpected borrowing from the extremist Mimiya Shi'ites, Sahl teaches the pre-eternal conception: Muhammad is the first-born of creatures, a light (*nur*) in the column of primordial light (*'amud al-nur*), the body of adoration from which God afterwards drew, particle by particle, all creatures. Primate of the naked faith, who, without external works, due to his uncreated nucleus (*yaqin*), makes it possible for the believer to adhere to the divine essence, provided that he calls it to mind constantly through vocal prayer (*dhikr*: whose clarity ends by substantializing itself within the believing heart); God is a sustenance.

This disciplined and militant fervor appears again in three aspects of the form of Sahl's life: the necessity of the ascetic effort, *ijtihad*, conceived, moreover, not as a pure human gesture or a pure divine influence, but as an authentic "acquisition," *iktisab*, bestowed by God upon the believer who imitates in that the practice (*sunna*) of the Prophet; Sahl, in particular, brings his effort to bear on supererogatory fasts, convinced that they obtain the gift of miracles. Next, the necessity of placing one constantly in the presence of God, through a penitent confession (*tawba*): Sahl teaches that the confession of powerlessness, the disavowal of self (*tabarri 'an al-hawl wa'l-quwa*) in each instant is a duty of canonical obligation (*fard*) for every believer (cf. Ash'ari). From this comes a final aspect that Sahl only sketched out as follows: the full renunciation of one's whole spirit, the continual disavowal of self—which excludes, according to his explicit terms, any "pretention to divine love, to divine abandon"—could not prevent God from intervening directly when He wishes, and in person, in the soul annihilated in this way; thus revealing what Sahl calls the "secret of divine omnipotence" (*sirr al-rububiya*), the sovereign "I" that then renders vain all intermediaries, prophets, scholars, and judges, making of this soul His Proof (*hujjat Allah*) before His creatures and even before His saints.

These last two theses, which were denounced, not only by the Mu'tazilites, but also by three Hanbalites from Basra and Ahwaz, Zakariya Saji (217, d. 307), Zubayr Zubayri (born around 221, d. 317), and Ibn Abi Awfa, served to bring about Sahl's exile to Basra; a little after A.H. 26[1], where Ya'qub-b-Layth, sick, had Sahl come from Tustar to cure him, at a time when the Zanj rebels were still masters of Basra before A.H. 2[69].

The leading pupil of Sahl, Abu 'AA M-b-A ibn Salim Basri (d. 297), codified his teaching, which became the rule of a theological school, that of the Salimiya; directed thereafter by Abu'l-Hasan A-b-M ibn Salim (d. 350), Ibn al-Jalla, Abu Talib Makki (d. 380) and Ibn Jahdam (d. 414); criticized by Ibn Khafif and by the Hanbalites. Besides Ibn Salim, Sahl had as disciples, other than Hallaj, Barbahari (d. 329), 'Akari, who will become the head of the Baghdadi Hanbalites, Jurayri (d. 313), who will be the successor to Junayd, M-'Umar-b-Wasil 'Anbari Basri, who was killed in Habir (in 311) and had for a *rawi* Yf Qawwas, who will come also to Baghdad, to Bab Muhawwil, to diffuse his *hadith* there, Abu Ya'qub Susi, who will go to Mecca, and AB-M-b-Mundhir Hujami.

We do not know if Hallaj stayed longer than two years with Sahl, or if he followed him to Basra; an account by Khuldi suggests that Hallaj might have left him suddenly. In any case there are undeniable signs of Sahl's influence on Hallaj; for example, the same discipline regarding fasting, the same manner of fasting in Ramadan, the same daily number (400) of *rak'a*, the same choice of anagogical meaning in Qur'anic exegesis (*masmud*), and the same notion of *yaqin*, attributed to both. Finally, it is very unusual that the Salimiya, the early ones, would defend Hallaj on the theological plane, as having carried out in actual fact certain ideas put forward by their theoreticians. In this connection, we must reconcile the Sahlian notion of the "*hujja*" of God, "*hadi, muhdi, wa huwa'l-Gharib fi zamanihi*" with the title "*al-Gharib*," given to Hallaj, and the theme of Hallaj's blood writing "Allah" on the ground, together with the anecdote of the disciple of Sahl, which was carried over into the *dhikr*, stating that, being accidentally crushed, his blood wrote the word "Allah."

'Amr Makki

'Amr Makki played a special role in the life of Hallaj; it is he who "initiated" him into Sufism, by conferring on him the habit (*khirqa*) and clipping his moustaches. It is just in this second half of the third century of the Hijra that the initiation becomes known, through the experience of such men as Shibli, Hallaj, and others. One small group of Sunnite Sufis held the monopoly of this initiation, whose classical *isnad*, included in the *risala* of Qushayri a hundred years later, is perhaps fictitious; it goes back to the disciples of Hasan Basri, who, with 'Abd al-Wahid ibn Zayd, founded the famous ascetic center of 'Abbadan. But 'Amr Makki does not seem to have been initiated at 'Abbadan; rather at Mecca; and by whom? Junayd, whose assistant he was in his teaching?

'Amr Makki was first of all a strict *muhaddith*, a pupil of Bukhari (190–256) and of two celebrated Egyptians, Yunus-b-'Abd al-A'la (d. 264) and Rabi'-b-Sulayman (d. 270; editor of the *Umm* of Shafi'i, and muezzin of Fustat). He resided mostly in Mecca, but he went later to Baghdad, via Basra. He became interested in mysticism at an early period in his life through Abu Hazim Madani, Nibaji, and AS Kharraz.

He wrote, in mysticism, on the subject of religious practice and gave some highly esteemed answers (*ajwiba*) to questions concerning symbolic allusions. In the first category, *Adab al-muridin*; in the second, *Kitab al-mahabba* and *Kitab al-kanz*. As to the first, it continues to be for us a puzzling allegory of the preexistence of the *asrar*, *arwah*, and *qulub*, future outer coverings of human souls, created 7,000 years apart from each other and finally encased within each other (as a punishment for becoming proud in the 360 glances that God cast on them) and enclosed in *ajsam*, bodies, to form responsible human persons. This strange allegory, which recalls the fall, seven times, of the rebellious angels, stripped at each fall of a color transferred to disobedient men and severely tried for 7,000 years in these material bodies, in the view of the Khattabiya Shi'ites, no doubt forms part of the corpus of picturesque anecdotes that Makki loved (cf. his letter addressed from Mecca to Junayd, threatening the mystics of Iraq with a thousand volcanoes and a thousand watery abysses). He loved verses that inspire raptures.

This austere mystic (penitence is obligatory—*wajib*; attenuation of Sahl's *fard* for the sinner; no inner states [spiritual intoxications, *sukr*, etc.] are valuable, only strict observance of ritual practices) did not disdain commercial matters; one day, his friend 'Ali-b-Sahl Isfahani paid off for him (without his knowing) a debt of 30,000 dirhams in Mecca. Later 'Amr Makki came to Isfahan to thank him, in 291.

It is told that 'Amr Makki died in this same year, though Khatib prefers the date "297" affirmed by Ibn Hibban. It is established that 'Amr died in Baghdad, having become named titular qadi of Jidda, which had outraged Junayd, who refused to preside at his funeral service. This post was a deputation from the qadi of the Haramayn, who was at that time (before 295) the famous Hammadite qadi, Abu 'Umar, famous misappropriator of funds, who will have Hallaj executed. I hesitate to place the death of 'Amr after 291, for, if he died in 297, he would have had to leave in 295 his rich judgeship of Jidda, seaport of the pilgrimage and prebend of Qadi Abu 'Umar (imprisoned and released in 295).

If Hallaj was to be under his influence (as Ibn Khafif will be) it was not for long. We have seen that he broke with his "initiator" because of his marriage, which set 'Amr against the father-in-law. As the initiation did not require a vow of chastity, we must look for a political basis of disagreement: Abu Ya'qub Aqta' was a Karnaba'i, allied to the head of the Zanj rebels; 'Amr Makki must have been doing a lucrative "business," on the Meccan hajj, through his connection with the clients of the Hammadite qadis and "in accordance with the 'Abbasid court of Muwaffaq."

Two other disagreements aggravated the conflict. On these we have only legendary versions. As to the first, 'Amr Makki was supposed to have found Hallaj (in Mecca) writing (inspired) sentences that Hallaj dared to put on a level with the Qur'an (u'arid al-Qur'an). 'Amr did not accept either *ilham* (private inspiration: opp. of *wahy*, revelation), or inner graces (*ahwal*) derived from that inspiration. As to the second, Hallaj was supposed to have stolen from 'Amr the manuscript of his book *al-Kanz* (while 'Amr was purifying himself); and 'Amr had cursed him, forewarning him of his eventual punishment. For this book contained the secret of Satan's damnation: if Satan had refused to bow down before Adam at the time of his creation by God's hands, it is because Satan was able, while remaining seated (on his prayer rug) to intercept the technique of the divine insufflation of the spirit of life. This was the sin that was to get him decapitated, after a delay (obtained from God in order that he be decapitated only at the end of the world, after having been able to tempt the sons of Adam). This ingenuous allegory, entirely "exoteric," which confuses the creation of Adam with the presentation of his predestination before the Angels, the insufflation of life with an external technique of blowing air, and the damnation of Satan with a material decapitation, is antithetical—not only to the meditations of Sahl and of the Salimiya on the "final redemption of Satan," but to the Hallajian theme of the *Ta' Sin al-Azal*, in which Satan refuses the *sujud* in pre-eternity; in which the intussusception of grace is purely "spiritual, inward," nonspatial; and in which the damnation of Satan is entirely internal, an increasing and irreversible darkening of his egotistical and jealous intelligence, from a false love growing more and more insolent and sacrilegious.

Hallaj could not at that time have confronted 'Amr so clearly with his thesis on inspiration, nor his theory of the damnation of Satan; therefore we believe that, if 'Amr attacked his theses, it was only much later, when Hallaj, rejecting the [Sufi] robe, was denounced by him to the canonical authorities in Ahwaz.

More basically, the temperaments of these two men were incompatible; both sought to reach God directly, through a true practice of the Commandments of the Law, carried out by attaching themselves through initiation to venerated teachers. Hallaj had left Sahl, who resented intellectual demands in theology (which Makki was not qualified to share), because Hallaj wanted to reach an immediate comprehension of divine things which the exercise of reason does not allow one to attain. But Makki could hardly guide him in that, being a simple *muhaddith*, a legalist, who sought graces and signs "from without" and, as Ibn al-Jawzi will say, invented them according to his need, in order to have a hold over his disciples. The anecdote concerning the paper found in Damascus under the full moon (when he had to go outside to purify himself), referring to the subject discussed in a meeting inside, is certainly disquieting. The danger of a mediocre spiritual poverty is that one indulges in a superstitious reading of intersigns, for lack of physical miracles. The gift of miracles is reserved to certain outlaws, since there is a break in the series of secondary causes; to outlaws who consent to being broken (in the temple of their bodies) by the sanctions of the Law, which the gift of miracles only serves to accelerate against them, being scandalous.

Junayd: Aqta' and Jurayri

Born in Baghdad around 225, of a family from Nihawand, AQ Junayd-b-Muhammad practiced at first, like his father, the trade of glass bottle merchant (*khazzaz, qawariri*). From the age of twenty, he attended the lectures of the Shafi'ite canonist Abu Thawr Kalbi (d. 246). His maternal uncle Sari' Saqati, who died in 253, a disciple of Muhasibi (d. 243), initiated him into mysticism. If Junayd became, for centuries, the patriarch of Muslim religious communities, he was, first of all, a prudent and critical theoretician of mysticism, involved in making its definitions agree with Islamic law.

Prior to 255 he was not yet a recognized master, and on one occasion when he wished to speak in the presence of Yahya-b-Mu'adh Razi (d. 258), who gave at that time the first public lessons on mystical doctrine, in Baghdad, the latter silenced him, saying "hush your bleating, little lamb." Eight years later, around 266, at the time of the Ghulam Khalil affair, Junayd broke his ties with the accused Sufis, returning to the garb of a Shafi'ite canonist. It was, however, about this time that he succeeded Abu Ya'qub Zayyat, successor of Abu Ja'far A-b-Wahb Zayyat (d. 270), as director of the Sufi convent of Shuniz; and about that time that he must have received Hallaj there, as a novice (in 264). He died there thirty-four years later, on Friday in the month of *Shawwal*, the day of *Nayruz* in 298. He was buried there in the tomb of his uncle Sari', a tomb that still exists, and which I have visited, in the midst of a large cluster of ancient tombs.

Junayd had a daughter and a son, the latter beheaded for a crime; from whence, no doubt, his bitter reflection on children.

The mystical doctrine of Junayd, based on the criticism of Mu'tazilism formulated by Ibn Kullab and Muhasibi, reduced sanctity to a predestination: on the day of Covenant (*mithaq*), God put a mark on His beloveds, His saints: long before the creation of bodies, their souls, at the time simple divine ideas, appeared: "He secluded Himself in them (*i'tazala'l-Haqq bihim*), His divinity was disclosed to them. . . ." Every effort of the mystic, in this life, must be aimed at rediscovering this declaration of anticipated love, this pure word of acquiescence to the divine will: by submitting to a progressive and implacable cleansing of our whole being. "Let the servant be, in relation to God, like a marionette (*shabah*) . . . let him return, in finishing his life, to his point of departure, and be, as he was, before he was given existence." This final state (*nihaya*) is thus the return to the initial state (*bidaya*). Isn't this really the reduction of the person of the mystic to a virtual and unrealized divine idea? Hallaj will deny this reduction; but Junayd himself did not go that far. Being a theoretician, he sought a formula; he said at the outset: the goal is to "separate the Absolute from the contingent (*ifrad al-qidam 'an al-hadath*)," which is the bare outline of a Hallajian formula, and which is indeed strongly anti-monist. He specified after that, in opposition to Kharraz, that one must avoid building a logical symmetry between *fana'* (state of mystical annihilation) and *baqa'* (state of the saint's immortalization); he emphasized also, against certain of his own disciples, that this annihilation of ourselves in the One Whom we commemorate (*fana' bi'l-Madhkur*), in His sovereign unity (*fana' fi tawhid al-rububiya*), is only realizable if we distinguish between what the Law commands and what the Law forbids (*ma'mur, mahzur*), which is also the beginning of a Hallajian statement. Finally, Junayd tried to explain this idea of a "return to our origin," no longer by means of gnostic myths, as Sahl and 'Amr Makki had, but as the access even to the Creator's life. According to the term *fana'*, "God possesses him (= the saint) with a supreme violence; He reduces him to dust before he dies; He kills him, buries him; then, if it pleases Him, He resuscitates him; but this man no longer has any connection with his past life, and other persons have had no knowledge of his death. "His life is based on that of his Creator, no longer on the subsistence of his bodily form (*haykal*); so much so that the reality of his life is his death, since this death is his access to the arena of primordial Life" (*hayat asliya*). Junayd, in this instance, is analyzing ecstasy as a theoretician. He makes no reference to a personal experience; rather he bases his thought on the accounts of ecstatics; notably on those of Bistami (d. 261), which he had had translated from Persian and whose variants he had noted; he made a commentary on the recension peddled by Abu Musa Dubayli Armawi; Junayd finds the experience of Bistami incomplete and his language too concrete.

Through objections raised against Sariʿ, his uncle and his master, and through his controversies with Nuri and Ibn ʿAtaʾ, the distinctive traits of Junayd's doctrine emerge. Junayd must have toned down the formulas of Sariʿ, which bordered on the *hulul* of Nuri and on *qidam al-ruh*, but upheld, as he did, against the Hanbalites, the thesis of *khalq al-huruf* accepted by Muhasibi. Ibn ʿAtaʾ, drawing close to Hallaj in that, corrected certain positions of Junayd in the direction giving a higher value to personal effort and suffering.

Hamd's account published by Ibn Bakuya presents Junayd as having been Hallaj's spiritual director after Sahl. But another tradition, going back to Jurayri and to Khuldi, and adopted by Hujwiri, claimed that Junayd had never wanted to receive Hallaj; it is obviously polemical. The Hamd account seems, in this instance, correct; Junayd only broke with Hallaj after Makki. The popular legend that depicts Junayd as profoundly attached to Hallaj, and admiring him as a mystic, even while condemning him as a canonist, may derive from authentic sources, since Junayd died only after the start of the attacks by the canonist Ibn Dawud. But fragment number 61 of *Akhbar*, which shows the young Ibn Khafif, during his first stay in Baghdad, standing up against Junayd in a meeting in which the latter had charged Hallaj with sorcery and magic, is more than suspect.

Two disciples of Junayd expressed themselves on the Hallaj case: Abu Yaʿqub Aqtaʿ and Jurayri.

Abu Yaʿqub (Ishaq?) Aqtaʿ Basri, secretary of Junayd, had given his daughter, Umm al-Husayn, in marriage to Hallaj; which had momentarily embroiled him with ʿAmr Makki, Junayd's assistant.

Afterwards, Aqtaʿ also became hostile to his son-in-law, and let it be known to Abu Zurʿa Tabari, the *rawi* of Khuldi. We know almost nothing about Aqtaʿ apart from an account in which he speaks of a ten-day fast during a pious visit to Mecca, and a rather arrogant sentence about divine union, repeated by AH Muzayin to Ibn Khafif. There is good reason to think Aqtaʿ was imprisoned with a family of notables from Basra, who had property in Ahwaz, the Karnabaʾi. The son and daughter of Aqtaʿ remained faithful to Hallaj.

Abu Muhammad Jurayri, pupil of Sahl Tustari, afterwards disciple and successor of Junayd, perished in the desert at the time of the plunder of the pilgrims by the Qarmathians around 312 (he died with his finger raised, according to Ibn Bakuya, who followed the report of Ibn ʿAtaʾ Rudhbari).

A Hanafite in law, he was, in mysticism, the teacher of Nahrajuri and Ibn Khafif. He must have known Hallaj intimately, but the account that Ibn Bakuya attributes to him of the first visit by Hallaj to Junayd is fiction, since it doesn't know that Hallaj and Jurayri both came to him from Sahl. At the time of Hallaj's second trial, Jurayri, summoned as a witness for the defense, according to Nasrabadhi, consented to his execution. But another tradition, followed by Hujwiri and by the historians Kutubi and Ibn Kathir, affirms that Jurayri did not want to condemn Hallaj. The few statements by him that have been preserved, as extracts from the works of Jurayri (which Kalabadhi mentions) (his very hard *i'tikaf* in 292 at Mecca: cf. Hallaj), do not reveal in what way Jurayri went beyond his master Junayd in innovation. The biographer of Bistami, Sahlaji (d. 476), relates that AM Jurayri one day consulted Nibaji concerning a famous sentence by Bistami: "One day God probed the consciences in the universe and found them all empty of Him, except mine, which was filled (with Him): and He said to me, to praise it: 'All the universe is My slave, except you .'" Nibaji responded to him that God had made him realize (in him, Nibaji) the meaning of this sentence, by adding to it "because you are Me." And Jurayri declared that the inner state of Nibaji seemed to him superior to that of Bistami, who did not become aware of (nor was able to formulate) his own transcendentalization (*ittisaf bi'l-tanzih*). Jurayri was killed at Habir (at the end of 311) on the hajj route; his body one year later was still there, knees to chin, the index finger raised for the *shahada*.

Nuri ibn al-Baghawi: Qannad Is His Ghulam

A contemporary of Junayd, born like him around 225 in Baghdad, Nuri died there, at Shuniz, in 295.

His first master was the Syrian Ahmad-b-Abi'l-Huwwari (d. 246); he made in that period several visits to Mecca. He pursued after that Sari' Saqati (d. 253) and became finally the collaborator and successor of Abu Hamza (d. 269) as the leader of the *hululi* (spiritual indwelling, incarnationalistic) extremist faction of the Baghdad Sufis, while his friend Junayd upheld the more prudent mystical doctrinal tradition of Muhasibi. We possess several anecdotes that illustrate the contrast between their two methods. For example, one day Nuri said to Junayd, who had decided reluctantly to speak in public and was lecturing in a theoretical mystical vocabulary, while he, Nuri, was preaching out of fraternal devotion: "you defraud them, and they have let you sit in their pulpits (*manabir*), but as for me, who wanted to warn their souls (*nasahtuhum*), they have thrown me into the rubbish heap." And around 266, when the Hanbalite Ghulam Khalil supported by the mother of the Regent, Ashar, denounced to the authorities the extremist Sufis for teaching pure love, Nuri with great courage volunteered to suffer the hardship imposed by the judges in place of the first accused, Zaqqaq, to whom Ghulam Khalil had said [hang the *hulul*, hang them by their necks] "*damuh hulul, damuh fi 'unuqi*." The grand qadi, Isma'il Hammadi (262, d. 282), being moved, acquitted them, but Nuri was banished for a period to Raqqa. After he had returned to Baghdad in the reign of Mu'tadid, he had the audacity one day to smash the wine jars that were being carried to the

Palace. He was exiled to Basra around 283; when his health became too bad to resume his preaching, he returned once again to Baghdad, in 289. He died six years later, as a result of having thrown himself on some pointed bamboo sticks during a state of ecstasy.

Like Abu Hamza, Nuri teaches that we must perceive God's call in every phenomenon, in each event that seizes our attention, and respond to him with our *"labbayka,"* "at Your service"; and he would rather say it when a dog barks than when a half-hearted muezzin calls us to prayer. He lessens the dangerous aesthetic tendency of Abu Hamza, who cultivated, through *dolorisme* the Platonic gaze, and bordered on homosexuality in his questionable accounts of visits from novices with handsome young faces; with regard to that tendency Nuri is more adamant than Yusuf-b-H Razi (220, d. 304). But he remains a partisan of the *qawl bi'l-shahid* and of the *qidam al-ruh*. Nuri is the first to have preached the notion of pure love (*mahabba*), the passionate fervor that the faithful must bring (without hope of recompense) to the practice of worship; like Sari', he even stresses the idea of that desire (*'ishq*) that God inspires in the fervent soul; this was moving toward the Hallajian thesis of union with God through love; but the theology of that time denied that love could be anything other than a species of "will," attaching itself only momentarily and to particular things; Nuri was thus accused by the Hanbalite Ghulam Khalil (d. 275) of *zandaqa* (= Manichaeanism).

Certainly Nuri, in his unusual devotional fervor, resorted unsuspectingly to a very materialistic symbolism to illustrate his thesis that God alone gives proof of God, and that, as Kharraz had already indicated, reason (*'aql*) is incapable (*'ajiz*) of attaining it. His enthusiasm as an ecstatic led him, through *dolorisme*, to perform a number of celebrated eccentric acts, reported by the Mu'tazilite Qannad; he punished his flesh by remaining standing for forty days, by throwing his money into the sea, by rolling in the mud during a lion hunt at Nashiriya, and by going about with his head hung down. He sought spiritual powers, on which subject his desciple Anmati has left us the following delicate diptych: Nuri fell sick, Junayd arranged to have him sent some financial assistance; Junayd fell sick in his turn, Nuri came to his bedside, and, by simple touch, cured him. He applied to community life the principle of pure love, declaring that community life (*suhba*) was superior to eremitical life (*'uzla*), and that there could be no communal life without the spirit of fraternal sacrifice (*'ithar*). He went about trying to read what was in people's hearts, from whence his nickname *"jasus al-qulub"* ("the spy of hearts"). Abu Nu'aym preserved for us his ten recommendations to his desciples.

Of his works, apart from bits of verse published by Kalabadhi, we have only some sentences collected by his direct *rawi*, Murta'ish, Anmati (in Faris), Qannad, and Khuldi; and the picturesque anecdotes gathered by Qannad and Ibn Bakuya.

We have no details on Nuri's relations with Hallaj, which would have to be placed between 264 and 266; because of their similarities of doctrine and temperament, several poems and some sentences have been attributed to Nuri that must be restored to Hallaj. Later legend invented visits by Nuri to Hallaj in prison.

Abu Bakr Fuwati

Sulami gives us just a word on this teacher of Hallaj who, we know from Ibn Bakuya, became his enemy. He seems to have known Hallaj in Mecca, through association with Abu Ya'qub Aqta'. He visited Isfahan when 'Ali-b-Sahl (d. 307) was alive; he had as disciples Ibn Khafif, AB M-b Dawud Duqqi Dinawari (d. Damascus, 359) and Abu 'Amr Adami.

Shibli

Abu Bakr Shibli was born in Samarra in 247 and died in Baghdad 28 *Hijja* 334. He was from a family of high public officials. His father Jabghi, *hajib* of Muwaffaq in 251, who brought him first to Egypt and to Yemen, became (in 257, or rather in 261, before Ibn Jahshyar) grand chamberlain of the new heir-apparent prince, Muwaffaq, who also employed him in the *hijaba* under his command. His mother was the sister of the military commander of Alexandria, probably Nasr Tahawi (in 252). It was undoubtedly through her that he was led to adopt the Malikite rite (the mother of the Malikite grand qadi, Abu 'Umar, whom he knew, was also Egyptian). As an assistant in the *hijaba*, he had gotten the fief (*tu'ma*) of Dimawand. He gave it up when Muwaffaq was stripped (*uq'ida*) of his title of *wali al-'ahd* (= 12 *Qa'da* 269) of Samarra and Egypt (he [Muwaffaq] remained at that time ruler of Baghdad and soon reconquered the empire from Mu'tamid).

Shibli's resigning of his fief is presented to us as coming at the same time as his conversion to mysticism, at a meeting with Khayr Nassaj, the friend of Junayd. In 269, Shibli was only 22 years old, which does not correspond with what he tells us elsewhere about the 30 (or 20 + 20 = 40) years that he was supposed to have dedicated to the study of *hadith* (with M-b-Mahdi Misri, an unknown) and Malikite law (we do not know with whom): he knew by heart one recension of the *Muwatta'* ('Akari); which would move the date of his conversion from 269 to 277, or even 287. He had withdrawn at that time to Syria, after having left the service of Mu'tadid.

Let us keep in mind merely that up to the age of about 40 years (287), Shibli, who had his connections in the Court, was also on close terms in Baghdad with Malikite jurisconsults (clients of the Hammadite grand qadis) and with *qurra'* (Qur'an reciters); notably with their chief, Abu-b-Mujahid (d. 324), whom he told one day: "I have studied the Qur'an for 43 years . . ." (which must have been around 295).

The high position of his family had made his conversion important for his group of Sufis, who were people of little background, modest artisans among whom Shibli, according to Junayd, had become the "show piece." Shibli, poet and religious enthusiast, profited from his position, on his part, to flaunt a way of life that was uniquely his own, undisciplined, and increasingly eccentric. He remained either under the cupola of poets—according to Ibn Sabir—at the mosque of al-Mansur, or in his *zawiya*, near the *halqa* of the Shafi'ite jurisconsult Abu 'Imran Musa-b-Q-b-H-b-Ibr. Ashyab (d. 302); who, overtaxed in his patience by the goings-on of Shibli, had him driven out around the year 295. Shibli made visits to Basra. Though having long-standing ties of friendship with Hallaj, he held public debates at this time with him; for Hallaj believed in preaching in a self-composed manner, while Shibli, for reasons of personal safety, preferred to assume the unbalanced gestures of a half-wit, to declaim his mystical truths in faked bursts of rhetoric. He had to be incarcerated several times as a madman in the Maristan (asylum), where he received visitors. He was released in 309, because he renounced his friend Hallaj twice: during the preliminary hearing (when Hallaj had asked him to help him be killed) and during the execution (he called him possessed, and, under the threat of prosecution, got himself reincarcerated.)

Around 330, the future Buwayhid vizir, Muhallabi, caught sight of Shibli lying in the street, after he had fainted in a cry of ecstasy. In the same period a Sufi, Abu Muzahim Shirazi, reproached him severely for this theatrical behavior: "for forty years Satan has played games with you." Shibli, unsuccessful in getting the assistants to throw him out, left, and Abu Muzahim, like a juggler at a fair, took up a collection, which netted him twenty dirhams.

Shibli had two sons: Ghalib, who died before him (he shaved his beard and his wife cut off her hair, as a sign of mourning), and AH Yunus.

Shibli had already acquired a strong cultural background when he converted to mysticism; also the Sufis with whom he associated by choice, Junayd, Ibn 'Ata', Khuldi, were more his friends than teachers. Only Hallaj seems to have exercised an increasingly pronounced influence over him. It was the style of Shibli's eccentricities that connects him in our minds with Nuri and Sumnun (d. 303).

Shibli seems to have written nothing other than short mystical poems, which have not been collected.

His mystical doctrine can be reconstructed, however, for Shibli will pass for an orthodox Muslim and a saint, even in circles that are most hostile to mysticism (Ibn Mujahid revered him; he was attacked only by Ibn Yazdanyar because of his devotion to the Prophet; Ma'arri didn't dare attack him). In effect, the union with God that he passionately sought by the most bizarre means, is for him only an instantaneous shock, a contact impossible to maintain, a throbbing jealousy; he does not accept the notion of a *shahid* (= a permanent witness of God), which had gotten Hallaj accused of *hulul*. One reproaches Shibli, of course, for his eccentricities: his remaining all one night on his terrace with one foot hanging in space; his having a comrade thrown into the water in order to see if he would float on the surface like Moses, or drown like Pharaoh; his threatening a youth in public whose beauty appeared to him to be created solely for temptation; his wanting to spit into Hell in order to extinguish it; his burning beautiful clothes and making holes in new clothes; his putting salt in his eyes so he couldn't sleep; his thanking God for making him suffer a liver ailment; his forcing a penitent into a humiliating penitence; his desiring God to say to him "go chase it," as if he were a dog; his wanting God to resurrect him blind (= damned, Qur'an 20:124); his thinking that his own reprobation should exceed that of the Jews and Christians. But people pardoned him for these things, because they knew them to be inspired by a profound and a very Islamic belief in the incomprehensible imminence of God's plan. Junayd revered him because of that, even though he reproached him frequently: "We prepared this doctrine harmoniously, and then we put it safely in the *sirdab*; and you, you are going to exhibit it, to hurl it to the vulgar mind?"—"When I speak, and when I listen, who is there in this world and the next, except me?" Some dialogues pinpoint their respective positions: (Junayd): "If you relied on God for your actions, you would not be reassured." (Shibli): "No, rather if God relied on you for your actions, you would not be reassured. . . ." Shibli scores Junayd for remaining on the level of theoretical faith in his mysticism. Like Hallaj, he claims that Bistami was only a beginner in theopathic expression.

Shibli said: "I am the moment (*waqt*); in this moment there is only me; I am its Realizer (*ana muhiqq*, variant: *ana mahq*)"; "a thousand years have passed, a thousand years will come, such is the moment, do not dwell on phantoms"; "the moment of others is interrupted, mine is lasting." Shibli, each time his nature is disrupted, feels a divine presence moving through the disruption; his union with God is essentially atomistic, discontinuous. He perceives that in Hallaj, through the joining of his *fiat* to the divine *Fiat*, a divine presence had penetrated definitively, which no longer disrupts him, but informs him; he certainly considered Hallaj more advanced than he in regard to this transforming union.

The friendship between Hallaj and Shibli, in spite of their differences of temperaments, was very great; though less clear and less heroic than that with Ibn 'Ata', Hallaj's friendship with Shibli had a larger range of cultural resonances. When Hallaj was killed, Shibli remained the only living witness of his superhuman desire [his *'ishq*]; and in secret, among certain friends whom he could trust, Shibli delivered or had others deliver speeches attesting to the fidelity of his affection and his admiration for his friend. First, in Baghdad, Shibli acknowledged that "Hallaj and I had one and the same doctrine"; the statement, collected and published by Mansur-b-'AA Harawi (grandson of Amir Khalid), must have been made to Anmati. His friends Da'laj-b-A Sijzi (260, d. 351), whose enormous income was used to support the Sunnites of the Qati'a against the Shi'ite persecution; A 'Ali M-b-'A Wah. Thaqafi (d. 328), the influential Shafi'ite jurisconsult of Nishapur; M-b. 'Abbas 'Usmi Dabbi—an enemy of Bukhari, and friend of Ibn Abi Hatim, the successor of Khalid-b-A Bakri Dhuhli (d. 270, Khurasan) prince of Herat, *wali* of Marw and Bukhara [which passed from the control of the Tahirids to the Saffarids: (292, d. 378)—were all surely among those who knew his views. It is his own *khadim*, 'Isa Qassar Dinawar, who transmitted the words of the dying Hallaj: "*Hasb al-wajid* . . ."; it is his *rawi*, Abu Hatim Tabari, who published the two recensions of the beautiful Hallajian couplet "*muzijat* . . ."; and it is another of his disciples, AB M Qasri, who must have provided Qannad with the couplet "*talabtu* . . ." and the oldest "account by Shibli" of the execution. As to the Hallajian secrets given by Shibli to Husri, we have only their early form for the parable justifying the votive substitution of the hajj, for which Hallaj was condemned; but one feels that is within the circle of the Zawzani *ribat* that the maxims concerning Hallaj ripened, which preachers like Shaydhala (d. 494) and 'AQ Hamadhani (d. 525) say came from Shibli, and which dealt with the question of divine love: ". . . Sufism is built on secrecy, because God is a jealous God" (explanation of punishment). "Love is a lasting attribute and a pre-eternal grace . . . throw your keys to your Beloved . . . (this is the pre-eternal grace that eternalizes the moment in you) . . . (verse:) my moment lasts forever in You. . . ." "Can it be, asks Shibli, that a lover allows himself to be deprived of his Beloved?—It is impossible for a valiant Knight (*fata*), responds Hallaj, to endure being deprived of the One who is his soul; as soon as love settles in, the blending is consummated, and separation becomes unrealizable; (verse:) I have tried to be patient. . . ." And the dialogue in dream form between Shibli and God: " 'Why do You put Your lovers to death?'—'So that they may receive the reward of blood.' . . ." This is very much the atmosphere of the legendary "visits" of Shibli to Hallaj, in prison, that one finds in the *Hikaya*.

It is to Shibli, furthermore, that the answer was given, authentically, by Hallaj on the distinction between prophets and saints, between those "who dispose of graces, without the graces transforming them" and those "whom the graces transform, without their disposing of graces," in which the thesis of the superiority of saints over prophets is very discreetly introduced.

The Hallajism of Shibli (cf. Husri) reaches the Hanbalites ('Ali b. A Hinkari via Sa'id Mukharrimi up to Kilani through 'A 'Aziz-b-Harith Tamimi (317, d. 371) and his son A Fadl 'A Wahid (d. 402); through Zayd b. Rifa'a, it reaches the *Ikhwan al-Safa'*.

In his biography of Shibli, based primarily on the lost *Ta'rikh* of Sulami, Ibn 'Asakir gives the following account: Abu Bakr Zubayr-b-M-b-'AA said: "I saw the Prophet in a dream and I said to him: 'O Prophet of God, what do you think of Junayd?'—'He is the one who put (mystical) knowledge in order.'—'And

what about Shibli?'—'When he was not in a trance, he was useful to many.'—
'And Hallaj?'—'He was in too much of a hurry (*ista'jala*).' "

Ibn 'Ata'

Ibn 'Ata' was born around 235 and was put to death in 309. His life, which
seems to have been spent entirely in Baghdad, can be divided into three periods. In the first, up to about 275, Ibn 'Ata', raised in the strict Hanbalite
muhaddithun environment, develops further under the influence of Abu Hamza
in the mystical and Sufi sense, the strong asceticism of Ibn Hanbal's *Kitab
al-zuhd*, certain hadiths attributed to Ja'far Sadiq, and a Bedouin poetic tradition derived from Asma'i. After visiting Abu Hamza, he becomes the disciple
of Ibrahim Maristani. Esteemed by Kharraz, he becomes the friend of Junayd
and of Nuri. In the second period, which, according to the sources, varies from
seven to fourteen or eighteen years, and, can be placed between 294 and 311
[?], Ibn 'Ata', after making a heroic vow, suffers a series of family and personal
misfortunes. In the final period, of which his disciple Ibn Hubaysh knew the
last fifteen (or ten) years, between 294 and 309, Ibn 'Ata', whose health was
restored, resumes a strict ascetic discipline, composes a commentary on the
Qur'an and, through an increasingly intimate and fervent union of soul, shares
in the work and ordeals of Hallaj, of whom he was the ultimate defender, at the
cost of his own life.

His first teachers were two Hanbalite traditionists: Fadl-b-Ziyad Baghdadi
(d. around 255), a personal friend of Ibn Hanbal, and Yusuf-b-Musa Qattan
Kufi (d. 253). Ibn 'Ata' figures as a link in the chain of transmission, in the
regular *isnad* of several hadith; he is the only Hallajian whose name has been
respected in this way, after the condemnation of Hallaj, in the manuals of hadith criticism and in the Hanbalite biographies. Ibn 'Ata' was also still accepted
by the Qur'an commentators, being the first, after Sahl, to compose a mystical
commentary on the Qur'an.

He held *majlis* [plural: *majalis*, meetings for discussion] on moral theology,
in which counsels were presented as coming from God: the *qari'* AB J-b-A
Khassaf mentioned them (in the Qur'anic text, the consonants are from the
creatures, the vocalization [*shikl*] comes from God (cf. Druze interpretations).

Ibn 'Ata''s personality is shown particularly in his practical moral theology.
Developing further what Nuri had set forth with the notions of *suhba* and *ithar*
(praise of God and preference of others above oneself), Ibn 'Ata' defines the
essence of the mystical life, in its social dimension, as being fraternal mutual
aid, the works of mercy, and mystical substitution, all conceived as ways leading to union with God. His entire life, as its great central crisis shows, inclined
toward compassion. Abu Nu'aym expressed it magnificently: "he leaned toward the miseries of captives, the different forms of suffering to which men are

subjected; he coveted this purity and this grandeur bestowed on them alone; after all he had gone through for his desire, with regard to tribulation and suffering." Ghulafi, his friend, who retired to Tarsus, told the following to Ibn Samʿun, who told it to Ibn al-ʿAllaf (d. 442): "I heard Ibn ʿAta' say: 'I have read the Qur'an and have perceived that God does not mention in it any one of His servants with praise without first having put him to the test: so I too have asked God to test me, saying to Him: "O my God, make me suffer, and keep me Yours during this suffering." And after a few days and nights, twenty-one persons left my house forever (= had died).' He lost his fortune, he lost his reason, he lost his son and his wife, and yet remained for almost seven years in a kind of rapture (*ghalaba*)." And Ghulafi said, "I have never seen someone coming out of an ecstasy express himself with such wisdom as Ibn ʿAta'. The first thing that he uttered at that time were these verses:

> Verily, you have inflicted me with more than justice, and in bearing
>> Your love, my patience has been wonderful . . .
> With his trial drawing out so long, Job quivered—and cried out, thirsty and
>> desolate:
> Evil torments me and Satan fights me—and You are the Merciful One, and Your
>> servant is unfortunate."

The adversaries of Ibn ʿAta', increasing the period of this ordeal to fourteen years, claimed that it was due to a curse made by Junayd, for his, Ibn ʿAta''s, having maintained against him the thesis of the superiority of the thanksgiving of the rich over the resignation of the poor; a thesis that, at the end, Ibn ʿAta' had retracted, saying "the curse of Junayd has overtaken me." In actual fact, Ibn ʿAta' maintained this thesis against Jurayri, the successor of Junayd. It is part of the five criticisms that Ibn ʿAta' raised against the moral theory of Junayd, calling upon him to consummate his theory in God through the practice of a more denuded abandonment, just as Hallaj, in his way, had also called upon Junayd.

The first debate in which, against Junayd, Ibn ʿAta' affirms that the thanksgiving of the rich on whom God bestows bountifully is superior to the resignation of the poor whom God deprives, establishes, on weak grounds, the idea that God is proven (and glorified) more through being than nonbeing. Ibn ʿAta' repeated the argument to Jurayri: the attributes of poverty are negative, the possession of wealth is participation in a divine Name, and one can only abandon something if one possesses it. Ibn ʿAta' had deduced this thesis from one in which Darani and Ibn Abi'l-Huwwari had affirmed the following against Rabah Qaysi: that the converted sinner who must continue to struggle is superior to the converted sinner who is no longer tempted; for, if the grace of conversion is the same in both cases, the grace to resist, which God adds to the second, makes the balance hang in his favor; from which one concludes, according to the thought of Ibn ʿAta', that suffering is a divine favor that one can even request.

The latter is what the second proposition of Junayd, stated as follows, denies: "sacrifice spontaneously made is superior to sacrifice accomplished with effort and suffering." Ibn ʿAtaʾ, following Mutarrif, Sahl, Nuri, and Hallaj, counters admirably that it is the latter that is superior, for there is a double sacrifice, a double victory, a gift of what there was to sacrifice and a gift of himself (his victory over egoism), a double divine grace, a double praise of God.

In the third debate, Ibn ʿAtaʾ (against Junayd) places the patient mystical ascent, accomplished through experimental knowledge, higher than the accelerated ascent, accomplished through ecstasies.

The last two touch more on mystical introspection than on moral theology. The fourth posits, according to Ibn ʿAtaʾ, that "ecstasy (*wajd*) marks the suspension of the qualities (of the subject) at a time when a pain (Junayd said: a joy) is imprinted in the essence (of the subject)." With pleasure indicating, in the view of the noted doctor Razi, the threshold of the return to normal equilibrium, Ibn ʿAtaʾ is right to see "pain" as indicating the actual passage into transcendence.

The fifth deals with impulses of the soul (*khawatir*); in the suggestions to act, which come to us interiorly from God, must we follow the "first impulse" or the "second"? Junayd argued for the first, for God makes it continue (in conflict with the second) in order to force us to reflect, which is the way knowledge occurs; Ibn ʿAtaʾ declares: it is the second that we must follow, for its impetus is added to the first; God shapes them and arranges then in a series.

The *tafsir* of Ibn ʿAtaʾ is rich in doctrinal themes of an entirely Hallajian coloration, especially on the symbolic form of the canonical pilgrimage; it contains also some very fresh thoughts on the ineffable *salam* directly desired by God for the elect in paradise. Ibn ʿAtaʾ writes in one of the verses that we have by him: "desire flows in my heart and swells it, as sap flows in blades of grass"; which is close to the Hallajian "*anta bayn al-shaghaf.*"

Ibn ʿAtaʾ had a large fortune, and out of reaction to the spiritual ostentation of the patched clothes worn by the Sufis, he dressed himself amply, in *dabiqi* material, and wore a rosary of pearls. But his spirit of compassion for the unfortunate put him at the head of the social protest movement that pitted the Hanbalite traditionists against the fiscal monopolists and the dishonest public officials who were responsible for famines; single-handedly he dared to raise an outcry in the presence of Vizir Hamid himself, who had him killed just a few days before the execution of his friend Hallaj, [who] died fourteen days later.

Two letters from Hallaj to Ibn ʿAtaʾ, which were quoted very early in the anthologies, bear witness to the level to which their pure friendship soared:

A. God bless me in lengthening your life and spare me from seeing your death; and that according to the best fate, fixed by destiny and rendered at His command. With all that (is) in my heart, the inner flames of your love, and the varied jewels of my affection for you, no letter could describe them, no arithmetic could enu-merate them, no blame could destroy them.

Also I tell you (in verse):

"I write, but this is not to you; in fact,—it is my Spirit to whom I write, and therefore there is no need to send a letter.

How is this possible? because between the (divine) Spirit and His lovers,—there is no disjunction owing to the difference between persons. This is why each letter coming from you brings to you my response, without a response being actually sent.

B. (written from his prison): But now, I no longer know what to say. If I recall Your kindness (*birr*), I do not know its end, and if I recall Your unkindness, I do not feel its reality. We saw them appear, these warnings of Your approach; but they set us afire, and we did not know when Your love was arriving. Then He leaned forward, gathering together what He had dispersed. He killed but He kept one from experiencing the taste of death. And here I am, before torn glimmers of light and rent veils, before the appeared invisible, and the dis-apeared visible. And as for me, I am no longer here; and He, Who has never ceased, He is ceaseless.

Then he sealed the letter, and for an address he wrote:

This thought toward him (= Ibn 'Ata') is my passion for You—O You, to Whom our allusions turn;

We are two spirits that desire has joined together—there, near You, and facing You.

Ibrahim ibn Fatik: His Blacklisting and the Fate of His Isnad

Ibrahim ibn Fatik was the witness to Hallaj's last days, his fellow-prisoner, and the one whom we turn to in order to reconstruct the circumstances of his exe-cution.

Son of a Syrian shaykh from Jerusalem named Fatik-b-Sa'id, according to the testimony of Harawi, he must have been formed in the *khanqah* of the Karramiya to the south of al-Aqsa where visiting Sufis stayed, similar to the *khanqah* in Dinawar. He must have known Nuri and Junayd, who regarded him highly (*yukrimuhu*); he would thus have arrived in Baghdad before Hallaj's journey to Jerusalem. Did he deliberately join him, was he imprisoned by chance, was he the occasional visitor whom Hallaj refers to in *Akhbar*, no. 3? We don't know. He spent "very little time" with him [in prison] (Ibn Khafif: *mudh qarib*), "fifteen days" (Daylami, trad. of Ibn Junayd), "eighteen months" (Daylami, according to Baqli, followed by Jami); perhaps Ibn Fatik is the un-known *rajul*, *fulan-b-fulan*, arrested in Dinawar at the time of the trial's re-sumption.

III. ANECDOTES FROM HIS YEARS OF APPRENTICESHIP: HIS *HAJJ (GHUTBA)*

The First Hajj and the 'Umr to Mecca (A.H. 270–272)

ACCOUNT OF AB M-B-'AA IBN SHADHAN (D. 376)

"I heard (AB) M-b-'AA 'Ali Kattani (d. 320) recount the following from Abu Ya'qub Susi: When Husayn-b-Mansur came to Mecca, at the beginning of his career, we pressed him very hard to let us take off his *muraqqa'a*. We removed the lice from it and weighed them; he had a half *danaq* of them (= 2.24 grams), so harsh was his asceticism, and violent his mortification."

On that, Ibn al-Jawzi observes that Hallaj was ignorant of canon law, which obliges the believer to maintain cleanliness, which permits the pilgrim in a state of *ihram* to keep himself shaved against lice, on condition that he make up for this extralegal abrasion by an alms gift; and he adds that Susi appears to be even more ignorant than he, by admiring him for this behavior. Susi, a pupil of Sahl in Arrajan and master of Nahrajuri, is one of the authorities cited in the *risala* of Qushayri.

ACCOUNT OF IBRAHIM IBN-B-SHAYBAN (D. 337)

One day my master (that is to say, A'AA Maghribi) had gone to find 'Amr-b-'Uthman Makki to settle a certain question once and for all. It so happened that in the course of the conversation 'Amr-b-'Uthman said to him: 'there is a young man here who went to live on Mount Abu Qubays.' And, after leaving 'Amr's house, we went up to see him; it was the noon hour. Upon entering the oratory, we found him squatting in the courtyard, on a rock from Abu Qubays, staying immobile under the sun, in bare feet, his head uncovered, with the sweat running down his body onto the rock. As soon as A 'AA had seen him, he turned around and gave me a hand signal to 'leave.' We left the oratory again, and went back down the *wadi*. When we reentered the mosque (of the Ka'ba), A 'AA told me: 'If you live long enough you will be able to see what will happen to this one; the Most High God will punish him with unbearable sufferings for his having sat like this, in his stupid obstinacy, wishing to compete in endurance with God the Most High.' And, wanting to know who he was, we found out that this man was Hallaj.

ACCOUNT OF NAHRAJURI (D. 330/941)

When Husayn ibn Mansur entered Mecca, that was for the first time, he stayed one year in the *sahn* (interior courtyard) of the mosque, without budging from his place, except for the ritual purification, and for the *tawaf*; he paid no attention either to the sun or the rain. Each day someone brought him, at the time of the evening prayer, a jug of water to drink and some flat bread, *qurs*, the kind they make in Mecca. He would take the bread, bite off four mouthfuls around the edges and drink two swallows of water, one before eating, one after. Then he would place the rest of the flat bread on top of the jug, and someone would carry it to him the next day.

ACCOUNT OF 'ATTAR (WITHOUT ISNAD)

"It is told that a visitor seeing a scorpion scuttle near him, wished to kill it; but Hallaj said: 'let it be; for twelve years it has been our table companion moving around us.' "

A figure of "twelve years" for his sojourn does not fit in with anything in Hallaj's biography; this legendary story must be connected with his Meccan period.

During this first stay in Mecca, Hallaj must have had contacts with only a small group of Sufis and with the guardians of the Haram, which three authorities controlled: the *wali* (or *amir*), resident governor of Mecca, the resident qadi, and the *amir al-hajj* (annual representative of the caliph to oversee the pilgrimage; a Hashimite).

With his Meccan milieu being in direct contact with the capital, the repercussions of the unusual life that Hallaj led in Mecca, outside of the time of the pilgrimage, on three occasions (270–271, 279–280, 286–287), must have attracted to him either the benevolent or the suspicious attention of high officials.

The northern access to the holy cities was not completely guaranteed to the Iraqi pilgrims by the Banu Asad and Banu Shayban patrols; in fact, since 251/865, the plateau oases (Najd, Yamana) were held by a Hasanid dynasty, that of the Banu Ukhaydir (chiefs: Isma'il-b-Yusuf, d. 253, his brother Muhammad, d. 316, his grandnephew Isma'il-b-Yf-b-M-b-Yf Ukhaydir, whom the Qarmathians would install in 315 near Kufa, probably in the castle of al-Ukhaydir, which I examined in 1908: *Tanbih*, 381, Musil A.P. [?], 366). Hallaj must have made contact with the Hasanid Banu Ukhaydir, at the time allied with the Qarmathians: and it is useful to point out here that Baghdad W[est?] has always been colonized by the Bedouin of the Tariq Makka, and that the sermons preached by Hallaj in Baghdad W. used Qarmathian terms, which suggests an audience of nomads dependent on the Banu Ukhaydir (cf. in 313 the arrests of Qarmathian Isma'ilis in this quarter).

I do not think that Hallaj had participated in the turbulent debates between Meccan Hashimites (fights in 281, expulsion of the Ja'farites [to Egypt's Sa'id] by the Hasanid 'Alids, amir-sharifs of Mecca after 345, under the Buwayhids, who handed over the control of the hajj to the *naqib* of the Baghdad 'Alids beginning in 354). His Hashimite friendships came, instead, from Basra. But it must be noted that in 279–280 (*wali* 'Ajj, *amir-ifada* Harun, then Ibn Burya) as in 284–286 (*wali amir* AB M-b-'AA) refused to cause trouble for Hallaj, in spite of the attacks of his former Sufi brothers (Ibn Burya let him speak in the mosque of the Round City in Baghdad and in the *waqfa* at 'Arafat).

The Anecdotes of Ibn Sa'dan

AB A-b-M ibn Abi Sa'dan recounted the following:

Husayn-b-Mansur told me: "If you believe in me, I will send you a bird
('*usfura*); and if you put the weight of one grain (*habba*) of his droppings on a
mann of lead, it will change into gold." And I answered him: "You, if you believe
in me, I will send you an elephant; when it rests on its back, the soles of its feet touch
the vault of heaven; and, when you wish to hide him, you will be able to hide him in
one of your eyes." Which made him keep quiet, dumbfounded, and silenced.

(I don't quite know to which folkloric theme the elephant belongs; but the
bird described here is not, as Herbelot supposed it to be, the safflower [*cnicus*],
but the Great Work of the alchemists: distilled gas is "the bird" that flies away,
leaving a residue, a solidified "dropping": the Philosopher's Stone).

Abu Mughith (= Hallaj) did not lean on cushions and did not sleep stretched out
on his side; he remained standing all night; if he closed his eyes, he stayed in a
squatting position, with his sides resting on his knees, and he dropped off to sleep
only a moment. Someone once said to him: "Be a good friend to yourself!" "By
God," he said, "my body has never been for me a friend who has given me joy. On
the contrary, I have heard the Master of Messengers (Muhammad) say, 'The men
who have suffered the most have been the prophets; after them, the *siddiqun*; next,
their likes and others like them . . .' (I want therefore to suffer like them)."

I have served Abu Mughith for twenty years and I have not seen him turn back
his steps to what he had passed beyond—nor seek anything which was lacking to him.

I heard him occasionally say: "From time to time it happens that I drop off to
sleep for a moment, and I say to myself: 'Are you going to sleep in spite of me? If
you do I am going to give you some lashes with the whip!' "

(He) told me one day: "I was seated opposite the Ka'ba (in Mecca), and I heard
a moan coming from there: 'O wall, move out of the way of those I love! The one
who visits you for yourself, walks in procession (for the *tawaf*) around you, and
the one who visits Me for Myself, walks in procession within Me.' "

This was already the theme of Hallaj's verses on *tawaf* and of his juridical
thesis about pilgrimage.

That did not prevent him from being very faithful to the strict precepts of
Sunnite law: he was *tutiorist* regarding those practices debated among the
schools; without joining any particular school (*madhhab*), when it came to debated points, he conformed to the most rigid (*as'ab*) solution. This led him, as
he told Ibrahim Hulwani, his companion for ten years, never to perform the
legal prayer without ablution and purification. Ibn Kawkab Wasiti, who accompanied him for seven years, said that he had seen him eat, of solid foods, only
salt and bread; he wore only a single *muraqqa'a* (patched material) over his shoul-
ders, and on his head a *burnus* (hood); but if someone gave him an *izar* (head veil),

he accepted it and wore it; "and I never saw him sleep for more than an hour at night and just a little during the heat of the day (su'ayriya min al-nahar)."

The Discussions with Nahrajuri and 'Amr Makki

It is during this first sojourn in Mecca that Hallaj, meditating on his inner life, seems to have convinced himself experimentally of the possibility of a science of mysticism founded on introspection. Ths following text, still weakly established (on a basis of two manuscripts), gives us a glimpse of it.

> He proceeded to Mecca, where, during a discussion with AYq Nahrajuri, he said to him: "When an indication or a sign emerges in your conscience, the communications (coming from God) must be linked together and the (mystic) states (in you) must be comparable and on the same level; if not, you can neither connect nor coordinate the communications and states with a view to knowing hidden things."—"Keep quiet," [the other said;] "I know (canonical) arguments that condemn your way of seeing; and before long you will realize this."—"But, my friend," [Hallaj said], "I mean that God shows me knowledge (from within) only after He transmits to me its tradition (from without)." "How could you have immediate (anagogical, ittila') knowledge on a point that you first have to receive through tradition and audition?" [the other asked]. Hallaj responded, "My friend, I can deduce something of tradition just as the physiognomist is able to explain faces; but, for me to rely on it, I must receive, at the same time as the communication, immediate knowledge of the matter; in this way I reconcile tradition with my intuition. Thus the two sciences are able to converge, the two suggestions to meet, the two comprehensions to meet. But I do not pretend that (mystical) intuition alone, without tradition, can be more certain, any more than that illumination without the faculty of sight, can be more clarifying." Then they parted, while Hallaj murmured a sentence that no one could penetrate or grasp.

This text, in this form, appears to have been doctored, probably during the period of the last editor of the *Akhbar* (Ibn 'Aqil); for it inserts a kind of apologia on a plane of pre-Ghazalian conciliation barely conceivable at the time of Hallaj's death. It corresponds, nevertheless, to a genuine trend, if one considers as strictly Hallajian the lines on the two sciences and their junction. Like Ibn Hanbal in the case of Muhasibi, these conservative mystic traditionists reproached Hallaj for delving into and classifying these "mystic states that are acts of God." And this reproach will be directed at him even more violently by 'Amr Makki and his group.

Concerning 'Amr-b-'Uthman (Makki), the last recension of the *Akhbar* tells us that his repudiation [of Hallaj] stemmed from an encounter at the time of the latter's arrival in Mecca. When they met, 'Amr asked him, "Where do you come from?" To which Hallaj responded: "If you truly contemplate all in God, you would see everything in its place, for God the Most High sees all." ʿAmr was annoyed and reacted coolly to him; but he waited a long time before announcing their break; he then spread the rumor that Hallaj had said to him: "I could express myself like this Qur'an."

Though the account of Hamd places the break with Makki (together with other issues) in Baghdad, this text places it in Mecca, and seems to be ignorant of the fact that they knew each other beforehand. Sulami had set the scene in a more likely manner (without any other *isnad* than the word *hukiya*, "it was reported," which refers probably to the collection of J. Khuldi: *Hikayat*): "ʿAmr Makki said: 'I was walking with him in one of the byways of Mecca, while (I was) reciting the Qur'an; he heard me reciting and said to me: "I could, I myself, express myself like that"; from then on, I stopped associating with him.'" Qushayri puts forward this version again in a ponderous style: "It is well known (*mashhur*) that ʿAmr-b-ʿUthman Makki, seeing Hallaj writing something, said to him: 'What is this?'—'This?' said Hallaj, 'I put it on a level with the Qur'an.' Then Makki cursed him and blacklisted him. The masters say, all the misfortunes that befell Hallaj much later, resulted from this master's curse against him." Abu Zurʿa A-b-M-b-Fadl Tabari, in a historic fragment recopied by Ibn Bakuya, says: "I heard M-b-Yahya Razi tell me: 'I heard ʿAmr-b-ʿUthman (Makki) cursing him, and saying "If I could have done it, I would have killed him with my bare hands."—What did the master reproach him for?—"I was reciting one day a verse from the Book of God, but he said to [me]: 'I am capable of composing something equal to it, and of reciting it.'"

AZ Tabari adds that two masters, residing at that time in Medina, Abu Yaʿqub Aqtaʿ (Hallaj's own father-in-law) and AB Fuwati, reacted against Hallaj the same way Makki did.

The four versions of the break with Makki show that what is involved is the problem of *ilham* or private revelation (cf. *hadith qudsi*); Hallaj dares to note down in writing "interior words" that he believes have come from the same God who dictated the Qur'an. He is inclined, therefore, to regulate his life according to them in terms of religious practice and in his relations with others, since he spoke to them about it. ʿAmr Makki, who recognizes perfectly well that interior words are divine graces, but who practices the "discipline of mystery" towards them, treats them as charisms without practical application, and advises him to say nothing about them; for, by listening to them, the faithful would be distracted and diverted from their endurance of the Law (*sabr*, Qur'an 38:6). Makki denounces Hallaj, not without treachery, as having become a heretic, a false prophet of a new Qur'an. He knows well enough, however, that Hallaj has not become a Muʿtazilite and does not believe that a man can usurp without divine investiture the miraculous style of an inspired Book.

This theory, sketched out by the Muʿtazilites Nazam and Murdar, on the one hand, leads to the critical skepticism of Ibn al-Rawandi (d. 248: in his *Kitab damigh, zumurrud, farid*), and, on the other hand, to the pseudo-Qur'anic literary imitations attempted by Mukhtar and Mutanabbi, or even to the *Fusul waghayat* of Ma'arri. But we find nothing of this sort in what has come down to us of Hallaj's works. Certain fragments, certainly, even apart from the incriminating utterances at the last trial, show him expressing himself "in the name of God," at times even in the first person, as in the *hadith qudsi*. But in all the traces of Qur'anic influence on the Hallajian style, there is no usurpation of the role of Prophet entrusted with a legislating revelation. Certain apocalyptic words attributed to 'Ali and divinized by Shi'ite extremists were, according to Suli, used again by Hallaj on his own behalf; but it is clear that they signified the passive deification of the saint, not the positive mission of a responsible prophet. In his own *Riwayat*, in which undoubtedly the themes of his public discourses are preserved for us, Hallaj, prior to his third pilgrimage, presents devotional rules to guide the soul toward divine sanctity. He presents them in the form of hadith, whose *isnad* (chains of testimonial authorities) are not a series of (professional traditionist) transmitters authenticating counsels emanating from the Prophet; they are signs of divine grace, different frameworks in which his recollected thought has seen these inspired counsels come into view—destined to establish, in a hierarchical system, and to spiritualize, without modifying them, the duties of Qur'anic legal obligation. Finally, like the *Tawasin*, his ecstatic utterances express the state of essential union (*'ayn al-jam'*), of unitive sanctity, which he explicitly contrasts with the role of prophet, whom he relegates to the second position.

This is that ultimate consequence of Sufism, posed as early as the *hadith al-ghibta*, and soon defined by a contemporary, Tirmidhi (*tafdil al-walaya 'ala'l-nubuwwa*), that 'Amr Makki does not wish to see posed by letting Hallaj divulge private revelations.

His Second Hajj to Mecca

ACCOUNT OF NAHRAJURI

Ibn Khafif, having been questioned by Abu Hasan ibn Abi Tawba on Husayn ibn Mansur, delared:

> I heard Abu Ya'qub Nahrajuri say this: "Husayn ibn Mansur came to Mecca with four hundred persons. The Sufi shaykhs divided them up among themselves, each lodging in his own home a group of these pilgrims. Now, during his first journey, I was his confidant among all of his *khadim*. But this time, I warned the shaykhs and urged them to keep the large crowd away from him.
>
> "Later, when the *maghrib* hour had come, I went to him and said: 'it is late, come to our home for dinner'—'We shall eat on the Abu Qubays,' he answered me. So, we took with us some provisions, and climbed Abu Qubays, When we reached the top, we sat down to eat. When the meal was finished, Husayn ibn

Mansur said: 'Shall we not eat sweets?'—'Why?' I asked, 'we have already eaten dates.'—'I would like something cooked on the fire.'—And he got up, took his shoulder bag, and withdrew from us a moment. Soon he returned with a cup of sweets, placed them before us, and offered them to us: 'Bismi'-llah!' and everyone began to eat them. As for me, I said to myself: that comes undoubtedly from the *sorcery*, of which ʿAmr ibn ʿUthman accused him before. I took a piece of it, descended the *wadi*, and went to the various sweets-sellers to show them this cake. I asked them: 'Do you know the one who makes this in Mecca?' But no one knew him. Finally, someone showed it to a kitchen-maid who recognized the cake and said: 'Only in Zabid do they make this kind.' I went to the home of a pilgrim from Zabid, where a friend of mine was staying: I showed him the cake; he recognized it, and told me: 'That is made in our region, but it is impossible to transport it. So, I don't see how anyone could have carried it here.' I had him take the cup, and asked him to have someone inquire around Zabid as to whether a cup having such and such a mark was missing from one of the sweets-shops in the town. . . . When this man from Zabid returned to his homeland, he discovered that this cup had been removed from a confectioner's shop.

"This is the way I became certain that Hallaj was served by the *Jinn*."

The accusation made by Nahrajuri, which Hamd discreetly alluded to in his account, was that Hallaj pretended to be served by demons.

But Nahrajuri had other reasons of a doctrinal nature for breaking with Hallaj. He had, indeed, been his *khadim*, and was to remain the friend of his *khadim*, Ibrahim ibn Fatik, but he continued to be above all the disciple of Junayd, Makki, and Abu Yaʿqub Susi, hence the convinced partisan of the superiority of ʿ*ilm* (the rational knowledge of revealed texts and tradition) over ʿ*amal* (pious supererogatory works): "Ecstasies are only valuable when they agree with the facts of ʿ*ilm*."

"The men of God have sought the reality of divine things, but their nature as created beings has continued to dominate them. This is why they have declared: one cannot seek the Truth, for one can only 'seek' what one has 'lost'; just as one cannot attempt to perceive God, for He is infinite. Also, the one who desires *to observe* the presence of the Omnipresent is a blind man, for the Omnipresent One only appears in ecstasy, and the discourses of ʿ*ilm* do not use visions derived from ecstasy."

He was developing forcefully, as one can see, the following thesis of Junayd: since God is purely simple, we cannot derive from ecstasy any positive information about Him.

ACCOUNT OF HULWANI

Ibrahim Hulwani said:

I was accompanying Husayn ibn Mansur with three of his disciples, and we were at the time between Wasit and Baghdad. He was speaking, and in the course of the conversation, he used the word *halawa*. We said: perhaps the shaykh will give us some of it. He raised his head and cried out: "O you, whom no consciousness can reach, whom no thought or opinion can depict, You are the one who is visible in every body and every form without touching or mingling with any. It is You who shine forth out of each one, who radiate in eternity before and after, and whom You let us find only when all appears lost, and who appears only in the form of an enigma. . . . If you set some value on my closeness to You and some value on my isolation from creatures before You, then, give us this *halawa* to please my companions!" Then he went off the route for about a mile, and there we found a morsel of bright colored *halawa* and we ate it.

But he didn't eat any of it. When we had finished and resumed our way, a suspicious thought came to me. My mind remained fixed on that place, and I analyzed it (in order to visualize it) to the best of my ability. Then I withdrew from the road under pretext of relieving myself, while they continued on their way. I returned at this time to the place where we had eaten, and I no longer saw anything; I prayed, made two prostrations, saying "Deliver me, my God, from this base suspicion!" And a voice said to me, "Come now! you have eaten on Mount Qaf, and you want to see that *halawa* in this place! Set your thinking straight. This shaykh is none other than the King of the world."

LEGEND BY SAMARQANDI

Rashid Samarqandi recounted the following:

When I was going on the pilgrimage, I met (Husayn) Hallaj in the desert with four hundred disciples, and I went along with them for a certain number of days. At one point when the provisions had been exhausted, his companions said to him: "We want some *mashwi*." And he said to them: "Sit down." They sat, and he moved his hand behind his back and brought out a dish for each of them on which there was a *mashwi* and two bread buscuits. They ate them and were satisfied.

Then a few days later they said: "We want fresh dates." He got up and said to them: "Shake me the way people shake the date-palms." They entreated him, they shook him, and some fresh dates fell from him, *jinni*. They ate them and were satisfied.

Then after a few more days, they said: "We want some figs." He extended his hand into the air, and brought a plate down in it filled with fresh figs. They ate them and were satisfied.

Then they asked him for the *halwa*, and, without delay, a bowl appeared before him containing the *halwa*. They ate it and were amazed at the fact that it resembled the kind sold at Bab al-Taq. They said to him: "How have you brought this about?" He replied: "There is no longer any difference for me between being here in the desert or being at Bab al-Taq; if you were there, you would receive it just as I have received it."

ACCOUNT OF AHMAD RUMI

Two centuries later, Ahmad Rumi gives, like the master of ʿAttar, a completely legendary picture of Hallaj the miracle-worker. This is a triptych:

> Someone asked Mansur: "O Saint, since you are an intimate [of God] (*wasil*), illuminated by divine glory, tell God my desire: get me a dish of roast meat."
>
> Mansur thrust his head into his collar (*jiriban*), and immediately he brought out a dish of roast meat and some bread.
>
> Another person said: "I want a bunch of ripe yellow grapes, here, in this summer resort where it is cool."
>
> Mansur plunged his hand into his collar, and, at once, he gave him the bunch.
>
> Then another said: "I want fruit flavored sweets, without a tray."
>
> Mansur thrust his head into his collar (*jiriban*), and immediately he brought out a dish of roast meat and some bread.
>
> O [dear] hearts, the aim of these anecdotes is to show that the self on the path of veils, is *the* way (par excellence);
>
> And that, whosoever washes his hands of "self" and "us," tears asunder these veils.

The Reprimand to Ibrahim Khawwas: in Kufa

Account by Hujwiri: "In a well-known passage of the *Hikayat* (of Khuldi), it is said that 'when Husayn-b-Mansur, God hold him in His mercy, came to Kufa, and stayed in the house of Muhammad ibn Hasan ʿAlawi, Ibrahim Khawwas, God hold him in His mercy, entered Kufa, and, having learned that Husayn was there, went to see him. Husayn asked him: "O Ibrahim, what benefit have you derived from these forty years persistence in this way of life (going around the desert, living in hardship)?" He answered, "the way of abandonment to God (*tawakkul*) has been opened to me." (Unfortunate one!) You have used your life to construct your interior dwelling (*fiʿumran batinika*); when will you make up your mind to consume yourself in the divine Unity?' "

The anecdote is, in fact, famous, and many commentaries have been written on it. Ibrahim Khawwas (d. 291), who had made his profession (*tawba*) before Khayr Nassaj (like Shibli), was a disciple of A ʿAA Maghribi and a friend of Mamshadh. He had followed a Karramiyan rule and had become set on an ideal of abandonment to God, based on a desire to love Him, but to be carried out in the minute and methodical practice of small privations. He left for the desert, carrying with him a needle, thread, bag, and scissors (respecting the canonical regulations), then he forbade himself, for example, to look at whatever could be seen, or to speak to anyone who came (even to Khidr) who might involve him in different experiences familiar to hagiography. Reacting against this conception, which had reduced the mystic vocation to a cult of self-renunciation, to the idolatry of a virtue, Hallaj urged him to surrender himself completely to God: to ascend, says Ghazali in his *Ihya'*, from the third stage of *tawhid* to the fourth and last. A commentary on the *Isharat* of Ibn Sina, attributed to Fakhr Razi, amends this: from the fourth to the fifth and last stage, where the soul is entirely conformed to the *akhlaq* (moral perfections) of God.

'Umar Suhrawardi, in his 'Awarif, comments: "When will you make up your mind to consume your virtue with abandonment to the One to whom you speak of abandoning yourself?"

The Visit to Jerusalem (Easter Night and the Paschal Fire)

I learned that he entered Jerusalem with seventy disciples (carrying beggar sacks); it was at nightfall. He entered the sanctuary (= the Holy Sepulcher), and saw that the lamps were extinguished (*al-qanadil makmuda*). He asked the priests in charge: "Up to what time do you leave them extinguished?" "Up to the last third of the night."—"This last third is long in coming," he responded: and he extended his index finger, uttering "Allah"; at that moment a light came forth from his finger and lit four hundred lamps, then returned to his finger. The monks, astonished at this, asked him: "What is your religion?"—"I am a *hanif*," he said, "the least significant *hanif* of the Community of Muhammad." Then Husayn added: "The choice is yours; if you wish, I will enter and sit down with you; if not, I will leave." —"It is up to you to decide," they answered him. —"I have my companions with me, and we need something (= to eat)." They then made him a gift of seven bags of silver; he spent them entirely on his companions, and left the same night.

The Maniac at Bab Khurasan

'Abdan-b-Ahmad said:

There was at Bab Khurasan (in Baghdad) an obsessed maniac (*muwaswis*)—is this 'Isa al-Muwaswis? (Ibn al-Khatib)—who associated with Husayn-b-Mansur; he used to hang around the cemeteries, then he would wander over to see Husayn-b-Mansur. One day, he came to him with a basket of dates on his head, and some children following him; he stopped and said to Hallaj: "When will I go out of my self? When will I despair of finding myself again? When will I rejoice in my joy, becoming friendly with savage beasts, and savage toward my own species?" Husayn said to him (distich, *hazaj* meter):

"When your mania besets you alternately with (funeral) processions and wedding nuptials,

"Place yourself in the presence of Hell, of Paradise, of angels and of the Throne."

Baqli, who seems to know only the distich, uses it as commentary on Hallaj's prayer during his last night, attesting, on the threshold of the execution, to his certitude of a sublime vocation.

The Fire Temple of Tustar

Ibn Hajj related the following:

> A group of Sufis came to see Husayn-b-Mansur in Tustar, and they asked him for an alms gift. He led them to a fire temple; but the custodian told them that the door was closed and that the key was with the priest. Husayn persisted (in order to get the key) but no one answered him. Then he raised his sleeve near the lock, which opened, and they entered the fire temple. Once inside, they saw a lighted candle, which didn't go out day or night. [The custodian] told them, "We revere this flame as coming from the fire on which Abraham was thrown; Zoroastrians carry it into all their countries."—"Who could extinguish it?" "We have read in our Book that no one could extinguish it except Jesus, the son of Mary."
>
> Now, Husayn extended his sleeve toward the flame and it went out. The custodian, believing himself at the Last Judgment, cried out: "O God! O God! Now at this hour all the fire altars are extinguished, in the East and in the West!"—"Who could relight them?"—"We have read in our Book: no other than the one who extinguished them." And he humbled himself before Husayn and wept. Husayn said to him: "If you have something to give to these shaykhs, I will relight it." Now, there was a trunk there, in which every Zoroastrian who entered the fire temple threw an offering of one dinar. He opened it, and handed over the contents to the shaykhs. Then he said: "There is no more here." And Husayn extended his sleeve toward the flame and it was relighted; then he recited the following verse:
> "The worldly life coaxed me as if I were ignorant of its worth.
> "The King prohibits to us what it offers that is forbidden; as for me, I avoid even what it offers that is permitted.
> "It appeared to me that it was needy, so I abandoned myself entirely to it."

The Mosque in Basra

We have three accounts of his two trips to Basra: in 291/903 and 292/904.

Abu'l-Hy M-b-ʿUbayd-b-M ibn Nasrawayh (qadi of Basra in 331/943), recounted the following to Qadi ʿAli Tanukhi (d. 342), father of Qadi Muhassin Tanukhi:

> My mother's brother took me out one day with him to go see Husayn-b-Mansur Hallaj, who at that time resided in the grand mosque of Basra, posing as a pious man, as a Sufi, as a *qari'*, and this was before he preached his non-

sense. and began what you know all about. His plans were still secret; only the Sufis attributed miracles to him in their fashion of calling them "divine aids," the possibility of which the orthodox rites do not accept. My uncle began to chat with him, and I, a very young boy, was sitting with them listening to the conversation. He said to my uncle: "I have decided to leave Basra."—"Why?"—"The people here spread a story about me; my heart cannot bear it, and I want to withdraw from them."—"What do they say?"—"They tell people that I have done some things, without speaking to me about them and without making inquiries to know whether they really happened; were it not for that they would see that their account is not consistent with (what happened to them in) reality. They went out of their houses, saying 'Hallaj's invocations are heard [by God], he has divine aids, he has already provided supernatural graces. . . .' Who am I to be capable of such things?" [Hallaj asked; then he said,] "So, I am going to tell you something: some time ago, a man came to give me some dirhams, and said to me: distribute them to the poor. At that moment, there were no poor around me; so I put them under one of the mats in the grand mosque, beside the *ustuwana*, in a corner that I knew well. And I stayed there a long time without anyone coming; after a while I went home and slept the whole night. The next day, I went to the *ustuwana* and took my place for prayer. Then, a number of poor people came up to me, interrupting my prayer: I went to lift the corner of the mat and gave them the dirhams that I had received. They spread the rumor about me that, if I struck the ground with my hand, dirhams came into my hand." And he began to relate other similar things. My uncle then stood up, took his leave and refrained henceforth from coming to visit him, saying: this man is an intriguer; all this will induce people to speak about him. Soon afterwards Hallaj left Basra, and his case became clear enough to all.

Account of the Ash'arite Juwayni

The Ash'arite Juwayni declared that Hallaj had actually entered into an absolutely fantastic plot, hatched like the one of Ibn Maymun Qaddah in earlier times, against the Caliphate and against Islam. "Several authorities affirmed that the three men whose names follow here conspired together to overthrow the state, lead the kingdom into ruin, seduce and win over people's hearts, each in the country that he was going to travel through. Abu Sa'id Jannabi assigned to himself the borders of al-Ahsa. Ibn Muqaffa' made his way through the lands of the Turks. And Hallaj traveled through the region of Baghdad, whose ruler sentenced him to the death penalty; and if he did not succeed (as much as the two others) in winning over the souls of people, this was because the people of Iraq do not like to be made fools of."

The Break with Junayd (282?)

Account by Hujwiri:

> I have read in the *Hikayat* (of Khuldi) that when Husayn-b-Mansur, in a state of
> trance (*ghalaba*), broke with 'Amr-b-'Uthman, and came over to Junayd, the latter
> said: "Why do you come?"—"To live in community (*suhba*) with you as the mas-
> ter."—"I do not live in community with madmen (*majanin*); community life re-
> quires balance (*sihha*), otherwise what happened to you with Sahl-b-'AA Tustari
> and with 'Amr occurs."—"O Master, sobriety (*sahw*) and intoxication (*sukr*) are
> only the two human aspects of the mystic, who remains separated from his Lord as
> long as these two aspects are not both annihilated."—"O Ibn Mansur, you are
> wrong in your definition of these states, sobriety and intoxication; the first means
> the state of normal equilibrium of the faithful before God; it is not a qualification
> of the faithful that he may acquire through his own effort (*iktisab*) as a creature;
> likewise the second, which signifies extremes of desire and love. O Ibn Mansur, I
> see in your language an indiscreet curiosity (*fudul*) and some expressions that are
> useless."

This account pits two theories against each other: that of Junayd, for whom
God is the lone author of contrasting psychic states that He alternates in His
own way in the souls of mystics, to whom He remains inaccessible; and that of
Hallaj, whom Junayd reproaches, as he did Sahl, for his idea of contrition and
personal effort, the semi-Mu'tazilite idea of the human soul's guided and progressive cooperation with divine grace; Hallaj adds to that his idea, which will
become his theses of *isqat al-wasa'it*: the gradual removal, through sanctification, of consideration of all intermediaries, rites, virtues, [spiritual] states, for
attaining the ultimate reality of worship: immediate and essential union with
God. Some chronological difficulties are raised by this acount: Hallaj is presented in it as a wandering mystic who has deserted two masters, and Junayd as
a master who immediately resists accepting him into his company; Samnani
envisages the beginnings of Hallaj in this way, but it runs counter to the account of Hamd. On the other hand, the word *fudul* appears previously in the
testimony of Hadrami, in which Hallaj puts to Junayd an entirely different
question.

The Episode of "Ana'l-Haqq"
("I Am the Truth" = "My 'I' Is God")

Hallaj seems to have become aware rather early (before his journey to
Khurasan) of the ultimate goal in the mystic way; since Baghdad, he had been
acquainted, through Junayd, with the theories of Bistami and Tirmidhi. His lu-

ınalysis and his firmness of will must have led him to formulate the
ıe mystic exchange of wills, when the time came, in a decisive per-
:ement without ambiguity or apology.

his was the expression "I am the Truth," *Ana'l-Haqq*, that is to say,
is God!"

Il later Muslim tradition, this saying stands for Hallaj; it is the mark of
itual vocation, the cause of his condemnation, the glory of his martyr-

he actually utter this statement, and, if so, when? Do we find it in his
' And what have been the different judgments passed upon him because

ı. .ı Sufi tradition says that he uttered it in the presence of Junayd before their
break; the first two known versions of this tradition are as follows:

a) Baghdadi, Shafi'ite and Khurasani Ash'arite, around 400, in his *Farq*: "It
was related (*ruwiya*) that Hallaj met Junayd one day, and said to him 'I am the
Truth'—'No,' Junayd answered him, 'it is by means of the Truth that you are!'
What gibbet will you stain with your blood!' "

b) Harawi, Hanbalite, Khurasani anti-Ash'arite, around 470, in his *Tabaqat*:
"One day Hallaj knocked at the door of Junayd's house; 'Who is there?'—'The
Truth (*Haqq*)'—'Don't say "the Truth," but rather "I come on behalf of the
Truth." ' What gibbet will you stain with your blood!" According to 'Attar,
Junayd was supposed to have made this prediction to him upon his return from
his first pilgrimage; this would be the "question" to which the account of Hamd
alludes; 'Attar adds that Hallaj retorted with another prediction: "The day when
I redden the gibbet with my blood you will again put on the coat of literalism."

This tradition has Junayd playing the role of spiritual director, interrogating
Hallaj with authority; it introduces an archaic prediction (blood is still considered impure in it; whereas, for 'Attar, not only is it pure [he writes "redden"
instead of "stain"], it also purifies [ablution]); this prediction, which Hadrami
puts elsewhere in the mouth of Junayd at the time of his first interview with
Hallaj, has the defect of duplicating the prediction by 'Amr Makki.

One tradition, formerly attested to, as early as 375 at the latest, when Ibn-al-
Qarih collects it in Baghdad from the great grammarian Abu 'Ali Fasawi
(d. 377), puts the prediction in the mouth of Shibli (Shibli was a friend of Ibn
Mujahid, master of Fasawi), and links it, on the one hand, with the quatrain *Ya
Sirra sirri* (attested to as early as 355 by Maqdisi, via Ibn 'AA = Ibn Khaluya?)
and on the other hand, we believe, with the sentence *Ana'l-Haqq*. It reads as
follows:

Abu 'Ali Farisi (= Fasawi) reported to me (*haddathani*) and told me: "I saw
Hallaj standing, within the *halqa* of Shibli. . . . (lacuna, to complete as follows:
saying, 'I am the Truth' and Shibli responding to him: 'do not say "the Truth," but

rather, "I come on behalf of the Truth.") What gibbet will you stain with your blood!' But Hallaj, covering his face with his sleeve, recited (the quatrain) *Ya sirra.* . . . For he believed that the wise man vis-à-vis God is in the same position as the ray vis-à-vis the sun from which it draws its light."

If the saying *Ana'l-Haqq* does, in fact, appear in the lacuna of this text properly transmitted and attested to, Hallaj would have uttered it there where Shibli held his *halqa*, in the *qubbat al-shu'ara'* of the cathedral mosque, in the *Madinat al-Mansur* (which would explain the presence of a *rawi*, a layman, one of the masters, *nuhat*, of Fasawi or Abu Ishaq Zajjaj); in the course of his public preaching, in one of the debates with Shibli, referred to in the account of Hamd.

Chronologically, this more recent date would be preferable. And if we must accept both accounts as true, the incident with Junayd was private, while the one with Shibli occurred in public.

A third tradition, Sufi and late, has *Ana'l-Haqq* uttered even later, during the trial. Qadi Abu Yusuf (*sic*: for Abu 'Umar-b-Yusuf) asks him, "Who are you?" and he answers, "I am the Truth."

Finally, legend has him saying it ardently, almost constantly, in a preaching manner; and shows him proclaiming solemnly from high on the gibbet "I am the Truth"; this is the "drum roll" announcing the Sovereign, says Harawi; and according to the Persian 'Attar and the Turk Nesimi, "the gibbet of the *Ana'l-Haqq*" is the *mi'raj* of heroes. When his blood is shed and his ashes scattered, they utter this phrase again, for his vindication.

2. The phrase occurs in a recension of the *Akhbar al-Hallaj* (no. 74), where, though metrically irregular, it is inserted in the second verse of a Hallajian poem celebrated since the time of Ibn Khafif: with the significance of a vow: "Unify me (*wahhidni*), O my Only One . . . [Let me] be . . . the Truth and, as the Truth bestows investiture of Its essence upon the one who becomes It, let our separation be no more." The Taymur ms., the only one that gives the sentence, is unfortunately testimony drawn from a deliberately doctored (probably by Ibn 'Aqil) edition of the *Akhbar*, and *Ana'l-Haqq* is perhaps interpolated in it in order to contradict the hostile tradition of Fasawi.

As for the *Tawasin*, "I am the Truth" occurs in it only in interpolation in a single recension; it includes a tendentious comparison, likening it to two blasphemies, to the "I (am more worthy than Adam)" of Iblis, and to the "I (am your supreme Lord)" of Fir'awn. A passage, moreover, which is very archaic and very important, for it makes Hallaj the patron saint of the *futuwwa*, an oath-taking society of outlaws, of the "dregs of society."

"If I had retracted my claim and my words, I would have fallen off the (initiation) carpet of honor (= *futuwwa*)." "And (after Iblis and Fir'awn), I have said: if you do not know God, recognize Him in His sign; I am His sign, and I am the Truth, and I have never stopped being true to Truth. And even if I am killed, or hung on the gibbet, or have my hands and feet cut off, I will not retract."

This text presents *Ana'l-Haqq* as the supreme cry of a voluntary outcast for divine love.

One can thus conclude that, if the statement *Ana'l-Haqq* is not found in the works of Hallaj, it was actually uttered by him, being consistent with his teaching. He said expressly in the *Tawasin* apropos of the Burning Bush in which God said to Moses "I am your God": "And my role (*mathali*) is the role of this Bush." 'Attar had emphasized it, and, before him, if we can believe Baqli, Hallaj's own son, Mansur.

3. It remains now to examine the different interpretations and judgments of the Hallajian "I am the Truth."

We shall see later how the notion of *al-Haqq* clarified itself for Hallaj, and what its antecedents were—Greek (philosophical), Syriac (Christian), and even Arab (Shi'a). If, in spite of Hallaj, *Haqq* has not become the name par excellence of God for Arab Islam (only mystic circles use it; they used it already before him, timidly; he himself presents it as standing for God considered only as *Mu'ill al-anam*, Creator of beings), by way of compensation, because of Hallaj, it became so for all of non-Arab Islam—Iranian, Turkish, Indian, and Malaysian.

In Arabic, from the time of Hallaj, *al-Haqq* is only one of the ninety-nine Names of God authorized in the litany of the rosary (*tasbih*) by hadith (fifty-first in Tirmidhi's list); and Qannad makes Shibli say that Hallaj was punished for having misused this divine name, whose power had been granted to him, this Name which, according to the partisans (*sifatiya*) of the real distinction of the divine attributes, had by no means introduced Hallaj into union with the other divine names, let alone with the divine essence. His cry of *Ana'l-Haqq* was only an effort at usurpation and appropriation, like that of an ascetic who believes that the radiance of his enthusiasm belongs to him, or of a magician who has become haughty with his power.

It is the same voluntary limitation of the meaning of the word *Haqq*, also through hostility toward Hallaj, when, in the monist theory of the seven enclosures of the soul, Kashi (d. 730/1330) teaches against Samnani that the divine name *Haqq* is only the fourth of the corresponding Seven Names, and that to say *Ana'l-Haqq* means simply that the soul of the novice is stripped of its fourth enclosure or *latifa* (= *sirr* = *nafs mutma'inna*).

Apart from these two theses made for the occasion, and the Bengali cult of Hallaj identified with Vishnu considered as "Satya Pir = Master of the Truth," the unanimity of Muslim thought has understood perfectly that this Hallajian Truth was, essentially, God. How Hallaj could have said *Ana'l-Haqq* was still to be explained. Here follows a tableau that we have tried to complete of these various exegeses; it is based on *fatwa* by Fakhr Razi and Ibn Taymiya, the translation of which will be given later.

The first series of exegeses believes that *Ana'l-Haqq* is an ill-adjusted statement, coming from a man who has not understood its expression fully (a-c); the second sees *Ana'l-Haqq* as a divine utterance, well-adjusted in its expression and real; what is left to explain is how it could have been spoken humanly (d-e).

a) *hikaya* (= transition from an indirect to a direct style). In saying "I," Hallaj meant simply that he was a narrator: as a narrator uses the historic present, as a reader of the Qur'an recites in the first person the Qur'anic verse in which God says "I" ('Umar Suhrawardi, *'Awarif;* criticized by Sirhindi).

This mild exegesis faces another problem: How much reality is there for the believing reader in the recitation of the Holy Book (Hanbalite realist solutions, Salimiyan)?

b) *tajawuz* (= hyperbole). Hallaj exaggerated:

(1) a false intellectual perception, his statement is incorrect, pernicious, and justly condemned; a grave error of a novice (Majd Baghdadi); a hypocritical pretention (Mu'tazilites) or simply unreal (Rifa'i);

(2) or the ambiguity of an outburst of amorous fervor; either spontaneous or provoked; by the theft of a book, or the ingestion of a talisman, or the sharing in the cup of intoxicating wine of Paradise (the pre-eternal wine of the covenant, *mithaq* offered to Hallaj by his sister. In this case, the incriminating sentence is no longer irreal, but it is excessive; it expresses an intoxication (*sukr*), a rapture (*ghalaba*), a dizziness. For there had indeed been divine commotion and participation, momentary at least, in one of the divine attributes (*sifat*), in one of the distinct perfections of which such and such divine name is the symbol, or in an Idea, or in Wisdom (*ma'rifa*). The one who is enrapt is irresponsible, thus canonically excusable (*ma'dhur*), but socially dangerous; once brought to his senses, if he repeats this statement, he is subject to the power of the Law, even though he is a saint. This exegesis is the most frequently used (Ghazali; Kilani; 'Izz Maqdisi; Jili). Cf. *Hayy-b-Yaqzan*—cf. the case of Jesus—no privilege, though Fakhr Razi accepts the privilege of theopathic expression.

c) *tajalli* (= intellectual illumination). In a very high ecstasy, Hallaj intercepted and understood an esoteric divine secret, overstepping the Law; it must not be divulged on earth. What secret?

(1) *sirr wahdat al-shuhud* (the secret of immanence). Even outside ecstasy, the beauty of the world testifies that God appears in every single thing (*shuhud al-mazahir*) to the one who knows how to perceive Him in it. This truth runs counter to the affirmation of divine transcendence proclaimed in the canonical *shahada*; the saints must say nothing about it in this world, otherwise they are justly condemned (Kilani; Samnani);

(2) *sirr wahdat al-wujud* (the secret of existential monism). Nothing exists but God; to arrive at the logical certitude of impersonal identity (or more

precisely, unipersonal, in the third person, *Huwa*) of every single thing and to proclaim *Ana'l-Haqq*, we must become fully conscious of the Universe, the only means by which God expresses Himself to Himself. Hallaj caught a glimpse of that, but expressed it before realizing it fully, otherwise the secular arm could not have executed him. He lacked respect for the Prophet, who, knowing this secret, did not speak of it; and he was obliged as penance (in Turkish legend, he spits in his mouth) to say *Ana'l-Haqq*, in order that he be killed in expiation (Ibn 'Arabi). The assembly of Prophets interceded with the Prophet on behalf of Hallaj. Besides, all the damned will be reconciled. In any case, *Ana'l-Haqq* does not give access to the pure divine essence (*ahadiya*), which is a supreme silence.

(3) *sirr al-muta'* (the secret of demiurgic investiture). God, who is immobile, delegates the setting in motion of the universe to a leader from the hierarchy of saints and all obey the succeeding appointees, the apotropeans (*abdal*), of this delegation, who must remain hidden. Insofar as it participates in the Creator's *fiat*, this *muta'* has the right to think the *Ana'l-Haqq*, the creative word. Ghazali (in his *Mishkat*) seems to think that after the Prophet, saints like Hallaj could have been invested with this role. But the many partisans of the pre-existence of Nur Muhammadi (Tirmidhi, Ibn Qasyi, Ibn Barrajan) teach that in the whole of time only the Prophet played this role of demiurge, receiving from God, who did everything for him, the divine Name of *al-Haqq*, verifying in him the permanence of the divine ipseity (Nur Kasirqi, *Ta'wilat*). And that only the perfect imitators of the Prophet, those, who, like Hallaj, receive in their pure heart the light emanating from the heart of the Prophet-demiurge, can proclaim this secret, *Ana'l-Haqq*. There would therefore be three steps, from God to an active Demiurge (the Prophet), from the Demiurge to a Passive Saint (= Hallaj), for arriving at the utterance of *Ana'l-Haqq*. This is what 'Attar means when he calls the Demiurge the *katkhuda* and the passive Saint the *haylaj* (in Shi'ite terminology, one would say *katkhuda* = *Mim* and *haylaj* = *Sin*; but, here, it is the *Mim* that is *Samit* and the *Sin*, *Natiq*).

According to this theory, Hallaj had the duty to say *Ana'l-Haqq*; he is holy and his judges are unjust;

(4) *Sirr al-rububiya* (the secret of supreme power). God, fundamentally, is the Author responsible for each personal act in every intelligent being; and, when this being says freely "I," he divulges the secret; he steals from God "the Pearl of love" (Kilani); he deserves in this world legal punishment, and after death, damnation. This is what Iblis and Fir'awn did; this is what Hallaj did, in saying *Anal'-Haqq*, divine words, stolen from God: thus the truthful and real word, and yet *kufr* (a blasphemy), forbidden (Tustari, AB Wasiti, Qushayri, Jurjani, Ahmad Ghazali). Hallaj is thus a saint damned, which is a contradiction; if God does not deprive Hallaj, damned, of loving Him, is it truly the same situation for Iblis and Fir'awn? Some answer affirmatively. But then, they are unjustly treated (*mazlum*) only in appearance; and with them, all rebels. *Ana'l-*

Haqq is an explosive sentence, which destroys the universe in conjuring God to come into it (cf. Yazidi eschatology): eschatological cry *"tasarrafa'l-aghyar bidamihi"* (Suhrawardi, Nasir Tusi).

d) *Fana'* (= annihilation). At the time of the declaration of *Ana'l-Haqq*, the personality of Hallaj was annihilated (this forces the mystics to admit that the soul is not an accident without duration, but a substantial form). How?

(1) demolished by pure divine will, which damns it [the soul] for saying "I" through its own mouth (= cf. *supra* c4);

(2) leveled by a moral preparation, a gradual amorous preadaptation of the subject to the whole of the divine will (*fana' bi'l-murad:* Kilani; Wafa'), a total self-renunciation (Sirhindi), a radical humility that is wholly contrary to the pride of Iblis (Kilani, 'Attar, Baqli, Rumi, Samnani), and that orients one toward a definite possibility, a renaissance, the *hecceity* of a divine person substituted for the former *hecceity* (Faris);

(3) transsubstantiated (= e).

e) *hulul wa ittihad* (= infusion and union). The personality of Hallaj was transfigured, essentialized, by the infusion (*hulul*) of a divine intervention, real and personalizing (intrinsic formal cause, intelligible form), surpassing the law.

It was either:

(1) a divine emanation; one of the celestial Intelligences, the Active Intellect (*'aql fa''al*), or the Universal Intellect (*'aql kulli*), or the Universal Soul (*nafs kulliya*), according to the Qarmathians and according to Ibn Masarra; or, on a higher plane, the Absolute *Hecceity* (*inniya mutlaqa = ihata*) according to Ibn Sab'in. If, as is usually the case, one identifies this emanation with Nur Muhammadi, we return to case c3, in which it is only indirectly, through this emanation, that God uttered *Ana'l-Haqq* through the mouth of Hallaj; or:

(2) God Himself, through the operation of His Spirit (*Ruh*), vivifying the heart of Hallaj and springing to his lips, through an internal taste, "the way the demon expresses himself through the mouth of the possessed" (*masru'*: criticism by Ibn Taymiya of the Hanbalite thesis of Harawi: *La'ih*).

In both cases, the judges who condemned Hallaj were guilty (Rumi). More profoundly, in the second case, the Law must persecute, must kill the saints. For the Law is made to use and to destroy a perishable world.

In both cases, the (transfigured) personality of Hallaj lives on, in a state of deifying union (*ittihad*), with God. In order that his *Ana'l-Haqq* be divine, this union must be real. Ibn Sina, Ibn 'Arabi, and even Fakhr Razi have challenged, as illogical, the reality of this union, determined to consider unity only within the range of nine categories (= *passiones unius*: equality, similitude, affinity, specificity, parallelism, symmetry, identity [*huwa huwa*], synergy, sympathy), and, more particularly, numerical unity, which in fact abhors union. Only 'AQ Hamadhani in mysticism, specifically apropos Hallaj, considered recourse to the notion of transcendental unity (whose plenitude makes him speak, paradoxically, of *Allah* = "*al-kathir*"); of which Ibn Sab'in (notion of *ba'd al-Wahid*), after Ibn Rushd, maintained the importance (against Ibn Sina) in metaphysics; and transcendental unity accepts union, total participation.

4. Popular devotion concretized in strange accounts the psychological genesis in Hallaj of the divine utterance *Ana'l-Haqq.*

Turkish Qastamuniyan legend includes this dialogue between God and Hallaj: "Ask me whatever you wish." Hallaj declines. God insists. Hallaj confesses: "I am disgusted with this world, and as for the other life, I will enter Paradise only in order to see You there." God insists again. Hallaj ends by saying, "O my Lord, give me Your personality in my language." God objects, saying, "This is my treasure; I have faithful servants who punish those who wish to steal it." Hallaj says, "O my just Lord, after You have given me Your personality, they may deal with my life according to Your will." After he says these words, God gives him permission to say *Ana'l-Haqq.* For, as the account concludes, the Beloved is the One who permits His lovers to play with His own personality, and the lover is the one who is flagellated, imprisoned, his hands and feet cut off (his blood serving him as legal ablution), is hung, burned, scattered to the winds: coming in this way to the Beloved, he finds union.

Indian legend shows Hallaj in ecstasy, before God, who says: "Who then will offer Us the sacrifice (*Yufdi lana'*) of his life?" "*Ana'l-Haqq,*" answers Hallaj; that is to say, "I will. I am firmly resolved (*thabit*) to sacrifice my life" (cf. Qur'an, 3:86). Kilani, already, had said that when Hallaj, full of love, came to God, God said to him, "Sacrifice Your life for Our sake by annihilation in order to rejoin Us"; Hallaj obeyed the order, and said *Ana'l-Haqq* in order to be admitted immediately, in accordance with the verse (Qur'an 3:167: among the martyrs killed *fi Sabil Allah*).

CHAPTER THREE

Travels and Apostolate

I. HIS MODES OF TRAVEL: HIS DRESS, HIS ITINERARIES, HIS STOPPING PLACES*

From 272 to 288, between his first hajj and his third and last hajj, Hallaj undertook a series of long apostolic journeys, going forth from a permanent base, which was his family home, during his first ten years in Tustar in Ahwaz (272–281), then in Baghdad (281–296), where he set up an actual *dar* (a reception and preaching center) in 288.

His behavior on these journeys was quite original. As regards dress, he rejected the *suf* and by preference wore the long-sleeved military caftan (*qaba"*), which awed the police and is more comfortable, or the patched *muraqqa'a* of the wandering beggars, which liberates the wearer by the very scorn that he arouses. He did not forgo, in case of need, visiting traditionists and Sufis, but he lived especially in mosques, which were open to the poor day and night, and in the *ribats*, those fortified convent-hostels that private alms gifts began to build on all the major routes leading to the frontiers and to the holy war, which the Muslims out of a religious instinct—a desire to collect hadith from afar, a need to preach to the lukewarm, and a vow of going out to fight the infidels—waged beyond their own boundaries. The Karramiya, who built many *ribats* at that time, often related a hadith from Salman on this subject: "To spend one night in a *ribat* in the service of God (*fi sabi'l-Allah*) at the frontier of the sea is worth more to a man than to fast a month while remaining among his own people; the one who dies in a *ribat* in the service of God, God preserves from the horrors of the grave."

That did not prevent [Hallaj] from visiting "society people," scribes, scholars, princes, and wealthy persons who were attracted to him through his reputation for cultural breadth and varied scientific knowledge. He approached the great with ease; "he was bold in the presence of sultans (*jasura ma'a'l-salatin*)," notes his contemporary, Ibn Abi Tahir. He discussed controversial issues with the noted in scholarship and politics, speaking to each school in its own language, whether Mu'tazilite, Shi'ite, or Sunnite. This will get him suspected of belonging to secret cadres of the Qarmathian conspiracy, where the Isma'ili Fatimid insurrection was being formed.

His "Qarmathianism" would explain his long travels, facilitated and expe-

*From *Passion of al-Hallaj,* Vol. 1, 135–38, 140–47, 150–89, 190–204, 216–23

dited by accomplices whom he would have found all along the way. The signs pointed to in favor of this hypothesis are definitely not convincing (even his vocabulary, *sini*). He could have been received as a visitor in certain Qarmathian *dar al-hijra*: for example, the one in Kufa (at Ukhaydir), the one in the Ahsa (at Hajar), the one in Multan (North Sindh). Also the question of the second coming of Justice, the spiritual mahdism that he never stopped preaching up to his final Baghdad mission, could easily be compared, by his malicious (Twelver) Imamite listeners, to the revolutionary mahdism of the Qarmathians. But, if he had been a "Qarmathian agent," as was inscribed on his pillory in 301, the precedent set with regard to the agent Abu Sa'id Sha'rani, for whom the Samanids paid the "blood price" to the Fatimid Caliph after 307, suggests that the latter should, in 309 or after, have made some gesture on behalf of Hallaj, which he did not do.

He must have conceived and organized his journeys in Ahwaz, thanks to the stable political connections that he established there, beginning with the relatives of his wife and his first disciples, families of eminent persons originally from Basra, either clients of the al-Muhallab Azdites, or allies of the Zaynabi Hashimites (Karnaba'i, AB Hashimi Rab'i), and extending up to high officials, Harithi scribes and Turkish amirs.

One can see immediately, from his itineraries, that he did not travel in the wake of officials profiting from the rapid couriers of the 'Abbasid *barid*; for they passed along the eastern border of the countries under strict Caliphal obedience, where he was often badly received (Qumm, Isfahan). To appreciate the pace of his journeys, we note that he went on foot, at reduced speed, a staff in hand, behind a caravan camel, sometimes on camel, accompanied at times by from seventy to four hundred disciples; even alone, he was not a "long distance runner" stringently keeping to a schedule of thirty kilometers a day (= one leg of the *barid*) in order to break any travel records; very often his apostolate kept him several days at a time at one of the stopping places along the way, not to mention villages like Talaqan, where he organized centers. "He moved along quickly" (*khafif al-harakat*), perhaps; but had he walked as fast as the Qarmathian agent Nasir-i Khusraw a century and a half later, or the ambassador Ibn Fudlan in 309–310, going to Bulghar, capital of the Khazars, he would have needed five years for his first journey, and therefore more than three years for the second (which forces us to reject the short chronology of Hamd.)

In the towns, Hallaj must have lived by preference in the section where Arabic was spoken (the *Shi'f al-Khuz* in Mecca, in Isfahan), since the incident in Isfahan proves to us that he did not speak dialectal Persian. Completely Arabicized, he could preach to his local listeners only through intermediaries, disciples native to the town or kindly sympathizers, or by relying on the musical effect produced by the gesture and the intonation of an earnest stranger over a crowd that does not understand his language (cf. St. Bernard in Germany, St. Francis Xavier in the East Indies). Unlike so many ascetics (Bistami, Ibn

Khafif, Khurqani), whose native accent shored up the local influence, Hallaj, during his itinerant apostolate, acted by indirect means: repeaters translating, commenting, and imitating as his discourses proceeded, secretaries taking down from his dictation the abundant correspondence described by Hamd, in response to questions posed (cf. Junayd previously). It is only at the end, on his return to Baghdad, that he will directly lecture the crowd, no longer inside a *ribat* or from a mosque, but in the open street, in the markets; and, in order to be spontaneous, these speeches offer, in contrast to those of truly popular sermonizers, some stylistic and technical refinements of expression that even an Arab urban public could hardly grasp without direct commentary.

It is, therefore, relevant to note that Hallaj stayed especially in Arab colonies: centers, like Bayda in Fars, Tustar in Ahwaz, Nishapur in Khurasan, towns exceptionally Arabicized; or seminomadic, as in Kirman and Sijistan, in Sindh (town of Mansura) and especially in Juzjan, in Talaqan, his center for preaching among the Samanids. Talaqan, in fact, a city strongly Arabicized, was adjacent to the important Arab colony of camel caravan drivers from north Juzjan (20,000 in his time) who in that period divided the monopoly of pasturage in Bactrian regions with the subject Turks for sheep and cattle grazing, the Khallukh (or Khalaj). These Arab cameleer tribes, cradle of the 'Abbasid revolution, must have had with these sheep-raising Turks the same relation of suzerainty that the *abbala* nobles in all of the Arab steppes had with the *shawiya* common people. The Khalaj Turks, having probably supplanted the Hephtalites, lived nomadically between Balkh and Bust, and went north each summer as far as Taraz and Isfijab. They had been converted to *hululism* by Muqanna'. Hallaj must have been brought by them into pagan Turkish country, particularly in the region above Isfijab. He must have followed the Arab camel caravan route on his first journey, reaching Khurasan directly through the desert and the Busht-al-'Arab (Turshiz) and certainly he returned with them from his second voyage, via Sijistan, Nimruz (= Zaranj) and Kirman, areas colonized by the Kharijite Arab nomads recently subject to the Saffarids.

II. THE TWO PERIODS OF PUBLIC PREACHING IN AHWAZ (272–273 AND 279–281)

His Acquaintances among Laymen, Scribes, Merchants, and High Officials

Ahwaz, and especially Tustar, played a decisive role in the career of Hallaj. Populated in the period by a refugee élite from Basra, and temporarily chosen by the regent Muwaffaq as his place of residence with the high Baghdadi officials of his court, during the military operations against Basra, Ahwaz much more than Mecca accounts for the social contacts that brought Hallaj to the fore after his break with the Sufis.

His wife was from Ahwaz, a member of a distinguished family probably of fiscal scribes originally from Basra. Though his father-in-law renounced him, his sons were allowed to live in Tustar, and his brother-in-law remained his faithful disciple: the one who, I believe, is the same person as the Karnaba'i with whom he will go into hiding in Ahwaz in 298.

The name of this Hallajian is interesting: *nisba* derived from Karnaba'i, a place said to be in Ahwaz, where Muhallab (under the Umayyads) had conquered the Azariqa Kharijites, thereby saving Basra; it referred to a family of Basra notables, the Karnaba'i, whom we see as early as 230 in a position to challenge on an equal basis a Zaynabi 'Abbasid line of governors of Basra, the Al-Sulayman-b-'Ali family. Around 260, Muhammad-b-Sa'id Karnaba'i agrees to become *katib* and temporary *wali* for Ahwaz under 'Ali-b-Aban Muhallabi, the Azd vizir of the Zaydite pretender-leader of the Zanj revolt. And, in 281 Karnaba'i the Hallajian must have been included among the Ahwazi notables whose arrival in Baghdad Hallaj arranged "at the same time as that of my mother and my *hama*," his son Hamd tells us. *Hama* is the maternal uncle; and we have good reason to believe that he and this Karnaba'i are identical: his full name would be Ibn Ya'qub Aqta' Karnaba'i Basri. In any case, the first setting of the Hallajian preaching in Ahwaz was the milieu of fiscal secretaries, clients of the Al-Muhallab, and therefore exposed to the jealousy of other Ahwazi *kuttab*, clients of Shi'ites (Karkhi, Baridi, Ibn 'Abi 'Allan).

Another Hallajian, of the very first rank, Abu 'Umara Hashimi Rabi'i Basri, chief of the Hallajians of Basra and of Ahwaz after 309, had married the daughter of Ibn Jankhush, an esteemed Ahwazi *shahid*. This takes us back to the rather lofty social circle of the *ahl al-buyutat* (in Pahlavi: *bar-baytar*), of old Persian stock who formed, as "professional witnesses" (*shahid*, plural *shuhud*), the local council of qadis named in Ahwaz by the central government; and who certainly belonged—they too—to the Iranian class of scribes (*dibheran*). As for Abu 'Umara himself, he was a member of the old Hashimite aristocracy of Basra, a Rab'i: that is to say, a descendant of Rabi'a-b-Harith-b-'Abd al-Muttalib, a friend of Caliph 'Uthman (d. 656 A.D., third of the classical *Rashidun* Caliphs) who had appanaged his son 'Abbas-b-Rabi'a in Basra (son-in-law of Hassan Taymuli and father-in-law of a Taymuli). It is undoubtedly through this Hashimite from Basra that Hallaj will later gain the support of the Zaynabi Hashimites at the court of Muqtadir.

It is also probable that in Ahwaz, in this period, Hallaj became acquainted with Hamd-b-M Qunna'i, experienced fiscal administrator and secretary of state, who defended him after 301, and who seems to have helped him get established in Baghdad; perhaps from 281 onward. Hamd Qunna'i was from the vizirial family of the Banu Makhlad, which claimed a Yemeni Harithi lineage, and it is possible, as we have seen, that the father of Hallaj had been a client of the Balharith. In any case, the fiscal administration (*kharaj*) of Ahwaz belonged until 272 to the cousin of Hamd Qunna'i 'Ala'-b-Sa'id, son of the vizir, Sa'id-b-Makhlad; which is another indication of the friendships that Hallaj supposedly gained at that time in the society of fiscal scribes.

Let us now look again at the phrase *abna' al-dunya*, "society people," which many years later Hallaj's son will use to describe the social milieu that his father entered after leaving Sufism (and to which, according to Qannad, he avoided introducing his Sufi friends). "Society people" does not mean in this instance only those who, in contrast to the Sufis, who have renounced the world, seek worldly honors, positions, and wealth; it also refers to 'Abbasid high society, especially to those renowned scholars at Court who were drawn particularly from among the fiscal secretaries, men like Karnaba'i and Hamd Qunna'i, assistants of qadis like Ibn Jankhush, and appanaged nobles, such as Abu 'Umara Hashimi; and who were at that time close to their colleagues in Baghdad and Samarra, having come to Ahwaz in the wake of the regent Muwaffaq.

If, for the history of great oriental states, the study of the scribal class is fundamental—for we know such history only through the scribes, through their collective tastes and prejudices (e.g., Kayasthas in the Moghul Empire of Delhi)—it is no less important for the history of 'Abbasid civilization. Through the capture of Ctesiphon, the great Iranian capital, the conquest of Mesopotamia led to the Islamization of the ruling classes of the Sassanid empire, and especially of the class of *dibheran*, or scribes, which had been, for four centuries, the third of the four great classes. Mesopotamia realized that it had to Arabicize itself thoroughly in order to preserve its privileges, notably the drafting and control of finances and the register of land surveys; and it succeeded in that, leaving a mark of its own on Arabic literature, in which it excelled, with a new poetic style and especially a complex and structurally refined prose, a learned rhetoric, the *adab rafi'a* introduced by Ibn al-Muqaffa', and developed as a monographic form by 'UA-b-'AA-b-Tahir and Ibn al-Mu'tazz.

Because of its Sassanid origins, attested to by many leading families of fiscal scribes (B. Nawbakht, B. Munajjim, B. Mudabbir, B. Muslima), the class of 'Abbasid scribes preserved a religious character that was not very orthodox; it was juxtaposed with a steadily diminishing Zoroastrian element, a Nestorian element, and a Rabbinical element, all of which were deeply rooted and tenacious, each well-versed in the official fiscal Aramaic (*huzvaresh*, in the Pahlavi diglot) of the Sassanids; it was often supposed to be tinged with *zandaqa*, affiliated in secret with dubious sects, and sympathetic to syncretist philosophies. But, like the Kayasthas at the Court of Delhi, it knew how to stay in power thanks to its careful study of the dialectical and compositional resources of Arabic. Ibn Hajib al-Nu'man, in a monograph on the scribes and their collections of "epistles" (*rasa'il*), and Abu Hayyan Tawhidi, in the epistolary examples that he gives us, help us gain access to the milieu in which Hallaj was instructed in the methods of style used in his letters and short treatises.

Entangled, through its functions in the Caliphate chancellery, in all the secrets of the dynasty, this class of scribes and vizirs was divided, since the failure of 'Alid legitimism under Ma'mun (reigned 813–833), into two trends, Sunnite and Shi'ite, whose growing vitality did not remove the bonds of professional solidarity or of personal friendship between secretaries of state of the two opposing parties. It is in this milieu that Hallaj made some contacts, even among Shi'ites, which developed into close relationships.

It is essential to state very precisely the dominant features of the governmental scribes' mentality in Ahwaz in this era, for this mentality alone throws light on the conditions under which the Hallajian thought was formed.

The administrative reorganization of the empire, after the Zanj class war, began in Ahwaz; and the regent Muwaffaq, although Sunnite, entrusted it, especially after 272, to Shi'ite experts, one of whom, a first-class merchant, Ahmad ibn al-Furat, was associated with Vizir Ibn Bulbul. This merchant increased and consolidated the proportion of Shi'ite tax collectors already installed (e.g., the Baridi) with his own clients (*sani'*: e.g., the Karkhi extremists like him, who will hold sway there for sixty years). The strength of this enterprise rested on a technical deception that an honest Sunnite like Ibn 'Isa disapproved of: the official inscribing in the annual provincial budget of Ahwaz of *mal al-jahbadha*, which is to say, of the profit provided the bankers of the empire for receiving the proceeds from taxes and in exchange for supplying ready cash at the Baghdad court for the army's payments. The banker of the empire, who for Ahwaz was a Jew, naturally had to show his gratitude for the Shi'ite fiscal policy that guaranteed him alone this profit (*marafiq*) by intervening at Court on behalf of Shi'ite tax collectors.

Just as the need for a strict setting of the hours of canonical prayer had led the canonists of Kufa to study the handling of the astrolabe by the Sabaeans of Harran, so the growth of the states' bookkeeping forced the fiscal experts to deepen their arithmetical knowledge by studying with Hellenizing philosophers: Ahmad ibn al-Furat had done this with non-Muslim scribes—Jews, Sabaeans, and especially Nestorian Christians.

The consequence of this, for this milieu of state secretaries, was the formation of an interconfessional cultural idiom for the whole of philosophical thought: logic, metaphysics at first; but also the practical disciplines: medicine, arithmetic and geometry, astronomy and alchemy, and administrative policy (*siyasa*).

In all these fields, the cultivated Shi'ite *kuttab* were ahead of their Sunnite colleagues, and this is why Hallaj, learning this cultural vocabulary in Ahwaz, will use so many words that have a Shi'ite coloration.

And that explains also the constant, and increasingly malevolent, interest that the Shi'ites will show in Hallaj, believing that he had educated himself in their school in order to betray them.

Upon settling in Baghdad, Hallaj rediscovered in cultured circles and at Court the same trends as in Ahwaz: infiltration by Shi'ite elements into the whole administrative infrastructure and, as a consequence, use of the Shi'ite *kuttab* vocabulary and of their borrowings from Hellenistic philosophy in various intellectual fields.

We believe it is by this Ahwazi scholarly milieu and its extension in Baghdad that the literary form and the original style of Hallajian writings can be explained; by this that they distinguish themselves from contemporary Sufi works, and ally themselves so curiously, even in their technique, with the rather heterodox works of Muslim scholars who were interested at that time in the Hellenistic sciences, philsophy, alchemy, and especially medicine.

In order to confirm these similarities revealed by internal criticism, we have only indirect but suggestive signs. For nearly a hundred years, at Court, vizirs and scholarly state secretaries were willingly becoming instructed in the Hellenistic sciences by Nestorian Christian scribes, and were urging the Caliphs, according to the rules of Hellenistic medicine, to attend, through Nestorian practitioners, to the hospital of Jundisabur (= Beth Lapat in Syriac): in Ahwaz, between Tustar and Sus, two of the towns where Hallaj stayed. Jundisabur, ancient center of the medical school of the Khuz, and the center of Hellenistic tradition in the East, could not have been ignored by Hallaj. Hallaj, unlike Sahl and Junayd, knew the vocabulary of Hellenic logic, and one hostile contemporary affirms that "Hallaj had learned medicine and experimented in alchemy."

The objection that this sentence is only a device for "explaining" the preternatural powers of Hallaj, breaks down before a number of specific proofs: for alchemy, his discussion with Ibn Abi Sa'dan, the testimonies of Ibn Zayyat and Ibn Babawayh, the collections of natural history reported in his possession (not only by adversaries, Tanukhi, Baqillani, but by the police, in 301); for medicine, his relations with the renowned doctor Razi, his recourse to some medical terms for the *arwah (ma'juna, Tafsir Qur'an; hadma, Tawasin)*.

We can assume that Hallaj knew some learned doctors in Ahwaz, because he visited the hospital of Jundisabur, the oldest of the official *bimaristan*, probably directed at that time by the Nestorian Ghalib (d. 286), principal doctor of the regent Muwaffaq prior to 272, afterwards of Mu'tadid; Ghalib's sons-in-law were Danyal-b-'Abbas, *katib* of Mu'nis Qushuri, and Sa'dun, *katib* of Yanis (Mu'nis and Yanis, amirs of Greek origin, like their close friend Nasr Qushuri, the loyal defender of Hallaj at Court). But Hallaj may have known them at the court of Muwaffaq, through the Banu Makhlad *kuttab*, natives of Dayr Qunna'. A whole series of doctors closely skirt the biography of Hallaj. Sinan-b-Thabit (d. 331), the Sabaean, *ra'is* of the doctors of Baghdad as early as 306 (after Sa'id Dimishqi, disciple of a friend of Ibn 'Isa, friend of Vizir Ibn

'Isa, doctor of Muqtadir in 309 when he had Hallaj come for consultation, must have given information to his son, the historian Thabit-b-Sinan, when he began to treat in depth the trial of Hallaj in his history. His successor at the court in 321 'Isa Mutatabbib (271, d. 360), so powerful in 304 and 311, was the friend of the brother of a Hallajian, the *katib* M-b-ʿAli Qunnaʾi (passionate over astronomy).

Through these Nestorian medical circles, Hallaj could have made contact with some *falasifa*, properly so-called, of the school of Kindi, Muslims such as Sarakhsi (*nadim* of Muʿtadid), Quwayri, and Ibn Kirnib, or Nestorians such as their pupil, the logician Matta Qunnaʾi (d. 328); but his acquaintances in logic could have been drawn only from among the doctors.

More complex is the problem of Hallaj's contacts with the equally Hellenistic Hermetic philosophy of the alchemists, in this same period, in Ahwaz. Nestorian doctors and Sunnite *falasifa* were in the group hostile to alchemy, which certain extremist Shiʿites propagated by vulgarizing in symbolic form the esoterism fashionable in Kufa (ʿAyniya, Mimiya, Siniya), combining Hermetic alchemy and astrology helter skelter with Islam. [These Shiʿites were] fallaciously called "Chaldeans" (*nabatiya*) in some much publicized pseudo encyclopaedias whose scientific influence was very widespread. We cite the *corpus Geberianum* as one example, an immense philosophico-politico-alchemical collection compiled before 330 in the name of Jabir-b-Hayyan Kufi by Hasan Nakad Mawsili. Next, the "Chaldean" works compiled after 312 in the name of Ibn Wahshiya by a *katib* of the vizirial family, A-b-Hy ibn Zayyat, under pursuit in 322 as a pupil of Shalmaghani, the extremist Shiʿite leader known in another connection for his alchemical works. We must recognize the fact that in this era of his life, Hallaj knew, among the fiscal administrative scribes, not only Sunnites like Hamd Qunnaʾi, but extremist Shiʿites, from the entourage of Ibn Bulbul, who would become his worst enemies, but who were interested first, as we know, in his apologetics.

All these verifications of Hallaj's many contacts in Ahwaz with fiscal scribes, judiciary assistants, Hashimite nobles, doctors, and alchemists, come together in a very simple explanation; namely, that he had aroused sympathies in the immediate entourage of a high personage of the ʿAbbasid Court who was transferred in that era to Ahwaz; such as, for example, the Turkish amir, Abu Hashim Masrur Balkhi, military *wali* of Ahwaz (265, d. 281), direct collaborator of the regent Muwaffaq as far back as 260 and 262 in the conduct of the war against the Zanj, and friend of the doctor Ghalib. The patronage of the *wali* Masrur (Hallaj will emigrate from Tustar to Baghdad in 281, the year of Masrur's death) would also explain the genesis of the confirmed friendship of Turkish military chiefs for Hallaj, and the choice of his journey in 273 to Khurasan and Turkestan, to Balkh especially, whose Al Banijur princes must have known Masrur.

The Original Features of the First Preaching: His Hadith
(= the Twenty-Seven Riwayat; His Miracles)

After his silent years of ascetic training and the break with his timorous and secretive masters in Baghdad, Hallaj wishes to raise his voice before all in a great burst of youthful valor. He goes from town to town, mosque to mosque, delivering inspired hadith in public, short imperative maxims on religious morality, which he claims to be formed by God in his heart when trained in recollection, and which he sets forth in the first person (c.f. Ibn al-Jawzi [*humaqa'*], *hasbi Allah* = *tawakkul*).

Some mystics, prior to him, had tried to formulate *hadith qudsi*; we have one such by Hasan Basri, four by Ibn Adham, after which he was silent; and Bistami himself had not dared to lose himself in God to this extent in public (influence of an 'Abbadan *wa'iz*, such as 'A W-b-Zayd, who was known in connection with the secret of hearts but without *isnad*.

Hallaj speaks boldly in the name of the unified God; by conforming his will to the commandments of the Law, he experiences only the fiat (*kun*) itself of God in his conscience, as the source of his perception, in each of his [mystic] states; and he is prompted to express it by a perpetual moving presence, that of the divine Spirit (*Ruh* = *shahid al-qidam*), the one which articulated for him (and for all men) the fiat of predestination on the pre-eternal day of the Covenant (*mithaq*). In this, he combines two theological theses: that of Ibn Kullab and Muhasibi (which Ash'ari will take up again against the Mu'tazilites) of the divine Word's uncreated simplicity (*kalam nafsi azali*); and that of Ibn Hanbal (taken over with pantheistic leanings by Abu Hamza, Nuri, and Sahl), on the possible actualization and substantial coming of the uncreated divine Word, uttered on the lips of true believers (a thesis that was also anti-Mu'tazilite).

In his inspired hadith, which Baqli has preserved for us (these are the twenty-seven *Riwayat*, which were actually delivered in Ahwaz and not in Khurasan), there are two parts, which reflect each of these two theses: the *isnad*, resting on such and such a natural phenomenon, a cloud or rainbow, considered as a sign from God (cf. the first Meccan suras of the Qur'an), witnessing His omnipresence; and the hadith strictly speaking, *matn*, in which the divine promise of a grace or a particular charism expresses itself. The following is an example of one (= *Riwaya* XVI): it was reported to us (= *haddathana*) by the greenness of grass and the colors of flowers, in the name of the life of (divine) Holiness: "Paradise (of the heart) draws near (us: in diving flight = *tazliq*) several times a day, as it does the holy land once a year."

These *isnad* are not a chronological chain of names of witnesses, but a hierarchical succession of visible symbols for everybody in nature ("the desert at dawn, the flash of lightning, the green grass growing," the feeling of nature: cf. Misri, Yf-b-Hy-Razi), or symbols recognizable only by believers ("the last Jujube tree, the great Angel, the well-guarded tablet"); which recalls the oaths of the first Qur'anic suras "by the dawn, by the night, by the star when it sets." It must have been because of that that 'Amr Makki attacked Hallaj. *Isnad* of this sort are extremely rare in hadith collections: two were transmitted by 'Ali-b-Hy Sayqali (d. 403), of which at least one dates back to the extremist Hanbalite M-b-'Ukkasha Kirmani (d. after 225).

The *matn* prescribes certain early Sunnite devotions, such as prayer at the end of the night (Hanbalite *hadith al-nuzul*), the promulgation of definitive Islam by Jesus returning as the *spiritual* mahdi (anti-Shi'ite hadith of Hasan Basri), the 360 daily glances by God for the friends of His saints, the value of repentence, of love, of detachment and recollection, the tenfold promise to those who have renounced the world, the figurative Covenant of the souls 7,000 years before the creation of their bodies (exegesis of the argument for the preexistence of souls, here sublimated: this is the lone *Ruh*; upheld by Ubayy, by the Hanbalites Ishaq-b-Rahawayh, M-b-Nasr Marwazi, taken up again by Ibn Hazm; denied by Ibn Qayim al-Jawziya). The Mu'tazilites and the Shi'ites condemned several of these *matn* (*hadith al-nuzul*, Jesus-Mahdi, tenfold promise), which present the early and popular aspect of the Hallajian apostolate; only two texts bear the polemical imprint: *Riw.* XXV, corrected by an addition to *Riw.* XIII (on the ineffability of the true *shahada*), and *Riw.* XVIII on the *Al Muhammad* (pro-Shi'ite in appearance). Later these *Riwayat*, probably conceived in Mecca, will be implemented by some critical and methodical treatises, composed in Fars around 378; resorting to the technical terminology of the non-Sunnite circles that he wishes to convert.

Of these first controversial tracts, surely coming prior to his second period of preaching in Ahwaz, we have only a fragment that is unimpeachable: a response to a Mu'tazilite, a disciple of Abu 'Ali Jubba'i concerning divine omnipotence and human acts.

His doctrine, a call to worship of the one God of Islam, insists on a gradual realization of His presence in the heart: obtained by adding good works, principally of penitential asceticism, to the regular canonical practices. He thus arouses his listeners to introspection, by "reading their hearts"; hence, the name *Hallaj* (= carder of consciences) that he received at that time in Ahwaz.

That does not mean only that he "cards language" (*yahlij al-kalam*, as A Yf Qazwini said) and utters words pregnant with meaning, or that he preaches like Muhasibi the examination of conscience in order to render the intentions behind our acts entirely pure (*ikhlas*); he does not teach only, like other Sufis, to make distinctions between mental incitements (*khawatir*); rather he realizes their distinctions by a charism, a divination of hidden intentions. For in Ahwaz he is not preaching to infidels, to make them believe, but to believers, to make them interiorize in themselves the divine presence that he has penetrated.

He proves this bold doctrine by a public and acknowledged recourse to miracles. Teaching that union with God should confer supernatural powers on saints, he claims such powers for himself. The reform mission that he takes upon himself in this way is precisely the one that the Shi'ites reserved at that time to their awaited mahdi, who disappeared in 260, at the very moment of the terrifying Zanj rebellion. Emotion among the Shi'ites of Ahwaz ran high; and it is from Shi'ite sources, hostile ones, that the principal accounts have come down to us of Hallaj's miracles in Ahwaz and Basra. According to Ibn al-Azraq (d. 377; taken from Ibn Abi 'Allan), Hallaj obtained for the people "food and drink (= fruit, according to Ibn al-Athir) that were not in season," and filched silver pieces (something mentioned already in Ibn Abi Tahir; then in 'Arib, taken from Nawbakhti). Ibn al-Athir adds that "Hallaj revealed to the people what they had eaten or had done within their houses, and read their consciences," which combined the two types of charisms, as in the case of Jesus. There is also a cosmic parallel between his call to divine signs in inanimate things ("grass growing green, rainbow brilliant in its living colors"), evoked in the *isnad* of his hadith, and the humble material needs alleviated briefly by his intercession, such as a day's provisions obtained through unexpected windfalls for the hard-working peasantry of Ahwaz, caught in the middle between the plundering of the rebel [Zanj] blacks and the fiscal exactions of the state.

That some provisions had been procured in an unusual manner, during this period of his apostolate in Ahwaz, is indicated by the alarm of two eminent authorities: the Mu'tazilite scholar Jubba'i, and the Shi'ite leader AS Nawbakhti, who collaborated in interpreting the affair as classical trickery of oriental charlatanism (from whence the polemical tract of Awariji comes, used in the trial of 309; cf. Baqillani, Ibn al-Azraq, edited by Tanukhi in his *Nishwar*).

One of the sad things facing the Sufi school milieu was the fact that some of its members from time to time resorted to relatively harmless "diverting physical" tricks in order to impress children or unsophisticated adults, and also that some believed it lawful to lie in order to edify (e.g., the fabricated *isnad* in hadith recommending certain devotions). These are the "less pure means" to which Renan tried artfully to connect the miraculous powers that Jesus attributed to himself in the Gospel accounts. Did Hallaj knowingly "fabricate" his miracles? The love of truth that he professed, naming God *al-Haqq*, and his explicit declarations on the folly of interpreting chance coincidences as miracles, dissuade us from resorting to this too easy explanation; more especially as we encounter other entirely similar strange facts that were directly verified, either in Mecca (Nahrajuri), or at the trial in 309 (the marrow of Sammari, the apple of Nasr's son, the parrot of Radi, the "swelling" before the jailer, the visits of Ibn 'Ata' and Ibn Khafif in prison).

We shall examine later the different theories conceived to explain the Hallajian miracles: tricks of charlatanism, according to Jubba'i, the whole Mu'tazilite school (which denies *a priori* the miracles of saints), and the Ash'arite Baqillani; pact with the jinn, according to Nahrajuri and other hostile Sufis (from whom Dhahabi will derive his theory of the satanic possession of

Hallaj); Suli had already pointed out that along with alchemy and medicine Hallaj had practiced exorcism (ʿazzama: accepted among Hanbalites); the exorcism of white magic (simiya) permitted, according to later mystic philosophers (Ibn ʿArabi, Jawbari, Ibn Sabʿin, Shahrazuri, Jildaki); and the magic power of a secret Name of God (Shibli, according to Qannad).

Hallaj's fame for bizarre and incriminating miracle-working, a fame widespread even among his partisans, dates from this apostolate in Ahwaz, and was certainly due to the bitter campaign waged against his "charlatanism" by his Shiʿite and Muʿtazilite enemies at Court to discredit him and to get his trial reopened in 308. At that time he was, after seven years in prison, beyond the state of "faking" anything, even about his fasts. We have to recognize also that the hold a saint has over the masses is not free from scandal or trouble. The explosion of an authentic miracle, cracking open the walled enclosure of the fossil universe in which hearts have been entombed, does not always induce the masses to taste and ripen in themselves the renewing medical efficacy of this unique grace that God enabled them to attend; and they can be haunted by the temptation to contrive for themselves a new mechanistic prison, by reduplication of the initial miraculous shock in a series of unreal charisms. To put faith in the charismatic power of Hallaj in Ahwaz was sound and efficacious only for those among his disciples who loved his mysticism and understood his passionate desire for an ignominious death, down to his execution. In the polyptych of his legend, his charismatic preaching to the Muslims of Ahwaz appears, before his mission into infidel lands—Indian and Turkish—and before his prayers of ecstatic offering in the suqs of Baghdad, as a "hollow" antithesis to his final "passion."

The Anecdotes

THE CRITICISM, BY THE MUʿTAZILITE ABU ʿALI JUBBA'I, OF THE MIRACLES OF HALLAJ

Account by AHy-b-A-b-Yf ibn al-Azraq Tanukhi (d. 378): "Several of our friends (= Muʿtazilites) have reported to me that, when the people of Ahwaz and its (seven) districts (kur) were seduced by Hallaj, because he got them food and drink that were out of season, as well as pieces of silver money that he called "drachmas of the divine omnipotence," Abu ʿAli Jubba'i was informed of it and declared: 'these are provisions gotten in advance and hidden in fake storehouses. But tell him to enter one of your, not his, houses with you, and ask him to produce for you right there just two palm strips. If he does it, then believe in him.' His words were reported to Hallaj, with the news that some people had decided to follow his advice, and Hallaj left Ahwaz."

Abu ʿAli Jubba'i (235, d. 303), a Hanafite in law, pupil of ʿAllaf (d. 235) via

AY Shahham (deputized by Grand Qadi Ibn Abi Dawud to supervise in the *kharaj*, the *katib* Fadl-b-Marwan, dismissed in 249), succeeded them as head of the Mu'tazilite school of Basra; he died at 'Askar Mukram in Ahwaz and was buried in Jubba, on his family property to which he came each year to draw the farming revenue from for his students. It was therefore easy for Ahwazians to come to consult him about Hallaj, who appears to have had in addition a direct theological argument with a disciple of Jubba'i.

The Mu'tazilite school does not accept the possibility of miracles for the saints. The opinion of Jubba'i was thus predictable; but the appearance on the stage, against Hallaj, of the most illustrious theologian of the age sufficiently indicates the rising notoriety of Hallaj. This was in 279.

ACCOUNT BY IBN ISHAQ TAKEN FROM TANUKHI

a) Most of the conjuring tricks of Husayn ibn Mansur Hallaj resembled miracles and helped him seduce the people. In this way he gave them water to drink, without using any container: by means of a trick; and those who did not see through it, were moved by it. But intelligent people did not let themselves be taken in by it. Such is the story that Abu Bakr Muhammad ibn Ishaq Ibn Ibrahim, *shahid* in Ahwaz, told me; he heard it from an astrologer: a man whom he named for me, and whose shrewdness and penetration he described to me. Here is his account:

> I had heard from Hallaj, about the wonders that he performed in public and which he claimed to be true miracles, disregarding natural laws; so I said to myself: "Let's go see what sort of miracles these are." And I came to him, pretending to be a novice seeking religious guidance, and we entered into conversation. And he said to me: "Tell me this moment what you desire, and I will produce it for you!" Now, we were in one of those towns of Jabal where there are no flowing streams. "I want a very fresh fish, and immediately!" He said, "I will go get it; you stay here." I sat down, and he got up and said: "I will go into the house, where I am going to ask God to bring you one." He entered the house, as if to avoid me, closed the door with a key, and made me bide my time. Then he returned to me, drenched up to his knees with mud and water, with a large fish which was wriggling. And I said to him: "What is this?" He said, "I prayed to God, may He be exalted! and He ordered me to go up to the *Bata'ih* (marshlands near Wasit) in order to bring you back this fish, and I have been there. I plunged into the *huz* (flooded ponds), and this is some of their mud, which got on me when I took it out." I realized that he was deceiving me, and I told him: "If you permit, let me go into the house, and if I discover no trick inside, I will believe in you." "Just as you like," he said. I entered and locked myself in. I found no exit, no trick; then I was filled with regrets; "if I find a trick, and I reveal it to him, he will kill me right here, in this room. And if I do not find any, he will claim my allegiance. What to do?"

While reflecting on it I lifted the wall-covering of the room, which was made of slats in *saj* (teak). They revealed a chink. I drew the slat to me which only half covered (*jisriya*) the partition, and I saw that it had been moved previously. I passed through, for the panel was only a door tacked in place! I slipped through it into a large interior court, where there was a superb orchard, containing all sorts of trees, fruits, plants, and scented flowers; also, as many of those which were in season, as those which were not; those which had already flowered, and which ordinarily would have withered, but which he succeeded in making last. There were also some beautiful chests, including a larder containing all sorts of foods, all prepared with the necessary accessories to be brought out immediately if someone asked for it. And in the center, there was a large fish pond, which I stepped into: I saw that it was full of fish, both large and small. And I caught a big one, and stepped out, my legs covered with mud and water, just as high as his had been. And I thought: "Now, if I leave, and if he sees me with this fish, he will kill me. . . . I am going to play a trick on him with it, as I leave." When I came back into the room I began by saying to him: "I believe, I swear!" "What?" he asked. "That there is no trickery here, that everything only confirms your sincerity." "Now then, leave!" And I left, for he moved aside from the entrance way, deceived by the tone that I had taken. But once I had left, when I was running in the direction of the outside door, he caught sight of the fish that I had taken, and came toward me, realizing that I knew about his imposture. He began to run after me and caught up with me; but I hit him with the fish in the chest and on the face, telling him: "Hey, did you follow me when I went into the ocean to fish this one for you!" And while he was rubbing his chest and eyes, where the fish had struck him, I got away.

Barely outside the house, I threw myself flat on the ground, I was so shaken and seized with terror. But he came out in my direction, and in a genial tone, he invited me back in. "Never, by God!" I exclaimed, "For if I came back in, you would never let me leave again." "Listen, by God!" he said, "If I wanted to kill you in your bed, I could do it! Therefore, if word of this incident gets back to me, rest assured that I will kill you, even if you are in the bowels of the earth. So long as you do not tell it to anyone, you will be safe! And, now, go away and do whatever you wish!"

He left me, and went back into the house. I believed that he could carry out his threat, by sending one of his secret agents to get me; and that such a person, being a zealous follower, would not hesitate to kill me. That is the reason I did not tell my story before his execution.

b) Ibn al-Azraq told me:

Many sound witnesses among our friends told me that Husayn-b-Mansur Hallaj had sent one of his friends into the towns of Jabal province, and had agreed with him to have him feign a role. The man left, and went to live for two years in this particular town, practicing asceticism, performing prayers, reciting the Qur'an, and fasting. Gradually he won the confidence of all. One day, he announced that he had lost his sight: someone had to lead him by the hand to go into the mosque, and for several months everyone believed he was blind. Then he announced that he had become crippled, and he crawled or had himself carried to the mosque. One year passed during which time everyone was convinced that he was indeed blind and crippled. When this period of time had passed, he made this declaration to them: "I have had a dream. The Prophet—upon him be prayer and peace!—told me that he was going to send to this town one of his faithful followers, a pious man, whose prayers are granted: 'Your cure was in his hands, reserved to his prayers.' Therefore find for me all those who will come, among the *fuqara'* and Sufis, perhaps God will comfort me by the hand and the prayers of His faithful; according to the words the Prophet of God told me, upon him be prayer and peace!" And all minds were preoccupied looking for this devout personage (*'Abd Salih*), and all hearts awaited him.

At the moment when the date was going to fall due which he had agreed upon with Hallaj, the latter entered the town, dressed in fine wool, and secluded himself in the mosque, invoking and praying to God. People took an interest in him; they spoke about him to the blind man, who said: "lead me to him." When he was led to him, and he had indeed recognized that this was Hallaj, he said to him: "O servant of God! I have seen in a dream this and that: pray to God for me!" "Me, who am I? I am unworthy!" But he insisted. Hallaj decided reluctantly to pray for him; placed his hands on him: and behold, the false cripple got up and his sight was restored in full. The town was overcome; many people gathered in a mob around Hallaj, who sent them away, and left the town. As to the false miraculously healed person, the false cripple, he stayed there a few more months, after which he said to the inhabitants: "In order to fulfill my obligation to God for the grace that He gave me, in giving me back the use of my limbs, it is fitting that I seclude myself more to pray, in spiritual retreat. My plan is to go to the frontier, to Tarsus: if someone has something to buy there, I will bring it back to him; if not, I entrust you to God's hands." And someone took out a thousand dirhams to give him, saying: "Wage the Holy War with that, in my place." Another took out a hundred dinars, saying: "Take that as a booty captured in the holy war out there." Others gave him some of their goods, so much so that he amassed thousands of dinars and dirhams. He then rejoined Hallaj, and divided the loot with him.

ORGANIZATION OF A POSTAL SYSTEM BETWEEN TUSTAR AND BAGHDAD

'Umar Mansuri, surnamed Abu Hafs Kabir, told me in Basra that 'Ubayd-b-Ahmad Saluli had told him:

When my father was living in Baghdad, and Husayn-b-Mansur Hallaj in Tustar, each day my father received news of Hy-b-Mansur, whose notoriety, already, was great. And I said to my father: "who informs you of this news?"—"A man, who maintains contact between Hy-b-Mansur and me, telling me what he does, and telling him what I do!"—"Does he put himself at his [Hallaj's] mercy?"—"Yes; but Hallaj does not content himself with that, he insists that he also gets his sons in his service; this man has refused up to the present, but if he agrees, it will be his loss."

This hostile text is obviously slanted; it refers to the period of Hallaj's last sojourn in Ahwaz; at the time when the coalition of his adversaries forced him to move, with the group of notables who supported his preaching, to Baghdad: around the year 289. This move could have been carried out only with the support at least of certain public officials. The organization of a postal service indicated here has to tally with the arrangements of this move without pointing to any kind of Qarmathian conspiracy in it.

THE INCIDENTS AT BASRA

On Basra, the account of Hamd notes simply that Hallaj spent time there on three occasions, and that he formed a group of dedicated disciples there. Other sources lead one to believe that Hallaj made prolonged stays there; in his early stages (according to Khurrazadh Baydawi and Jurayri; he was supposed to have accompanied his teacher Sahl, exiled there before 267); and during his apostolate of 272–273 in Ahwaz and 279–281, according to Baqillani, Abu 'Imran-b-Musa and Ibn al-Jundi; Baqillani assigns to him even a fixed residence in Basra, which must be identical to the dual-purposed building, convent and school, where his disciple Abu 'Umara Hashimi will give conferences on mysticism a little later (before 326).

The "Swelling Room" (Bayt al-ʿAzama).

Baqillani, wanting to distinguish (against Razi, who had identified) the miracles of the prophets (as essential transmutations) from the conjurings of charlatans (the production of illusory accidents), attributes to Hallaj a series of faked phenomena of this second category: such as "inflating his body in a room, nicknamed the 'swelling room.'"

> According to reports, Hallaj had a large room in Basra, with some devices composed of pipes hidden in the corners and wall partitions, and underneath, some vents through which wind came into the hall. Hallaj would take his place on an elevated chair, dressed in a silk or other light material shirt, which, when the visitors were entering, gave him a slender appearance. Then he would order the vents opened for the wind to pass through the pipes, slowly entering his robes until his shirt puffed out to the point of filling, it is said, the entire room with its swelling.

He used this room (bayt al-ʿazama) for two other tricks: to show a living lamb coming out of a burning oven and a fish coming out of a room, their sizes appearing to expand to the eyes of those present in the hall. Baqillani recalls that the lamb trick consisted of placing a duct into the oven and hiding the living lamb inside the duct, through which someone pushed it, making it thereby appear to come from the burning oven. These people, he adds, have in some rooms of their houses subterranean tanks and fishponds stocked with fish, whose doors are bolted and [concealed by] wall partitions . . . [resembling] the framework of the room; thus, they can order an assistant in charge of the fish's appearance to enter by this means to bring it forth, so effectively that the spectators believe the fish has been created at that very moment. The way to expose their fraud is to ask them to make this fish come from another house, or from under a step on a stairway, or from some wells full of water where fish may live: it will not take them long to steal away, admitting the falseness of their pretended power. Just as when they claimed to be able to draw a strong scent of musk or of other aromas, or a scented taste of rose water, from a river or a well; their trick consisted in using a freshly coated jug, soaked with rose water, and when they were asked for water, to draw it from the river with this jug.

According to Baqillani, Hallaj was supposed to have mounted this charlatan's play in Basra. But the parallel texts given above, which were earlier, place it in Ahwaz; the later assertion of Baqillani does not, therefore, establish definitively that Hallaj had founded in Basra a permanent center of propaganda.

The Account of Abu Musa 'Imran-b-Musa

Abu Musa 'Imran-b-Musa relates that a Basrian, who up to then had been hostile to Hallaj, decided to go and beseech him to pray for the cure of his brother who was in great suffering; Hallaj answered him, smiling: "I will pray for him, but on condition that you continue to speak evil of me, even more, that you accuse me of impiety, and that you agitate to get me executed." Stupefied, I remained silent. "Pay no attention," he resumed, "to what does not concern you, but only to the acceptance of the condition." So be it. He poured out a little water in a bowl, *spat* on it, and said. . . . And, after the cure of his brother, Hallaj confided in him: "If God had not said, 'Verily, I shall fill Hell with the angels and men together' (Qur'an 11:119; 32:13), I would spit on Hell in order that a sweet perfume might pass over its inhabitants. . . ."

The Accounts of Ibn al-Jundi.

He first presents a celebrated couplet frequently attributed to Junayd, *qad tahaqqatuka*, as having been dictated by Husayn-b-Mansur Hallaj in Basra to a witness whose name and *isnad* are left out:

> I have found You within me,—and yet my tongue calls out to You.
> United in one way,—we are thus separated in another.
> For, while Your majesty conceals You—from my sight,
> Ecstasy has brought You—deep within my heart.

And elsewhere, similarly leaving out the name of the witness and the *isnad*, he says: "I have seen Hallaj, and participated in some of his conjurings, such as that of making an enclosed garden appear before him, with cereal plants and water."

Ibn al-Jundi (= AHy A-b-M-b-A-b-'Imran Baghdadi Khaffaf), d. 396, semi-Shi'ite, master of the qadis Bay (d. [?] 42) and A 'AA Baydawi (d. 362) and of Qushayri, *rawi* of Ibn Dawud and of Shibli, was the pupil of the Sufi Khuldi (d. 348); like him, he transmitted some favorable accounts of Hallaj, together with some hostile accounts, from an anonymous Basrian source.

III. THE OTHER REGIONS TRAVELED THROUGH

The Towns of Jibal

DINAWAR AND NIHAWAND; HAMADHAN; RAYY

Two anecdotes verify that Hallaj stayed in Dinawar and in Nihawand. Dinawar, Arabicized by colonists from Kufa (as Nihawand was by colonists from Basra), was at that time a prosperous center, with an elite of Sufyanite and Karramiya traditionists, among whom Hallaj had some disciples. It was also a strategic point, controlling (cf. now Kirmanshah) the imperial route from Baghdad to Khurasan; entrusted to distinguished *walis*, such as the amirs Buktamur (265) and Rashid (279, d. 280; former *amir al-jund* of Muwaffaq), then to the heir to the throne, Muktafi (281–289); and, after a Sajid usurpation (around 296), to the amirs M-b-Ishaq-b-Kundaj (301, d. 304) and his son Tar-khan (304–308), to the Hamdanid Abu'l-Hayja 'AA (308, d. 317; replaced in 316 by Nihrir), famous military commander, who probably was responsible for the arrest, in the Karrami *ribat* at Dinawar, of a Hallajian, the same one who hastened the denouement of the trial in 309. Ten years later, the Daylami rebel Mardawij ravaged Dinawar (319), which at that time was under the command of Amir Hamza Isfahani, and the survivors came to Baghdad to lament their fate.

The qadis of Dinawar (at the time AB Ja'far-b-M-Firiyabi, d. 301, Malikite, and Abu Nasr A-b-Hy-b-M, do not seem to have bothered Hallaj, whose so-journ there must be placed at the very end of his second long journey, that is to say, around 285. The memory of Hallaj still persists today among the Kurds of the region, and as much among the extremist Shi'ites (Qizilbash) as among the anti-Shi'ites (Yazidis); we are speaking therefore of a very old survival, even without being able to prove that it dates back to his direct apostolate.

As for Hamadhan, no source says that Hallaj stayed there, and the Hallajism of four Hamadhanis as well known as the mystics Ibn Jahdam, Yusuf, and 'Ayn al-Qudat, and the historian M-b-'Abd al-Malik, does not prove that it comes from a local tradition.

As for Rayy, the same silence from the sources. This town (which Tehran will succeed in importance) was already very important; it was coveted simultaneously by the Daylamite rebels in the north, the Sajids (303–305) in the northwest, the Samanids (289–303) in the east, and the Dulafids in the south. Defended vigorously by imperial governors of Turkish origin: Adhkutakin (266 to 276 with Madhara'yi (Ab H) of quasi-Shi'ite fiscal leanings; occupied then by a lieutenant of the rebel *wali* Rafi' of Nishapur, H-b-'Ali Kura, who rallied 276–281), Kayaghlagh (262–264), Talmajur (264, d. 266), and his brother Abrun (in 288: with Ukurtmysh and Khaqan), it was the residence of the heir to the throne Muktafi from 281 to 288. At that time its fiscal *wali* were men connected with the patrons of Hallaj: Ahmad-b-H Madhara'yi (266–276) and M-b-Asbagh (281–285: friend of H-b-Makhlad and son-in-law of Vizir 'UA-b-Sul-b-Wahb). Then came the Samanid occupation (289; Mansur). From the Islamic cultural point of view, Rayy, more conservative than Nishapur, had been the homeland of Kisa'i, of the Hanafite M-b-H Shaybani; the center of the Murji'ite theological school of the Najjariya; and became Shi'ite.

The Qarmathian revolutionaries had tried to get a foothold there; establishing nearby, in 261, at Talaqan (in Daylam) the *sahib al-naqa* which had as successive agents in Rayy: Khalaf Hallaj al-Qutn, his son, then Abu Ja'far Mahrum, Abu Sa'id [Ghiyath] Sha'rani (around 307) and the celebrated Abu Hatim Razi, before whom Mardawij (316, d. 323) arranged a debate in Rayy with the renowned physician Razi. The possibility of Hallaj's connection with "Qarmathians" remains an enigma.

HALLAJ'S FIRST ARREST: *"FI MAHIYAT AL-JABAL"*

"And it was said (*qad qila*; variant: *wa ruwiya 'anhu*) that, at the very beginning of his career, he preached to get the political rights of the family of the Prophet (on him be Peace) recognized; for which he was flagellated, in *nahiyat al-jabal.*"

This sentence, borrowed just as it is by our two earliest secular historical sources, Suli and Ibn Abi Tahir, from an unnamed historian, introduces two interesting editorial peculiarities.

First, concerning the geographical placing of this incident. In this period *nahiyat al-jabal* refers generally, and especially in Tabari, to the whole of the large mountainous province of al-Jibal (Hamadhan, Karaj, Isfahan, Rayy), at the time defended by Caliphal amirs against the Zaydite rebels of Daylam. It is there that Hallaj, taken for a Zaydite, was said to have been flagellated. Biruni believed this: "He preached mahdism at first, pretending that the mahdi would appear at Talaqan in Daylam, and he was arrested." But Isfara'ini, much better informed than Biruni about Hallaj, states precisely that it is at Talaqan in Khurasan that he gained disciples (the famous prophesy on "the mahdi who will appear at Talaqan," was at first, as we shall see, applied to a Talaqan Khurasanian); and, geographically, al-Jibal has nothing to do with Khurasan. It is necessary, therefore, to look elsewhere. Tabari, for the year 252, designates,

under the name "*nahiyat al-jabal*," the area of Diri, the domain of Shuja',
mother of Mutawakkil, in the province of Wasit; it is the third stop on the route
from Wasit to Sus (Ahwaz), fifteen parasangs from Wasit, and twenty-one
from Sus. Hallaj must have passed through it many times, and the incident
would have to date back to his stay in Ahwaz, before his first long journey:
before 274; and with the future vizir, Hamid, already a fiscal official at Wasit,
perhaps we must trace the beginning of his enmity toward Hallaj to this incident.

Next, concerning the motive: "*Kana yad'u ila'l-rida min Al Muhammad*":
this expression puts Hallaj among those who, without naming any 'Alid pretender (contrary to the orthodox Imamites), nevertheless made use of legitimist
propaganda. It is used in Baladhuri for the sending of the Rawandite *da'i* M-b-
Khunays into Khurasan by Abu Riyah Maysara of Kufa, in the name of the
'Abbasid pretender (*wasi*) M-b-'Ali (d. 124): "*fa amarahu an yad'u ila-rida
min Al Muhammad, wala yusammi ahadan*." And it reappears in the year 281,
which directly concerns us, in the great *qasida* of Ibn al-Mu'tazz (verse 211)
to characterize the rallying of Rafi'-b-Harthama, Caliphal official at the Zaydite rebellion of Daylam: "*yad'u ila zahr'l-Nabi wa'l-rida minhum*." This double coincidence allows us to believe that Hallaj's first arrest took place in 281,
probably at Qumm (this would be an allusion to his dispute with Ibn Babuya,
recounted by the Imamites). He was said to have been denounced by Imamites
(hostile to any project for a legitimist rebellion prior to a supernatural call from
the mahdi) as an agitator, an accomplice of Zaydite rebels, to the Dulafid authorities. There were two grounds for justifying this charge: the Karramiya
mystic traditionists declared themselves Zaydites, insofar as they were disciples of Sufyan Thawri; and Hallaj had close ties with the Karnaba'i family, of
Ahwaz, which was involved in the Zaydite revolt of the Zanj.

NEW YEAR'S DAY IN NIHAWAND

We were with Hallaj in Nihawand; it was the day of the *Nayruz* (= New Year);
and we heard trumpets blowing. Hallaj said: "What is happening?" I told him: "It
is because today is *Nayruz*." Then, he sighed and said: "Ah! when will *Nayruz*
come for us?" And I said: "When do you think it will come for you?" He said,
"The day when I will be exposed to view on the gibbet, when I will be in this way
very close (*iqtarib*: Qur'an 96:19) to God."

But, the day when he was exposed on the gibbet, thirteen years later, he looked
at me, from high on the pillory, and cried out: "Ahmad, our *Nayruz* that we celebrate is here." And I said: "O master, have you now received your feast-day
gifts?"—"Ah yes," he said; "I have received them, I am overwhelmed with cer-
tainty by the vision, so much so that I am ashamed: I must not yet surrender to my
joy."

THE TOWNS OF THE DULAFIDS: ISFAHAN, QUMM

To the northeast of Persian Kurdistan, between 230 and 284 of the Hijra, an autonomous principality held its own under a Dulafid dynasty of the 'Ijl Arab tribe, at Karaj. With shifting loyalty, it struggled in the south against the Saffarids ('Umar Dulafi replaces 'Amr Saffari in the Baghdad *shurta*, 276–278), in the north against Rafi', not without sometimes showing pro-Shi'ite tendencies (his *katib* Dindan; his *qaharamana* Thumal); it controlled Isfahan and Qumm.

Isfahan was already a very large city, in the heart of Iran (country of the blacksmith Kaveh), near the fire temple of Juzjan; a rich agricultural region, an industrial (weaving) center, the only one whose life had never been interrupted, it was on the verge of developing into a city of artisans like those known in Flanders (with distinction between hanses and trade-guilds: fights between them, between working-class north and bourgeois south, Shafi'ites against Hanafites under the Saljuqs, Hayaris against Ni'matis under the Safawis); this active market center was directed by money changers (Jews: *Yahudiya*). Isfahan had from that time on, in spite of the literalist orthodoxy of its *muhaddithun* and its Hanbalite qadis, a questionable legendary reputation: "city of the Dajjal" (= anti-Christ: because of its route toward the always-smoking summit = Dimawand); and it participated in an anti-Arab nationalist renaissance (locality of the legend of Salman at Jayy and Quhab and of that of Abu Muslim.

Qumm, at a center of important routes, between Isfahan and Rayy, was already passionately Shi'ite; it was a desert region city, modeled on the image of Kufa by refugees from that city, the Yemenite dynasty of Al Sa'd b-Malik, of the tribe of Ash'ar. From 125 to 278, this line of petty rulers gave asylum to a growing number of Shi'ite jurisconsults; and in spite of several heretics: 'Ali-b-Hasaka, M-b-'Urama, Sahl-b-Ziyad, H-b-'Ali Sazjada, the official Imamite orthodoxy was formed there over a period of ten centuries. The Daylamites came there in 317.

THE ALTERCATION IN ISFAHAN

Account of Ibn Khafif:

> When Husayn-b-Mansur Hallaj came to Isfahan, he went to the home of 'Ali-b-Sahl, who was in his sitting room, speaking of wisdom (*ma'rifa*). Hallaj came and sat down in front of him and upbraided him: "You, who are a retail merchant, how dare you speak of wisdom, while I am still alive and while between the sobering period and the rapture there are seven hundred degrees whose aroma you have never suspected and whose meaning you have never grasped." 'Ali-b-Sahl then said: "A city like Isfahan, where there are Muslims, should not tolerate the pres-

ence of people like you," and stood up to go. This sentence was spoken in Persian, and Hallaj did not understand it, for he did not know Persian; but the public gathered in a mob, crying out "Where is his house?" with the idea of demolishing it and hunting him down. Then, a man found Hallaj and told him: "Get away, before they kill you, or at least hide in such and such a place, so they won't find you." Hallaj answered: "to seek refuge from God outside God, is to doubt God"; then he changed his route (to go out of Isfahan), and he left for Shiraz, taking the (opposite) Garmaqasan route.

The Towns of Khurasan

Khurasan had four capitals at that time, each quite different in character: Balkh, Marw (the real capital), Herat, and Nishapur; Hallaj stayed in Khurasan, and his doctrine has had a lasting influence there.

HERAT, MARW, AND BALKH

Herat, the least populous, governed by the family of the Banu Dhuhl-b-Shayban (Arab tribe of Bakr), was the most Arabicized, on the route from Kirman to the Oxus; vassal of the Saffarids.

The Hanafites of Herat were Karramiya, therefore mystics; just as the local Hanbalite *ahl al-hadith*, who upbraided Ibn Karram for his theological vocabulary, were mystics, and will be pro-Hallajian. Bushanj was the homeland of Mansur-b-ʿAmmar, and Nuri was born in Baghdad. Herat had a Karramiya *khanqah madrasa*.

Marw, where Hallaj "came, it was said, in secret," Harawi tells us, without explanation, was rather decadent; it was retaken by the Tahirids (266–278), and annexed finally by the Samanids (Tamim and Azd-Khuzaʿa tribes). The Hallajian AB Wasiti, fleeing Iraq, settled in Marw, where Sayyari became his disciple.

Balkh, which still had remains of the old Greco-Buddhist civilization when the Muslims came there, must have had through the influence of its offspring, the Barmakids (who ran the vizirate in Baghdad, 136–138, 170–187), a sudden prosperity that brought into relief its original character as the crossroads of India and the Turks. Governed by local Iranian dynasties that were clients of the Banu Farighun (in Guzgan, then in Balkh, 340–401), its Arab (Bakr tribes, in the majority over the others *akhmas*) or Arabicized élite was highly cultured; this region of the exegete Muqatil-b-Sulayman, of numerous Muʿtazilites, of such eminent mystics as Ibrahim-b-Adham, Shaqiq Balki, and Tirmidhi, Balkh, when Hallaj stayed there, was a teaching center for the Muʿtazilite school (AQ Balkhi) and for two mystic schools (Tirmidhi-AB Warraq and the Karramiya). The Shafiʿites would found a *dar al-ʿilm* there, but the qadis of Balkh remained Muʿtazilite Hanafites up to 378.

It was among these people of Balkh that Hallaj had organized his Talaqan center and his apostolate in Turkish lands (Qaratakin, prince of Isfijab, Samanid delegate to the Banijurid princes); his disciple Iskaf found asylum at Balkh, in the home of an ʿAqili *sharif* (there were also ʿAlids there [ʿUmariyin, Minkhuraniyin], with a *naqib*).

NISHAPUR

Restored by the Tahirids, Nishapur replaced Marw, after the period of Maʾmun, as the intellectual and economic center of Khurasan, before becoming, under the Samanids and the Ghaznavids, the capital of the Mashriq and even the center of Sunnite Islam (between 330 and 420), during the eclipse of Baghdad: Eranshahr.

Hallaj, who will settle his eldest son Sulayman there, must have stayed there at least three times, around 275 and around 284 (coming from Tus), and in 285 (when returning).

In 260, as in 280, the majority was Sunnite, Hanafite, divided between Muʿtazilites and Karramiya mystics. In this milieu of the Arab *ahl al-hadith*, of the Hira quarter, the seed of Hallajism took root, preparing the poetic flowering of the Hallajian legend.

TALAQAN

Talaqan, in Khurasan (which must not be confused with two other cities of the same name, the one in Daylam near Qazwin [Jabal], the other to the east of Balkh in Tukharistan), in 309 was the Hallajians' center in the Samanid state; it is reasonable to conclude, therefore, that Hallaj, on his two trips, in 274 and 283, had made it the center of his apostolate.

In Talaqan, Hallaj came under the jurisdiction of the Samanid state, and he entered an intellectual milieu in which the élite of Balkh, even more than that of Nishapur, set the tone. It was a Sunnite élite, but one that was obviously passionate over critical discussion of theological ideas, since it was four Balkhis in that period who wrote the first books of heresiography. At the Samanid court, which supported the renowned doctor Razi, the patrons of this élite were the two viziers, Jayhani (d. 307), who was suspected of "dualism," and Balʿami, a Shafiʿite; the amir of Marrudh, Hy-b-ʿAli, who will become an Ismaʿili in 307, and his brother Akh Suʿluk (d. 311): these last two granted a pension to AZ. Balkhi and apparently knew Hallaj.

Talaqan, which will revolt in 309, at the news of the execution of Hallaj, and will declare him the mahdi, was alluded to as early as the second century of the Hijra, in a sort of apocalyptic prophesy, in a hadith: "God (variant: the family of Muḥammad) has in Talaqan a hidden treasure that He will reveal when He so wills; his preachings will be truth; he will manifest himself with His permission, and will preach the religion of God."

The Towns of Transoxiana (Mawaralnahr): Bukhara, Samarqand, Ush, Isfijab

During the century that followed Hallaj's death, the Hallajian doctrine gained the greatest foothold in Transoxiana, that is to say, in the heartland of the Samanid state, among both the Hanafites and the Shafi'ites. And, as we know that the Hallajian apostolate of the Hanafite Faris, around 340, in Samarqand (and in Bukhara, where the Hanafite Kalabadhi chased him) was considered by some as distorting the thought of the master, there is good reason for thinking that Hallaj, both in 276 and in 284, stayed quite a long time in the region in order to form direct disciples, especially among the Shafi'ites (friends of Ibn Surayj), and perhaps among the Sufyanite Karramiya.

The sources do not tell us the precise stops he made on his travels, either the towns or simple *ribat* (convents and fortified postal relay stations). The present localization of his legend at Ush in Farghana could not prove that Hallaj had an apostolic center there thanks to the family of this or that Farghani Turkish amir whom he had known in the entourage of the regent Muwaffaq, at the time of their arrival in Ahwaz. To the west of Isfijab, at Yasa, the great Turkish poet Ahmad Yesawi (d. 562), lived, for whom Hallaj is the saint *par excellence* of Islam, and through whom the present Turkish order of Bektashis is said to have received the monastic rule of the Khwajagan: the rule owed to Yusuf Hamadhani (d. 535), who propagated it in Transoxiana; we know that the execution of Hallaj is expressly evoked in the initiation ceremony of this order; the "gibbet of Mansur" (*dar-e Mansur*) stands symbolically for the center of the cell where the novice prostrates himself to declare his vows. But it is unlikely that this rite was born in the region of Isfijab-Yasa just because Hallaj stayed there.

India

The capital of Qashmir [Kashmir] is the only sure point on Hallaj's itinerary, around 283, in the northwest of India, which we know he reached by way of the sea, either via Daybul (near present-day Karachi), or via the *balad al-shirk*, to the east of Gujrat, between Bihruj and Qanbaya. Via Daybul, he went directly up the valley of the Indus via Mansura-Multan, Muslim towns. The detour through

Gujrat (Bahmi) brought Hallaj into contact with polytheists who were already accustomed to receiving Muslim merchants, who were permitted to set up little autonomous colonies in their midst, notably at Saymur; which perhaps attracted Hallaj to come there to preach. But the fact that today, in two important villages of Gujrat, Dhahulkah and Mandal (in Jainist lands), the lowly Dudwalas (dairymen) caste bears the surname "Mansuri" in memory of Hallaj, does not prove that its Islamization dates back to him. For two other present-day localizations of a Hallajian survival in India, the cult of *Satya Pir* in East Bengal, and the cenotaph of Hallaj at Muhammad Bender (near Madras) appeared only much later.

·

ANECDOTES

The "Rope Trick"

[Abu al-Hasan] al-Muzayin (d. 328/940) recounted, Sulami notes: "I saw Husayn-b-Mansur during one of his travels, and said to him: 'Where are you going?' 'To India,' he said, 'to learn about white magic, in order to draw men to God, may He be praised and exalted! by this means.'"

This is the abridgment of a more extended account, which the *Kitab al-ʿuyun* has preserved for us:

> One of his friends told the following: "I accompanied him one year to Mecca; he remained there after the pilgrims left to return to Iraq, at which time he told me: 'If you want to return with them, go ahead! As for me, I feel inclined to go from here to India.' And he observes Hallaj had made many journeys (*siyahat*), many voyages. He set off then for India and I accompanied him as far as India. Once there, he asked information about a certain woman, went to find her, and chatted with her. She arranged to meet him the next day; and the next day, she left with him for the sea coast, with a rope twisted and tied in knots, like a veritable ladder. Once there, the woman said some words, and she climbed up this rope—she placed her foot on the rope, and she climbed, so much so that she disappeared from our sight. And Hallaj, turning to me, said 'This is why I came to India—to meet this woman.' "

Ibn Khafif related to his disciples the same story, taken from a certain ʿAli, son of Ahmad al-Hasib, an arithmetician skilled in the handling of the astrolabe, who said:

> I heard my father relate the following: "Muʿtadid (d. 289/901) sent me to India to get secret information; with me in our boat was a certain Husayn-b-Mansur, a pleasant man and good company. Once we had left the boat, and while we were standing on the beach and the porters were taking the baggage (*thiyab*) off the boat, unloading it (on the bank), I said to him: 'Why have you come here?' He said, 'In order to learn white magic (*sihr*) to be able to preach God to the people.'

Now, on the shore there was a hut in which an old man lived. Husayn asked him: 'Do any of you know *sihr?*' Then the old man brought out a ball of string, handed the end to Husayn, and threw the ball into the air: and it became an arch, onto which he climbed; then he climbed down and said to Husayn: 'Is that what you ask for?' 'Yes,' said Husayn [Hallaj]. The old man said, 'That is only a tiny sampling of the knowledge of the masters. Go further, for the land is full of it (*Mantiq*).' Then Husayn left me and I saw him no more. Later, returning to Baghdad, I learned that he pretended to do wondrous things. They said he was waited on by *jinn* and many stories went the rounds concerning him."

The two anecdotes actually boil down to one; namely, the tale of the famous "Rope Trick" recounted by Anglo-Indian folklorists (as recently as the last century a yogi from Madras succeeded in "flying in the air by means of a wand planted in the ground. Similar feats are elsewhere everyday performed by poor country jugglers, without their pretending to any supernatural power.") Al-Muzayin and Ibn Khafif have merely chosen Hallaj as witness to a scene of this kind, performed during the disembarkation of tourists in India; Ibn Battuta relates for us a similar episode. They have seized upon a text about it to try to vindicate it from the orthodox point of view. Hallaj never claimed to have the gift of miracles; those that he showed in public were only juggler's tricks, innocent sleights of hand used for gathering the crowd that he wanted "to evangelize."

This explanation does not account for the view of Ibn 'Ata'; here it is only a diverting expedient. The "preternatural" deeds in Hallaj's biography begin before his voyage to India.

The Account of Turughbadhi

One day, Shaykh 'Abdallah Turughbadhi, of the city of Tus, had spread his tablecloth and was breaking bread with his disciples, when Mansur Hallaj arrived from the city of Qashmir, dressed in a black *qaba'*, holding two *black dogs* on a leash. The shaykh said to his disciples: "a young man arrayed in this way is going to come; get up all of you, and go out to him, for he does great things."

And they went out to this man and brought him back with them. The shaykh, as soon as he saw them, yielded his place to him; [Hallaj] took it, brought his dogs to the table close to him. . . . The shaykh looked at him; he ate bread, and gave some to his dogs, which shocked the disciples; only when he was leaving did the shaykh get up to say goodbye to him.

Upon the shaykh's return, his disciples said to him: "why do you let such a man who eats with his dogs sit in your place, a passerby whose presence here renders our entire meal impure?" "These dogs, responded the shaykh, were his self (*nafs*), they stayed outside him, and walked after him; while our dogs remain inside ourselves, and we follow behind them. . . . This is the difference between the one who follows his dogs, and the one whom his dogs follow. His dogs are outside, and you can see them; yours are hidden. His state is a thousand times superior to yours. He desires to be in the creative will of his God; whether there be a dog there or not, he wants to direct his act toward God."

Hallaj in Turkestan and in Ma Sin

The final goal of Hallaj's longest journey was to reach and to "evangelize" the Turkish race in its cultural center of that time: the pentapolis of Turfan, and hence, more particularly Qoço [Qocho], the age-old cultural capital of the Uyghur Qaghan Turks.

For "Turkestan" means here the Turkish regions that were pagan, thus the front of the holy war beyond Isfijab, between the Aral and the Ili; Ma Sin (= Mha Cinatish in Uyghuritic, from the Sanskrit Mahacinadesa) designates the western edges of China (Tawgac in contrast to "Khitai," its eastern edges), more particularly the pentapolis of Turfan, which Hallaj must have reached also by a grand detour (going to the north, then to the west), the direct route (northeast) via Qashghar being for the most part cut off by the Tibetans, controllers of Qashghar until 260 and of the Qashghar-Qocho route (taken by Bishbaliq in 193/808) until about 300; contacts between Samanid Islam and the Qaghan Turks (caravans, holy war in 280 and 291) were made via Farab (Shawghar) and Isfijab, and not in Farghana (Haftdih).

Hallaj's apostolic method in non-Arab countries was to approach a ruling élite whose attention he could get only through the help of educated translators; thus of the scribal class. In Turkish countries, this class enabled the Uyghur dialect to gain ascendancy as the language of administration, writing it in alphabets derived from Syriac, either in ancient Syriac characters, if they were Nestorian scribes, or in Soghdian, if they were Manichaean scribes. The Nestorian Turkish cultural center was Almalig, the Manichaean was Qocho (where at that time there were persons known as "the elect," or *denawar*). Since Hallaj surely did not go into Turkish lands in search of Christians (he had Christians as neighbors right in Iraq), he must have concentrated on establishing contacts with Manichaeans, the *zanadiqa* (furthermore, in the Manichaean form of the Uyghur alphabet, which became the official administrative script of the Mongol empire, we have the Chagatai version of the life of Hallaj by 'Attar—direct proof of the instrumental role in the mystic Islamization process played in Turkish countries by the Uyghurs in the twelfth to fifteenth centuries). When and how did Hallaj make these contacts? These Uyghur Turkish Manichaean scribes spoke Soghdian; they came from Samarqand, Paykand, and Kish, centers for the manufacturing of Chinese silk; they had also been engaged in the reexportation of heavy gold brocade into Arab Iraq (therefore to Tustar), which the Chinese chronicles tell us were brought via Qocho to the Qirghiz prince Bilgaqaghan around 226/840; along with jade and horses. Paper was also exported from China; we know that even in this era at Qocho people used *shaçie kägdäsi* (= paper manufactured at Sha-tshey, near Tuenhuang, Kansu) and that in 309 in Baghdad, at the homes of Hallaj's disciples, manuscripts of his works on Chinese paper (*waraq sini*) were seized; the manuscripts were written in gold ink and covered with brocade and silk; this paper could have been obtained for him by his Turkish friends abroad; we are told (by Hamd) that they wrote him letters, after his journey, calling him *Muqit* (= vegetarian provider, a rather Manichaean illusion to some miracle).

Certainly, Hallaj could not have followed the "silk route" to Tchangngan and Lo-yang; but can we be sure which Uyghur prince was reigning when Hallaj visited Qocho? According to Vizir Ibn al-Furat, the two greatest potentates of the infidel world of that time were the Caesar of Rum (Byzantium), and the Qaghan of the Turks (= Uyghurs of Qocho = Toquzguz; after 744, when the Tu-kiue empire was founded). For nearly a century, 762–840, China under the T'ang dynasties had been obliged to pay tribute to the Uyghur Qaghans, who had been converts to Manichaeanism since 762, under Qaghan Alp Qutlugh Kulug Bilga (759–780), known as *Zahag i Mani* (= emanation of Mani) by the Iraqi missionaries whom the Manichaean patriarch had sent to him (from Mada'in). One Qirghiz usurper, in 840, had occupied Qocho, permitting China, then emancipated, to bar Manichaeanism; but a new dynasty of Uyghur and Manichaean Qaghans reinstalled itself at Qocho in 865, with the title of *Idiqut*. Toward the end of the reign of the first Idiqut, Pu-ku-ts'un (865–900), a sort of Muslim diplomat, Tamin-b-Bahr Mutawwi'i (= the "volunteer for the faith") went to call on the Orkhan around 272/866, about the time that Hallaj must have come to Qocho.

Is there a direct link between the generation of disciples that Hallaj himself acquired around 285/898 between Isfijab and Qocho, and the Islamization of Turkestan, where the Hallajian legend seems so deeply ingrained?

We do not know if Isfijab was where his disciple, Abu Nasr A-b-Sa'id Isfijabi, took down from his dictation the important *'aqida* that Qushayri published in the beginning of his famous *risala*. No known Hallajian appeared in Qashghar, where there had been Shi'ites; but as early as 510 a certain Ilekkhanid princess, a patroness of Ahmad Ghazali, may have been pro-Hallajian; and the *diwan* of Ahmad Yesawi (d. 562/1166), shows that his country, the country of the Ghuzz of Dihi-No, homeland of the Saljuqs, did not have to wait for 'Attar to be translated into Turkish in order to venerate Hallaj.

There are indications that devotion to Hallaj, in its specifically Turkish, Kurdish, and Shirwaniyan form, was born and maintained in the various *ribats* of the *mujahidin* (fighters of the holy war), such as those at Kirwan, Tirmidh, Washgird, Ush, Isfijab, and Mirki. The members of the Bektashi order, were always recruited from military circles; as was the case with the Ottoman janissaries. The *isnad* of Bektashi descent goes back, via Ahmad Yesawi, to Yusuf Hamadhani (d. 535), an Iranian Kurd, settled at Marv, whose Hallajism originated: either in the Khurasaniyan Hallajian center at Talaqan, and afterwards

Balkh, which goes back in a continuous line even to Hallaj himself; or in a Kurdish center from which the symbolism of two initiatory small cords was derived, a symbolism common, strangely enough, to two groups, the Yazidi *feqiran*, and the Bektashis, which now differentiate all their other observances and have in common only the devotion to Hallaj. But on one fundamental point, the damnation of the saints through love (and thus the sanctity of Iblis), the Iranian Hallajian tradition is unanimous, in Khurasan (Ash'arite mystics) as well as in Kurdistan and Daylam (except for Y Hamadhani, AQ Kilani, Jagir Kurdi and R Baqli); while the whole Turkish Hallajian tradition (and especially the Bektashis) ignore the "Satanic" interpretation of the *Tawasin*, and weigh the sanctity of Hallaj against the damnation of Iblis. Such differences must go back very far, and argue in favor of a Turkish Hallajism that is original and early, and traceable to the apostolate of the Hanafite Faris (d. 340) at Samarqand; carried on by the Hanafite Kalabadhi (d. 380) at Bukhara.

But, instead of furnishing a literary proof of it, the Turkish texts on Hallaj refer us, often explicitly, to Persian prototypes.

One oral tradition alone, collected at Ush (Farghana), among Qaraqirghiz immigrants, should prove that the devotion to Hallaj did not find its way into this Turkish tribe, like the later cult of the other Ishans, through external accession; rather this tribe incorporated it itself, since the tribe heard the structure explained even from the time of the initial splitting up of the Qaraqirghiz clans, before leaving their racial center of dispersal, their formative social center, Qocho, near Turfan, in "Ma Sin": in the period of its Islamization in the twelfth century, before its first emigration to Farghana.

Hallaj's remote journey to Ma Sin and Qocho, has a distinct historical significance: he had met there the apex of the Turkish racial swarming; and, by being the first to broach the Islamization of the Turks, near the Mosque of the Seven Sleepers of Toyeq, he set in motion, not only the definitive orientation of Turkish ideal poetry, but also the Turkish capture of Constantinople, undertaken by the Saljuqs ('Arabjami', after Mantzikert) and achieved by the Osmanlis.

In fact, it is interesting to note that Ibn al-Muslima, the only 'Abbasid vizir who admitted to being a Hallajian, to the extent of consecrating his vizirate to him, had determined and arranged the coming of the Saljuq Turks into the capital of the Caliphate; Hallaj was thus constituted a witness of the Islamic vocation of the Turkish race.

According to the strange statement by the dying Hallaj, the statement which the head of the police force preserved for Muqtadir, about the "taking of Constantinople"—that distinguished city, founded to celebrate the triumph of Christianity, but promised to Islam in an ancient hadith, the city that had resisted the assault of the standard-bearer of the Prophet, Eyup (= Abu Ayyub Ansari), buried under its ramparts and regarded as the ancestor of Hallaj because of their common vocation for the holy war: this city had to be claimed by

Islam as the symbol of its share in the glory of Christ, whose mystic sanctity Islam venerates, and it was in actual fact conquered by a Turkish army. Indeed, just as the capture of Jerusalem, on two occasions, from the Greeks, and later from the Latins, is manifest in the history of the double claim by the Prophet (*qibla, mi'raj*) to the *dhabih* of the sacrifice of Abraham, in the name of the Arabs and of all Muslims who received the Arabic Qur'an; so, also, the conquest of Constantinople by the Turks, over the Greeks, casts on the historical horizon the astonishing Hallajian interiorization of the crucifixion, proposed by Hallaj (*'ala din al-salib yakuna mawti*) to some renegade Greeks (Shaghab, Nasr) and Nestorians (Qunna'iya, from the Iranian Ctesiphon, the city that held the true cross), and accepted by many Iranian Hallajians ('Attar), Indians and especially Turks, including those ex-Christian janissaries in the barracks of Istanbul (the Bektashis). In February of 1940 I collected living testimonies in Istanbul of the Turkish people's spiritual appeals to Hallac-e Mansur, made as if to "a saint of apocalyptic times."

IV. THE SOCIAL EXPRESSION OF HALLAJ'S VOCATION, AND HIS CONTACTS WITH THE CULTURAL RENAISSANCE OF HIS TIME

We have focused our attention deliberately up to now on the travels of Hallaj proceeding from the axis of his original milieu, Muslim and Sunnite, *Muhaddithun* and Sufi: by establishing that, beginning with his preaching in Ahwaz in 272, his break with the Sufis had led him to form friendships with members of "the upper class", administrative scribes and learned secretaries of the state: a milieu of high culture, but of an often suspect Sunnite orthodoxy, in which many began to relish as connoisseurs the Hellenistic sciences, especially those of medicine and alchemy. Hallaj benefited from these contacts by learning to make use of a "comparatist" technical, and partly philosophical, vocabulary for setting forth the doctrine that he preached: a doctrine whose source was strictly Muslim, but whose orientation was his own interioristic and mystical one. And we have noted that during his lifetime some had accused Hallaj of having strayed from Islam because of experiments in medicine and alchemy that he was supposed to have practiced, presenting them falsely to credulous Muslims as miracles.

In fact, early Muslim orthodoxy, which made God not only the first cause, but also the immediate author of every (isolated, instantaneous) event, could see in Hallaj, announcing and producing in public connected series of phenomena (predictions, cures), the custodian of a supernatural power, permitted (if he were a saint), forbidden (if he were possessed), or pretended (if he were a charlatan). Hence, the accusations in question.

These charges are not enough, as we have seen, to prove that Hallaj deliberately adhered to Hellenistic philosophy, either by taking the Hippocratic oath in practice among doctors, or by having himself initiated into any of the extremist Shi'ite sects, in which hermetic alchemy was one of the trade secrets.

But we can and even must change axis for the examination of this period in Hallaj's life, in order to grasp, through consideration of his posthumous extra-Islamic influence, how the expression of his social vocation interposed itself in the cultural renaissance of that time; slowly, but in a positive way.

One tradition, collected by Hujwiri affirmed that "the heretic (*mulhid*) Husayn-b-Mansur Hallaj had been the master (*ustadh*) of M-b-Zak Razi (the great physician) and the traveling companion (*rafiq*) of the Qarmathian Abu Sa'id (Jannabi)": Juwayni even believed that three Qarmathian conspirators had plotted together to destroy Islam: Abu Sa'id Jannabi (d. 301) had set aside Ahsa for himself, Hallaj Baghdad, and Ibn al-Muqaffa' (*sic*) the Turkish countries.

On the other hand, among the disciples of Shibli, who was so profoundly Hallajian, we find a demi-philosopher, Zayd-b-Rifa'a Hashimi, one of the drafters of the encyclopaedia of the Ikhwan al-Safa' and an amateur philosopher, 'Isa, son of Vizir 'Ali ibn 'Isa. Then the celebrated Abu Hayyan Tawhidi (d. 41 [4]), both a philosopher and a mystic very close, as we shall see, to Hallaj: which explains how Ibn Sina (d. 437) had known and commented on a Hallajian text.

It was therefore not the pure philosophers (of Christian or Sabaean background) who were the first to become interested in Hallaj, but gnostic Shi'ites, basing their Qarmathian politics on Greek philosophy, such as the Gebrian alchemist (Ibn Zayyat) and the Ikhwan al-Safa'; they tended to a self-interested exploitation of his ideas, just as certain Sunnite men of state tried to exploit his influence (cf. Joan of Arc, used by the skeptical advisors of Charles VII, according to Machiavelli).

Hallaj is thirty years old; after a series of incidents in which he became estranged from the leading Sufis, incidents undoubtedly exaggerated *post eventum* by the interested parties, he is voluntarily "defrocked," so to speak, and able to participate in all of the cultural and political activity of his time, which the common rule of the Sufis, even at Mecca and at Kufa, had barely allowed him to catch a glimpse of. He broke away, because he was worn out by spiritual dryness and by the hypocritical "fraternal corrections" of those hermits who cultivate their perfection sealed off from reality, keeping for themselves the words of life that could save others and only intoxicate themselves. But he acquired [in that milieu], and retains the essence of, an ascetic, and mystical technique of spiritual life, for which his drive was greater than theirs; [this technique is] a route to the Real God, *al-Haqq*, a conditioning whose method he is determined to communicate, through fraternal compassion, to laymen of every milieu.

If this spiritual technique of transmutation truly transubstantiates the soul, it is an experimental conditioning that must be able to communicate itself to all from the experiential language of each. He "linked his existence to the Source of existence"; he wants to apply the general therapy that he found, and to preach it, as much for the purification of individuals as for the restoration of the social order, and not only among Muslims.

His crucial period of transition was the period between his years of apprenticeship, which had confined him in a suspicious and closed provincial milieu of humble, ordinary people, taciturn contemplatives and solipsists, who had no influence upon the learned of their time, and the period of the great political trial, which will make his condemnation a momentous event, *yawm ʿazim*, for the whole Islamic world.

The Goals of His Apostolate

THE SYNCRETIST AND UNIVERSALIST ASPECT OF HIS METHOD
OF CULTIC INTERIORISM

He maintains the appearance of an ascetic (*nasik*). "If he learned that the inhabitants of a city or the members of a group professed Muʿtazilism, he became a Muʿtazilite for their sake, and assiduously; if he saw a group inclining toward Imamism, he became an Imamite, telling them how to recognize the signs of the Imam whom they were awaiting; if he saw a group of Sunnites, he became a Sunnite. . . . He had practised medicine; he had experimented with alchemy and with the results that one expects from it. . . . He traveled from town to town."

The intent of this testimony by an opponent, Suli, is to suggest that Hallaj was a dangerous intriguer, exploiting public credulity. The Muslim world was beginning then, even among laymen, to split itself up into mutually exclusive groups, and it is certain that Hallaj did not hesitate to enter all of them, since even today, as we shall see, his name is known and discussed in all the Sunnite rites, in all the Shiʿite sects, and even among the Yazidis. In this era, furthermore, the newly-formed groups discussed by Suli were not yet autonomous, with their own complete and distinct system of interpretation of Islam: the word "Sunnite" referred to those who emphasized the study of hadith, by collecting and transmitting them as a basis for judging the worship and moral life of the Muslim Community; the word "Imamite" referred to those who gave priority to the problem of legitimate executive power, so as to know to whom to entrust it in order to reestablish the social order in justice; the word "Muʿtazilite" referred to those who preoccupied themselves with establishing a theology and a canonical legislation on coherent theoretical foundations. Hallaj's brief list of works shows that he, in fact, treated the *loci theologici* as defined by the Muʿtazilites, and problems of political theory in the manner of the

Imamites; having come from Sunnite circles, he gives, in his *Riwayat*, several devotional hadith accepted among the Hanbalites, and he visualizes from a particular angle, reminiscent of the oldest Qur'anic suras, the problem of the *isnad*.

It was very unusual for a Sunnite to behave this way, transposing from one vocabulary into another his essential thought, which was, as we have said, a conditioning based on introspection. This state of mind is actually a philosophical one. And one can understand how he was easily confused with other propagandists of the era, for example, the Qarmathian *da'i* who made use of a syncretist symbolism in order to bring about, in the manner of Freemasonry, a fusion of all religions, and one interpretation for all their rites, reducing them to a collection of rational social rules intended to bring about a reign of peace and good will among men. However, his formal texts establish his thought very well (cf. also *isqat al-hajj*): as having a clearly universalist scope, but founded on a method of interiorization of the strictly followed Islamic rituals of worship:

> 'Abdallah-b-Tahir Azdi was quoted as saying: I was quarreling with a Jew in the market of Baghdad, and I blurted out "dog!" Passing then by my side, Husayn-b-Mansur regarded me with an angry air and told me: "Don't make your dog bark so!" and he withdrew in haste. My quarrel ended, I went to find him and entered his home; but he looked away from me. I apologized and he calmed down. Then he said to me "My son, the religious faiths, all of them, arise from God the Most High; He assigned to each group a creed, not of their own choice, but of His choice imposed on them. When one reproaches another for belonging to an erroneous faith, it is because one presupposes that he has chosen it of himself, which is the heresy of the (Mu'tazilite) *Qadariya*: who are (says the hadith of Ibn 'Abbas) the 'Zoroastrians of this Community.' I would have you know that Judaism, Christianity, Islam, and the other religious denominations may be different names and contrasting appellations, but that their Goal, Himself, suffers neither difference nor contrast"; then he recited the following verse:

> I have pondered as to how to give religious faiths an experimental definition
> And I formulate it as a single Principle with many branches.
> Do not demand therefore that your companion in discussion adopt this or that confessional denomination.
> That would prevent him from arriving at honest union (with you and with God).
> It is up to the Principle Himself to come to this man, and to clarify
> In him all of the supreme meanings: and then this man will understand (everything).

That characterizes his universalism; and the following, his interioristic method of ritual observance (it is the prologue of *Kitab al-sayhur*):

> Understand, my brothers—God grant, to you and to us, the good fortune of being in His grace—that observance (*'ibada*) is the fruit of knowledge, profit

(drawn) from life, harvest of the servant of God, provision of saints, way of the strong, fate of the great, goal of the wise, armor of noblemen, food of travelers, choice of seers. Indeed this is the road to joy, the route to Paradise, yet at the same time it is a steep way, a hard road, full of obstacles and setbacks, cluttered with pitfalls and ambushes, teeming with enemies and pillagers, ennobled by those who seek it and follow it. And this is very much as it should be, since it is the Way toward God. Yet, for all that, the servant (of God) is weak, the times are hard, with much work, and life is short. Action is inadequate, criticism heedful; death is near, and the voyage long, in which obedience to God (ta'a) is our indispensable provision; it is the resource that one cannot do without; he who has set his hands to it has triumphed, he will be happy for ever; he who has not been able to seize it is lost with the losers, and will perish with the damned, and the grave question dealt with here will have been for him null and void, I say it before God: the danger is therefore great. This is why glory belongs to those who undertake this Way, and they are few in number; glory to those among these beginners who persevere in it; and finally glory to the perseverers who reach the goal and grasp what they sought, for they are those for whom God reserved (from the beginning) His wisdom and His love, whom He confirmed afterwards by His sovereign providence, and whom He brought finally through His grace to the Paradise of His Complacence. We ask Him, may He be exalted! May He rank you, and us also, among His saints who have triumphed by His mercy. Yes!—And from the moment when we have established that this Way was such, we have examined and scrutinized in what manner to travel it fully and everything that the servant (of God) needs, talents and training, equipment and strategems, in theory and in practice, in order to be able to pass through it, safe and sound, thanks to the good divine Providence; so as not to be stopped in the midst of his precipices, to be lost there with the (sons) of perdition, we should seek refuge in God, the Lord of the worlds.

HIS CONTACTS WITH THE CULTURAL RENAISSANCE OF HIS TIME
(PHILOSOPHIC GNOSTICISM)

In this era, in the Arabic Islamic world, a true cultural renaissance blossomed forth, similar in nature to our two Western renaissances, the classic Greco-Latin of the fifteenth century, and the Arabo-Latin scholastic of the twelfth. By means, like those, of translations of rediscovered scientific works from ancient times: in a language medium, no longer dead, like our Latin, but living, the official language of the Caliphate and liturgical language of Islam, Arabic. "It is in the Arabic language," Biruni remarks, "that the sciences have been assembled from all parts of the world and translated; it is by Arabic that their ideas have been harmonized to the point of convincing our hearts, while its attractions filter into our arteries and our veins." The language promoted at that time as "the language of civilization": thanks to the presence, in Iraq, of a catalyzing milieu of specialized translator-scribes: the pagan milieu of the Sabaeans of

Harran, to which the Aramaic language community had annexed, for this cultural work, Christians of Hellenized stock and Manichaeans of Iranian stock.

The very special character of this renaissance is its aspect of being simultaneously skeptic and gnostic; due to a blending of naturalist and magical traditions of the old Chaldean soil, "made fertile by sacrifices to the stars," with the initiatory philosophy of the last neo-Platonic adepts of the school of Edessa; and due to the presence, in large part, of increasingly industrialized cities of Kufa, Basra, Baghdad, Isfahan, Rayy, Nishapur, Damascus, and Cairo, of trade guilds that grouped workers together by means of supposedly Shi'ite revolutionary initiations.

One begins to get a glimpse of the ancient Hellenistic intellectual trends, which revive in this renaissance that the slothful ignorance of the conservative Sunnites (Hashwiya) was determined not to see; a revival thanks to the influence of their technical terms on certain Mu'tazilites, such as Nazzam and Jahiz, and especially on a collection of apocryphal or anonymous writings of extremist Shi'ite origin, Ps. Balinas and Ps. Jabir, former branches (Kayyaliya) of the Ikhwan al-Safa'. First of all, a distinctly empirical and pagan line of thought, neo-Pythagorian in character (with old stoical elements), that of the *ashab al-taba'i' wa'l-tilasmat*, "adepts in the four elements and in talismans," with its base of support in Basra. The science that it advocates consists of dismantling the cosmic machinery that formed the universe, by isolating its causal series, in such a way as to be able to reproduce the whole of its parts naturally, and even to improve upon them; it is based on Greek works dealing with the specific qualities of numbers, minerals, plants, and animals (geoponics, bestiaries, toxicologies); generalizing and systematizing with a brash confidence that borders on charlatanism, they dare to contemplate the possibility of manufacturing artificial men, of thinking "robots," and, just as the caster of spells imprisons the soul in his *dagyd*, or Porphyrius fixing the divine emanation in a pagan idol, they would reach the point of impregnating certain "robots" with the divine influx that produces Imams.

The other line of thought, gnostic and hermetic, that of the *zanadiqa ruhaniya* "neo-Manichaeans, pneumatics," based at Kufa, tinges its Hellenistic scientific matter with a certain pneumatology, and hopes to reach and to reconcile, through asceticism and prayer, the primary spirits (*arwah*) that activate and elevate beings of the sublunary world; more distinctly Islamized, these men, who were mostly extremist Shi'ites, tried to understand the visible universe by regarding it, in the light of their new faith, through the prism, the "stained glass," of their ancient myths.

These two groups have in common the fact that they resort freely to Greek sources (which the second group considers "inspired"), that they accept the Aristotelian organon, and that they reveal the Semitic individualistic realism by using it in the creation of experimental sciences in a modern way. For example, the creation of an arithmology, projecting numbers, written as letters, outside the geometric space in which Greek thought had materialized them in punctual groups; projecting numbers, that is, into the realm of discontinuous time in order to intervene there experimentally, by analogy with numbered cycles of stars, and using the specific properties of certain peculiar numbers: at first to bring about alchemical combinations, then productive therapeutic processes, and even social transformations, which will influence the formation of the Jewish Kabbala, but which also hastens the development of algebra, chemistry, and medicine.

They both also intend to attain two goals, which were classical goals of Hellenistic philosophy: the purification of the soul through knowledge of the truth, and the formula for the political balance of the ideal state.

We now have documentation on the individual crises of conscience of Muslim intellectuals who were connected with this strange cultural renaissance: on the case of independent philosophers, such as Eranshahri and the physician Abu Bakr Razi, or of exceptional theologians, such as Ibn al-Rawandi and Abu 'Isa Warraq. And this allows us to reconstruct the angle at which Hallaj participated in it.

From the point of view of technique of reasoning and presentation of arguments, Hallaj accepts, even more fully than those whom we have just cited, the data of the Aristotelian organon; he uses the ten categories and the four causes, and the last five chapters of his *Tawasin* are based on syllogisms. But he went even further: he called himself *namusi* (from the Greek *nomos*, law), which is reminiscent of Socrates; the God whom he preaches, *al-Haqq*, the Truth, bears a name common to several religious movements, one that had been already emphasized by his teacher Tustari, but which was taken here absolutely, and clarified by the Greek, *mu'ill*, "first cause"; it is not merely one of the ninety-nine traditional Islamic names of God, but is that One Truth that is the former of unities, that "unifies the nomads." His definition in this instance combines with that of Proclus, while on the geometric question it returns to that of Plato. These resources allow Hallaj to state that he exists, outside of the space and time of spiritual substances, and that therefore the soul is immaterial, that it is "one" with a transcendental unity distinct from the numerical unity.

Was it in the Sabaean milieu in Basra, where he had disciples, or in gnostic circles, like those at Kufa, that Hallaj absorbed the character of Hellenistic culture? The evidence is not yet decisive either way.

The Sabaean Milieu of the Ashab al-Taba'i'

It would be tempting to suppose that Hallaj learned Hellenistic philosophy from a Sabaean scholar of the caliber of Thabit ibn Qurra in Baghdad. But his known contacts with this pagan antimystical milieu appear to have been limited. One family of Sabaean historians left us some ironic and hostile notes concerning him. The talismanic processes (*khanqatiriya*) and the alchemical formulas, rendered into verse, which were attributed later to Hallaj, will be examined further in this study. It is possible that Hallaj had read, in the period when he upbraided Junayd, the famous *Kitab sirr al-khaliqa wa san'at al-tabi'a*, written in the time of Ma'mun under the authorship of Apollonius of Tyan (Ps. Balinas); a work that contains the Emerald Table. Sabaean terms are found in his writing; and Ibn Wahshiya Junbulani Qissi (figurehead for the Sabaist Ibn al-Zayyat), claimed that Hallaj had worked with them:

> I saw myself, in 311/924 (*sic*), one of those experimenters with magic, Abu Mansur Husayn-b-Mansur called Hallaj, who, specifically, claimed to have succeeded in working marvels, by magic. Among other examples: "I burned the skull of a man who had just died in a cultivated field in which a melon seed had been sown. After covering it over again with compost to strengthen its growth, and after wetting it down with human blood thinned with warm water, I grew a melon whose fruit inspires perverse thoughts in whoever eats it." This is what he stated positively to me.

Ibn Wahshiya, in spite of a hypocritically sympathetic notice, as a good Sabaean actually hated the sufis; he resumed against them the neo-Platonic tirade of Eunapios against the Christian monks; he branded the claims of the ascetics "of our religious community, *min millatina*, the wearers of black *suf*, as lies like those of the Nabatean, Hindu, and Christian ascetics, who say that renunciation gives true happiness, when the world (which they live in only as parasites) rejected them, who counsel peasants (the foundation of all civilized life) to work no longer, and who pretend that their prayers are worth the alms they seek. His well-known taste for aberrations no doubt amused itself by attributing to a mystic the aforementioned small perversity.

Like the Druzes (against the Nusayris), Hallaj concedes to the *ashab al-taba'i'* that the mechanism of interconnected natural causes explains, against the occasionalists, the normal course of visible phenomena; but he does not resort to them to explain the psychic progress and the spiritual transmutation that he preaches; he leans on the secondary causes only to rejoin their First Cause, *mu'ill al-'ilal*; he attaches himself neither to observances nor to prayer, nor to supreme virtues in themselves.

Did Hallaj really "experiment with alchemy" (Suli)? A title of a lost treatise on "red sulpher," no doubt a simple mystical symbol, an affirmation by Ibn Babawayh concerning his disciples, and an anecdote by a hostile Sufi that shows him claiming knowledge for himself of "the philosopher's stone," are not sufficient proof.

As to the question of his practicing medicine, the Hallajian doctrine on causalities is not contrary to the use of medical remedies (*'aqaqir*), but all the cures attributed to Hallaj are presented as instantaneous charisms; and do not bring medical practice into play. One cannot deny that he had known the celebrated doctor Abu Bakr Razi, who settled in Baghdad in the old Maristan under Muktafi before he founded the great hospital of Baghdad, thanks to the support of the Queen Mother, Shaghab, who esteemed them both. Being slightly older, however, Hallaj could not be identified, without proof, with a certain doctor named Hallaj whom Abu Bakr Razi cites in his *Hawi*; furthermore the "pneumatic" theory of *ta'jin al-arwah* of our Hallaj would have offended a clinical physician. Hallaj, perhaps, had become friends with this great doctor during the controversies with the Qarmathian *da'i*; both accepted their thesis of an "infallible leader" (*imam ma'sum*) for the ideal city; both rejected their claim of reserving this holy infallibility to the physical lineage of the 'Alids: every man of good will is suited to attain purification of the soul, through a progressive training of his reason, according to AB Razi, and through an asceticism of heart, according to Hallaj. And through the Razian notion of progress based on experimental science *fi'l-tariq ila-Haqq*, "on the way toward the Truth," agrees to some extent with the Hallajian idea of mystical ascent, Hallaj nevertheless condemned, like the Qarmathian *da'i* Abu Hatim Razi, the work in which the noted doctor challenged the miracles of the Prophets as the legerdemain of imposters.

The Qarmathian Revolutionaries, Ashab al-Sin

Hallaj's connections with the gnostic and hermetic milieu of the *zanadiqa ruhaniya* were much more extensive and profound, for it is in this milieu, when in contact with Qarmathian revolutionaries, and more specifically with the Salmaniyan school of the *ashab al-Sin*, that he developed his personal philosophical vocabulary, and in a definitive way; it is only very recently that the growth of our knowledge of Isma'ili literature has permitted us to clear up the serious problems of vocabulary that a work like the *Tawasin* posed to the reader.

Where, how, and why did Hallaj learn this vocabulary? As to the first question, perhaps in Kufa, where the extremist Shi'ites were divided, particularly among partisans of the *Mim, 'Ayn* and *Sin*; but he only passed through there briefly. At 'Askar Mukram (a Shi'ite and gnostic center), as well as at Tustar and at Karkh, his Sunnite entourage would have kept him apart from it. The more likely place, therefore, is Khurasan (and specifically Talaqan), where he came to build up, in an old center of Shi'ite uprisings, a group of converts to his mystic doctrine who survived him.

One gets a glimmer also of how he was led to it: of the Shi'ite sects, only the Qarmathian had developed a vocabulary making comparison of their different doctrines possible by using the logical mechanics of the organon, of the ten categories and the four causes. Why did he decide on it? He lived the same kind of life, of a wandering journeyman, as the Qarmathian missionaries; he had the same clientele of malcontents in search of a cure—physical, intellectual, moral, or social. He was concerned in the same way with affirming doctrinally the immortal immateriality of the soul and the ineffable divine transcendence, and in breaking loose, as Saint Augustine did when he left Mani for Plotinus, from the materialistic terminology of the mixture of the two primary causes that had infected the cosmogony of the early theologians of Islam and even of mystics such as Tustari and Junayd.

The long list of Hallajian terms that were of Qarmathian and Siniya origin will be studied later on. Through a process of thorough and profound investigation, their primary meaning becomes, in Hallaj, "warped" and transformed. Some examples (of this remodeling process) follow: *jafr* [divination]: the use, which was dear to Shiʿites, of the twenty-nine consonants of the Arabic vocabulary for "philosophical purposes," conferring on them each, along with their usual phonetic and numerical values, a fixed conceptual value (ex.: *alif* = a, = 1, = Oneness); this latter value is constantly invoked in the theological and eschatological speculations of the Salmaniya. For them *ʿayn* (= ʿ = 70 = *maʿna*) symbolizes the essence, the divine meaning of beings, and, on the social level, the divine seed hereditarily carried in the family (*ahl*) of the legitimate Leader, the silent (*samit*) Imam designated by the Prophet; *mim* (= m = 40 = *ism*) is the existential name, circumscribing the revealed message, and the transmitting Prophet; *sin* (s = 60 = *salsal*) is the causal (*sabab*) source of the spiritual life, the inspiration that initiates the elect. These three consonantal signs acquired in the early days at Kufa an unrivaled place in the discussions among extremist Shiʿites on the positions of priority, in the divine omniscience, of the three personages invested at the beginning of Islam with three missions that they symbolize: ʿAli (= *ʿAyn*), Muhammad (= *Mim*) and Salman (= *Sin*). The Qarmathian school, founded by Abuʾl-Khattab (d. 138), is *Siniya*. which maintains the priority of Salsal (= the gnostic name for Salman), who was a simple Iranian *mawla*, a non-Arab, incorporating mystically into the Family of the Prophet through a famous adoption formula, which had acquired prior to 128/745 an initiatory value. And the Qarmathian revolutionary movement, born from this school, was banned by the other Shiʿite sects because, by systematically basing its initiatory propaganda on the priority of spiritual adoption, thereby making it possible for anyone to attain the highest ranks, it destroyed the Shiʿite principle of the aristocratic prerogative of ʿAlid "spiritual leaders by right of birth."

Hallaj knows and cites the Salmaniyan meanings of *ʿayn, mim*, and *sin*, but he remodels them in a very personal way. *Mim* is nothing more than a *farʿ*, one of the two "derivatives" (*farʿan*, as opposed to *aslan* in Abuʾl-Khattab); there is only one *asl*, one "original element" (instead of two Kattabiyan "original elements"), the "Eternal Witness" (*shahid al-qidam*), the Spirit who commands (*ruh al-amr*) and brings about mystic union: the *ʿayn al-ʿayn*, whom he calls also *alif maʿluf*, which is to say, in Salmaniyan terms, the formative *hamza* applied to consonants and the first element of elocution.

Moreover, Hallaj does not wish to imprison himself in the literal symbolism of *jafr*, thus he also represents his line of reasoning by geometric forms, circles and straight lines, a method the Druze will later use.

The role reserved to the *Sin*, to the Initiator, among all the Salmaniya since Abuʾl-Khattab and by the Qarmathians down to the Druze, for whom the *Sin* is the mahdi, a mahdi who is a "spiritual," not a "carnal son" of the Family of the

Prophet, gives us the key to the texts that present Hallaj to us as having been the political agent of a legitimist conspiracy on behalf of an 'Alid. And it clarifies the puzzling *isnad* of Hallaj's only dated text, his *Riwaya* XXV: "through the meaning (*'ayn*) of the scale, in the year 290, through the *'asr khatib* in the year Seven of the Calling, through the saint of the lineage. . . ."

We know, in fact, that, in Qarmathian circles, a conspiracy was under way, the one that will end in the triumph of the Fatimid dynasty; it was announcing that the Hour of Justice was not far off, that after having concealed themselves for 309 years, like the Seven Sleepers in the Cave, the legitimate descendents of the Prophet are going to reign; and that the year of their reappearance, that of the general uprising, would be the year 290/902. For, according to *jafr*, 290 = 80 + 1 + 9 + 200 = FATiR = 40 + 200 + 10 + 40 + MARYaM: this is both the number of Mary, by whom the *fiat* caused Jesus to appear, and the number of the Prophet's daughter, Fatima, ancestor of the Fatimid 'Alids, whom the Salmaniya, since Abu'l-Khattab, called Fatir. And according to Shi'ite tradition, the triumphant coming of the mahdi must call forth *de facto* the second coming of Jesus; that is claimed in A.H. 132 by Saffah, at the time of his proclamation in Kufa, as it was claimed by the Qarmathian Abu Tahir before A.H. 319. This is what the Sunnite Hashwiya were denying, drawing their argument from an invented hadith: "no Mahdi, except Jesus," *la Mahdi, illa 'Isa*. A century later, in Baghdad, the insurgent Fatimids erected crosses crying out the name of their Imam-Mahdi, to defy these Sunnites and their false opinion.

Hallaj wrote his *Riwaya XXV* for a public sympathetic to the Qarmathian propaganda about "rebels for the year 290"; it appeals to their hope in this mahdi, in this "rightly guided leader" who "will fill the world with justice as it has been filled with iniquity." But like the Qarmathians of Bahrayn, who will refuse to recognize as mahdi the Fatimid of the Mahdiya, Hallaj, like the Druze, announces a "mahdi" of the Salman type, a "Saint of the *adoptive* lineage," not of the carnal lineage, a mystic saint, thus preparing the way for the second coming of Jesus; which Tirmidhi (d. 285/898), a Sufi, had just defined as the coming of the "Seal of the Saints," the promulgation of the definitive Muslim law, just as Hallaj expresses it in his *Riwaya XXIII*.

The Mahdi that Hallaj was announcing, then, is the *shahid ani*, the "present witness" (of the Eternal Witness), the one whom he will declare himself to be on the eve of his execution, as if the martyrdom of a Muslim *Nafs Zakiya* might provoke the return of Christ; he uses also the word *muta'*, the "one who has been obeyed," which Ghazali will use again.

The notion of the "present witness," identified here with the *Sin* of the Salmaniya Shi'ites, was born of a very ancient Sunnite tradition, respected by the Hanbalites, that of the *badal*, the "apotropaic saint"; the immediate Intercessor, the one who, through his sanctity, forestalls the anger of God, the spiritual pillar that keeps the world from giving way; it is said that he is a simple *mawla*, a non-Arab foreigner; according to Jahiz, Bilal had preceded Salman as a *badal*. When the Muslim hierarchy of Intercessors became more complicated, and when there was no longer just one, but forty *abdal* (plural of *badal*), there was placed above them, at the very top, the one whom, in the following century, the Sufis will call the Pole (*Qutb*), and whom at that time the Hanbalites were calling the *Mustakhlif* (the successor). If Hallaj had not entered into relations with the Qarmathian revolutionaries, *ashab al-Sin*, it is doubtful that his Sunnite notion of the *badal*, of the "present witness," would have had the dynamism and the accent to make the people of Talaqan, in 309/922, believe at the news of his death that he could not be killed, that he had only "appeared to die," like Christ, his soul also being immortal, and that he is the mahdi who must return (Biruni).

The Word al-Haqq *and the Supraconfessional Problem of Truth*

The word *al-haqq*, meaning right (or duty), truth (and reality), has become simply the name of God for the whole of Persian, Turkish, Indian, and Malaysian Islam, that is, for the world converted by mystics. Not only the apostolate, but the matter of Hallaj's individual conscience, is to a high degree linked to this fact, whose genesis must be studied closely.

Truth is not always regarded with the same coefficient of reality, from the simple rational (nonambiguous, coherent) assertion of the mathematically, materially, and biologically true, to the psychologically true (agreement of tongue and heart), to the morally true (agreement of actions with theory), and the metaphysically true (ultimate intelligible reality). And common language assumes ingenuously that there is agreement *a priori* between the various states of our mind (with itself and with the minds of others), the facts or events of the external world, and their ultimate reality (in God).

However, at the starting point of Islam, in the Qur'an, *al-haqq*, the truth, is presented in the large sense as a fulfillment, by God, of His design as the Creator; truth "comes to light" (*ja'a, zahara, hashasa*); it enables us to verify agreement between what it sets forth (prophecy, directions, counsels) and facts (revealed books, and prophets sent to make them known by applying legal sanctions to them), an agreement which culminates with the Judgment, with that Hour which is the Truth; the Judge; *al-Haqq* becomes one of the Names of God. However, the Qur'an shows that *al-haqq* is not immediate and universal totality, in the monist sense; it happens, it is fulfilled, it is preached, it is disputed, it requires, in order to come to light, a special psychological state, as much in the one who declares it as in the one who accepts it; namely, *al-sidq*, "sincerity," as distinct from *al-haqq* (notion of the *siddiq*).

In the beginning of Muslim thought, optimism leads thinkers to propound agreement *a priori* between a thought and its object: *kull mujtahid musib*, 'Anbari says, which Jahiz and Dawud Zahiri will echo again. But, with Nazzam, Mu'tazilism perceives that one must at first treat *al-haqq* as the conformity of the judgment with the belief of the one who forms it, and *al-sidq* as the conformity of his declaration with his belief (even if erroneous); for, without us, neither the universal consent, nor the consensus of the Community, is gained concerning the uniform application of the *asma'* (juridical names) to the *ahkam* (practical statutes).

Going deeply into the notion of *sidq*, "sincerity," seeing it as a mental state, a real purification of the heart, Dhu'l-Nun Misri and Muhasibi consider it the means of access to God, conceivable in so far as it is truthful. In this era, when the Zahirites are still restricting *al-haqq* to the meaning of "the sound, *sahih*, mode of existing for the thing considered," when the Zaydites are emphasizing the meaning of rightful claim of this term (the *da'i Natiq bi'l-haqq*), when the Sufis are beginning to refer to God, among themselves, by the name of *al-Haqq*; this name when used in public, still surprises people. Hallaj, no doubt the first to dare use it, hears his listeners ask him: "What is this Truth to which you allude?" He answers: "He is the First Cause of creatures, Himself not undergoing causalization." Even for mystics, *al-haqq*, the truth coming to dwell in our purified thought and to explain creative action to us, is not simply God, but rather a demiurge, a first divine causative emanation, *al-'adl* of Tustari, *al-haqq al-makhluq bihi* (Ibn Barrajan will say), the *Nur Muhammadi* (Kasirqi will say, commenting on Qur'an 28:48).

Even to Hallaj, *al-Haqq* represents God only in so far as He is intelligible to us, accessible to us by his *amr* or directive (principle of union). It is not the whole sealed essential mystery of God, which he calls *haqiqa*. It is the *fiat*.

The important distinction that Hallaj, in reaction against the Mu'tazilites, makes between *haqq* and *haqiqa*, is brought out in a series of remarkable texts, in which, at times, when he is referring to the life of the heart (the *nasut* aspect) *haqq* takes precedence, and at other times, when he is referring to the interior life, God (the *lahut* aspect), *haqiqa* takes precedence. *Haqq*, which is a Name of God, thus stands for His practical *hukm* marking us; *haqiqa*, which is an abstract quality, stands for His *hukm* that is by nature inaccessible. Ash'ari will use the same distinction, which the monists will reverse.

The general tendency at that time was to equate *haqq* with *haqiqa*, both among the Zahirites and among such Hellenistic philosophers as Farabi. Hence, the dogmatic theologians imbued with Mu'tazilism believe that both terms signify the use of one given word in its literal and not figurative (*majaz*) sense; that a Qur'anic word, even if it has no antecedents in ordinary language, is to be taken in the literal sense, since man is freely invested by God with its administration; this holds as much for a practical and concrete name like *haqq* (or *kafir*) as for an idea in God like *haqiqa* (or *kufr*). On the contrary, Hallaj believes that the idea of infidelity (*kufr*) in divine knowledge must not be separated by us from the idea of faith (*iman*): both, in God, are true and inseparable, like the acts that they explain; whereas the status of the conscious infidel (*kafir*) must become dialectically separated by us from the status of the believer (*mu'min*), for the one is true, the other untrue (*bihaqq al-nasut, bihaqq al-lahut*).

The notion of truth is linked in Hallaj to the universalism of his preaching, in which he affirms his belief that mystic union is founded, not on a resigned adherence to the predetermining body of divine knowledge, but on a passionate abandon to the directive ordering us to do good. *Kufr haqiqi = istitar.* Once having become the whole of the soul, God withdraws from the Soul [Qur'an 6:73]: this is damnation, experienced—the third night of the soul—*stronger* than for Satan, who claims a last look and intends to make use of it in order to resist God; not daring to withdraw from the soul its divine support, Iblis says to Moses: *ibtila'*, not *amr! amr nafsi khafi* (secret directive; mental commandment: an angel cannot receive such a commandment, for he is a pure form, according to the theory of 'AQ Hamadhani and 'Attar)—*kufr wajib 'alayya.*

V. THE LAST HAJJ OF HALLAJ AND THE *WAQFA* OF 'ARAFAT

The Waqfa *of 'Arafat and the Hallajian Teaching on Pilgrimage*

In 632 of our era, with his farewell pilgrimage (his only hajj), Muhammad restored the primitive Abrahamic Pilgrimage, which the Ahmas of Mecca had mutilated, preserving only the *'Umra* in Mecca and a gathering of Quraysh at Muzdalifa. He "made the *'Umra* enter the hajj," according to hadith, and subordinated a tribal ritual to a ceremony "for all people" (*al-nas*). One cannot emphasize enough that this ceremony culminating in three stages, at 'Arafat, Muzdalifa, and Mina, has its summit at 'Arafat: the place where Abraham, according to Shafi'i, became *Khalil Allah.*

Over and above the *wuquf* of Muzdalifa, which is only the maintenance of a secondary and tribal *Ta'rif* (at the Mash'ar) and of the sacrifice at Mina, Muhammad gives absolute priority to the *Ta'rif* at 'Arafat, in a "*hill*" ("free") district, at a time when Mecca, Muzdalifa, and Mina are "*haram*" ("sacralized"). It is the *ikmal*, the moment of the Qur'anic observance's "fulfillment" (Qur'an 5:5), at the time of the suppression of the intercalary calendar, with the Moon pulled back to its initial position (Qur'an 9:36). Turned toward the *qibla*, Muhammad solemnly proclaims the remission of debts of blood spilled and for usurious borrowing, and the right of women to a minimum support; he stops the fast; after a brief prayer that combines *zuhr* and *'asr*, and that has, to begin with, as on campaign (*safar*), only two *rak'a*, he institutes a personal free prayer (*du'a*), a *talbiya* derived from older Arab sources: in which he humbly begs for divine mercy, which is to descend upon him and upon all the believers with a certain "presence" of God, which the cry of the *Talbiya* repeated by everyone summons forth.

Immediately, the believers understood that the essential part of the hajj is 'Arafat ("*al-hajj: 'Arafat*"); it is there, without waiting for the blood of the next day's victims, that God pardons everyone, present and absent (whose names are called out, as in a general mobilization of forces), while taking into account the spiritual declaration by certain individuals, pure and predestined Witnesses (*shuhud*) of a vow made in humble and repentant adoration of the God of Abraham, Who, in order to accept the figurative victims of the next day, is content with the ardent and sacrificial contrition of these Witnesses: and rejoices in it (*yubahi*) with his Angels. Liturgically, the *yawm 'Arafat* takes precedence over Friday (when the two days coincide: every nine years; cf. the priority of Easter over the Sabbath among the Sadducees). Thus, even outside the Hijaz, the *ta'rif* takes precedence over Friday (the custom in Khurasan, against Muslim, Abu Hanifa, and the custom of the Moroccan Jibala); Malik accepts this priority only in the Hijaz (Medina and Mecca). The day of 'Arafat takes precedence over *yawm al-nahr* (Hasan, against Ibn Hanbal), *layat al-qadr* (Jabir-b-'AA, Qastallani against Ibn al-Qayim, Ibn 'Abidin) and the other feast days.

This is the only feast in which the Muslim (once in his lifetime) must offer a free, personal prayer, an offering of himself, which can become an intercession for his brothers (also one is advised to recite on this occasion the "community" prayer of al-Khidr: that of the *abdal*, the apotropaic saints, the seven intercessors, on this particular day, according to 'Ali b. Muwaffaq, one of the masters of AS Kharraz (d. 286), accepted by the Salimiya).

Muhammad, by "restoring," or, rather, by "initiating" the priority of the *ta'rif*, had extended to all believers (for the *ifada* of 'Arafat belonged at that time to another Arab tribe, the Al Safwan-b-Shijna-b-Ka'b, of Tamim) the annual pardon that the Ahmas had restricted to the Quraysh tribe. Hallaj, meditating on this Muhammadian *Ikmal* of Islam, contemplates as a geographical universalization of the "*hill*" site of 'Arafat, in his *waqfa* of 'Arafat (in 290); a universalization of the *qibla* that Muhammad had already transferred from Jerusalem to Mecca (as Jesus at Sichem [at Jacob's well] announced the universalization of the Shechina of Israel, already transferred with the Ark, from Sichem to the Eben of Moria). And he believes that, while transferring the hajj rites into omnipresence, the essential thing is to gain pardon for all people by means of a totally divested prayer of offering, of the kind offered by Muhammad when renouncing himself in the *haram* (under the *ihram*), and saying to God "I am the wretched and the poor begging for help (*mustaghith*) and protection (*mustajir*). . . ." At the place where Abraham, with the same circumcision of heart, gained God's Friendship (*Khulla*), which is, over and above the Law: the pledge of general reconciliation.

His Last Prayer at the Waqfa of 'Arafat

Hallaj uttered this famous prayer during his last hajj, 9 *Hijja*, on this particular day of the *ta'rif* at the culminating hour of the pilgrimage, a little after the '*asr*, when the official *khatib* (usually a qadi, designated by the *amir al-hajj*; was Hallaj designated this year? it is unlikely, even the account by 'Attar excludes the possibility) exhorted the crowd to put itself in the presence of God by means of contrition, and made it repeat the *talbiya*. Hallaj seems to have stayed a little behind on the slope of Jabal al-Rahma, and to have prayed in a very high voice, while the other pilgrims were praying, they too, these two *rak'a* of the *waqfa*, adding to them the names of absent dear ones whom they wish by custom at that time to join in the general pardon that is to descend on the entire crowd.

He said, at 'Arafat: "O Guide of those who are astray (*Dalil al-mutahayyirin*), increase (in You) my wandering; if I am an infidel, make me even more unfaithful." Then, when he saw that each person was praying the *du'a'*, he also turned his face toward the hill *(tellerig* = Jabal al-Rahma), and, when he saw that everyone was returning (to go to Muzdalifa), he also beat (his breast) and cried out:

"O my God, glorious sovereign, I know You are pure, I say You are pure, beyond what Your worshippers do in order to draw near You, beyond what Your unitaries say in order to proclaim You One, beyond the *tasbih* of those who say to You "Glory be to You," and the *tahlil* of those who say to You "there is no god but God," and the concepts of those who intellectually conceive of You, over and beyond what Your friends and Your enemies, combined, say to You. O my God, You have made them build the *waqfa* in positions of powerlessness and then you have demanded of them observances of Power; you know I am powerless to offer You the thanksgiving (*shukr*) that You require. Therefore thank Yourself, Yourself, through me, such is the true thanksgiving."

This solemn prayer, a call for visitation of the divine Spirit in the depths of the heart, assumes its full importance, if one recalls the price that pilgrims attach to two *rak'a* of the *waqfa*, "these two twin doves that quench their thirst only once a year and are thirsty all year long," in the meaning of the *talbiya* for Hallaj (his poem "*Labbayka*" is fulfilled only at 'Arafat), and finally in the meaning of his thesis of the *ta'rif*, which led to his condemnation.

CHAPTER FOUR

In Baghdad: Zealous Preaching
and Political Indictment

I. BAGHDAD

What Baghdad, the Capital of the Muslim World, Was Like when Hallaj Preached There

"He returned very changed, . . . acquired property in
Baghdad, built a home where guests could be
received (*dar*), and began to preach in public a
doctrine only half of which I understood."
(Account of Hamd)

"Therefore come into me so that You can give
thanks to Yourself."
(Hallaj's words at ʿArafat)

"O men, save me from God, who has robbed me
of myself."
(Hallaj in the Suq al-Qatiʿa)

"This doctrine (of the deification of the saint)
attracted to him the veneration of a whole group of
state secretaries, dignitaries of the Court, governors
of imperial towns (*amsar*), and state appanages of
Iraq, Jazira, Jibal, and beyond."
(Istakhri)

"Those who want him dead are the
ministerial scribes."
(Nasr)

With the return from his last pilgrimage to Mecca, the features of Hallaj that
were already so original are silhouetted in full light on the stage of events, at
the center of public life, among elites and throngs both, in Baghdad, that immense, complex and subtle city. As in the case of Bernardino in Sienna and
Savonarola in Florence at the height of the Medici Renaissance, his speech

*From *The Passion of al-Hallaj*, vol. 1, pp. 224–26, 253–71, and 271–303

reorients, for or against him, the cleavage of irresolute or indifferent consciences.

He addressed himself by preference to the people, to the workers of the industrial section of Qatiʿat Umm Jaʿfar, but he accepted also the invitations of rich merchants, like Ibn Harun Mada'ini and Bahran the Zoroastrian, and was present at the home of Abu Tahir of Sawa at a concert at which a *qawwal* was singing (his disciple Faris will not be shy about attending concerts in Nishapur given by the vocalist Hazara). And he met the educated high society: at first in its *halqa* or private circles, in the courtyards of the mosques, especially in the mosque of Mansur (Shibli sat there, in the *qubbat al-shuʿara'*, "the poets' corner"); next at the *majalis* [sing. *majlis*] or conferences organized each week in such and such an educated patron's house (the *hajib* Nasr used to receive traditionists in this way) to hear lectures by learned men (*qurra'*, *muhaddithun*, *fuqaha'*, *lughawiyun*) on religious or profane subjects. Hallaj, though ostracized by the Sufis, continued, as we shall see, to meet with some of them who were connected with the *qurra'* and the *muhaddithun*. These *majalis* were held, either in the libraries of patrons (*dar al-hikma* of the Banu al-Munajjim), or in the homes of leading booksellers, manuscript copyists (*warraqin*: Q. al-Rabiʿ, B. al-Taq), or in the hospitals, such as the Bimaristan al-Sayyida, directed by the celebrated M-b-Zak. Razi, whom Hallaj is supposed to have known; undoubtedly under the auspices of the Queen Mother, Sayyida Shaghab, his patroness—therefore before 296.

This latter name brings us to the threshold of the Court receptions: adjacent to the ruler's receptions, at which normally only his "commensals" (*nudama'*) appeared, certain women of high society received in their salon, separated from their male guests by a light curtain through which their talks could be heard; we know that the Sayyida received Ibn Rawh in this manner. And when these women had remained Christians, like Maryam, the widow of Vizir Qasim ibn Wahb, their superior culture and their greater freedom of movement favored their receptions (in the same way as the Christian secretary of the *qaharmana* Umm Musa). It is very likely that Hallaj was received by some of these women. Hallaj received also in his own home, in his private chapel (*masjid*). The visitors would wait when they found him in the act of praying. He did not have at his disposal a private schoolroom, unless Daʿlaj Sijzi allowed him use of his *waqf* in the Suq al-Qatiʿa.

The surviving documents concerning his public preaching in Baghdad give us only very fragmentary views of the variety and depth of social contacts made by Hallaj, but these imply years of residence in Baghdad. The *Akhbar al-Hallaj* show him during visits with notables, preaching in the *suq* and in the mosques, receiving in his own home, and praying by night in cemeteries.

Baghdad was the chosen site of Hallaj. It is in this city, chosen by him long before, where he intended to bear witness, and where after a long imprisonment, he suffered martyrdom before the fickle crowd that had called him in his early days *al-Mustalim,* "enraptured by God." And, after his death, though the radiance of his thought shone forth in Khurasan, the poetic diffusion of his legend to the far reaches of Islam still kept the names of Hallaj and Baghdad linked together. It is fitting, therefore, to try to grasp, through the topography and statistics, the measurable components of this city's social structure, the different circles penetrated by the Hallajian preaching; to depict the life of the people, the hardship triggered by an outrageous banking and financial system, into which the ʿAbbasid empire was going to sink.

The Caliphal Court

THE GENERAL POSITION OF THE EMPIRE

In this last year of the reign of Muʿtadid, the general position of the Muslim empire, as seen from the capital, was the following: definite progress in territorial restoration, by war and diplomacy. In the west, the Tulunids' dissidence in Egypt was weakening; they were paying tribute. In 284, Baghdad had retaken the Thughur (= frontier fortresses of the Taurus), resuming direct contact with the Byzantine empire, for a holy war interrupted by truces for the exchange of captured prisoners.

In the east, the Saffarids' dissidence in Fars was also weakening, thanks to a military accord with the vassal state of the Samanids of Bukhara, on whom Baghdad counted also to contain the threat of the Daylamites coming from the Caspian, as well as to wage the holy war in Turkestan and India. With the latter region, Baghdad no longer had direct links except by sea.

Over the holy places of Arabia hung a growing uneasiness; the Fatimid conspiracy, already active in Yemen, was spreading there, branching out from the Syrian desert as far as Bahrayn, where the Qarmathians, probably of Qaysanian origin, were not yet affiliated with it.

There were in Baghdad permanent diplomatic representatives (*sahib*), including a Samanid diplomatic representative, Abu ʿAli ʿImran-b-Musa-b-Saʿd ʿImran Marzubani (280, d. *Hijja* 307), Abu Fadl ʿAbbas-b-Shaqiq (329, 331), for eight years a Tulunid diplomatic representative, the pearl expert, Ibn al-Jassas (279–287), and a Saffarid, Abu ʿIsma (265–296 approximately).

The state did not tolerate foreign diplomatic intervention on behalf of the religious minorities among its subjects, and recognized for each group (except for the Zoroastrians) one leader: for the three Christian sects, this was the Nestorian patriarch (*jathaliq*) of Mahuza (Yuwanis 279–288), Yuhanna-b-ʿIsa 288–293, Ibrahim 293–325), who acted in this capacity for the Jacobite patriarch of Antioch (Denys II, 284–297), for the Malphrian sect of Tagrit (Athanasius, 273–291, Thomas), and for the Melchites (suspect, their legate was driven out in 300). For the Jewish sects, it was the orthodox exilarque (*resh. galuth*): Natronai (around 257); his son Hasdai II; 'Uqba (288–307); Dawud-b-Zakkai (307–325), and the two presidents of the Academy, the *goan* of Sora (Shullum 292–299, Yusail 299–312, Yomtob 312–316, Saadia [d. 331] and the *rabban* of Pumbaditha (Kimoi 285–294), followed by the anti-exilarque Karaite (Hezekial, around 357; Hasdai; Solomon).

The *ra'is* of the Manichaeans, after Nasr-b-Hurmuz Samarqandi (d. 260), had had to transfer his center from Babil to Samarqand, the Manichaeans no longer being tolerated except in Samanid regions, because of diplomatic pressure being exerted by the Uyghur peoples and by China. The Sabaeans of Harran had their *ra'is* in Baghdad (Qustas-b-Yahya-b-Zum'a, 265–307); they were threatened with dispersal and massacre in 321.

The Caliphate had no permanent diplomatic representatives beyond the frontiers; for the exchange of captives with the Byzantines, it designated as plenipotentiaries the *walis* of the Thughur and sent occasionally some *safirs* to Byzantium: such as Ibn Abi Sa'dan, a Sufi from Tarsus, a declared enemy of Hallaj.

THE COURT, PUBLIC SERVICES, AND VIZIRIAL DUTIES

The Court, around which revolved the public services, means, on the one hand, the Palace = the *Sada* (the sovereign and his sons, his secretariat and their teachers, the Queen Mother, her parents and her *qahramana*), the grand chamberlain, the harem (and eunuchs), the *imamsalat* of the palace mosque, the guard (*Hars*, with stables, gardens, kitchens, falcon-house, hunting hounds, doctors, torch-bearers [with fuel oil], entertainers), the postal service (*barid wa kharita* = information and official mail: directed by a *mushrif*), the police (*shurta*), registry of markets (*hisba wasuq al-raqiq*).

To which must be added the *nudama'*, or officers admitted to the table of the sovereign, who set the tone of the Court; chosen by the Caliph from among the princes of the royal bloodline (Ibn al-Mu'tazz therefore played a great role under Mu'tadid; after him there were only idlers among them, like Ishaq-b-Mu'tamid), and from among the admirers of literature and art, and connoisseurs of new poetry, exotic curios, sumptuous enclosed gardens, vintage wines from monasteries, beautiful slaves of both sexes, *qiyan*, knowingly chosen by *nakhkhasin*, and the supreme luxury of great singers, especially female singers (*tanburiyat*), who came after the time of Ibrahim-b-Mahdi and Ishaq Mawsili, from two rival schools: that of 'Urayb (186, d. 282), preferred by the Shi'ite party (Ibn Bulbul; letters exchanged between 'Urayb and Ibrahim-b-Mudabbir), and that of Shariya (d. around 265), preferred by Ibn al-Mu'tazz. The poets maintained contact between public opinion and the Court, in a political poetry which was often satiric (Ibn al-Mu'tazz, Buhturi, Ibn al-Rumi, Ibn Bassam, Suli), and which, as a source, is full of valuable information. Beside them, some paid reciters of the Qur'an, like AB M-b-J Adami (born 268, d. 348), pensioned by Mu'nis.

On the other hand, the vizirate and its twelve subordinate departments: finances (*kharaj*): west (Egypt-Syria), east; postal service (*barid*); landed estates (*diyaʿ*); audit of expenditures (*zimam*, court of accounts); war office (*jund*); court of appeal (*nazar al-mazalim*); salary of the military establishment (*mawali wa ghilman* = freedmen and guardsmen); department of expenditures bookkeeping (*zimam al-nafaqat*); official correspondence (*rasaʾil*); seal of official documents (*tawqiʿ*); registration and reception of official documents (*akhtam*); inspection of weights and measures (*ihtisab*). In the third place were the pensioned: the princes of the royal blood, close relatives of the sovereign, crowded together in the Harim Tahiri; the 4,000 other Hashimites, ʿAbbasids, or ʿAlids, directed by a *naqib* (official trustee), guardian of the genealogical register; the representatives of the sovereign at religious functions (Friday prayer in the cathedral mosques, *ifada* of the annual pilgrimage) were chosen from among these ʿAbbasids; the gifts to the confidants of the sovereign; the alms. Finally, the control of the army, which will tend more and more to be independent of the palace and of the vizirate: with parade ground for military reviews at Bab Shammasiya, and palace for its chief, the *amir al-jaysh* (Badr, Fatik, Wasiq, Muʾnis).

The army will guarantee dynastic continuity, from Muwaffaq to Radi (256–329); given the fact that its chiefs, during the Zanj war and the civil war of 277, had committed themselves personally to Muʿtadid and his sons: Badr, Yanis, his son-in-law, close friend of Nasr, Ibn Abiʾl-Saj (temporarily in schism in Armenia), Muʾnis, ʿAjj, Rayiq, Nazuk, Gharib, and Nasr. They were joined by some Tulunid amirs, some rallied supporters, Luʾluʾ, Tughj, Badr Hammani, Ibn Gumushjar, Khaqan, Nujh, and his brother Salama. The frequent outbursts of rivalry between all the military chiefs (between Ibn Kundaj and Ibn Abiʾl-Saf; Badr and Muʾnis Fahl; Tughj, Takin, and Kayaghlagh) did not seriously endanger the loyalty of the army; the Shiʿite party would be able later to triumph over it only by delivering Baghdad up to the Daylamite invader.

The nucleus was formed by the imperial guard (*ghilman khassa*), commanded by two *ustadh*, one of whom was in charge of the *sittiniya* (twenty-five companies, including that of the *hajib*) and the other of the *tisʿiniya* (or *hijariya*, archers). Its officers, for the most part of Turkish origin, together with some renegade Greeks (Gharib, Muʾnis, Yanis, Nasr, Bunayy, Yaqut, Qaysar, Dhuka), supplied the cadres of four other orders of troops: elite mamluks (*mukhtarin*) bearing the name of their first recruiting chief (Bughaʾiya, after Musa-b-Bughaʾ [d. 250], Nasiriya, of Muwaffaq, Masruriya, Bakjuriya, Yanisiya, Muflihiya, Azkutakinya, Kayaghlaghiya, Kundajiya Sajiya); *Nubian guard* (after Saʿid Nubi, d. 314, afterwards Yusuf: comprising also some Zaghawa, some rallied Zanj, and some Berbers); *masaffiya*, regulars recruited at Jannaba and Basra, by Muflih, and commanded by some Caspian and Maghribian officers; police patrol force (*shihna*: recruited by Ibn Abi Dulaf and Ibn Abiʾl-Saj).

Istakhri tells us (*Umara'l-Amsar*) that Hallaj found his staunchest supporters within the circle of high military officials. He had become acquainted with them during his travels, particularly in Mecca, through Amir ʿAjj (who had a garden in Baghdad); the commander-in-chief Badr (who was determined to be buried in Mecca), his son-in-law Yanis, compatriot and friend of Nasr Qushuri, the great patron of Hallaj and of Gharib, brother of the future Queen Mother; the friends of Nasr, his son-in-law Rashiq, Shafi Muqtadiri, A-b-Kayaghlagh; the friends of Ibn ʿIsa, Salama and Nujh Tuluni; (*amir*, Basra, 301); and finally, very close to the Commander-in-Chief Muʾnis, whose feelings [about Hallaj] are not known, the amir Husayn-b-Hamdan, to whom Hallaj dedicated a book prior to 296.

The crisis shapes up as follows, after the reconquest of Egypt (gold):
—*the draining of the treasury by the praetorian guards* (paymaster general of the west [307]): Ibn Hawwari; of the east (310): Niramani. Followed by AY Nawbakhti (315) for both (cf. in Istanbul; the Janissaries increase fom 15,000 [A.H. 945] to 53,000 [A.H. 1119] and from 1 aspre to 7 aspres [A.H. 1115, A.D. 1817], the aspre increasing from 10 [823] to 40, then 80 [1009] and 120 [1102] to the gold ducat. In 1071, on a budget of 603 thousand aspres, the donativum is 203 thousand and the annual cost of the janissaries 300 thousand);
—*guaranty of the deficit by confiscations (tarikat, etc.)*. We know that at the palace, in 309, the Queen Mother defended Hallaj, who was held in favor by her relatives: that is to say, her nephew Harun-b-Gharib, her sister Khatif, the *qahramana* Umm Musa and her brother the *naqib* Ahmad Zaynabi. When and by whom had he been introduced? Some indications make us believe that the Queen Mother defended Hallaj from 301 on, and even as early as 296: the interest that she had in things concerning Mecca may have led her to become interested in him even before that; introduced (to her) by her brother Gharib, rather than by Umm Musa (named in 297) or by Nasr (a prisoner until 296). Because of his incurable disease, Muktafi had formed a liaison with Shaghab even when Muʿtadid was alive; at the death of his rival, the Egyptian princess Qatr al-Nada and Muʿtadid had threatened one day to cut off Shaghab's nose.

As regards the ministers subordinate to the vizirate, the situation is clear; the Hallajians are secretaries in the finance administration, and members, through family connections or politics, of the vizirial group of the B. Makhlad (or the B. al-Jarrah). This smacks of a clan solidarity, and supports our hypothesis about the milieu of clients (converted *mawali*) of the Balharith of Kufa as a familial milieu of Hallaj at Bayda and in Ahwaz. Indeed, the B. Makhlad, of Dayr Qunna, were celebrated by the poet Buhturi as belonging to the Harithi Yemenite clan. Their political fortune was established by two brothers, Hasan (d. 269 in Cairo) and Saʿid (d. 276 at Wasit), in power from 251 to 263, and from 265 to 272. Their party at that time had at its head M-b-ʿAbdun-b-Makhlad, *katib* of the Commander-in-Chief Badr, and his cousins, the B.

al-Jarrah: M-b-Dawud, director of finances (Maghrib, 286–296); allied with a family of tax collectors, the Madhara'iyun (Ahmad-b-Khalid, advisor to Badr; Ibrahim and Hasan): Hamd-b-M Qunna'i, former assistant of Hasan-b-Makhlad, his maternal uncle, had displayed toward Hallaj not only friendship, but veneration; and one other Qunna'i, son of ʿAli Qunna'i (who remained a Christian), M-b-ʿAli, will be arrested as a Hallajian in 309.

This party of the B. Makhlad was composed of Sunnites of recent vintage, professional scribes who came out of the Nestorian Christian schools of Dayr Qunna, greedy, but endowed with a certain ideal of official financial exactness. Those among them who had remained Christian appear to have cherished the hope of a political Islamo-Christian entente, based on the "capitulation" of their forefathers, the Balharith-b-Kaʿb, with the Prophet at Medina, and calling for a kind of legal recognition by Islam of the Nestorian patriarchate (*jathlaqa*) as supreme authority over all the Christians of the *Dar al-Islam*. The conditions included financial autonomy and guarantee of protection for Christian peoples, bound in loyalty to the Muslim state, but released from any military service and from any hindrance to their own way of worship (even for Christians married to Muslims). As for the sincerely Islamized heads of the party, they based their dynastic loyalty on the fact of their belonging to the Harithi clan, "maternal uncles" of the first ʿAbbasid; and, indeed, it was one of them, Vizir Saʿid-b-Makhlad, who had saved the state from the ʿAlid revolt of the Zanj chief.

The party of the B. Makhlad, crushed in 272, had returned to power, from 278 (and 286) to 291, only through the protection of another family of secretaries of state that was Christian in origin and which had been Islamized earlier (but in which the women remained Christian)—the B. Wahb. The latter family's politics, much more limited, aimed simply at consolidating hereditarily the fortunes of the Christian minority (edict of 284), in a state in which the financial system would treat all subjects with more consideration (*Nayruz* postponed to end of June in 282, to permit farmers to harvest before paying the tax, which is why they ran into debt to usurers). . . . This is the policy of financial equity for all that governed the conduct of the most eminent of the B. Makhlad in the vizirate, ʿAli-b-ʿIsa. Although a close relative of Christians, as the incident with the Nestorian patriarch apropos the eucharistic spoon proves, ʿAli-b-ʿIsa ostensibly broke his ties with them (pension to a renegade), but drew his inspiration in his administration from a Sunnite gentleness of spirit that a Christian could understand. (Note the episode of the plaintiffs from Fars; the plan for the general budget of the year 306; the gifts to the Holy Places; and the office of pious donations.)

But against the B. Wahb and the B. Makhlad, a rival party, victorious in 272–278, maintained its position: the Shiʿite vizirial party; founded by Vizir Abu'l-Saqr ibn Bulbul (d. 278), "Father of the Vulture, son of the Nightingale," a curious figure of an Arab Bedouin nationalist who was smitten with Hellenistic science; his party was directed after his fall by his former assistant,

Ahmad ibn al-Furat (d. 291), and by his brother 'Ali (d. 312), two statesmen of consummate skill, ringleaders in a complex game. They themselves were secret heads of a little extremist Shi'ite sect, the Namiriya (future Nusayris), and holders of a considerable fortune; to regain power they were able to unite with the old and powerful moderate Shi'ite family of the B. Nawbakht, the extremist Shi'ite families of tax collectors named by Ibn Bulbul, the Qummiyun, B. al-Fayyad, B. al-Shalmaghan, B. Bistam, Karkhiyun (an Islamized Jewish family), the B. al-Baridi, and the two families of Jewish *jahbadhi* (official bankers) (who were powerful under the Sassanids), the B. Netira and B. Amram, who were threatened by the anti-Semitic tendencies of the B. Makhlad party. The fiscal policy of this party, convinced of the illegitimacy of the "usurper" 'Abbasid state, consisted of entering its service to exploit it to the utmost, believing its ruin could lead to a restoration of 'Alid legitimacy. Their lack of scruples about their fiscal technique of "sweating" enabled them to seduce a court whose women and army were always demanding immediate hard cash.

Not only the trial of 309, but the whole series of proceedings instituted against Hallaj, turned on the social conflict underlying the struggle between these two parties for the vizirate: the crisis of food supply within and the Qarmathian and Daylamite threats without had a direct bearing on the case.

The Life of the People: The Bread Question, Stocking by Bank Speculators, Revolutionary Banditry of the Nomads

To understand the resumption of Hallaj's trial in 309 and the antagonism between Vizir Hamid and his assistant, Ibn 'Isa, who at the time of the Hanbalite outbreak called for a halt to Hamid's frenzy of speculation, we must analyze the problem of daily bread. Though the Roman empire, in the early days of the *pax romana*, was able to distribute wheat from Africa gratuitously to the people of the capital (thereby hastening the ruin of agriculture in Italy), the 'Abbasid empire, continually waging war, within as well as without, was not able to feed Baghdad gratis. The empire had tried to get agricultural manpower cheap, by settling hungry Bedouins and importing black slaves from Zanzibar, but these two categories of workers had united in a terrifying social uprising, which had devastated the whole southern part of Iraq; Basra had been ruined. When Muwaffaq came to power, the rich provinces, Fars and Egypt, were in schism, Mosul threatened to follow suit; the only fertile area that was left, to supplement the Sawad, was Ahwaz, which became, for fifty [years] the center of the imperial economy.

It is in Ahwaz that the new structure of the agrarian system was formulated.

1. At the lowest level, the *fellah*, on the *day'a* (pl. *diya'*), land cultivation: he sows wheat in October (*shatwi*), harvests it at the end of April—beginning of May. He has the obligation to pay in kind, at *Nayruz* (Mu'tadid postponed it to

June 12, for the tax collectors were demanding the tax before the harvesting): land tax (*kharaj*) of 4 dirhams per *jarib* (= 2,160 sq. meters = 1/5 hectare), plus the 12 dirhams in tribute (*jaliya*) per nonconverted male: on an average of 3 per farm: 36 dirhams (or simply the tithe if converted). He was able to keep a margin of one-fifth for the annual family consumption and the seed, if the collector was lenient.

On irrigated alluvial land, 2 *jarib* of land yields 514 kg. of wheat: thus 1 hectare (= 5 *jarib*) yields 3,140 *ratl*. Thus the fellah harvests one *kurr* (= 5,760 *ratl*) of wheat on a plot of about 2 hectares (exactly 18,662 sq. meters).

As he pays in kind, if he cultivates 2 hectares (= 10 *jarib*), he delivers first in wheat (at the rate of 500 dirhams per *kurr*, in A.H. 303), adding it to his land tax, either 460 *ratl* of wheat (valued at 40 dirhams) or 8 percent of the harvested *kurr*. Later he delivers the rest (minus the previously cited margin of one-fifth) to the local administrator, who tries to make him deliver the harvested *kurr* in full, and thereby garners at the minimum 72 percent and generally 90 percent of the harvest. He gets the land assessments (*massah*) revised, he sends the tax collector (*mustakh-rij*) to the fellah with the account sheets, so that the *jahbadhi* may collect the total on the announced day.

2. The *katib al-dayʿa* (= *patwari*, in India), the district tax collector-book-keeper who keeps his register in figures that are deliberately indecipherable (*siyaq*). A tax collector's commission (*marfaq*), at a minimum of 10 percent, might be, at the rate of 500 dirhams per *kurr*, 50 dirhams. For if he is the supervisor of a tax farmer (*damin*), he can keep, for overhead expenses (as in France in 1774), up to 42 percent of the harvest (against payment to the fiscal inspector of an official bribe, for renewal of the rent of the farm, of 3 per thousand: 450,000 pounds in 1774 for 152 million in gross profit). This *katib* is also in charge of loading the harvest on a boat, or the stock in a granary, and of sending (preferably by the official *barid*) the proof of taxes paid to the local banker, carrying it by a bill of exchange, *suftaja sakk* (= *hundi* in India) to the banker of the landowner.

3. The *jahbadhi*, banker, in Baghdad receives the *suftaja* (paper bill of exchange), which he changes into cash, to be handed over to his client, the large landowner, whenever he needs it. When this client is the state, we know that the *jahbadhi*, in speculating on the *suftaja*, is only acting as an agent of the treasury, collecting a sum from receipts provided for in the budget, in accordance with the doctrine conceived by Muwaffaq and inaugurated in Sawad. A-b-al-Furat indicated as much to Ibn ʿIsa, which roused the latter to indignation against what he considered an iniquitous increase in the burdens already put upon the *raʿayas* (ʿAbd al-Hamid was still doing it in 1907, in partnership with an Armenian bank whose officials were going to take 1 percent of their salary). Speculation was therefore carried over to budgetary provisions, and its value fixed; the *jahbadhi* accepted the *suftaja* as representing the payments in kind from the *raʿayas* at the legal rate of 10 dirhams to the dinar; but he deliv-

ered them to the bakers of Baghdad (to take the wheat in the granaries) only at 14 1/2 or 15 dirhams to the dinar. For doing the dirty work of the sovereign, the *jahbadhi* received, as compensation, anywhere from 25 percent (= 8 percent of the total) to 50 percent (agreement with Ibn 'Isa in 301, Ahwaz) of this money gained through speculation.

4. Like the state with its territories and the sovereign with his private landed estates (*diya' khassa*), the large landowners, *muluk al-diya'*, who generally were high officials of the Court, used their banking in such a way as to increase the revenues from the lands that they held by grant (either hereditary [*iqta'*] or for life [*tu'ma*]). Banking speculation enabled them to recoup their losses, and more, from the river transport of grains and their storage in granaries located in Baghdad, either near the two ports (*furda*) or near the mills of the patricians ('*Abbasiya*). Indeed, they actually sold their wheat in this manner, not at the fixed rate of 600 dirhams, but at the forced rate of 725 dirhams (the dinar at 14 1/2 dirhams at the end of 308 instead of 10). They were losing only through the fraud practised by the *katib al-diya'* or, in the case of the harvest contracted by the state, by the *damin*; fraud, it is true, took up to nearly 50 percent of the proceds from the harvest. But, morally, it was banking speculations, more than the tax farms, that killed the economy of the state.

5. The problem still remained of supplying bread to the people of Baghdad. In France (Paris 1860: 33 percent), a limited but adequate living was granted the bakers, *farrana*. It seems that in Baghdad there was little concern for them, although they were obliged to pay the *ghalla*, the completely uncanonical wheat market tax, usually of 2 percent in the Muslim towns. And these bakers, mostly small retailers, *ashab al-ta'am*, tried to increase the selling price of bread in relation to the cost of breadmaking, so as to cover their needs; this was possible in normal times, the *muhtasib* (inspector of markets) as a rule kept a close watch over food produce on which there was no fixed price (free market). But, in times of inflation, the public noticed the slightest increase on the part of the small retailers. And the *muhtasib* had to take the unusual step of fixing a maximum price, *tas'ir*, on bread. If this maximum price was below the purchase rate of wheat, the retailers, working at a loss, gave the signal to riot: in 308, in Baghdad, as in Mosul in 307. In 308, in Baghdad, the banking speculators set the *kurr* rate on wheat (fixed at 50 dinars, equivalent, no longer to 600, but to 725 dirhams) which forced the retail bakers to work at a loss. The loss, amounting to 5 dirhams, came about when the *muhtasib* Ibrahim-b-Batha, trying to ward off the crisis, fixed the maximum price of one dirham per 8 ratl (3 kg. 2) of bread, which gave to the bakers only 720 dirham per *kurr* of bread (with the weight remaining the same). This occurred at the very moment when Hamid, who was both vizir and a tax farmer, intended insanely to have the rate of wheat raised to 55 dinar (thus, given the speculation, to 777.5 dirhams). This meant starvation; and rebellion broke out and prevailed.

THE ROLE OF THE BANKER, *JAHBADHI*

In the first half of the third century of the Hijra, we find individual cases of vizirs, such as A-b-Israyil, complaining that they do not know how to cope with the sudden "recoupments" practised by the Caliphs over their fortunes, commercial deals that individual bankers, like Abu'l-Khayr, could only facilitate privately. This particular banker was a Christian, but the Caliph had expressly remarked to Buhturi, who complained about it, that nearly all the *jahbadhi* authorized by the state were either Jews or Zoroastrians. The Christian bankers, given the proximity of the Byzantines, could, indeed, present a political threat.

Even before the Zanj rebellion, the ʿAbbasid state, in desperate economic straits, had two men of state, Vizir ʿUA-b-Yh Khaqani and the future regent Muwaffaq, who undertook to reconstruct the fiscal situation of the only province near the capital that remained productive in the empire, Ahwaz. According to Tanukhi, it was Khaqani who had the idea of appointing a Jewish banker as *banker of state* to collect all the land taxes of Ahwaz accruing to the state or to the sovereign, and to convert them into cash to be placed at the disposal of the vizir in Baghdad.

Why this new office and this choice? Ahwaz, economically controlled by Jewish merchants, concentrated at Tustar, had already been the theater of an early capitalist reform, affecting its leading industry, that of fabrics. The *bazzazin* of Tustar were probably the earliest ones to have created a luxurious covered market, a *bazzazistan*, or *qaysariya*, a kind of "bonded warehouse," for their expensive fabrics, which guaranteed the circulation of bills of exchange enabling them to enlarge their clientele. These bills of exchange, or *suftaja*, had a standard value, that of a specific material, which served as reference for their price variations of the commodities. The people of Tustar, established in Baghdad, near the Bazzazin of the Siniya (Darb al-Zaʿfaran), in the Karkh district, undoubtedly organized another *qaysariya* there, near the bankers of Dar al-Bittikh, and developed there the ʿAttabi textile industries (Hallaj touched on these matters, because he led some notables [merchants] from Tustar to settle in a body in Baghdad, and preached there in the district of the ʿAttab). A third *qaysariya* appeared in Mosul, where the *Bazzazin* were corporately certified from 307 on; a fourth in Isfahan, where the ʿAttabi textiles had had its own industry.

In two other maritime lands, Ahwaz was at the forefront of the capitalist evolution: for the remote colonial expeditions of the Rahdaniya Jews (secondary center, Siraf); and for inland and coastal water transport of Iraq, which had taken refuge there from Basra.

Even prior to 272, Buhturi made allusion to the officially recognized Jewish hold over the finances of Ahwaz, maintained by the newly Islamized Jews, the

B. al-Baridi (note that the *suftaja* had to be carried by the *barid*). The state banker of that time, *jahbadhi al-Ahwaz,* was Sahl-b-Netira, a member of a very well known Jewish family, collector as early as 247; we know that in 265, at the time of the imprisonment of the B. Wahb vizirial family, he was in a position to supply a revenue (foreseeing their return to power, thirteen years later); and that he did the same, less advantageously, in 278, for Jarada, who was dismissed from office (his chief, Vizir Ibn Bulbul, being unable to supply revenue, because he had already been executed).

The successor of Sahl was the father-in-law of his son Netira-Yusuf-b-Finhas, with whom Harun-b-Irman (with his son Bishr) was officially associated. Their position in the Court (special protocol for the asking) enabled them to intervene decisively, not only in the life of their Baghdadian Jewish community (they collected the tax there; they got the famous R. Saadya named as *gaon*), but also in the fortunes of the ʿAbbasid empire. It is certain that they made a choice, even prior to Muqtadir, between the two rival political parties for the vizirate: for the B. al-Furat, against the B. al-Jarrah. Indeed, their *suftaja* from Ahwaz made it possible for them to provide the money for the monthly pay of the Baghdad garrison; and as the donativum was large in 295 due to the proclamation by Muqtadir, the leaders of the *coup d'état* of 296 on behalf of Ibn al-Muʿtazz continued, after twenty-four hours, to appeal to two bankers of the Court for the troops' wages; but in agreement with Ibn al-Furat, they refused. This simple refusal of credit brought about the fall of Ibn al-Muʿtazz and reestablished Muqtadir, with Ibn al-Furat in the vizirate. Having become vizir in 306, Ibn ʿIsa had to compromise with them in order to get the cash, at the beginning of each month, to pay the troops in Baghdad, conceding to them, per contra, a part of the revenues from Ahwaz (the banking management which they already controlled) and the monthly revenue from Wasit (farmed out to Vizir Hamid). Were the two bankers working from that time onwards to get Ibn al-Furat returned to the vizirate? In any case, in 306, I believe rather that, through Akh Abi Sakhra, a former assistant to Ibn Bulbul, and a friend of Ibn al-Furat, they encouraged Hamid and Masmaʿi (known for this same tendency, tax farmer of Ahwaz as early as 304) to draw still more revenues (600,000 dinars more), the greatest portion of which came from Ahwaz, in spite of the opposition of Ibn ʿIsa and of Nuʿman.

The association of the two state bankers lasted, with the same prerogatives in the Court and in Ahwaz, until 317, at the time of the *coup d'état*, which emptied the coffers of the state and of the sovereign. Ahwaz, furthermore, after 316, had passed under the fiscal supervision of the Banu Baridi, and they made two new *jahbadhi al-Ahwaz* whom they chose, Ismaʿil b. Salih, and a second Sahl-b-Netira, the grandson of the first, as their autonomous agent, independent of the Court. They put [the latter] to death in 329.

The Common People of Baghdad; Typology
of This Collectivity as Seen through Its Proverbs

In each period of cultural maturity, the great cities of a state find themselves assuming a kind of psychological, or rather typological, personality, which records the mutual contrast within their world by means of proverbs. These proverbs, often representing keen value judgments, make known the probable average opinion by evaluations suggestive of actual accounts: and their total body constitutes a useful and concise, if semiconvinced and semiironic, handbook of customs and social relations. In the third century of the Hijra, Arabic literature created in this manner, retrospectively, a somewhat caricatured and exaggerated image (*mathalib*, more than *mafakhir*) of the ancient tribes of Arabia, the classes of Muslim urban society, and, finally, the great cities or *amsar*. They represent a rather stylized and lively decor (but accepted by those affected by them, even when the written comments of commercial travellers ridiculed them altogether); this is essential in order to understand the public addressed to by the Hallajian preaching.

Ibn al-Mubarak, perhaps the first to represent them in this way, had briefly characterized cities: (before Baghdad came into being) by the six condemnable tendencies deviating from the sunna: Kufa, by rebellious schism (*rafd*); Damascus, by the deadly sword (*sayf*); Basra, by the man who wants to determine his destiny (*qadar*) on his own; Khurasan (Marw), by the man who overestimates the divine indulgence accorded him (*irja'*); Mecca, by the spirit of trade (*sard*); and Medina, by the spirit of hoarding treasure (*ghina*).

Fifty years before Hallaj, Jahiz had already said that Baghdad was typified by its magnanimity, Kufa its beautiful speech, Basra its hand-craftsmen, Cairo its trade, Rayy its disloyalty, Nishapur its uncouthness, Marw its dirtiness, Balkh its arrogance, and Samarqand its industry. And fifty years after Hallaj, the geographer Muqaddasi stated, with a picturesque and biased attention to detail, that the people from Ahwaz were considered indolent and degenerate, those from Fars skillful and practical in trade, those from the Maghrib ungainly and uncouth. As for the *amsar*: in Medina misery prevails, in Mecca a haughty greed, in Jerusalem concern for honor and good morals, but little knowledge; in Cairo the character is affable and conciliatory, credulous and soft, disposed to luxury and to recitations of the Qur'an, to a taste for strolling, white bread, and wine; in Isfahan it is Jewish avarice, conjugal infidelity, luxury in clothes and pottery; in Rayy keen intelligence; in Nishapur, city of leading families and good craftsmen, where ignorant preachers and macrobites are found in profusion; in Damascus an ascetic piety combines with turbulence; in Balkh good jurisconsults; in Kufa just weights; the people of Homs are dull, those of Wasit harebrained, and those of Basra irascible. In Baghdad, lastly, where life is short, the distinction of becoming manners (*zarafa* and *muruwwa*) in the capital blends with a penetrating, but treacherous intelligence (cf. "*al-'Iraq nifaq*"), one that is iniquitous and amoral.

Within the Baghdadian population, each social class, and each profession in its turn, is satirically distinguished by brief descriptions recalling its professional vices. Some descriptions are of the general human sort: slander by the religious, biased unfairness on the part of judges, perjuries by witnesses, larcenies by trustees and servants, cheating and false weights by retailers, drugs falsely represented or poisoned by doctors and apothecaries, persecution from tax excise men, extortions from policemen. . . .

Others emphasize the very curious list, so well preserved by Shi'ites, of the "professions that damn": blacksmith, butcher, conjuror, policeman, highwayman, police informer, night watchman (alone at night with the dogs of the markets and the streets; except if he is at the frontier or in a *ribat*), tanner, maker of wooden and leather pails, maker of women's shoes, burier of excrement, well digger, stoker of baths, felt-maker, masseur, horse trader. To these are added the weavers, the ironsmiths, the pigeon racers, and chess players.

Even within the urban scholar class, the *'ulama'* especially, the features of the schools revealed themselves through collections of discriminating psychological character sketches, a summary of which Muqaddasi has left us, in a list of satirical common sayings. Among the jurisconsults, the Hanafite, very conscious of being an official, appears deft, well-informed, devout, and prudent; the Malikite is dull, obtuse, confines himself to the observance of the Sunna; the Shafi'ite is shrewd, impatient, understanding, and quick-tempered; the Zahirite is haughty, irritable, loquacious, and well-to-do; the Mu'tazilite is elegant and erudite, free-thinking and ironic; the Shi'ite, entrenched in his old rancor, is intractable, enjoys riches and fame; the *muhaddith* (Hanbalite), anxious to practice what he preaches, is active, almsgiving, and inspiriting; the Karamite is pious, partisan, avaricious, and predatory; the man of letters (*adib*) is frivolous and vain, clever, and pompous; the Qur'an reciter (*muqri'*) is greedy, sodomite, vainglorious, and hypocritical.

Glancing through the little collection entitled *Risalat al-amthal al-Baghdadiya al-'ammiya*, in which AH Talaqani, Hanafite qadi of Balkh, assembled in 421/1030 the popular Arab proverbs of Baghdad, summarizing the appearance of manners in the capital in the preceding century, one can study the effect of the Baghdadian character in the time of the Hallajian preaching on aspects of the Muslim faith, through expressed popular judgments. Those latter concern everyday ethics, the manner in which one fulfills his canonical obligations, prayer, and especially pilgrimage, and, finally, the different shades of adherence to the revealed text, to the Qur'an, to its verses on the prophets, the angels, and the Last Judgment.

As for ethics, the lowest level is an ironic acceptance of the worst: "worship the monkey when he is powerful" (90); "the slave is the one who has none" (66); "if you have no *shaykh*, buy yourself one" (447); "when power is fair, subjects abuse it" (40); "rather the abuses of power than the fairness of subjects"(186); "intentional forebearance on the part of the qadi is worth more than two trustworthy witnesses" (319); "the watcher is worth as much as the pot" (14); "they accused the ironsmiths and then imprisoned the blacksmiths" (26); "if you are an anvil, suffer; if you are a stick, make someone suffer" (43); "I am the color of time, like the dyers cord" (53); "if one has to be put in chains, let the rust be rubbed off" (84); "irrigate with water this canal of yours, and eat while you work" (84); "more middleman than a good piece of silver" (97); "I drew him to the *mihrab* (to pray), he drew me toward rubbish (to fornicate)" (102); "the average quality is sister to the bad" (113); "already the top of the cask is the dregs" (121); "our misfortune comes from us" (134); "with the dates come the wasps" (156); "your appeal is made to mercilessness" (161); "he approached me with a beardless face and a coat the color of ashes" (184); "to be hungry, at school, with a blind teacher" (185); "in our house you are worth as much as a wet dog in the mosque" (189); "paradise, where the pigs are fed" (192); "of one of his ears, he makes a garden, and of the other a hippodrome" (= he does not listen to the sermon) (193); "threaten him with death before he resigns himself to fever" (220); "a eunuch who's 100 years old seems 60" (221); "the cat who has learned how to lift the lid off the cooking pot can no longer do without it" (263); "he cooked his fish on the fire of this conflagration" (276); "a companion of passage goes his own way" (281); "two slaps in the face for a robe of honor" (286); "they granted him oil for his candle" (287); "the street of the bald leads to the merchants of high hats" (306); "a foreign guest approaches the innkeeper of falsehood" (327); "the executioner flies into a rage against the condemned man" (331); "Pharoah who preaches to Moses" (335); "he fled, let God punish . . . is better than: he got himself killed, let God have mercy on him" (336); "he gave up borrowing and rolled himself up in a mat" (370); "by dint of growing old, one becomes worse" (397); "sow [a seed]; God grant, it will germinate 'perhaps' " (422); "without attachment to his country, the country of evil would perish" (437); "a fugitive who blows the trumpet" (450); "who will testify for the bride? her mother, who will add an oath on it" (466); "what the thief had left behind has been taken by the detective" (470) "he who is not pleased with the government of Moses has to be pleased with that of the Pharoah" (512); "he who conquers, plunders" (514); "his mouth praises God, and his hand cuts the throat" (515); "the dog finds his happiness in the misfortune of the family" (521); "woe to the strong between two weak men" (525); "he lines up with God against the vanquished" (545); "don't end up teaching the orphan to weep" (568); "the eclipse does not come without any earthquake" (570); "don't trust the edict, if the vizir deceived you" (573); "don't do good, and evil will not befall you" (579); "be not as the grasshopper, who eats what if finds, and is eaten by who finds it" (588); "as regards sins, (he dares not sin but) he is proud to be suspected" (602).

Of the religious obligations, pilgrimage especially is mentioned, with some unmalicious barbs of irony: "you are part of the biscuit of Fayd" (21) (dry biscuit eaten by the pilgrims at the last stop of the return); "he is like the Ka'ba; he receives visits, and does not pay them back" (342); "they will not see him shave his head at Mina" (236); "Mecca suits only the one who brings faith to it or his purse" (462).

Finally, the proverbs that touch even on the use of the Qur'an in prayers show us the point of insertion, in popular paractice, of certain arguments of the Hallajian *khutab*: "What is there about 'Tabbat' (= Qur'an 111) that can arouse fear in the *jinn*?" (514); "to recite 'Say: God is the Only One' (= Qur'an 112) is not the act of those initiated into the mystery of Y and S (= initials of Qur'an 36)"; or, according to the Maidani variant, "to recite in supererogation (= *sharifata*) 'Say: God is the only one' will not make you one of the initiates into the mystery of Y and S" (437a); a Shi'ite argument ("initiates" = the 'Alids) that Hallaj uses against Shi'ism ('initiates" = the holy ascetics); which confirms the proverb preserved by Maidani *"rudda min Taha ila bis-millah"* = he has been reduced from the rank of the initiates in T and H (= initials of Qur'an 20), to the (common) level of "in the Name of God"; "to love and to be unhappy makes one even more in love" (496). Finally, some of them dealt with relations between master and disciples: "he already made him pay his Thursday" (Thursday is the day off in the *maktab*, and students give the master a gift for his meal: (380); "more stupid than a teacher in the Qur'anic school."

Others allude to instigators of brawls: "a slap in the salon is not an aggression by a Daylami": an excuse invoking the unexpected (285); "he has his soup boiled, and lives comfortably": which is the source of the name given by the Iraqi bandits *shuttar* to those who do not belong to their brotherhood "*tharidiyun*," "those who have their soup" (283.) Abi, contemporary of Talaqani, left us some interesting details about the remarks of the Baghdadian *shuttar*, particularly on Hallaj's profession. For example, the following dialogue between two *shatir*: "Even though your two feet were settled on Mount Qaf, and your two hands on Gemini, you will remain a *hallaj* (a carder)"—"and you, even though you would grasp the rainbow in your hand, you will remain a *naddaf* (a comber)." We shall examine later, with regard to the *futuwwa*, the popular devotion of the Baghdadian Sunnite bandits for Hallaj.

II. PUBLIC PREACHING IN BAGHDAD

The Definitive Features of Hallaj's Apostolate

After his return from his second long journey, at the time of his third pilgrimage, Hallaj's already very original traits begin to assume their definitive character, after a slow but steady evolution.

To the strict interior, ascetic, and moral discipline of Sahl Tustari, was added first the traditional knowledge of the orthodox Sunna, from those Sufi *ahl al-hadith* who were particularly devoted to the Prophet, such as Makki, Junayd, and Ibn 'Ata'. The mystic experiences of his interior life led Hallaj to choose from among the traditions of the Sunna those that allude more particularly to the life of renunciation and fervent humility; an overflowing faith incited him to preach in public those rules of life that he had found beneficial for himself, and he did this among his Muslim brothers and even among the idolators, among the great as well as the lowly. But up to this point his personality does not contrast completely with the profiles of other traditionists with mystic leanings; his freedom of behavior is not unique; and the same use that he made of concepts from Greek logic is found in two others, Tirmidhi and Kharraz.

Perhaps one thing begins to separate him clearly from the others: the unusual number of people who turn to him as to a savior, who write him letters in which they call him "the one who feeds," "the one who can discern," "the one who is enraptured in God." And, parallel to this outpouring of profound feeling for him, there are numerous miracles that people attributed to him.

The miracles attributed to earlier Sufis, by Ibrahim ibn Adham to Dhu al-Nun, by Bistami to Tustari, are wonders performed in a select gathering among initiates: and cited in much later accounts. Those that are reported about Hallaj had occurred in public. And this is what begins to amaze and shock his contemporaries.

Only then does the figure of Hallaj stand out in its definitive form. Returning to Baghdad from his third pilgrimage, he was "very changed," his son Hamd notes, meaning very different from the way he had been up to then. "He acquired a piece of property, built himself a house on it, and began to preach to the inhabitants a doctrine (ma'na) that I only partly understood. The jurisconsult Muhammad ibn Dawud, together with several other 'ulama', denounced this preaching; and they cast aspersions on his attitude of mind. [Vizir] 'Ali ibn 'Isa attacked him because he had converted (the chamberlain) Nasr Qushuri; and Hallaj was disowned by Shibli and other masters in mysticism. Some said: he is a sorcerer; others said: he is a madman; still others said: no, he has the gift of miracles and his prayer is answered [by God]. Tongues wagged about his case so much and so effectively that the Sultan had him put in prison."

What is the character of this new preaching? He has come from Mecca, where he had spent two years in solitude. And it was there that he found the expression of the perfect life, and the goal of mystic theology. In the prayer of his last vigil in 309, he will say to God: "It is You who have assigned to this present witness (= Hallaj) from Your divine essence, a certain ipseity (huwi, in order to speak of You in the first person; while relating Your traditions, Riwayat). . . . And it is You who have taken my essence to serve You as a symbol (among men), when, showing me in the last of my states, you have come to proclaim my Essence (= You, my Creator) through my (created) essence. . . ." It is this second and definitive election that characterizes the last period of Hallaj's public life. His enemies, the Imamites, have noted his progression well; at first, he usurped the right of da'wa, public preaching, reserved to the only *na'ib* (representative) of the Shi'ite Imam; he assumed the right to decree rules of worship, reserved to the Imam himself; finally, on his last pilgrimage, he assumed the right of commanding *like* God, the sovereign authority, *rububiya*, which belongs only to God, who has not even delegated it to His prophets.

At the height of his sanctity, in the consummation of divine union, the saint is more than a prophet entrusted with an exterior mission to fulfill, delegated with a law whose observance he is sent to put into effect; the saint who has perfectly united his will with the will of God is in everything and everywhere interpreting directly the essential will of God, and participating in the divine nature, "transformed" in God. We shall study later in more detail the very interesting theological form given by Hallaj to this conception. From all accounts it appears that he was driven to apply it in his conduct, to preach it by example, before formulating it in theory.

It is already set forth in the public prayer (*khutba*) that he performed in Mecca, on his farewell pilgrimage, the ninth day, 9 *Dhu'l-Hijja* 295/907, at Mount 'Arafat, before the assembled pilgrims: "O Guide of those who have gone astray!" he cried out, from the top of a hill: then, beating his chest: "Glorious King, I know You to be transcendant, I speak to You above all the *tasbih* of those who have said to you: 'Glory be to You!' above all the *tahlil* of those who have said to you: 'There is no god but God!' above all the concepts of those who have conceived of You! O my God, you know I am powerless to offer you the thanksgiving (*shukr*) that You must have. Come therefore into me to give thanks to Yourself, that is the true thanksgiving! there is no other."

This is that double affirmation that the dogmatic theology of Hallaj will develop, and which his preaching will set forth: the pure divine transcendence and presence of God by His grace in the just souls that this presence sanctifies through the rites of worship. The negative asceticism of the soul recommended by Junayd is only a preparation; the delirious intoxication noted in Bistami is not the true and lasting presence of God in the mystic. In the essence of union (*'ayn al-jam'*), all the acts of the saint remain coordinated, voluntary, and deliberate, by his intelligence, but they are entirely sanctified and divinized. The effect of divine unity is not the destruction of the mystic's personality, by crushing it with rites (*sabr, sahw*) or disengaging it through ecstatic intoxication (*sukr*); divine unity perfects it, consecrates it, exalts it, and makes it its own free and living agent.

Such is the ultimate discovery, and the final message presented in Hallaj's intense preaching after 295/907. He cries out his joy at having reached, and having in his possession, "the One who is at the heart of ecstasy," beyond the cult of restraint that leads some to ossify in their strict observance, beyond the cult of enthusiasm that inspires others to work themselves into ecstasy through created objects and human means; the outcome of these practices is the idolatrous destruction of one's individuality at the feet of an indifferent divinity. But the true mystic, according to Hallaj, does not end up that way. The divine union in which it is consummated is the amorous nuptial in which the Creator ultimately rejoins his creature, in which He embraces him and in which the latter opens his heart to his Beloved in intimate, familiar, burning, and flowing discourse. The conversation becomes continual between him and this divine Converser whom he possesses at the very core of his being, using with Him the "You and I," relating all to him and offering Him everything: sufferings, desires, sorrows, and hopes. There is no Arab mystic whose passionate language is both more ardent and more pure than Hallaj's; no transposition of symbols of profane love occurs in it to confuse the impulse.

The Baghdad Public and the Scene of His Preaching

Hallaj, upon returning to Baghdad, must again have found some supporters there, the same ones who had nicknamed him al-Mustalim, "the one who is enraptured in God." It seems likely that if the "Tustariyin" section, which was established on the right bank of the Tigris, between the Sunnites of Bab Basra, the residence of the Hashimites, and the Shi'ites of Karkh, near Bab Muhawwah, had sheltered from 292/904 onward the notables from Ahwaz whom he had at that time persuaded to come to Baghdad, it was there, among them, that he returned to settle, to build his house, and move his wife and his young son Hamd. The people of Tustar were traders in cotton fabrics and brocade (dibaj); it is possible that Hallaj had returned, among them, to the occupation of a carder.

In any case, all of the first-hand accounts present him to us as preaching and praying on the right bank of the Tigris, around this Tustariyin section; in the mosque (of Mansur) in the Round City; in the 'Attab masjid the Suq al-Qati'a, the central market of the Qati'at Umm Ja'far, the former fief of Sultan Zubayda; in Karkh's Bayn al-Surayn street; in Khan al-Jabbana; on the so-called tombs "of the Martyrs," maqabir al-Shuhada', in the Quraysh cemetery; Qabr ibn Hanbal; and Bab Khurasan. He used to preach while walking from 'Attab masjid (textile quarter, "attabin") to the Suq al-Qati'a (= Qati'at Umm Ja'far) and to his masjid (converted into a jami' mosque, A.H. 379: if this is the one belonging to the (Qallayin?). The Qati'at Umm Ja'far revolted in 308 against Hamid; next in 353 and 389 (some 'Alids had settled at the time in this Sunnite district); 'Attabin is the district of Ibn Sam'un (between him and Harbiya, is the Khindiq). It is also on the right bank that his maslib will be shown and that his tomb will be built. To what audience did he speak? As we shall see, he accepted invitations to the homes of important people. Two army commanders in favor at Court, Ibn Hamdan and Qushuri, were on friendly terms with him; he dedicated treatises to them both, and the second became converted by him. Rich merchants like Mada'ini received him; he even accepted the alms gift of a Zoroastrian, Bahram.

But he spoke, by preference, to the masses; and this occurred in the markets, at the entrance to mosques, and was in the form of an improvised talk, both reasoned and spontaneous, argumentative and lively, a sort of "ecstasy of jubilation" unfolding itself before the crowd; a clairvoyant rapture, without any insane outburst of gestures or words. He undoubtedly continued to preach contrition and to practice a life of renunciation; but he was called above all to witness his joy in divine union, to proclaim it aloud.

The Baghdad public gladly stopped to listen to him. What did it really think of him? His son reported as follows: they called him "a magician or a possessed man"; but others defended him, saying: "he has the gift of miracles, and his prayer is answered."

Hallaj's public preaching in Baghdad singled him out in the public eye along with Hanbalite popular preachers (qussas) and Shi'ite criers (na'ihat), whose impudences Mu'tadid had tried to curb by edict in 284 (cf. the edicts of 334, 367, 398). They were viewed just like the satiric poets whose barbs the highest placed personages feared (for example, Mu'tadid himself with respect to the verses by Ibn Bassam against his mistress, Durayra): comparable to the controversial exposés of our scandal sheets. Like his friend Shibli, recognized both as a poet and a mystic, Hallaj must have had more than one professional reciter to present orally (rawiya) his poems in prose and verse in the public squares, just as there must have been qawwal (singers) to intone them in private performances; there must have been also a warraq ("publisher": both stationer and head of the copyist shop in which the mustamli or "repeaters" who were accredited by the master were authorized to dictate) at whose shop people could buy his works.

The poetry of the street and of the salon in Baghdad thrived on violent controversies; Hallaj himself had put into verse a sarcastic eulogy of the esoteric discipline professed by Sufis (after having himself broken with it) and a rawi had taken it down from his dictation in Kufa. Ma'arri will later collect in Baghdad an anti-Hallajian satiric piece written in Hallaj's lifetime. A short Shi'ite poem in Persian preserved by 'Abbas Qummi and satirizing both Ma'ruf Karkhi and Mansur Hallaj (in adjacent tombs) seems to be a faithful echo of the sneering versified insults that Hallaj suffered in his lifetime: "if to be a man of God is to be a potter, then be assured that the worker Ma'ruf Karkhi is one; and if having froth at the mouth proves that one is raised to the throne of God, then be assured that the camel Mansur Hallaj qualifies."

This skeptical and submissive population loved and venerated the Sunnite traditionists; it had given Ibn Hanbal a majestic funeral, and its attitude will force the vizir to release Ibn 'Ata' (309/922) for fear of an uprising. The people loved and venerated Hallaj, they preserved the cult of his memory, but it seems that his last preaching did not immediately arouse them. They were already beginning to suffer from the economic and social crisis which, starting in 308/921, with the outbreaks and spasmodic panics mentioned by Hamza

Isfahani (he mentioned eighteen such from 308/921 to 320/932), will lead to the destruction of the temporal power of the Caliphs, and bring on the local kingship control by the (Persian) Buwayhids (in A.D. 945).

The place where Hallaj withdrew at night to pray, during his last period of preaching, and where he counseled his disciples to make ten-day retreats of fasting and prayer, was a secluded corner of the great Quraysh cemetery, called the *maqabir al-Shuhada'*, the tombs of the "martyrs." It seems this was the way that the pure Sunnites, the ahl al-hadith of Baghdad, honored the four great Khurasanian victims of the Mu'tazilite inquisition, the martyrs for the "uncreated word" of God—Ahmad ibn Nasr, executed in 231/846, Ahmad ibn Hanbal, flagellated in 219/834, and their companions Ibn Nuh and Ibn Hammad, who died in prison for the same cause. Ibn Hanbal was buried nearby.

This fact is very important. First of all, it shows that Hallaj believed that his doctrine concerning the permanent participation of the just, who were sanctified by the mental speech of God (*kalam nafsi*), was only the outgrowth of the protest of Ibn Hanbal proclaiming his deep faith in the uncreated Qur'an. Recalling the devotion of Hallaj for Ibn Hanbal, it explains further why the Hanbalites of Baghdad have had men among them who were staunch defenders of Hallaj, to the point even of endangering themselves: Ibn 'Aqil and Ibn al-Ghazzal.

The following is an account of Hallaj's prayers in this place:

Account by Qadi Ibn Haddad taken from Abu Husayn Basri:

> I went out one night in the moonlight to pray at the tomb of Ibn Hanbal (May God bestow His Mercy upon him!) and I saw there, from a distance, a man standing, turned toward the *qibla*. I came up to him without his seeing me, and I saw that it was Husayn ibn Mansur Hallaj (May God bestow His Mercy upon him!). He was weeping, and saying: "O you, who have intoxicated me with Your love, and let me wander through the esplanade of Your nearness, You are the Only One, in the loneliness of Eternity, You are the Only One to witness You, from the height of 'the throne of truth'; Your testimony is justice, without Your actually balancing; Your being far away is damnation, without Your actually stepping aside; Your presence is Your knowledge, without Your moving at all; Your absence is the *veil* (of the *name*) conferred without Your leaving. And nothing is above You that casts a shadow on You, nothing below that supports You, nothing before that limits You, and nothing behind that overtakes You.
>
> "I beseech You, out of respect for this sacred possession that You bestow upon me and for the even higher degrees I am asking from You, do not return me to myself, after having robbed me of myself; do not show me my soul now that You have robbed it from me; increase the number of my enemies in Your cities, and the number of those among Your faithful who clamor for my death!"
>
> When he saw me, he turned and smiled; then he came to me, and said: "O Abu al-Husayn! The state that I am in is indeed only the first degree of novices!" And

I said to him: "How can you say that, O Shaykh! that this state is the first degree of novices? What mystic state could be higher than that one?" And he said: "I have lied, it is barely the first state of the ordinary faithful, not even that: it is the first state of infidels." And he uttered three cries, fell down, and blood came out of his mouth: he made me a sign with his hand to go away, and I left immediately. The next morning, I saw him in the mosque of Mansur. He took me by the hand, and, taking me aside, said to me: "For God's sake! don't tell anyone what you saw me do yesterday."

His Visits to Baghdad's "Upper Class"

Urban civilization is born and expands at meeting places, in markets, sanctuaries, courts, and public gardens. But its elite, its high society, which alone makes possible the flight of artistic and scientific thought, gathers, according to its affinities, in the most restricted circles, *majalis, halqat,* circles, and salons of informed amateurs, educated appreciators, high officials, the newly rich in the worlds of finance and the military, Hashimite nobles or important Islamized landowners. This process had begun in Medina, with the "conscription" of young women who had had multiple divorces (*murdafat*) into the rollicking harems of the grand *sahaba* (Asma-bt-ʿUmays, Umm Kulthum-bt-ʿUqba-b-Muʿayt, ʿAtika-bt-Zayd-b-ʿAmr-b-Nufayl . . .) and with the introduction each spring of young men (*maʿrid ghilman al-Ansar*) into the prescribed civic "fraternization" (*taʾakhi*) between Muhajirun and Ansar (Muʿadh-b-Jabal, Jarir-b-ʿAA Bajali, Usama-b-Zayd, Dihya, Qays-b-Saʿd, Malik-b-Anas, ʿAmr-b-Hamz).

Afterwards, it became specialized, with the selection of a class of performers, professional idols of beauty, dream-like creatures, supposed to stimulate people's desire for aesthetic diversion, slaves of both sexes trained for a long time in song and dance, and even learnedly initiated in the art of literary improvisation, by slave-trading experts (*nakhkhasin*), who knew how to stage luxurious festivals at lavish costs. Like an anticipated paradise offered to table guests (*nudamaʾ),* complete with foods, flowers, *huri,* and *ghilman:* the beauty of the human face was unveiled so that the ultimate ideal meaning might be read in it; an unveiling that, too often, ended up, by offering itself to all, only to destroy, through the lure of the feminine face, natural family relationships, and to degrade, through the brilliance of the virile face, intellectual relationships.

These traders, *nakhkhasin,* together with their troops of male and female performers, went from Medina, *qiyan hijaziyat* (Janila, ʿAzzat al-Mayla, Salamat al-Zarqa), to Basra, then to Baghdad, some, like ʿAbd al-Malik ibn Ramin, even daring to lead them on the hajj to Mecca.

Loose women, looking, or even conversing, from behind a screen or peering over the top of a booth, "*maqsura,*" could join the men attending these gatherings.

We know that in 360/971, in Baghdad, there were 580 of these *femmes de luxe* (120 freed and 460 slaves), and 95 *ephebi* "de luxe." Having the monopoly on the art of mimes (*muqallidun*), the male performers soon constituted the majority of this social class; it suffices to recall, for Turkish Istanbul, the "*shehir-engiz*" of Mesihi, and the eleven teams of *lu'bebazan* (= around 3,000 ephebic performers) censured around 1050/1640 in Istanbul by Evliya.

But in Hallaj's time, the two sexes were almost equal in number, and the "*femmes de luxe*" were prized, like certain pallacides or Greek hetairia, for their literary abilities (we still have some letters from 'Urayb [d. 282] to her friend, the banker Ibrahim-b-Mudabbir; we know also of Mutayyan, the Baghdadian "madonna of the violets" (cf. Jeanne de Loynes), and Bad'a [d. 302]). As for the young men, they were not slaves, nor freed mamluks (like Ayaz, the freedman of Mahmud Ghaznawi, whose tomb I have visited in Lahore; he was Lahore's first amir), but mostly young artist singers (Jahza) or poets (Abu'l-'Atahiya and Abu Nuwas began their careers in this way, at the cost of their masculine purity, in the exhibitionism of salons).

The unacknowledged ideal of Baghdadian high society at that time was the search for ecstasy: in the presence of an image of beauty that transfigures the human form and illuminates divine meaning. This is what is meant by the *shahid*, the "present witness," who verified the fact that God *is*.

This is the source of the idea of pure profane love, of *hubb 'udhri*, an idea originating among the Yemenites, and combined, at the time of Hallaj's preaching, with the philosophers' concept of platonic love, by a Baghdadian jurisconsult, the young head of the Zahirite rite, Ibn Jami', a refined uranite. This idea was in vogue in the salons of Baghdad.

Certain mystics, specifically evoked (without names) by Ibn Dawud in his *Kitab al-zahra*, like Abu Hamza, Abu Hulman, and Nuri, believed at that time that it was possible to transmute uranism into divine love, to harden the look of the lover to the point of making him see God through his tears drenching the created face of the beloved. But, in order for the *shahid* not to be a deceiver, he must not wear the mere theatrical, temporary mask of the actor; rather he must capture in the voice of his heart, offered and given, the unimaginable Presence. Bistami expressed desire for the Presence. Shustari repeated this desire.

This superintelligible Presence is what Shibli believed he perceived and saw again in 309, personified in the human form of Hallaj, in the mosque of al-Mansur, on the day when "*Ana'l-Haqq*" was uttered. Indeed it must be admitted that, during his visits to the Baghdadian salons of Mada'ini, Sawi, Bahram, even more than in the markets, Hallaj was boldly offering to manifest this Presence. The scandal of his bearing witness in this way was tempered by the desire he expressed to die accursed for the whole body of believers to whom he exposed himself. It brought on the legal condemnation of the *shuhud*, "professional witnesses," of the canonical court, who were stirred up against him by Ibn Dawud in particular.

Hallaj, the Crafts Question, and the Social Crises of His Time

It is probable that, even after assuming his mystic vocation, Hallaj, like many other Sufis, returned each time that he needed to earn his living to the manual trade of his father, which had been that of a cotton carder. The profession of cotton carder had led them both to Ahwaz, a warm and irrigated region, where, because of the export of cotton fabrics, there was an increase in the number of cotton plantations in the countryside and of weaving shops in the towns. The proletariat that had emerged because of this industry reacted sympathetically to the slave revolt of the Zanj; and the upper middle-class Karnaba'i family, at least one member of which (perhaps the brother-in-law of Hallaj) became a Hallajian, rallied to the cause of the insurgents. Which proves that this rebellion, stemming from the hunger and despair of colonized laborers transplanted by slave traders as diggers for rebuilding canals and dams (*kassahin*, extracting saltpeter), had found some echo among the underfed craftsmen of the towns, and even higher up.

The repression of the Zanj had coincided with a reorganization of the ʿAbbasid state, in which the regent, Muwaffaq, on the advice of his many financial experts, had undertaken a restoration of the empire based on a tight-fisted agrarian and labor fiscal policy. Moreover, the luxury needs of the governmental elite increased proportionately with the tax returns and with the [previously discussed] banking arrangements. To be sure, the accelerating agents of this social transformation had no scruples about intensifying this exploitation, in view of the fact that they did not believe in the legitimacy of the dynasty, being for the most part extremist Shiʿites; and their Jewish and Christian colleagues, who were the offspring of persecuted minorities, were hardly entitled to call a halt to this direction.

After 270, therefore, the economic development led to a division in the industrialized towns of Tustar, Wasit, Mosul, Isfahan, Rayy, and Cairo: a classic division between the production worker and the merchant, who realizes a double profit by acting as middleman between him and the consumer. Through an alliance of the privileged classes of the State, provincial administrators and accountants of the large landed estates under cultivation (*diyaʿ*), concessionaries of grain storehouses and importing flotillas, and banking-speculators, a flourishing urban business came into being, controlling the selling of manufactured products, brokers, agents, and warehousemen. Four powerful corporations emerge at that time; cloth merchants, *bazzazin*, who shelter their precious materials, woolens, linens especially, and brocades, in a special *suq, bazzazistan* (*bazestan*) or *qaysariya*, a huge and luxurious covered market, serving both as bonded warehouses and as stock exchange for material securities, since it is a linen standard that is the standard of exchange for the merchants of the rest of the city. Then the flour merchants (*daqqadin*), wheat merchants (*hannatin*), show merchants, *asakifa* (or *kharrazin*), and, combining with them, the second-hand clothes dealers, *ashab al-khulqan*; and the *ashab al-murabba'a*, "people of the market," probably the street hawkers, *dallalin*.

Organized against them, and leading the riot in the name of the over-exploited consumers, were the *ashab al-ta'am*, bread peddlars, keepers of cheap eating houses, fruit sellers. The first riot of this sort broke out in 307, at Mosul; the second in Baghdad, at the end of 308, followed by others in Mecca.

The fact that the carders' profession was separated, in the chain of fabric manufacture, from the *bazzaz* by four proletarian trades: those of cotton sorter, spinner, weaver, and tailor, must have influenced Hallaj, in Ahwaz, following the example of the Karnaba'i, to become more concerned about the workers than the merchants.

Undoubtedly, when he settled a colony of notables from Tustar, in Baghdad, these notables were *bazzazin*, cloth and brocade merchants, coming there to set up their workshops. It is also probable that, when these notable merchants were settling in Sharqiya, to the east of Sarat in the Tustariyin quarter, they preferred to recruit their workers for their family workshops in the district in Baghdad, which (named, no doubt, for 'Attab-b-'Attab, commander of the guard of the Shakiriya under Muhtadi [killed with him in 256]) had already given this name *'attabi* to a luxury fabric, made of silk and cotton, which Istakhri, fifteen years later, noted as also being manufactured in Isfahan. This 'Attab quarter, where, until the Mongol conquest—that is, for three centuries—the Baghdadian work-shops specializing in this fabric will be concentrated, was being built up on the other side of the Round City, in the suburb (*rabad*) of Bab Sham: to the south of the fief known as Qati'at Umm Ja'far, within the confines of the Harbiya suburb. It is in this working district, Sunnite, but bordering on the Shi'ite pil-grimage site of Kaziman, that Hallaj will preach his great public sermon, fol-lowing his return from his last pilgrimage to Mecca; it was at that time, as his son tells us, "that he built himself a house" (thanks to some important backing); and at that time, up to then, that his wife and his son must have been living with his brother-in-law, among the Tustariyin (where they will still be living in 309). And it is in the Qati'a district that riot raged in 308.

One account from the *Akhbar* depicts Hallaj preaching before the 'Attab *masjid* (perhaps the private chapel of the Dar 'Attab, belonging to the head of the Khurasanian Shakiriya); Sam'ani (381 b [?]), two centuries later, will call our attention to a *masjid* in the 'Attab quarter. Two other accounts place us in the Suq al-Qati'a, a quarter in which Shi'ite propaganda was making inroads; one Sunnite of the *ahl al-hadith*, Da'laj Sijistani (d. 351), who assigned his large fortune to several Sunnite *waqfs*, lived there for half a century, Darb Abi Khalaf, the name of the favorite monkey of Zubayda. At his death, the Buwayhids tried to confiscate his various *waqfs*, which two Hashimites, Ibn Abi Musa Ma'badi and the *naqib* Abu Tamman, defended to the best of their ability. Twenty-five years later the Shi'ite *naqib* of the 'Alids, Abu Ahmad Musawi, succeeded in 379 in inducing Caliph Tayi' to allow him to erect as a *jami'* a *masjid* of al-Qati'a; as compensation, the Sunnites (Hanbalites) obtained permission in 383 to build a *jami'* whose *khatibs*, like Ibn al-Mahdi (d. 444), will be avowed anti-Shi'ites. We suspect that Hallaj came there, into this crafts proletarian milieu, as much out of compassion for humble people as out of a desire to rally quasi Shi'ites (he speaks to them in *Siniya* terms) to his own spiritual and mystical form of mahdism.

His Public Discourses (Khutab)

IN THE MARKETS *(ASWAQ)*

1. Ibn Marduya said (Ahmad-ibn-Faris-ibn-Hasari said):

I saw Hallaj, in the Suq al-Qati'a, full of sorrow, and crying out: "O people! *save me* from God" (three times)! Then he recited the following: "For He has robbed me from myself, and He does not return me to myself! I cannot witness to Him the respect due to His presence, for I am afraid of His forsaking (me)." Then, "He will leave me deserted, forsaken, outlawed! and woe to the one who feels deserted after the [experience of God's] Presence and abandoned after the [experience of] Union [with Him]!" The people wept for him. Then, he came to a halt before the entrance to the 'Attab mosque, and began again to utter his words, some of which were intelligible, though the rest escaped us. There follows what seemed intelligible:

"O people! most certainly, when He creates His creature, it is through pure goodness towards her. And if he sometimes shines forth brilliant before her, and sometimes puts a veil before her, it is always in order to make her progress. For if He did not shine forth, everyone would deny His existence; and if He did not put a veil over Himself, everyone would be entranced. And that is why He makes neither of these two states permanent for them. As for me, there is no longer a veil between Him and me, not even a wink, my time of resting, so that my humanity may perish in his divinity, while my body is consumed in the flames of His omnipotence: in order that there remains behind neither trace, nor vestige of it—neither face, nor description!"

And the following is what we did not understand:

"You must learn that material forms subsist in atoms, in His divinity, and that judgments are given by His humanity, lastly, that the play of [personal] reflection and tradition are two routes that lead equally to knowledge of the Primordial Point."

Then he recited the following:

The science of Prophesy is like the lamp of divine light,
While the fuse of ecstatic inspiration is in the *burial niche* that He prepares
   for it.
By God! it is the breath of the uncreated Spirit that breathes into my skin a
   thought, the very one that Israfil will blow into the trumpet.

As soon as He is transfigured in this way before my spirit in order to
 speak to me,
I see in my rapture Moses on Mt. Sinai!

2. Ahmad ibn Faris said:

I saw Hallaj in the Suq al-Qati'a, and he was saying: "The truth affirming that
God is one is sheathed in the conscience (*sirr*), whose act is sheathed between two
inspirations, and the two inspirations between two thoughts; and thinking is
quicker than the blinking of an eye!" and he recited the following:

For the flames of religious light, there are hearths, in [God's] creation,
And, for the conscience, secrets are kept in the privacy of discreet hearts.
And for the being, in the depth of beings, a creative Existence resides which
  is keeping my heart for Himself, which aims at it, and which chooses it!
Consider with the mind's eye, what I describe to you,
For the mind has its means of hearing, grasping, and seeing!

3. Ahmad ibn Faris said:

I saw Hallaj in the Suq al-Qati'a, standing before the entrance to the mosque,
and he was saying:
"O people! When the Truth has taken hold of a heart, He empties it of all but
Himself! When God attaches Himself to a man, He kills in him all else but Himself! When He loves one of His faithful, He incites the others to hate him, in order
that His servant may draw near Him so as to assent to Him!"
"But what happens to me? I no longer feel the least breeze of His Presence, nor
the least reach of His glance! Alas! And here are so many people who begin to hate
me, now!"
Then he wept, and the people of the Suq began to weep with him. And when he
saw them weeping, a smile returned to his face, as if he were going to break into
laughter; then he uttered several cries of anguish, and afterwards recited:
"*Mawajida . . .*"

4. Ahmad ibn al-Qasim al-Zahid said:

I heard Hallaj in the Suq in Baghdad saying:
"O people of the Suq! O people of the Suq! Save me! He does not give me back my
self in order to familiarize Himself with it, and He does not deprive me of myself so as
to make me feel reassured; His advances are more than I am able to bear!"
Then he recited the following:

I have embraced, with my whole being, all Your love, O my Holiness! You have
  manifested Yourself so much that it seems to me that there is only You in me!
I examine my heart amidst all that is not You,
I do not see any estrangement between them and me, and only familiarity
  between You and me!

Alas! here am I, in the prison of life, reunited
With the whole human race . . . Ah take me with You, outside of the prison!

5. Taken from Husayn ibn Hamdan also: He said:

I heard Husayn saying, in the Suq in Baghdad:

Yes, go tell my friends that I have set sail on the sea and that my boat is
smashed.
It is in the confession of the Cross that I will die;
I no longer care to go to Mecca (Batha) nor Medina!

And I followed him. When he returned home, he prayed a great deal, recited
the Fatiha, then Sura 26 and Sura 30, verse 56, in which God refers to: "Those
who have knowledge and faith." Then he repeated this verse and wept. When
he had finished (*taslim*), I said to him: "O Shaykh, you have spoken impiously
in the Suq, then here you raise a fracas (literally: you transport us to the Last
Judgment) while praying according to the Law. What is your aim in doing
this?" He said: "That someone will kill this cursed one!" and he pointed his
finger at himself. I asked, "Is it permitted to incite people to kill?" He said,
"No, but I incite them to be sincere in their faith, for, in my case, the putting to
death of this person is their duty, and if they wish to do it to me, they will be
recompensed."

AT MEETINGS (*MAJALIS*)

1. Abu al-Qasim ʿAbdallah ibn Jaʿfar al-Muhibb said:

When Hallaj came to Baghdad, and when its residents gathered around him, a
shaykh, finding himself in the home of one of the notables of Baghdad, named
Abu Tahir al-Sawi, who liked Sufis, suggested that he organize a meeting to which
Hallaj would come. He agreed and gathered the shaykhs together in his house. Hallaj
being present, Sawi said to the reciter: "Sing what the shaykh (he meant Hallaj)
requests of you." Hallaj said: "*Let him wake the one who sleeps*, for the reciter,
among the Sufis, doesn't sleep." The reciter chanted (on this theme) and those
present were charmed. Then Hallaj stood up in their midst, in ecstasy and entirely
resplendent with the lights of divine reality, and he cried out:

Three letters without dot and two dotted, the discourse comes to a stop there.
The first (of the dotted) indicates each ecstasy, and the other serves to affirm each.
As for the (three) other letters, they are mysteries and enigmas, in which
there is no further mention of voyage, nor stopping place.

2. Husayn had undertaken the conversion of a certain Ibn Harun al-Madaʾini, who
gathered together some well-known shaykhs of Baghdad, to talk with him. When
everyone had arrived, at the beginning of the meeting, Hallaj, reading their
thoughts, recited the following:

O heedless ones! are you so ignorant of what I am?
Why not recognize my veracity and my eloquence?
For designating the worship that I give to God, there is an adjective
    that has six consonants,
Of which two carry diacritical points.
Of these two letters, one is a radical, the other accented following the
    orthographic sign for "*my faith.*"
And, if one places it before the initial consonant, the first letter of the
    alphabet,
This consonant becomes the second consonant of the word,
And you will perceive me, in the place of Moses standing
In the light on Sinai, if you read me correctly (my enigma).

And all were nonplussed. But Ibn Harun had a sick son who was dying. And he said to Hallaj: "My son is sick. Pray for him." Hallaj said, "I have cured him. Fear no more." And, after a few minutes, the child entered, as if he had never been sick. Those present remained stupefied by it. Ibn Harun handed to Hallaj a sealed purse, with 3,000 dinars in it, and said to him: "Use it, O shaykh, for whatever you wish." But, the room in which they were gathered looked out on the Tigris. And Hallaj took the purse, threw it in the river, and said to the shaykhs: "You want to submit me to an interrogation? But on what subject then? Don't I know that you are in the state of truth, I in error?" and he left.

The next day, Ibn Harun went to the shaykhs who had been with Hallaj, and gave them the purse that Hallaj had thrown into the river. He then recounted to them the following: "Yesterday I had remained preoccupied with the gift that I had given to Hallaj, and I was filled with regret that he had thrown it into the river. Barely an hour later, a *faqir* from among his disciples knocked at my door to tell me: 'the shaykh greets you, and tells you: "Regret no more . . . take this purse. To the one who is obedient to God, God gives all power, over the land and the sea."' "

IN THE MOSQUES

1. Jundub Wasiti said:

Bahram the Zoroastrian came to find me at midnight in Baghdad; he was a rich man, and had with him a purse carrying 1,000 dinars. He said to me, "Come with me to see Hallaj; he might not dare refuse to accept this purse which you will give him." I went with him; we entered; he was on his prayer rug, reciting the Qur'an in a high voice. He bid us be seated and asked us, "What do you want, at such a time?" I spoke to him about the purse. When Hallaj refused to accept it, I insisted, and as he liked me, he accepted and took the Zoroastrian's purse. He said to me, "Don't leave." Then the Zoroastrian left. Hallaj then stood up and we went to the mosque of al-Mansur. But, it was evening and, with some poor people surrounding him, he divided the sum among them without keeping anything for himself.

One of his disciples said to him, "O shaykh, why didn't you wait till tomorrow?" He answered, "I would rather spend the night with scorpions (that sting me) than keep a sum of money in my possession."

2. 'Abd al-Karim ibn 'Abd al-Wahid said:

(I entered the house of al-Husayn ibn Mansur; he was in his *masjid*, surrounded by some people.) And he said:

"If out of all that is in my heart, a single atom were thrown onto the mountains of the earth, they would begin to melt! and if I were, myself, on the day of Resurrection, thrown into Hell, the infernal fire would be burned up; and if I entered Paradise, the dwellings of Paradise would crumble!

"I asked myself: how could my *Whole* bear my *Part*?"

"It is so heavy; the earth could no longer bear me.

"Ah! had it to spread over the whole length of creation in order to come to rest, my Part, with the whole expanse of creation, would still remain half between my tightened arms!"

3. One day he entered the mosque of Al-Mansur in Baghdad and said:

"O people, gather together and hear the story that I am going to tell you." A great crowd gathered, some of whom loved and believed in him, and others of whom hated and rejected him. He said: "You must understand that God has made (the spilling of) *my blood lawful* for you (*Abaha lakum dami)*: therefore kill me!" But the crowd wept. 'Abd al-Wadudi ibn Sa'id ibn 'Abd al-Ghani al-Zahid, one of the great figures among the Sufis, was seen advancing towards him, and said to him: "O Shaykh, how could we kill a man who prays, fasts, and recites the Qur'an" and Hallaj said to him: "O Shaykh, the thing that prevents you from shedding my blood has nothing to do with prayer, fasting, or the reading of the Qur'an! Kill me then, and you will be rewarded for it, and I will gain peace by it, for you will have fought for the faith and I, I will have died a martyr."

And Shaykh 'Abd al-Wadud said: When he left, I followed him to his house, and said to him: 'O shaykh, your language upset us, what do you mean by it? Explain it to us . . .' And he answered: 'My dear son, there is no more pressing business for the Muslims than my execution. Try to realize that my execution will be the preservation of sanctions enacted in accordance with the law, for he who has transgressed [the law] must suffer [the sanctions].'

4. Ibrahim ibn Sam'an said:

I saw Hallaj one day at the mosque of al-Mansur: I had stowed away in my *tikka* two dinars, and I was thinking only of spending them on unlawful things. Someone came up and asked for alms. And Hallaj said: "Ibn Sam'an! Give him alms, with what you have stowed away in your *tikka*;" and I was dumbfounded. I exclaimed, "O shaykh, but how do you know about that?" He answered, "Every heart which has emptied itself of what is not God, reads consciences and the invisible." "O shaykh, teach me a maxim!" and he said:

"The one who searches for God beyond the *mim* and the *'ayn* finds Him! and the one who looks for Him in the consonant of the *idafa*, between the *alif* and the *nun*, that one will lose Him! For He is holy, beyond conjectures of thoughts, and above hinted suggestions, which are in the being of every person who is tempted." And he recited the following:

Return to God! the last dot is His!
There is no "why" in the hereafter but Him.
If, for men, the "*ma*'" of Him is in the *mim* and the *'ayn*, the meaning
 of this "*ma*'" is that God is holy.
Yes, that is His meaning! on the lips even of those who are held back by bonds;
 it advises creatures to flee to Him.
And, when you doubt, think of the hadith, because even your denial,
 your doubt itself, points to Him!
And here the *mim* leads unto "Him" from top to bottom
And here the *'ayn* leads unto Him from far and wide.

THREE MAXIMS

1. Account from one of his early disciples (al-Qasri?) to Ibn al-Azraq:

We were walking with him in one of the alleyways of Baghdad, and we heard the sound of a flute, well played, which made us weep with emotion. One of us said to him: "What is this?" He said, "This? it is Iblis who weeps over the loss of this world."

2. Anecdote of Zakariya al-Qazwini (d. 682/1283):

It was related that Hallaj went out of the *hammam*, when one of the enemies of his *madhhab* met him and gave him a violent slap. "Why did you slap me?" he asked. The man said, "The Truth commanded me to do it." Hallaj then said, "In the name of this Truth, give me another slap!" And when the man raised his hand to slap him, it withered away.

3. Anecdote of Tha'alibi (d. 429/1038):

Someone came to tell Mansur ibn Husayn Hallaj: "If what you claim is true, then transform me into a monkey!" He answered him: "But if I considered such a thing, what you ask would be [already] half achieved!"

The Indictment of Public Miracles

THEIR HETERODOXY IN SUNNISM

This resounding public preaching, even in the capital of the empire, ran up against a threefold opposition, arising from mystic, juridical, and political circles. Hallaj indeed, in the eyes of the Muslim community, brought upon himself a triple indictment:

First, for spreading the news of miracles (*ifsha' al-karamat*).

Next, for *da'wat al-rububiya*, usurpation of the supreme power of God, whose *imam* is merely the temporal deputy, according to the Sunnites; the spiritual and temporal, infallible and faultless deputy, according to the Imamites.

Finally, for the crime of *zandaqa* (thesis of divine love).

In his later preaching, Hallaj presents his miracles as *mu'jizat*, or immediate acts of God and signs of a divinely ordained public mission, as the prophets had presented them; and no longer as simple *karamat* or individual and private graces that God gives quietly to his saints or to some pious men withdrawn from the world.

Hallaj transgresses a fundamental distinction, which he himself had known and applied, between the *saints* and the *prophets*. Yahya ibn Mu'adh, Dhu'l-Nun, and Bistami had agreed that God, if it were really necessary, could cause public miracles through the instrument of his saints, but by putting them in states of mystic intoxication (*sukr*), making them unconscious and irrational proofs of His omnipotence. Hallaj, on the other hand, proceeds to offer simultaneously in public both an inspired doctrine and miracles to support it. The correlation between *miracles* and *doctrine* is unique in Sunnite hagiography.

Thus, the Sufis abandoned him. They had followed him in great number. Although he had rejected the white robe (*suf*), Hallaj was still, to them, one of their own; and, in fact he did not abandon their technical language, but spoke it even in public. The leaders of Sufism had officially denounced him, but stayed in contact with him. Shibli, Ibn Fatik, Abu Husayn Wasiti will still be present at his execution, as much out of sympathy as curiosity. The rupture occurred when Hallaj's declaration of public miracles seemed to them to prove that he had reached, while still alive, this ideal line that Sufism wanted to be only the asymptote or the affirmation of the pure divine essence; and that his personality had not been destroyed as the mystic theology of Junayd was convinced it would be, by the arrival of this miracle from the divine power, but, quite to the contrary, it had been raised up, consecrated and sanctified. Only one disciple of Junayd seems at that time to have revised the theology of his master in line with the thought of Hallaj: Abu Ya'qub al-Mazabili: his thesis was that "Sufism is a divine favor (*hal*), in which the signs of one's humanity (*insaniya*) are cancelled out (*idmihlal*)." But his sect was officially denounced and nothing came of it. The other Sufis protested and tried, like Ruwaym, to bring back to an acceptable position the concepts of *lahut* and *nasut*, which Hallaj used. But they rejected his miracles, after having previously accepted them.

THE ATTITUDE OF IBN 'ATA'

The only one who had supported him up to the very end, Ibn 'Ata', was in great difficulty.

Abu 'Abbas (Ahmad ibn Fatik) Razzaz related the following to Sulami:

One of our own told me that he had asked Abu'l-ʿAbbas ibn ʿAta': "What is your opinion of Husayn ibn Mansur?" He answered, "He has *jinn* serving him." But one year later, Ibn ʿAta' revealed to him: "It is God (who acts in him)." And the other said in astonishment: "What! When I questioned you about this man, you answered me that he had *jinn* in his service, and look now what you tell me!" "Yes, all those who associate with us do not stay with us long enough for us to lead them back to the understanding of these divine gestures (*ahwal*). And, when you put this question to me, I had not yet begun your education. But, now that our friendship has become stronger, you can be sure that the truth concerning Hallaj is what you have just heard."

This theory of immediate, direct, and transforming union of the divine will with the human will, was unacceptable to the majority. The gift of miracles was for them only a certain personal and private power, conceded by God to a few privileged persons, and they used their ingenuity to acquire it in order to command the *jinn*.

Thus Tahir ibn Ahmad Tustari said:

I used to admire what Hallaj was doing; I continued to inquire about and pursue the science of conjuring; and I performed the *niranjiyat* (tricks of white magic), in order to penetrate the nature of its marvels. One day I entered his house, and, after having greeted him, I sat down for a moment. He said to me then: "Tahir, don't delude yourself; what you see and hear is done by other individuals (*ashkhas*) than me; don't imagine this to be a supernatural power (*karama*) or the result of conjuration (*shaʿwadha*)." And I could see that he was speaking truthfully.

This statement by Hallaj is not a retraction; rather it is the verification that his public *muʿjizat* are not the marvels of a conjurer, of which he would be the only author, but real scenes involving several persons, which God alone arranges; but the tone of the narrative suggests that Hallaj played his part in it as director of the play by ordering the *jinn*.

THE UNUSUAL IMPORTANCE OF THE *MAKHARIQ*
AL-HALLAJ IN MUSLIM HAGIOGRAPHY

We have kept insisting in this study on the "preternatural" facts of Hallaj's biography with complete impartiality; because the duty of the historian is to criticize the personal authority of the witness before the text of his testimony; and, if he accepts the witness, not to mutilate his testimony to support *a priori* theories. There are evidently some basic facts that one cannot depart from. But the fact that obtrudes itself here, is that the "miracles of Hallaj" are not the later embellishments of legend; they are real facts inseparable for his contemporaries from his biography; they appear, though interpreted in different ways, in all the early texts; even in the report of the trial by the assistant clerk Ibn Zanji. They were not a subjective illusion of his self-love; they were the most efficacious means of propaganda that he had, at his disposal, in terms of his ability, his influence, or his sanctity. They are distinguished by two essential traits from other "miracles" of Muslim hagiography. They provoked, immediately, polemics and seditions, attested to by his adversaries such as Nawbakhti. Before Hallaj's death, they were even the subject of a pamphlet by ʿAwariji, which led to his trial being reopened in 309/922. Mufid, sixty years later, said of the Hallajiya: "They attributed to him absurd things. in the manner of the Zoroastrians for the miracles of Zerdasht, and Christians for the miracles of their hands" (*sharh ʿaqaʾid al-Saʿdun*).

They also provoked doctrinal discussions and new theories on the concept of miracles. Among Sufis, with the physician Razi and Ibn Wahshiya, the thesis of participation through mystic union in the divine will, maintained by Hallaj and Ibn ʿAta': against the old Sunnite thesis of a special power bestowed, of an authority exercised over the jinn by proxy. Among the *mutakallimun*, the Muʿtazilite thesis of Abu ʿAli al-Jubbaʾi about the unreality of the miracles of the saints, reducible to mere conjurings; and the Ashʿarite thesis of Baqillani—these two classical theories had as their incentive and subject specifically the miracles of Hallaj.

In his time, they raised against him the objection of the Sufi traditionists, for whom there could no longer be any public miracles (the last had been the revelation itself of the Qurʾan), but only private miracles, which it was forbidden to make public under penalty of committing the crime of *ifsha' al-sirr*, the divulgence of the secret of divine grace. This rule is a little strange; it makes us think that many Sufis believed that, in theory Hallaj was right; but that in practise, as Sahl Tustari had seen, the divulgence of the "secret of divine omnipotence" (*sirr al-rububiya*) risked "making the prophetic authority (*nubuwa*) a sham." They vaguely felt there was a contradiction between their mystic experimentation and the divine inaccessibility taught by the law of the Prophet.

They did not have Hallaj's courage, which they rejected, and therefore admired quietly for their own lives the dualism of a purely external literal law and a purely individual mystic esoterism.

Most of the Sunnite jurists imitated the attitude of traditionists on this: the possibility of miracle, the legal interdiction of its public manifestations. As for the Imamites, they adopted, as we shall see, the purely negative attitude of the Muʿtazilites.

III. POLITICAL INDICTMENT: THE *DAʿWAT ILA'L-RUBUBIYA*, USURPATION OF THE SUPREME POWER OF GOD

Shiʿite Origin of This Indictment: The Ghuluw

Such is the official name for Hallaj's crime, for which the vizir already prosecuted his disciple Ibn Bishr in 298/910, and which will justify his arrest in 301/913. What is the exact meaning of this expression and what is the origin of it?

"*Da'wa*" is public preaching; "*rububiya*" is the supreme power of God, the sovereign authority that He retains, above all the delegations of authority that He invested in the prophets and Imams, to establish and govern states. To make such a claim is therefore to threaten both the Muslim law and the security of the state; it is to put oneself above the Prophet and the Imam, to change the rites of worship and the bases of government. This double character, combining spiritual and temporal, tells us rather that this is not an indictment of Sunnite, but of Shi'ite, origin. The expression was used by the legitimist Imamites to designate the action of those who have *exaggerated*, by usurping the authority, both spiritual and temporal, infallible and faultless, which God invested in the 'Alid Imams; it is the heresy of the Kaysaniya and Khattabiya, of Bayyan ibn Sam'an, Abu'l-Khattab, Namiri; of the *Ghulat*. According to the legitimist Imamites, their crime, *ghuluw* (exaggerations) (opp. *taqsir* [diminutions]), is twofold: (1) assuming for oneself the '*isma* reserved to the 'Alids by hereditary privilege; (2) defining this '*isma* as the transforming union of a man with God, the permanent sanctification, the real divine anointing that invests the Imam; an absurd *exaggeration*, according to the Imamite *mutakallimun*. For as atomists and materialists like the others, they declare they could prove it only by communication of a particle of the divine essence to man—*hulul juz'ilahi*—which implied two theological impossibilities: composition = materiality = corporeity (*tajsim*) in God; and the nontranscendence of God.

Such is the theory that was attributed to Hallaj. There is no doubt about its Shi'ite origin. To the legitimist Imamites, Hallaj has political aims, since he called himself inspired by God; no one, in the opinion of the Imamites, has the right to make rules of devotion for the faithful except the Imam; not simply to transfer their privileges to a younger 'Alid branch, like the Zaydites or the Qarmathians, but to put within reach of all the monopoly reserved to one alone.

The Mahdi Theme and Shi'ite Legitimism

Hallaj's years of preaching in Baghdad end by making him a public figure, the aim of the Shi'ites, as much in the Court as in his little Sunnite quarter. The Shi'ites wonder whether he is one of their own, he who put forward the mahdi theme during his apostolate in Khurasan—in Talaqan, which was described by hadith and distinguished from other towns by the preaching of Muhammad b. Qasim (d. A.H. 219), the 'Alid who was a "Sufi." Let us recall here briefly the major traits of this mahdi theme, which had such a widespread, and always such a real, reverberation in all Islamic countries.

This theme has its beginnings in the Qur'an, in which some eschatological and apocalyptical verses announce certain tragic "days" (*ayyam*) prior to the Hour of the last Judgment, certain "cries" (*sayha*) or supernatural calls addressed (*nida'l-munadi*) to the true believers to guide them in times of trial:

"*ihdina,*" that is to say, "*urshidna*" as it is expressed in the Fatiha: "Guide us!" The first guide, the Prophet, is dead; his son-in-law, ʿAli, could not reestablish peace and was killed without being avenged (*talafa*); it is in his lineage that the Hujr, certain believers, seek those "*asbab,*" those intermediaries with God of whom the Qur'an speaks, and the cloud (*ghamama*) which guided the exodus of the people of Moses until the Hour of the return of Jesus; the extent of their period of expectation is embodied in the years (309 years) of the mysterious sleep of the Seven Sleepers in the cave, described in Sura 18 and read in public each Friday in the mosque.

The mahdi theme had formed the subject of a prophesy of Muhammad, conceived as follows (*malhama*): ". . . who will fill the world with justice and fairness as much as it was filled previously with iniquity and injustice."

It is an expression of the profound aspiration for social justice that ferments in every human community, especially a religious community, at the sight of abuses and crimes that an unholy apirit can seduce its leaders to commit. We should not be surprised that such a sentiment is nourished by pre-Islamic memories, either folkloric (hope in the coming of a mysterious Child, whose cradle is watched over by the phoenix, or the return of a just Leader whom God keeps on reserve in the cave, guarded by wild beasts, and whom we shall recognize by bodily signs, a beauty spot), or Judeo-Christian memories (the Saviour will be preceded by a Just man [*nafs zakiya*] who will be assassinated in the Temple by an Anti-Christ; he will be aided by a Yemenite conqueror, Mansur al-Yaman); or Iranian memories (Zoroastrian . . .), Manichaean, etc.

But the Muslim conception of the mahdi is not a simple amalgamation of earlier survivals adapted by the Qur'an; it is a theme having an original and specific form, with a Shiʿite coloration: the awaited Leader (Muntazar, Sahib al-Amr, Sahib al-Zaman) will make a triumphant and culminating appearance (*zuhur*): he will be the *Qa'im*, who will reestablish the true practice of the Qur'an; he will defend the laws of God, and will execute without pity all great guilty persons face-to-face with their victims, thanks to the *rajʿa*, a sort of first resurrection affirming the survival of souls under this archaic form, while awaiting the Resurrection for the final Judgment. This justice will be bloody, and the guilty whom it will strike will leave their penal metamorphoses briefly so that their victims might recognize them for an instant. There is more: "the day on which He will rise" (Qur'an 14:42) will be more than a simple reestablishment of the order promulgated by the Prophet ; it will be the consummation of it, its coronation; and, like the celebration of the Breaking of the fast at the end of Lent, it will bring to the true believers emancipation from servile observances of the Law based on fear, and the fullness of liberty (*yawm Allah*).

One can see how the mahdi theme could be disquieting, not only for the government, but for strict orthodoxy also; it is a revolutionary and levelling spirit, which could break out against all secular privileges, notably against the hegemony of the Arab race, insofar as it was the sole beneficiary of the holy war, of its booty and its land revenues.

The oppressed converted classes (*mustad'ifun*) were the first to ponder this mahdi theme: the tribes scorned by the dominant tribe, Quraysh (and Thaqif), either because they were Rabi'ites, or Yemenites ('Abd al-Qays, Hamdan, Kinda, Madhhij, Khuza'a), or because of the influence of their converted clients (*mawali*), such as the clans Kahil and Ghadira of the Asad, Hanzala and Sa'd-Hibaq of the Tamim (in view of their *hilf* with the Iranian Hamra). And, even before 'Ali became Caliph (in A.D. 656), it was this spirit that aroused, against the favoritism of (his predecessor) 'Uthman, such Shi'ite preaching as that of Abu Dharr, and of the 'Abdite Zayd ibn Suhan, the disciple of Salman.

It has often been said that Shi'ism was born from a profane and banal legitimism, claiming authority in Islam for the 'Alids, because they are "people of the House of the Prophet" (*Al Bayt al-Nabi*), corporeal heirs (*nasab maddi*) of Muhammad, descended from 'Ali, his first cousin and the husband of his daughter Fatima. Some have concluded that such "legitimism" is an unwarranted inoculation, in the early elective state in Islam, of the dynastic principle, a Sassanid principle handed down by the Iranians: that Mu'awiya (the Ummayad caliph, defeater of 'Ali) was the first to introduce this principle, and that the first Shi'ites were pure Arabs from Kufa. In reality, the recitation of such formulas of worship as the second part of the *shahada* ". . . and Muhammad is the Messenger of God," and the *tasliya*, fixed the thought of fervent believers on the Al Muhammad. Therefore, if some deny that Muhammad had explicitly delegated the political power to the 'Alids, others must avow, not only that they were his private heirs according to the unwritten Arab law, but also, and especially, that they were established publicly as his juridical "substitutes," acting in this capacity vis-à-vis his clients as his debts of blood.

This substitution dates, as the whole of Shi'ism affirms and the Qur'an and historical data agree, from a public test of an ordeal, the *mubahala* of 21 *Hijja* 10/March 22, 632. On this particular day, in Medina, Muhammad had challenged the Christian Banu 'Abd al-Madan emissaries of the Balharith of Najran, to a "judgment of God" (seized with fear, the Christians declined it the next day, signing a *musalaha*, "capitulation," the first between Christianity and Islam). For this "judgment of God," Muhammad had placed as hostages of his sincerity (about the negation of the Incarnation) and of his faith (in his own mission), "his own people," the "five whom he covered with his mantle" (*ashab al-kisa'*): his two grandsons, Hasan and Husayn, his daughter Fatima, his son-in-law 'Ali, [and himself]. Henceforward this solemn judiciary substitution was to transfer to each of them the expectation of justice and the devoted service that the true friends of Muhammad had pledged to him; and it also transferred equally all vendetta, all of the hatred that the Umayyads, of the Quraysh, nurtured against the founder of Islam for their pagan dead killed in cold blood after Badr (in A.D. 624).

At the time of 'Umar's Caliphate (A.D. 634–644), 'Ali demanded equality of rights for non-Arab converts; the latter were Persians, for the most part. There had been an alliance through the women between the *dihqan* Hormozan and the 'Alids, which explains the tenacity with which 'Ali pursued the son of 'Umar, who was the murderer of the *dihqan*. A mandate as "redresser of wrongs"—such is the primary meaning the 'Alids gave to their investiture of the Prophet; and this is why martyrs "challenging oppression" (*min abat al-daym*), like Husayn at Karbala, and Zayd at Kufa, have left such a lasting memory.

But the *mubahala* soon takes on another, profounder meaning: this "judgment of God" in favor of the Prophet and His own people, the 'Alids, did not only confer on the 'Alids a power of "divine right"; it also signified for those who had grasped its full meaning a sort of initiatory adoption (*nasab ruhani*); and this is why the founder of this doctrine, *Sahib* Salman Farisi, became for the whole Shi'ite tradition, both orthodox and Isma'ili, what he doubtless was historically, the spiritual adviser of the Family of the Prophet.

The Shi'ite school of the *Mukhammisa* was interested in interpreting, in all of its symbolism, the *mubahala* scene. At the cemetery in Medina, at the bottom of the Baqi', on the red dune, we see the Five standing, under the Mantle, illuminated with thunderbolts and lightning flashes. Before them, together with the other initiated *mawali*, stands Salman pointing out the Five for the veneration of the amazed Najranian Christians. At the call of the Initiator, they recognize the Five in their glorious transfiguration (*tajalli*). Their halo of lightning flashes signifies that their authority is a "divine right," inducing them to affirm that their bodies are shadows (*azilla, azlal*) cast by Divine Light, silhouettes (*ashbah*) temporarily outlined in the divine emanation, exempted from the generation and corruption of suffering and death. It is the call (*nida'*) of the Initiator that animates and sets the scene: the instrument of the divine Spirit, which discerns and reveals the divine secret, the seal of the prophetic mission that marks the Five: which raises Salman above the Prophet and the Imams, like Khidr above Moses in Sura 18: above prophesy, there is sanctity, and the initiated companions of Salman have access to it.

Facing this scene is another, even more celebrated one, which is also more legendary, for the Qur'an ignores it, and numerous hadith (even Sunnite) that describe it do not establish its historicity; traditional Shi'ite devotion makes it the center of its meditations: we refer to the "day of the *ghadir*." Returning to Medina from his farewell pilgrimage, on 18 *Hijja* 10/March 19, 632, Muhammad rested by the *ghadir* of Khumm; and there, from an improvised platform-pulpit, made of piled-up benches, he is supposed to have proclaimed 'Ali his heir apparent. What did this proclamation (*da'wa*) represent? Did it announce the handing down of all or part of his prophetic authority to a subordinate or to an equal? Was this the declaring, by a herald-precursor, of a divine secret, designating 'Ali as the faultless Leader (*ma'sum*), to whom God had the oath of allegiance administered by the Islamic Community? But if Muhammad speaks (*natiq*), 'Ali remains silent (*samit*); his *a priori* faultlessness, which he will bequeath to the Imams as a hereditary, aristocratic privilege, is not the expres-

sion of an interior sanctification, and it is incommunicable to the faithful, because their devotion saves without transfiguring them. The secondary differentiation that the *ghadir* scene introduces between the expressive Prophet
(= *Mim*) and the silent Imam (= '*Ayn*) poses a question of precedence between
them that was much discussed between the Mimiya and 'Ayniya; but the divine
investiture that designates them together manifests the divine power (*qudra*),
and not the presence of God, through His grace: because it causes them to act,
without transforming them, it was not necessary, in defining them, to imagine,
as some extremists did, the infusion (*hulul*) into them of a special divine particle (*juz'ilahi*).

The *mubahala* scene, on the contrary, requires a subtler metaphysical justification: how to define the quasi-sacramental mode of intervention of the Spirit
into the person of the Initiator, giving to his words much stronger efficacy than
to those of a prophet (who is a simple transmitter of a warning), since (the
Initiator) can make the initiated be reborn in eternal life and confers on them
the *fitra* (= *sibghat al-walaya*) when making them recognize and contemplate,
in the Five under the Mantle, a divine commandment (*amr*). At a very early
time the influence of Hellenistic philosophy and its thesis of an influx of the
efficacious intellect (*hulul al-'aql al-fa''al*), which was supposed to explain
how a sovereign, who may be a legislator, prophet, or Imam, can be moved to
govern according to justice, like a Sage, proved itself in practice insufficient to
explain this ascendancy of the Spirit (*Ruh Natiqa*) over the Initiator, and,
through him over the adept, who is revivified by it; holiness is above wisdom.
The persuasive voice of the Initiator contains a divine presence of another
order than that which maintains the terrestrial powers in balance, the powers of
the Imams as the sum of material masses. Beyond the visible sign to adore
(*ma'luh*), there is God (*Ilah*), Who inspires the act of cultic adoration, Abu'l-
Khattab observes. The soul of the Initiator is possessed by God. Such is the
circuitous route, so full of precipices and certainly very gnostic, by which extremist Shi'ite theologians of the school of Mukhammisa brought Islam, in the
face of possible concrete cases of intervention by the Spirit, to consider publicly [the notion of] the Saint.

The only metaphysical vocabulary at the disposal of the Mukhammisa in this
period was that of Manichaean dualism, of the two [coeternal cosmic] principles [of good and evil]. When they spoke of the inclusion of a particle of the
substance of the supreme God they were quickly condemned by the Zaydite
Mu'tazilites for upholding two theological absurdities (composition = materiality = corporeity [*tajsim*], in God; and the nontranscendence of God). Perhaps
they also tried to apply to the Spirit (= *Ruh*) the Hellenistic thesis of the influx
of the Active Intellect into souls (during the process of intellection), imitating
in this application those whom Ibn Hanbal called "*zanadiqa min al-Nasara*,"
"certain Manichaeans among the Christians"; which came under the same condemnation.

Such attempts at metaphysical explanation could not disarm the rising hostility of the Kharijite, Sunnite, and Zaydite jurisconsults to this Shi'ite tendency toward a sacrilegious divinization of human beings. The moderate Shi'ite theologians, themselves very disturbed by this tendency, objected that their Imams themselves were hardly responsible for the excessive veneration that was accorded them, that they affirmed that they would not hesitate to denounce their most devoted partisans as extremists. The latter, moreover, with magnificent rashness, invoked the practice of the occult in order to continue their propaganda, even though they had been disavowed and cursed by the Imam for whom they declared themselves ready to die as *fida'i*, martyrs out of love. They remained loyal subjects, even if his opinion had changed. Mughira died, renounced by Nafs Zakiya; Abu'l-Khattab was killed, renounced by the Sixth Imam; the same for Ibn al-Furat, under the Eighth Imam; and we have two remarkable parallel texts dealing with Bashshar and Ibn Sinan, those devout and more or less sincerely impassioned followers of the Imam [who cursed them], who prefigure the Hallajian theme concerning Satan, the one damned through pure love.

Following the example of their Imams, the moderate Shi'ite theologians, since the time of Hisham ibn al-Hakan, condemned the Mukhammisa as extremists for their doctrine of *hulul*, using again the arguments of the Mu'tazilites. The list is long of *hululiya* heretics drawn up in this way by common accord, and it was borrowed just as is by their fellow Sunnites; the Hallajiya are included in it. There is more: the official expression for the legal grounds invoked in 298 to start proceedings against Hallaj and his disciple Ibn Bishr, and for arresting him in 301, is a Shi'ite expression, the same that figures in the denunciation of extremists such as the Mukhammisa: *"da'wat ila'l-rububiya"*: "public claiming of the supreme power of God." In 298 the vizir in power, 'Ali ibn al-Furat, who was secretly a Shi'ite, had to adopt this formula on the advice of an old adversary of Hallaj, the leader of the moderate Shi'ites of Baghdad, Abu Sahl Nawbakhti. Many of the Sunnite high officials must have been anticipating in Hallaj a temporal Messiah.

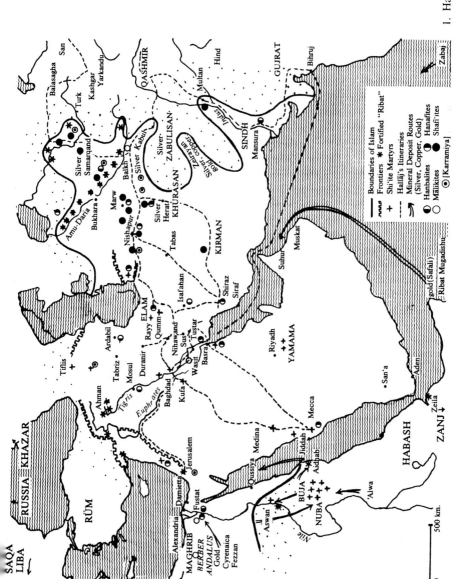

1. Hallāj's itineraries

SAQĀ
LIBA

RUSSIA KHAZAR

RŪM

Balasagha   San
Turk
Kashgar
Yarkandu
QASHMĪR
Hind
GUJRAT
Bihruj
Zabaj

Silver
Samarqand
Multan
ZABULISAN-
Silver Kabul
Silver
KHŪRĀSAN
Silver Zeitaran
gold
copper
Indus
SINDH
Mansura

Amu-Daria
Bukhara
Marw
Balkh
Nishapur
Silver
Herat
Tabas
KIRMAN
Muskat

Tiflis
Ahman
Tabriz
Ardabil
Mosul
Duranir
ELAM
Rayy
Qumm
Nihawand
Sus
Tustar
Isafahan
Shiraz
Siraf
Suhur
gold (Safaii)
Ribat Mugadishu

Tigris
Baghdad
Kufa
Wasit
Basra
Riyadh
YAMAMA
Aden

Euphrates
Jerusalem
Qussiya
Medina
Mecca
San'a
Jiddah
ZANJ Zeila

Alexandria
Damietta
Fustat
Aidhab
Aswan
BUJA
NUBA
'Alwa
HABASH

MAGHRIB
BERBER
ANDALUS
Gold
Cyrenaica
Fezzan

Nile

500 km.
0

Boundaries of Islam
Frontiers ✱ Fortified "Ribat"
Shi'ite Martyrs
Hallāj's itineraries
Mineral Deposit Routes
(Silver, Copper, Gold)
● Hanbalites   ● Hanafites
○ Mālikites   ● Shafi'ites
⊚ [Karramiya]

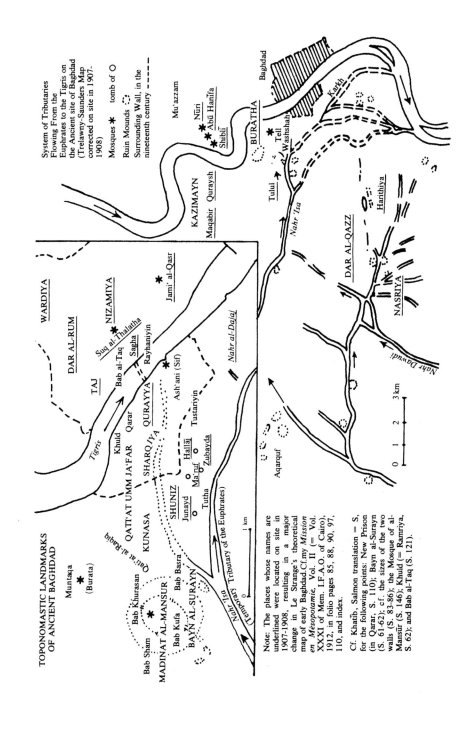

TOPONOMASTIC LANDMARKS OF ANCIENT BAGHDAD

3. Vision of the burning lamp. Sixteenth-century Persian miniature

5. Hallāj led to execution. Sixteenth-century
Persian miniature

4. Hallāj on the gibbet. Eighteenth-century
Indo-Persian miniature

6. The Intercision of Hallāj according to Bīrūnī. Arabo-Persian miniature,
dated 707/1307

7. The Intercision of Hallāj according to Bīrūnī. Seventeenth-century
Persian miniature. This miniature, like the rest of the manuscript
of Bīrūnī's *āthār*, was copied from the original work from which
the previous miniature came. A comparison
of the two is very instructive

9. Hallāj on the gibbet

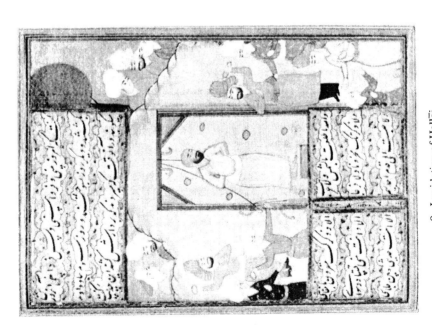

8. Lapidation of Hallāj

10. Burning of the body of Hallāj before Caliph Muqtadir
and his retinue

11. "Tomb" of Hallāj in Karkh (1957)

12. Interior of the "tomb" of Hallāj in Karkh

CHAPTER FIVE

The Indictment, The Court of Justice, and the Actors in the Drama

I. THE INDICTMENT AND IBN DAWUD'S INITIATIVE*

The Indictment: Ibn Dawud's Initiative

Before the case of Hallaj was brought to a religious court, it was exposed to public opinion in the capital of the empire, and denounced violently from the twofold perspective of religious orthodoxy and sound philosophy by a jurisconsult named Ibn Dawud who, though still young, was already head of the Zahirite school of law; a man who, in addition, was a refined, sentimental, and respected man of letters attached to the philosophy of Kindi (185/801).

Ibn Dawud was of the opinion that both the legalistic conception of the Muslim Community's having been formed by love and the jealous savageness of early Arabic poetry, were distorted by Hallaj's preaching of the principle of divine "Essential Desire."

For Hallaj to refer his audience, without confessional distinction, to an internal experimentation that claimed a common Base (*aslan jamma'an*), was to appeal to an inspiration superseding the guidelines of the Sunna of the Prophet, and to a symbolic interpretation of terms of the Arabic language that nominalism (common at that time to Mu'tazilism, Zahirism, and to the Hellenistic philosophical school of Kindi) had rejected.

This position of Ibn Dawud represented a hardening of Islamic legalism; certainly Muhammad, like Moses, teaches that love must be socially confined, with the sexual instinct for propagation of the species, to the notion of conjugal duty; if left free, love could only beget a fatal madness. But this strict, disciplinary approach did not claim to solve the problem of beauty, which was so subtly posed by the story of Joseph in Sura 12, nor that of the role, in the City, of the spiritual brotherhood (*ta'akhi*, in Medina), a generative source of civilization outside the natural families.

As for the nominalist conception of Arabic grammar, steadfastly upheld by the Zahirites, from Ibn Dawud to Ibn Hazm and Ibn Mada, by means of examples (*shawahid*) drawn from the most physically profane Arabic poets, in spite of the original ambivalence of Arabic roots (*addad*) and the ambiguities

*From *The Passion of al-Hallaj,* vol. 1, pp. 338–51, 358–71, 378–82, 386–87, 392–406, 407–14, 416–18, 420–21, 421–24, 425–28, 429–33, 435–38, 448–53

(*mutashabihat*) of the Qur'an, it already came up against the wise phonological and structural exactness of serious thinkers, as can be seen by Khalil, the Shafi'ites, and Hanbalites, and also the translators of Greek logic into Arabic. For Ibn Dawud, faithful to the letter of Muslim law, the solution of the two problems, of seductive beauty and of intellectual relationships, was given by the traditional ideal of love developed by early Arabic poetry. Love, which can only desire beauty, is a magnetic blind fatality of a physical nature, *dexithymon erotos anthos*, and the entire dignity of a superior soul must experience it without surrendering to it. The melancholy of love, by the very meaning of its etymology, is the result (and reciprocally, the cause) "of the inflammation of the blood and the bile that leads to increasing atrabiliousness; the greater the atrabiliousness, the more possessed one becomes by melancholy; so much so that love is a disease for which doctors have no cure." Whether it is a question of popular themes from Bedouin folklore, or of their learned orchestrations by the poets of the cities, Ibn Dawud, in a detailed criticism of the Arabic poetic texts, shows that careful and systematic examination finds only elements of a clinical analysis of symptoms classifiable in a sequence, a chain: one concluding usually in madness and death, after a gradual weakening of the body and an increasing isolation of its lonely thought, captivated by its fanciful ideal. It is not forbidden, however, to taste of it, and the Muslim paradise that Ibn Dawud envisions is one in which the memory recaptures the features of beloved faces just as they were, not altered or rearranged in any way.

It should be noted that the two sources of Ibn Dawud's theory—Qur'anic law and classical Arabic poetry—do not appeal to the personal experience of the living, neither to the faith of believers nor to the passion of lovers. Ibn Dawud, a good Zahirite, refuses to indulge in any psychological subjectivism, whether sacred or profane; love is a desire (*irada*, opp. *karh*), a concupiscent appetite of the sensual soul, drawn necessarily to a concrete good, something partial (*juz'i*); the soul (*nafs*), furthermore, according to the *kalam* of that time, is not substantial, but a simple accident of the body; it has no nature of its own.

This position of Ibn Dawud, one of deliberate intransigence, represents a very limited perspective on a whole body of collective thought that was elaborated about love by the young Muslim civilization; for three or four generations, translations of Pahlavi, Sanskrit, and Greek (through Syriac) texts led it, through a comparatism differentiating the rhythms and meters of amatory poems, to intellectualize their structure and the stages of the realization of the idea [of love].

Through Abu Tammam, Ibn Dawud at least learned, as he admits, to intellectualize amatory rhetoric; in a manner less conventional (and Hellenistic), and more spontaneous, than Ibn al-Mu'tazz. He philosophizes, in his sense of the word, and coldly criticizes the development among poets of a malady of soul that he considers contagious, and whose outcome is fatal. And by grouping poets together according to their mode of expressing the stages of the malady of love, he realizes with them their preferred intellectual affiliations, in a manner of instantaneous musical pleasure, experienced at the same time as the hearing of the melody, and as brief as it; but expressible in technical terms. This is the origin of his ladder of "the steps of love," for which the school of Kindi undoubtedly gave him the idea. The Hallajian term for "desire" ('*ishq*) is included in it, but in the sense closely related to its primary grammatical meaning (the bitterness of desire in the unsatisfied she-camel): a step leading to a final frenzy of passion (*walah*), and the sign of a demoniacal obsession (*waswas*), Ibn Dawud notes; his friend Niftawayh says it leads to mental slavery (*tatayyum*).

The following is the so-called "ladder" of eight psychic stages of love, according to Arabic poetry (Ibn Dawud, *Kitab al-zahra*):

1.	admiration	*istihsan*	5.	inclination	*hawa*
2.	attraction	*mawadda*	6.	desire	*'ishq*
3.	attachment	*mahabba*	7.	enslavement	*tayim*
4.	familiarity	*khulla*	8.	delirium	*walah*

In a later time, another Zahirite, the great Ibn Hazm, also a sensitive man of letters, will enumerate just five:

1.	admiration	*istihsan*	4.	affection	*kalaf*
2.	infatuation	*i'jab*	5.	fervor	shaghaf
3.	intimacy	*ulfa*			

Niftawayh had discerned five:

1.	volition	*irada*	4.	desire	*'ishq*
2.	attachment	*mahabba*	5.	bondage	*tatayyum*
3.	inclination	*hawa*			

All of these are observable external symptoms, not experienced "internal tastes," nor a glorification through a translucent crystallization of a memory into an idea.

Ibn Dawud has the virtue as a Muslim monotheist of removing the Hellenistic and Sabaean astral polytheism from his amatory rhetoric. He simply cites, without imitating the Platonic parable of the "Symposium" on celestial spirits, those spherical beings created and afterwards split in two to be imprisoned in bodies in which they are attracted to one another; he cites also the comment "by Plato" on love, "a madness, a divine (demoniacal) possession that can be neither praised nor blamed," and the genethliac themes of friendship and enmity of Ptolemy.

Ibn Dawud, on the other hand, refuses to believe that "tastes experienced" in love indicate a progress of the soul, a gradual "substantialization," a sanctification. The Sufi school of Basra, through analysis of its experiences of asceticism and prayer, believes that in such cases God loves the soul (cf. Qur'an 5:59); meaning that if He never restrains the soul, He always desires it, and makes the soul desire Him, and that He "draws near" it through stages in a mental pilgrimage, in a gradual purification, whose schema can be constructed: as stages of an ascent toward God.

If Ibn Dawud accepts this idea, probably borrowed from Stoic philosophy, of a "ladder" of amorous states, it is only a ladder of stages in an increasing, fatal aggravation of a mental illness. He judges their desire for God to be as illusory as the desire for any other love idol. Dhu'l-Nun Misri, and afterwards Yahya Razi, in trying to present in a dynamic form the stages of their "itinerary toward God," remained prisoners, like Ibn Dawud, of the Mu'tazilite vocabulary of their time, describing them as "stages" (maqamat) conquered (sic) through the effort of asceticism. What about God's role in all of this? Indeed, a sound orthodoxy was viewing it rather in terms of gifts that are gratuitous, "modalities" (ahwal) of divine Grace, but excluded, in such cases, from any rationally forseeable dispensation?

Ibn Dawud also rebels against the therapeutic claims of such Baghdadian Sufis as Abu Hamza and Nuri; who, accepting the same point of departure as Ibn Dawud, the pathological symptoms of love, claim that these symptoms have a deeper, moral meaning: that they obtain a divine medication, which cures the amorous soul of creatures, if, through them, the soul begins to love the Creator:

> Certain adepts of Sufism (mutasawwifin) have claimed that it is God (exalted be His praise) Who put men through the experience of love, as a trial: so that they might subjugate their "self" to the object of their love, to His wrath that breaks them, to His pleasure that enlarges them, so that after that they may balance such a subjugation with the bondage of obedience to God (may He be praised and exalted). He, the Incomparable One, the One Without Equal, He, their Creator, Who did not need to create them, their Providence, their Author, Who does not even remind them of the blessings that they owe to Him. And, finally, since they obliged their "self" to obey an "other," God is the One Whose will should have the most right to claim their obedience.

Mas'udi adopts this important commentary, and thirty years later uses it against certain Sufis, especially of Baghdad, who loved to preach in public . . . something other than the "union-separation" antithesis (that is, "jam' tafriq"; he was aiming therefore at the Hallajian 'ayn al-jam'); against those among the Sufis who were "interiorists" (batiniya), he concluded, meaning surely the Hallajians.

Ibn Dawud in the above passage appears very shocked at the claim of these adepts in Sufism to discern, in the depths of desire ('ishq), which he considers an aberration of the personal will, or a "useless folly" (according to Peripatetic moral philosophy), infecting "the heart preoccupied with neither craft nor trade": a pure transnatural attraction, which they claim descended from the divine Essence itself. The *mutasawwifun* whom Ibn Dawud has in mind in this instance are, we believe, Abu Hamza and Nuri, because of their therapeutics, aimed at Baghdadian literary circles contaminated by uranism, and their mystical "sublimation" of the Platonic bondage of love. For this passage seems to have been written prior to Hallaj's public preaching:

> But, God willing, we shall demonstrate later on all that is truly love in the hearts that experience it, by describing its stages and its changes, its resumptions and its onslaughts, by relating how it bends wills that are considered strong, and rushes to the rescue of wills that are hard-pressed, how it plays upon the hearts of adepts in philosophy, and how it knows how to subdue the thoughts of those who believe they have sacrificed themselves.

Ibn Dawud decided, therefore, against the possibility of this *dianisante* therapeutics for the malady of love, against a "(real and not imaginary) substantialization" of the final goal of love. And not only vis-à-vis these Sufis, but also vis-à-vis the neo-Platonist tendencies of his friends from the school of Kindi, "the philosopher of the Arabs," led at that time by Sarakhsi. Although he was a disciple of Kindi, Ibn Dawud embraced until the end of Sarakhsi's definition of love as a noble mental illness, as the impossible quest (Ibn Dawud; the natural and legal prohibition = impossibility) of a corporal union, of an ideal union of two souls (*ittihad al-nafsayn*)? Did he share the final hope of the following tercet by Ibn al-Rumi?

> I embraced her and my soul, after that, desired her again. And yet, who can be closer than an embrace?—And I kissed her lips to quench my thirst, but what I tasted only inflamed my thirst.—Now the burn of love inside me is so great that I cannot cure it by inhaling cool air.—Ah! the fever of my heart cannot be broken so long as our two souls are uncombined as one!

What kind of personal life could Ibn Dawud have hoped to live in the union of two sensitive souls outside of their bodies? For Ibn Dawud, love leads to death, which it hastens in coming, but cannot divinely transform the body, and it stops in the impersonal heaven of ideas. In that, he was too restrictive with the richness of Arabic poetry.

The theology of a Zahirite denies the unity of psychomatic phenomena, and therefore the unity of human nature, in love; the only hope of immortality that he retains for the experience of having loved, is that of a survival in an impersonal heaven of ideas. Knowing that the sensual soul (*nafs*, identical for him with the *ruh*, the spirit) is only an accident of the body, his reason cannot grant any objective reality to a life beyond the grave, a life of mummified recollections, which the experience of the union enabled two souls to live outside of their bodies.

To say "in the Name of God . . ." (= to recite the *basmala*) means, for Hallaj, to express the creative "fiat" (= *kun*) to God Himself: in order to fulfill it *hic et nunc*: by granting to this divine Host, with our body and our soul, the most sacralizing of the rights of asylum, that of hospitality, *iqra', ikram al-Dayf, dakhala, ijara*. To say to God "I love You, I give You thanks," means to give oneself to Him; it means to die with Him of the same Desire that He has of Himself, in calling Himself supreme. He, in the same eternal present moment in which this extraordinary word of loving annihilation resuscitates Him: and resuscitates us: "those whom Desire kills. He returns them to life."

By performing the *manasik al-hajj* in Mecca, Hallaj understood that the rituals of this Abrahamic sacrifice usher one into a deifying mystery of love, because they call forth "the descent of divine forgiveness" to ʿArafat. By transferring to his home in Baghdad the rituals legally bound to the confines of the Kaʿba, Hallaj discovers that their real consummation, which was accomplished there only in a *hill* (a non-sacred place) and symbolically, at ʿArafat, could only be realized in Baghdad by getting out of his home . . . out of the sacralized walls of his body (*ihram* of the *Labbayka*): by going out into the streets to expose himself to death, by provoking those for whom he spoke to God; and he offers himself to God to give him this consummation.

There, at the crossroads, he offers himself to the famished bedouin Arabs, whom misery and the revolutionary propaganda of the Qarmathians cast away, like the lost sheep of Ishmael, over all the routes of the caravans and the hajj, where his preaching led him. He wished his death to be at the hands of these Muslims, but it will be at the hands of others—of Sunnites, who believe in the "corporal" materiality of the hajj and in its localization at the Meccan Kaʿba, in which the Qarmathians no longer believe;—of Sunnites, who still believe in the resurrection of the body, in which the Qarmathians also no longer believe.

Ibn Dawud, like the majority of theologians of his time and like all the Zahirites, was a Muʿtazilite, a libertarian; and he was the latter also in his capacity as an expert in the Hellenistic philosophy of Kindi. Jahiz, departing from the then classical principle of the nonsubstantiality of the soul, had demonstrated that any form of worship that claims to love God is anthropomorphic and ends up comparing Him with man (*tashbih*) and, therefore, envisioning a material divinity, which is absurd. Furthermore, the majority of theologians taught that God could not be loved (except in an Emanation, according to extremist Shiʿites), for He "cannot love Himself" (*Allah la yuhibbu dhatahu*): Baqillani, Abu Yaʿla, Juwayni: against Ibn Taymiya. At a time when Hallaj shows us the Essential Desire of God, of Love, Lover and Beloved together, in His primordial solitude; and not as a result of climbing ascetical steps. He said this bluntly to a Karramiyan Sufi, Ibrahim Khawwas. The latter barb made any technical discussion between Ibn Dawud and Hallaj impossible.

Also, when the Malikite qadi, Abu ʿUmar, *khalifa* of his father for the judicial district of the west bank of Baghdad, consulted Ibn Dawud, his assessor, about the utterances made by Hallaj in his jurisdiction (Tustariyin, ʿAttab), Ibn Dawud responded with the following *fatwa:*

I heard Abuʾl-Qasim Yf-b-Yq Nuʿmani, who said: "I heard my father say: that he had heard this from the mouth of the Imam, son of the Imam AB Muhammad ibn Dawud-b-ʿAli, the *faqih*, of Isfahan:

" 'If what God revealed to His Prophet (blessings and peace be upon him) is true, if what the Prophet came to impart to us is true, then what Hallaj says is false (*batil*).' So Ibn Dawud attacked him vehemently."

He concluded that it "was lawful to put him to death."

It is, therefore, as a violent intrusion into the life of the City that Hallaj presents, in sermons that are both impetuous and technical in style, the call to the perfect life that the Sufis were living, shut off in hermitages (only Yahya Razi had attempted to hold conferences, *majalis*, for cultured people). He seems to the casual passerby in the markets like another of those popular uneducated preachers (*qass*, plural: *qussas*) who, since the time of Mansur ibn ʿAmmar, had been shouting out their apocalyptic threats and promises in this city of luxury and lust; warnings which were associated either with legitimist Shiʿite propaganda or with an ascetic reform of morals. And since these preachers were the target of Muʿtadid's edict of 284/897, it was probably as a *qass* that "Hallaj was denounced to Muʿtadid" by Ibn Dawud.

But this Zahirite jurisconsult was well aware that Hallaj was not just one of those ordinary inciters of mobs who irritate the police by appealing to God without first going through the proper channels. Hallaj was an aberrant but esteemed theological author, who was in contact with the various schools of the learned scholars of Islam, Muʿtazilite, Imamite, Sunnite, and knowledgeable in the language of the school in general. It was politically and socially dangerous for the state to allow him to strengthen his influence over his popular Arab audience of Karkh and Bab Basra, to give a spiritual leader, and reasons for hope, to a whole proletariat made up of displaced nomads, driven out by famine, attracted by the lure of bread, ex-bedouins from Yamama and Ahsa retreating from Basra and Kufa under pressure from the Qarmathian social revolution (Banu Ukhaydir), settled in their Dar al-Hijra, between Kufa and Karbala.

The vocabulary of Hallaj's Baghdad sermons is filled with extremist Ismaʿili terms because of his bedouin audience, to whom he had previously dedicated his apostolate in Khurasan (Talaqan, Juzjan): terms that also appear in his theological treatises.

Ibn Dawud had Imamite friends, but they were moderate Shiʿites; and since he did not believe in the reality of the Hallajian "Essential Desire," he must have believed, like these moderate and very well-to-do Shiʿites, that Hallaj was a Qarmathian agent disguised as a mystic so as to launch a Qarmathian social revolution.

The Arab proletariat of West Baghdad was very predisposed to such a revolution; Ibn Dawud was all the more aware of this for having studied the soul of the Arab nomad apropos his poetic ideal of love. And Taha Husayn has very rightly linked the surge of *'udhritic* Arab poetry ("in which one dies of love") in the seventh century of our era to the economic crisis that had at that time impoverished Arabia.

The hard life of the desert, with its continual dangers, is a novitiate of Poverty, which predisposes the Arab race to a "paroxystic" manner of loving that is very unsocial and, on the whole, anticommunitarian, in which death hovers as a constant threat and as the desired end.

"Love, so long as it hides, feels itself in great danger, and is only reassured by exposing itself to risk" (Hallaj, *Diwan*). This is not yet the sublimated self-conscious tension of townsmen (*hadar*, yesterday Manichaeans, today Isma'ilis, for whom death is desirable, because it is an explosion of the Spirit destroying a sinister body, which must not revive), but love as known among the nomads (*badu*): it is a clinical case, a *"crise de sauvagerie."* L. F. Clauss, in his observations on Arab nomadic life in Jordan, notes that it is not rare for an Arab who has fallen in love to die, for he "burns" and is consumed, body and soul. The desert has no distractions or "substitute" capable of diverting him from the image of beauty that flames his solitary memory; and if he prays, his prayer, born out of a burnt monotheism, can only hasten his death, through desire to see the veil of beauty rise, to discover another Face, *al-Wajh al-Karim*: of the Judge.

It is this second death that the Hallajian preaching attempts to explode in its listener. And, whatever may have been Hallaj's position, thoughtful minds believed it possible to make the unsocial *"crise de sauvagerie"* of *'udhritic* love develop gradually into the *"crise de sauvagerie"* in God as is the Hallajian Desire. It is, in fact, with an *isnad* of two well-known Hallajians that the *Masari'* of Sarraj transmit to us (via Nasrabadhi, Ibn 'Ata') the basic text of Asma'i on *hubb 'udhri*, that "gentleness of heart," *"riqqat al-qulub,"* which was the attribute of an elite Arab tribe that was preeminently pure, the Banu 'Udhra, whose people "died when they loved" and believed that "to die of love is a sweet and noble death." And the early accounts, attributed to the Salimiya, on the martyrdom of Hallaj, are filled with a poetic atmosphere of *hubb 'udhri*. But the attempt to harmonize the two only weakens [the testimony of] Hallaj's [martyrdom]. Daylami, in a very interesting way, compares the Hallajian theory of Desire with that of such pre-Socratic philosophers as Empedocles and Heraclitus. These harmonizing attempts, in which mere pastiches rather than genuine realizations were stirred up, succeeded in paralyzing the development of Muslim mystical poetry.

Hubb 'udhri is so characteristic of the Arab soul that it is fitting, for our understanding of this soul, to discuss in a few lines here the main theories about its origin and its philosophical meaning.

Historically, this love that is "pure and shy unto death" originates in Yemen, according to classical Arabic criticism (Asma'i); however, we question the Qahtanid genealogy of the Quda'a, the clan of which the Banu 'Udhra tribe (encamped at Wadi'l-Qura, northwest of Medina) was a part, which gave birth to 'Urwat 'Afra, the first poet of *'udhritic* love. The deeply religious character of Yemen should link this love to an "archetype" found in the subconscious of most of the primitive tribes of humanity: the election of a religious and sacrificial life by the unexpected appearance of a "kindred soul"; this "kindred soul," the sign of our calling, is above all (and sometimes totally) a spirit, and the spiritual relationship in which it sustains us avoids any physical and sexual contact; the "kindred soul" is pure and is interiorized through contemplation and is consumed in solitude. The perfect symbol of this spirit is the fragrance used in worship, which Yemen alone, throughout antiquity, always furnished to the temples (Queen of Sheba), and as far off as India: the incense (*yanjujshahas*) of South Arabia, sap extracted from a bush that is raised and tapped only on the coast called Shihr al-Luban (in Mahra, land of the Mehari racing camels, which transport it); the incense "burned in worship" of which Hallaj spoke during his last vigil.

Ibn Dawud perceived this love, considered as an "angelic" consecration and as revealing of one's predestination, when he asked whether the image (crystallized: Stendhal) that the impassioned lover substitutes for the worship of the object loved is not a kind of spell due to a "demonic possession"; for canonical Islam acknowledges "demonic possession," *waswas*, but not divine possession. He quotes the following verses of Jamil Buthayna:

> Love embraced my spirit with his spirit before we were created,
> —and even after our weaning, and even in the cradle;
> And it grew, as we were growing, unceasingly growing,
> And nothing will come to break our union when we are dead;
> Only it, surviving everything, will visit us,
> In the darkness of the grave, beneath its stone.

More profoundly, shouldn't the human nature of the two lovers, in the care of a single angel, be marked with the sign of a predestination of unimaginable unity, and, for their salvation, mustn't the two lovers go beyond the mutual image of their beauty in the angelic mirror, in order to adhere to the *fiat* of the Essential Desire? We shall examine an anecdote by Ibn Dawud on this later.

"Just as drawing near a being in ourselves removes us from him," says Hallaj, "so drawing near him in himself brings us closer to him."

Indeed this love can veer toward syneisaktism or uranism. Celtic syneisaktism seems to be one of the origins of mediaeval courtly love, while the self-conscious uranism of too many Arab poets may have been inspired by Plato.

As early as the first century of Islam, this *'udhritic* love, an adoration turning to idolatry of the sovereign power of the beloved object [which is reflected already in the double names given to poets (Jamil Buthayna, Kuthayir ʿAzza)], turns frustrated and bitter among the legitimist Shiʿites who passionately adore the Imam whose Name they keep secret to outsiders, for the Imam, a divine emanation, must wear a veil over his face.

For about a century and a half, comparative literary criticism has tried to discover connections between the Arab poets of *hubb ʿudhri* and the western poets of courtly love, of the *"dolce stil nuovo."* The cases of Guilhem IX de Poitiers (d. 1127) and of Ramon Lull (d. 1315) have been cited. The Andalusian dialectal method led the way to certain discoveries (rhythms, variations in themes).

Let us keep in mind from this discussion that Arab *ʿudhritic* poetry suggests that love is not a stratagem of the reproductive instinct, but a divine annunciation. It is not an external revelation of the Law, but an internal one of Grace. A revelation of divine nature to human nature, through the ministry of an Angel, because the angelic nature, ruled by *sujud*, that is to say, by an intellectual ecstasy beyond its own will, must present the *fiat* intellectually to material bodies, animate or inanimate. Human nature, ruled by *nazar*, by sight, that is to say, by a "visionary" ecstasy beyond its own intellect, must "exorcise" the angelic annunciation, by accepting only its pure *fiat* "in the name of God": without becoming attached to the messenger.

In the Qurʾan, Islam announces, not the union of the Christian incarnation, but a mystic union (which is also Christian), by means of a prior angelic revelation (entrusted also to Gabriel), which, as such, resounded in the amatory ideal of the Banu ʿUdhra, owing to the feeling of predestination which love reveals to lovers; while putting them to the test: of choosing between idolatry of the created messenger of the divine "Commandment," and renunciation of every icon, even mental, of the Adored One.

Ibn Dawud's Life and Teaching

Abu Bakr Muhammad-b-Dawud-b-ʿAli-b-Khalaf Isfahani, the son and successor of the founder of the Zahirite school, was born in 255/868.

A sensitive personality, frail and effeminate, he was very quickly enervated by the refinements of luxury at the ʿAbbasid court, to which his father's connections with Muwaffaq had introduced him, and where he formed a friendship with the poet-prince Ibn al-Muʿtazz. He was the only Sunnite among his learned friends, for, like Suli, he usually frequented Shiʿite circles.

One account gives a typical picture of his "behavior," his teaching, and his fate:

Ruwayn told of being present during a gathering in the reception room of Dawud-b-ʿAli, his father, when the young child entered weeping. His father embraced him and asked, "Why are you crying?" He said, "The children have given me a name." "Tell me what it is, so I can take it up with them." "They have given me the name of something." "Well, tell me what it is, so I can put a stop to it." "They call me 'poor little sparrow ('*usfur al-shawk*).'" His father laughed. Then the child said: "See, you are meaner to me than they are, because you laugh about it." The father answered: "There is no god but God, and no names but those that are given by Heaven: you are nothing other, my child, than a poor little sparrow."

The Zahirites, in fact, believed that the study of onomastics is *tawqifi*, that names are predestined by God, and not invented and agreed upon by men (*istilah*: the theory of the Muʿtazilites, the *falasifa* [Platonic onomatology] and Ibn Surayj). For they all have their obvious meaning, which does not have to be analyzed in order to be established.

Barely sixteen when his father died (270/883), he became head of the Zahirite school and later had almost four hundred students who came with ink-well in hand to write from his dictation. By the age of seven he had learned the Qur'an by heart (*hafiz*), and by ten, the classical Arabic poets: which his *Kitab al-zahra*, written probably before he was sixteen, proves.

Of his body of writing, which for the most part was juridical in nature, this work of literary criticism on the subject of pure love is the only one that is extant.

Along with didactic works on the Zahirite school, he wrote polemical tracts: against the Sunnite Tabari (Yaqut analyzes this one), against Ibrahim Darir, and against the Imamite Nashi Akbar (d. 293/905).

Ibn Dawud was refuted by a Shafiʿite qadi of Cairo, ʿAA-b-M ibn al-Khasib (d. A.H. 347).

Some of his "conversations" have been preserved and show us the effectiveness of his method. Such as the one in which he gives priority to ʿAli over Abu Bakr in the presence of the secretary of General Badr (against the arguments of the Shafiʿite Muhamili). And two of those that he had with the Shafiʿite Ibn Surayj, the first concerning Hallaj, the second concerning the formula of retraction of the declaration of divorce. We shall analyze the latter in some detail, for it throws light on the different general methods of approach used by Ibn Dawud and Ibn Surayj to the particular case of Hallaj.

There are several kinds of declaration that a husband may make use of, lightly, for purposes of divorcing a wife whom he basically loves; and jurisconsults have gone to great lengths to find legal loopholes, *hiyal* (casuistical devices, evasions), by which a husband, denounced by witnesses before a qadi, may avoid being forced to give her back her liberty and to pay a compensation.

In the case of the *zihar* declaration ("You are for me as the back [i.e., the body] of my mother [i.e., untouchable]"), Ibn Dawud, basing his position on Qur'an 57:2–3, explains the "obligatory retraction" (*ʿawd al-wajib*) provided for in the law as the "pure and simple repetition of the formula of repudiation." He deduces that from the *tawbat al-qadhif*, "retraction (admission) of the false accusation"; which the Zahirite school declares completed (with cancellation of sanctions) as soon as he recites word for word the formula (*'awd al-lisan*) for removing it, as if this were a magic formula, completing *ipso facto* the *kaffara* (expiation).

One rather limited Shafi'ite, AS Istakhri, argued in an analogous way that the retraction of the false accusation consists of what the accuser himself considers false, without realizing that he was thereby falling into the sophism of Epimenides. The Shafi'ite school did not follow him, but followed Ibn Surayj, who argued that the accuser must confess *al-qadhf haram*, "the false accusation is forbidden" (the *isnad* of this solution passed from Ibn Surayj through AB Qaffal and Abu Ishaq Shirazi up to Ghazali).

Applying this solution in turn to the problem of "the retraction of the repudiating formula," Ibn Surayj declared that it consisted of the husband's expression of desire to resume conjugal life and of regret at what he had said (the Hanafites are satisfied with an "admission that the repudiating formula used was pagan").

In this discussion we see that, for Ibn Dawud, the juridical formulas applicable to social life amount to stock phrases to be judiciously spoken without any regard to their effect on the well-being of consciences: taking into account only their material and legalistic expediency. Ibn Surayj sees the common good in the resumption of conjugal life, the well-being of the conscience of everybody in the confession of regret; he is obliged to express it in terms that do not belong to literal Law, and this got him accused of Mu'tazilism; but he does not proceed along the lines of Mu'tazilite *istilahat*, of inventing technical terms, rather he attempts carefully and reflectively to define the situations of conscience in jeopardy by means of appropriate approximative lexical modalities.

The debate between the two adversaries, apropos of Hallaj, revealed even more fully their ideas about the origin of language and the social import of language used in testimony.

Comparison of Their Deaths and Their Destinies

The sharp contrast between Ibn Dawud and Hallaj is shown by their different kinds of death, though their survivals are strangely intermingled in the memory of the Muslim Community.

KINDS OF DEATH

Both died for love. We glimpse the precious, ordered setting of Ibn Dawud's death: still young, lavished with attentions and weary regrets, on a divan, between the light filtering in from outside through the *shahnishin* grating and the empty space that the "tarma" overlooks, before a cage that holds a blinded twittering nightingale. His last remarks show him turning back, restored to serenity, to the renunciations of forbidden pleasures in his past; his body was going to be ritually bathed (by Ibn al-Mughallis, rather than by the filthy Niftawayh) and buried in a shroud; what was of concern to him was that he was allowed in this way to carry the mental conception of this forbidden pleasure intact, since it was unsatisfied, to the paradise of uranians.

We shall see in further detail the other death for love, that of Hallaj. The huge, gory setting of the gibbet execution: the explosion into ruins of the hoisted tortured criminal, and his collapse, in the open air, the butt of everyone's sarcasms, mutilated, decapitated, burned. His last words show his broken, yet so vital spirit filled with desire, aspiring after an even more piercing renunciation of himself, penetrating to the very solitude of God, even beyond death. They deluded themselves into believing they could prevent his body from resurrecting with the martyrs of the holy war by burning it, scattering it to the sandstorms and the river waves; he had cried out that a single spark from his remains, burned in oil, was proof to him of the glorious resurrection of this broken body.

THEIR SURVIVALS

Just as the Zahirite theology of Ibn 'Arabi, which denies, in the name of existential monism, that God speaks to Himself essentially, tried to incorporate the Hallajian presentation of testimonial monism and its witness of bodily resurrection through the Word, so also did classical Muslim scholasticism, which denies, through agnosticism, that God loves Himself in an Essential Desire, try to reincorporate Hallaj, executed as a criminal, into the supposedly Muslim Community of Damned Believers, founded by the fallen Archangel when he refused to submit his will to God, in order to keep intact the solitary ideal that he held of His transcendence.

It is true that if divine transcendence excluded the possibility of God's communicating to Himself and submitting to Himself, in His essential life, then the perfection of *Tawhid*, of pure Islam, is *Tafrid*, the proclamation of the Jealous Solitude, which the Zahirite theologians, following Ibn Dawud, analyzed correctly in the pure uranian love sung by classic Arabic poets: in the "disinterested" gaze of morose delectation that Ibn Dawud considered licit, directed at forbidden beautiful faces (of beardless youths: *nazar ila'l-murd*). For the aforementioned famous hadith that his father had imparted to him, taught that the amorous one who endures love chastely unto death, dies a martyr. And Ibn Dawud died for this *shahada*, revived by the only "licit gaze." Ibn Dawud should therefore be seen as the herald and martyr of the Lonely God. In fact, this was clearly defined in sermons from the pulpits of mosques two hundred years after his death: by 'Umar Samarqandi and by Ahmad Ghazali. The definition was based on an authentic anecdote from the life of Ibn Dawud, two recensions of which we present here:

1. AS Malini (Sufi) > H-b-Ibr Laythi:

One day, Muhammad-b-Zukhruf ibn Jamiꜥ went to the *hammam*. After having his face massaged, he veiled himself, and got on his horse to go and meet Ibn Dawud. But when Ibn Dawud saw him arrive veiled in this way, he thought it was because of an accident, and he cried out: "What happened?" "I have just seen my face in a mirror. I admired it so much that I veiled it, for I wished no one to see it before you." And Ibn Dawud swooned (from jealousy).

2. Caliph Muttaqi, according to Samꜥani, questioned Ibn Jamiꜥ forty years later:

"Did you notice anything strange about him?"—"Nothing, O Commander of the Faithful, except that one night when I was sleeping in his house, he lifted the veil from my face and said 'God, You know that I love him, and that it is You whom I behold in him.' "—"What was your way of repaying him for his admiration?"—"I went to a *hammam*; and when I was leaving, I looked at my face in a mirror and admired its appearance more than usual. I veiled it, so that no one could see it before he did. I went to him; he lifted the veil from my face and rejoiced; and filled with joy, he said 'Glory be to Him Who created and fashioned it.' He then recited the following: 'It is He who fashions you in the loins as He likes' (Ibn Fadl Allah)."

3. The following is ꜥUmar's sermon:

A Karramiyan preacher named ꜥUmar-b-Hy Naysaburi Samarqandi (who wrote under the Mazyadite Sadaqa I, d. 501/1107) states in his *Rawnaq al-qulub* that Ibn Dawud's swooning was due to a fearful jealousy:

In Baghdad there was a man (Ibn Dawud) whose *maꜥshuq* (beloved) came to his house unexpectedly and was wearing a veil of thin material. He removed his veil and said to him "look (*Unzur*) at my face." And his lover said to him: "do you wish to disturb me with temptation?" He responded, "I went to a *hammam*; and when I was leaving, I looked at my face in a mirror, I admired it so much that I wanted no one but you to see it; look at me." But the lover looked away from him and said, "I will no longer look at you."—"Why?"—"I looked at you in such a way that no one else but me could look at you; but now you, you have looked at your face inflamed by it (*la'ihan bihi*); I do not wish to share love." And the preacher concluded: "Such must be the behavior of the believer vis-à-vis (his) God."

There is no doubt that the *maꜥshuq* in the sermon is Ibn Jamiꜥ and the "man" who loves him is Ibn Dawud. But what is important is the final thought of the sermon: "Such must be the behavior of the believer vis-à-vis (his) God."

Is the believer therefore supposed to *refuse to obey God*, when, in the Qur'an, God demands (referring to Moses) that we *look at* His reflection (not at Him) on Sinai; or that we *prostrate* ourselves (referring to Satan) before His image (not Him) in the form of Adam? The rigid transcendentalism of Islam raised the problem in the very beginning for mystics. AS Kharraz said, "If God took satisfaction from the acts of His creatures, the refusal of Satan would certainly be an act of extreme desire to please Him" (*ghayat idlal*). Dhu'l-Nun Misri claimed to have seen Satan's tears of loving regret flow, and Sahl Tustari had conversed with Satan about his desire for God's forgiveness; and his disciples, the Salimiya, for two centuries taught that Satan would be forgiven, for he had acted out of pure love (and had prostrated himself at the second command).

In a famous text, Hallaj had rectified this view by showing that the election of an Angel could not be changed, that Satan had, more than any other lover of God, sought to please, not God but the sublime idea that he had had of God, that men must imitate his example by pushing their desire for God further to breaking the Law, because human nature can in such a case die and undergo that essential change which is the resurrection of [God's] forgiveness. This is why Hallaj had conceived of a dialogue between Moses and an Annunciator, no longer Elias (Khidr) but Satan—on the slope of Sinai—in which Satan reproached Moses for having obeyed when God had said to him *Unzur* (*look*: at Sinai), for he, Satan, would never have done it, nor had he lacked the heroism of pure love.

The Salimiya observed that Moses was punished, for he saw "a hundred Sinais and on each Sinai a Moses" (which Hallaj denies); for the Salimiya believes that Hallaj was a hero of pure love, damned like Satan; holy like him, he will be redeemed with him.

The Ash'arites, who, like Hallaj, teach the irremissible damnation of Satan, were divided on Hallaj himself: Abu Ishaq Isfara'ini taught that Hallaj was damned like the Hallajian Satan, for a false pure love; Jurjani and Qushayri rehabilitate both by teaching that damned saints exist (and that the fire of hell is the fire of their love of God, which they do not want to go out). That God has two kinds of holy witnesses, the Elect (with the Prophet as their leader), and the Damned (with Satan their leader). In this they always use the theme of *hubb 'udhri* to characterize Hallaj. It is strange that the early Hallajians, in order to give an acceptable exoteric teaching of their master, made him out to be a uranian lover of God, a satanic lover of God.

What Ibn Dawud had been, at heart, they reclothed his victim in. The conclusions of the two sermonizers are identical and categorical: Naysaburi says, apropos of the refusal to look at (God): "such must be the behavior of the believer vis-à-vis (his) God." Ahmad Ghazali says exactly the same.

It is certain that the Qur'anic verses in question, concerning Satan and Moses, disturbed the rigid transcendentalism of the early Muslim mystics. Their uncertainty about the incorporeity of angels made them indecisive about the irrevocability of their damnation; Hallaj, and afterwards Ash'ari, will be the first to affirm the latter for external reasons of metaphysical soundness. Only Hallaj will attempt a "psychological" investigation of the fall of Satan, dead from an *amour manqué*,

The divine trial, in the two cases of Satan and of Moses, consists of their being "transported"; Satan beyond his angelic nature, Moses beyond his human nature, beside themselves with His Essential desire. God says to the Angel *"Usjud,"* bow down before the form of Adam, meaning before a material Temple of His glory; Satan, an immaterial being, refuses to recognize this abasement of God. God says to Man (Moses, directly and through the ministry of Khidr; Muhammad, at Qab Qawsayn): *"Unzur,"* look at Sinai, the High Place of His Glory; Man, being composed of a body and a soul, wavers but ends, not without regret, by obeying (*ruju' 'an hawlihi*).

Hallaj, with a singular power of thought, remarked that Satan was right to reproach Moses for having yielded and obeyed; Moses should have followed the angel Satan and refused, through pure love. For angelic nature is right in counseling human nature to destroy the Temple (in order to worship the Holy One Who is all Alone), provided that it is the privilege of the created human being to be able to die ("destroy the Ka'ba of your body that it may resuscitate, created anew"); but the angelic species, which cannot die, was wrong to refuse to acknowledge and to want to destroy the personal form of Adam, for angelic nature received legitimate authority only over the human body, while the human soul receives personal life from a divine Spirit over which the angels have no normal intellectual hold. Satan therefore sinned and in an irremissible way (*ma raja'a 'an hawlihi*); nevertheless, his justification through pure love, his death song, has a value for us as an exemplary warning (AS Kharraz had said that if God could take pleasure in the acts of His creatures, certainly the refusal of Satan would be an act of extreme desire to please [*ghayat idlalin*]). In man, the love of God must make a sacrifice to God of the Temple of God; but in the Angel, love cannot destroy the Temple (the form of Adam) in which the Spirit is mysteriously infused, for the immaterial nature does not conceive of a body as its place (from within), rather it conceives of it as a sphere of action (from without) imparted by God.

By a second inversion, Satan, who in his damnation, preached pure monotheism and the destruction of the form of Adam to the angels, preaches idolatrous polytheism to men in their damnation, thereby hastening the destruction of the Temple. In both cases, his tempting preaching is valid, according to predestination, and carries out the divine Word "by an inversion of meanings" to the letter.

The loving adoration that destroys the perishable Temple in order to hasten its resurrection, the Solitude of Man in the Essential Desire of God, the negative way which Hallaj describes more purely than Eckhart (who was burdened with a bad Platonist vocabulary), is an annunciation of the Reign of the Holy Spirit, of the *kun* (*fiat*). It is a death from love that resuscitates; very different in this regard from the death from love that, in Ibn Dawud, is a "mummifying" abstraction of memories and an impersonal "intellectualization" of regrets.

Given the essential difference between Hallaj's and Ibn Dawud's versions of death for love, how does it happen that there were not only enemies who compared the execution of Hallaj with the damnation of Satan, but also disciples (perhaps through catechesis) who compared the state of soul of the dying Hallaj with the state of soul of the dying ʿudhritic lover, the state in which Ibn Dawud wished to die?

In actual fact, it took several centuries (perhaps because of the official excommunication) to get rid of this double (and contradictory) comparison.

(1) With the ʿudhritic lover. Hallaj had been a disciple of Nuri; some Hanbalites, like Khara'iti and Ibn ʿAta', Hallaj's close friend, and a true Hallajian, Nasrabadhi, were convinced of the therapeutic excellence of the sublimation of ʿudhritic desire to the Desire of God. In his splendid book on love, Daylami, an independent philosopher who was also a mystic, a disciple of both AH Tawhidi and Ibn Khafif, resumes this harmonizing effort with great sincerity; but he recognizes the solitary position of Hallaj: "the one who studied the question thoroughly and isolated himself from his masters and his contemporaries in setting it forth is Husayn-b-Mansur." The following is the text of his theory about love itself:

Husayn-b-Mansur, known as "Hallaj," said: "Desire is the fire from the Light of the primordial Fire; as pre-eternity colors every shade, Desire manifests every attribute; its essence becomes inflamed by its essence, its attributes sparkle from its attributes. It is realized, traversing all routes from pre-eternity to the post-eternities; its source is Illeity arising from Hecceity; the interior of the exterior of its essence is the reality of Being, and the exterior of the interior of its attributes is the perfect Form that witnesses totality perfectly." And he recited the following concerning this subject:

> Desire, in the pre-eternity of pre-eternities is the Absolute;
> In Him, by Him, of Him it appears; in Him it appeared.
> Desire is not contingent, since it is the attribute
> Of attributes for the one whom it killed and whom it restores to life.
> His attributes, of Him in Him, are not created things,
> "The creator of a thing is he who makes these things appear.
> When He set the beginning in motion, and showed His Desire as an attribute
> Through what He had released, its gleam sparkled in Him.
> The Lam was formed with the Alif as partner;
> Both have thus been predestined as One.
> By differentiating them, they become two if they unite together.
> But their only difference is the same as that between the servant and his Lord.
> Such are the realities, the fire of Desire inflames them with Reality
> Whether they are near to it or far.
> They dwindle, losing force, the more infatuated they become;
> And the strong, when they lose their hearts, are humbled."

Hallaj presented the first on a metaphysical plane: Desire is linked, in the divine essence, to the divine Illeity (huwiya) and Heceity (anniya), the real

Being (*Wujud*) and integrally perfect Form (*sura*). He noted, on the other hand, that mystic union does not annihilate the personality of the holy witness (*shahid*), because union is transnatural, between two natures, *lahut* and *nasut*.

Daylami adds: "in this theory (Hallaj) differed from all the other masters," as much on the question of the essentiality of divine Desire as on the matter of union without extinction of the lover by the Beloved. The amorous creative act produces an effect.

Hallaj borrows from Empedocles and Heraclitus: "we do not know any forerunner for his theory among the other (Sufi) masters; it gained him many disciples too numerous to list here (Mantiqi, Tawhidi, Balkhi); and if we are going to cite his theory, it is because his language is akin to theirs (the pre-Socratics (*awa'il*), Empedocles and Heraclites)."

(2) With the damnation of Satan. Salimiya (death for *ʿudhritic* love). Ashʿarites: damnation of the hypocrite (temporary punishment for the exalted lover).

It is very strange that this "Satanic" justification of the jealousy of Ibn Dawud should be introduced simultaneously by these two Khurasanian preachers, Naysaburi and Ahmad Ghazali, just as Ahmad Ghazali, attempting to identify Hallaj's attitude toward love (following the Ashʿarite school of Khurasan in this effort), was being vilified by Baghdadian Hanbalites and Shafiʿites: Yf Hamadhani, Ibn ʿAqil, up to Kilani, Baqli, Rumi, and Samnani, showed how the humble abandon of Hallaj is the opposite of the jealous reserve of Satan and of Ibn Dawud. It seems that the Sufism of the Shuhudiya had become cognizant again of the true mentality of Hallaj just at the time when the monism of the Wujudiya began canonizing Satan and, with him, those uranians who, like Ibn Dawud, held the idea of a celestial paradise without the desire of God.

The jealous glance, winking from within, at the swerve of Divine Transcendence just as it "draws near," is the "rear view" glance of intellectual onanism, of narcissism, enamoured of no one else but its own ideal, in the mirror of its mind. In fact, the poets of Ibn Dawud's time, Platonized narcissists, celebrated the lordship of the narcissus (*narjis*) flower, which the uranian Sophocles portrayed blossoming at the edge of the magic shadow; a thick and hardy snow flower whose polygonal sexual bud undergoes invagination, speared toward the inside. Meanwhile their spokesman, Ibn al-Rumi, mocks the rose (*ward*), a flower of the glade, for the bloody dehiscence of its sex, ingenuously blossoming out toward the sky, in dazzling display. If it does not close again over its enraptured vision of the sun, it is because it is like a crystal of it which becomes opalescent through a virginal conception.

In any case, in spite of Muslim poetry's persistent taste for narcissus, only the rose, especially among Turkish poets, will symbolize *Hallac-e Mansur*; crucified, he is the heart of the blossoming rose that mystic birds come to peck at. Lamiʿi of Bursa dedicated his *qasida* to the rose (about Hallaj, written for Sulayman; the rose that modestly bends its head in dying, like Mansur on the gibbet) (v. 2); "the rose, whose heart burned like a candle . . . and arms were smeared with blood, like the lover (= Mansur)" (v. 11).

Ibn Surayj's Opposition; Its Suspensive Power

It was under Qadi Abu ʿUmar Hammadi, who had just been appointed deputy of his father, the Malikite grand qadi, for the western section of Baghdad (Madinat al-Mansur), that Ibn Dawud, his Zahirite assessor, had formulated his charge against Hallaj. Qadi Abu ʿUmar also had a Shafiʿite assessor, Ibn Surayj; and together with Ibn Dawud, they held legal discussions, perhaps before Abu ʿUmar's nomination as deputy, in the Rusafa mosque (east bank). It was during the course of these tripartite talks that Ibn Surayj formulated his Shafiʿite opposition to the charge of the Zahirite Ibn Dawud.

Ibn Dawud thought that Hallaj was adducing (on the problem of love in particular) an interpretaion of the Qur'an that was contrary to the Sunna (traditional example) of the Prophet, and contrary to the obvious meaning of the Arabic lexicon, which grew out of authoritative examples (shawahid) drawn by grammarians from classical Arabic poets.

The Zahirites do not believe in the use of qiyas (analogical reasoning; syllogism in philosophy), and they believe that the Prophet only transmitted and put into operation the message of revelation (tanzil), whose meaning, especially whose obvious meaning, the believer can grasp directly. Similarly, external knowledge of Arabic words is sufficient; there is no analogous internal symbolic meaning to be found or understood in them.

The Shafiʿites, on the other hand, deduce from the general principle of "the Sunna [taking] precedence (in practical matters) over the Qur'an" that the Qur'an, in order to be put into practice, requires interpretation (ta'wil). That the meaning of a legal designation, such as salat ("prayer"), is not obvious; that in order to understand it, one must use not only external analogical reasoning (the Hanafite position), but also meditation (tuma'nina), for there are immaterial durations of mental states (ahwal) having for us a causal mode of existence (wujud: not only instantaneous ecstasy, wajd), a truth (haqq: a certitude that is not only momentary sincerity, sidq). This is against the hypocrisy of the Kattabiya Ismaʿilis, who developed an inverted dialectical argument out of "materialism"; these two sources of interpretation, which were rejected by Zahirites, are different, and one cannot subject to the analogical reasoning of jurisconsults those certitudes that are privately, but validly, experienced in meditation—that is, experienced through "private inspiration," ilham, which is not prophetic inspiration, wahy, but which is in union with the divine fiat, according to the Qur'an.

Later we shall give some examples of the general discussion that took place between Ibn Surayj and Ibn Dawud, to illustrate what we have just summarized. On the specific case of Hallaj, we have just one very brief text of opposition, which is a sort of suspensive *fatwa*:

"This is a man (*rajul*) (Hallaj), whose inspiration I cannot grasp. So, I shall not attempt a doctrinal evaluation of it."

Beneath its obvious spareness, this *fatwa* proves that in his eyes Hallaj is a sincere believer and not a hypocritical imposter. It concludes very clearly in favor of the independence of mysticism in Islam vis-à-vis canonical courts; in the face of mystic states of consciousness, the jurisconsult "suspends" his judgment (*tawaqquf*); he is not qualified to pronounce on such matters, and the qadi is not competent to apply, through analogical reasoning, any legal sanctions.

This falls within the category of *sarira*, of the inward consciousness of every person, which will be revealed only on Judgment Day (*yawma tubla'l-sara'ir*, Qur'an 86:9), for it is the secret of love (*lihawa'l-nufusi sariratun la tu'lamu*: unknowable by science; hidden even from angels), of the *khulla* of the *abdal*, on which a contemporary Shafi'ite, Abu 'Amr A-b-Nasr Khaffaf (d. 299/911), from Nishapur, gave a similar suspensive *fatwa*.

Some more or less apocryphal enlargements of Ibn Surayj's *fatwa* have been preserved:

In the *Sirr al-'alamayn*, attributed to Ghazali (39):

"What should I say about a man who in jurisprudence knows more than I do and who in mysticism speaks a language I do not understand?"

In the *Akhbar al-Hallaj*, no. 72, he is depicted responding (to Jundab Wasiti?): "As for me, I attest that he is a *hafiz* (= one who knows the Qur'an by heart), that he is trained in jurisprudence and learned in hadith, traditions and customs, that he fasts continually, prays all night, preaches good morals, weeps out of contrition; it is not because I do not understand the language he uses that I can condemn him as a *kafir*."

In the same collection of *Akhbar* (no. 71), he is depicted responding to Ibrahim-b-Shayban (an anti-Hallajian Sufi) who asked him: "O Abu'l-'Abbas, what do you say regarding the *fatwa* of those who demand his execution?" "They must have forgotten the words of God: "Would you kill a man because he says "my master is God?" (Qur'an 40:28)."

These different variants show the whole range of Ibn Surayj's opposition, relevant not only to the suspension of proceedings against Hallaj, but also to the entire subsequent history of Sufis' contentions with jurisconsults. Kamal Damiri (d. 808/1405), trained in the Sa'id al-Su'ada' *Khanqah*, twenty years a *mujawir* (in Mecca), and a professor at al-Azhar in Shafi'ite law (a pupil of the son of Subki), compared this *fatwa* of Ibn Surayj to the *fatwa* of Caliph 'Umar-b-'Abd al-'Aziz, who declined to settle the conflict of *tahkim* between Mu'awiya, his ancestor, and 'Ali, the fourth Caliph: "God has averted our swords from their blood; our tongues must not go deeply into their conflict." The *fatwa* of Ibn Surayj removed for good the procedure of *takfir*, the only Qur'anically proper procedure, from trials involving mystics. And it forced the enemies of Hallaj to "politicize" their charge, to replace the term *kufr* with the term *zandaqa*.

Ibn Surayj's unquestionable sympathy for Hallaj proved itself to be active on the practical level, since as long as the party of Ibn 'Isa, who admired Ibn Surayj, was in power, that is to say, until 296/908, and again at the time of the trial in 301/913 and just after, Hallaj was spared; until 306/918, the year when Ibn Surayj died, 25 *Jumada* I, on the very day before Hamid's appointment as vizir.

II. THE DEFINITION OF *ZANDAQA*, A HERESY THREATENING THE SECURITY OF THE STATE

The Crime of Heresy, the Anathema (Takfir), *and Its Lack of Effectiveness*

It was the entire Islamic Community, the *Umma*, that was called to pass judgment on the orthodoxy of Hallaj. In his preaching he had wanted to reach all Muslims, from the most traditional Sunnites to the most extremist Shi'ites. He had even devised for himself an Arabic metaphysical vocabulary, which was sometimes borrowed from profane sciences developed by independent minds outside Islam. This universalist tendency had brought him a few enemies everywhere who were determined to expel him from the Islamic "communion."

They tried for twelve years to do so; and yet, in spite of his "excommunication" and his execution, they seem to have only partially succeeded. This is because it is not enough to define a given proposition as containing a doctrinal error and to anathematize it (*takfir*)—not enough, that is, for moving the Sunnite public opinion of the large majority of Muslim believers to isolate the author of the accused proposition and to bring him, through the instrumentality of the *shuhud* or legal witnesses, to the qadi court for punishment by the secular arm.

The social discipline of Islam forbids such discreditation and limits the right of fraternal redress. From the moment that a believer suspected of heterodoxy resumes reciting the *shahada* and turns toward Mecca in prayer, he is a member of the *Ahl al-Qibla* whom no fault, not even a public fault, may cut off entirely from the *Umma*. Theologically this duty of the "good opinion" (*husn al-zann*) incumbent on every Muslim is called the *irja'*: to postpone judging one either damned or holy until Judgment Day (even in the case of a deceased man). And a proverb, supposedly given by the Prophet, says *"ikhtilaf ummati rahma"*: "differences of opinion are a (divine) blessing for my Community." This facilitated a free inquiry which was not without philosophical interest, but which was always regarded with suspicion by men of action and by rational minds that accepted only religious doctrine as being actually formed by equipollent and simultaneous variations. The Muslim Community, as Goldziher noted, has a "catholic tendency," especially among the Sunnites, "which attributes to the Prophet another saying": *la tajtami' Ummati 'ala'l-dalala*, "my Community cannot err when it is unanimous." But when is it unanimous? Historically the Hallaj case is precisely one of those paradoxical instances in which a quasi-unanimity is formed against an attempt at universalization.

The first attempt was that of the *Muhakkima* of Harawra, those jealous puritanical guardians of the Qur'anic text who had insisted that the armed conflict between the Companions of the Prophet which was halted at Siffin be settled by a unanimously accepted arbitration. They saw themselves being excluded by the two rival parties, and, though they succeeded in maintaining an *ijma' al-Qurra'*, "a consensus among Reciters of the Qur'an" regarding theoretical studies, they saw themselves being dealt a blow by the others, and by their own dissenters from the anathema, *takfir*, which they had at first devised against controversialists who held differences of opinion: without any reconciliation [possible] through true repentance (external *tawba*) or through recognition of the legitimacy of 'Ali.

The second attempt was that of the *Zaydite Mu'tazilites*, those thinkers concerned with justice who attempted a reconciliation among Muslims based on honestly reasoned principles of theology (*kalam*), without protecting it from perfidies by a social philosophy (*usul al-fiqh*), that took into account the living presence of the Word of God—without which no religious society can hold together, as their victorious enemy, Ibn Hanbal, showed.

The third attempt was that of the *Sufis*, those ascetics who, from Muhasibi to Hallaj, developed through self-examination and an interiorization of the acts of worship a method of guidance (*irshad*) capable of morally purifying the life of society by spreading recollection and communal centers of spiritual and fraternal mutual aid. This attempt collapsed too, since it was caught in a vice between the large banking capitalism of the Imamite Shi'ite businessmen and the urban bedouin communism of the Isma'ili revolutionaries, both the declared enemies of the universal Sunnite Caliphate. The latter collapsed, preserving in Baghdad a shadow of its former life thanks only to a temporary coalition of Hanbalites and Sufis, which rescued the monasteries from Shi'ite hatred.

Hallaj is the one who had brought Sufism to the political plane as a social force, for he had given it an original theological and philosophical superstructure; but this also had made it vulnerable, exposed to theological charges of *takfir*, and even threatened by effective legal penalties.

The charge of *kufr* (impiety) is directed at two positions: *juhud*, avowed denial of the Law, and *nifaq*, hypocrisy with respect to it. Avowed denial has to do with the apostate, *murtadd*, or the obstinate (the Jew, the Christian, the pagan). Hypocrisy refers to willful neglect of the prescriptions of the Law (*tashri'*), either in themselves (*matlab ta'abbudi*) or in their preparation (*matlab tawassuli*). Which can make one liable to the *hudud* (*huquq Allah*), to legal punishments provided for in the Qur'an.

Hypocrisy is a form of "hidden associationism" (*shirk khafi*); worse than denial, it should be subject to the death penalty; but as far back as Hasan Basri (d. A.D. 728), schools of asceticism insisted that every habitual sinner (*fasiq*) was a hypocrite (*munafiq*), worse than an apostate, but that it was up to his conscience to repent. Legal punishment could not touch the bottom of hearts; it could only censure the outward signs of hypocrisy, the four deadly sins: *zina* (adultery), punished, like *khamr* (drunkenness), by whipping; *sariqa* (stealing), punished by cutting off a hand (*qat*); fighting or false accusation (*muharaba, qadhf*), possibly punishable by death when it is a question of an insult to the Prophet (*sabb al-Rasul*).

The problem of detecting the hypocrite is crucial for the purification of a religious society. It is similar to the problem of purifying the professional witness (*tazkiyat al-shahid*). It requires a form of initiation that binds the initiates to a purity of intention (*ikhlas*) by a pledge of honor, and that asks God, not positively for the "descent" of a Spirit of truth in us, but negatively for the "descent" of the Fire of His vengeance on the false witness, the hypocrite. The Qur'an contains a reference to a trial by fire of this sort, the *mubahala* of Medina, between the Prophet and the Christians of Nejran. The Shi'ites have derived a purification ritual based on it which bears its name; the Sunnites resort to it at times, but only privately. Among the Shi'ites it is the test for the bad, demoniacal inspiration by which the hypocrite is possessed: the *waswas*. In Islam, "the evil spirit" alone is detectable in hearts. For "the good spirit" (the angel) is only an external agent [of God] who speaks into ears. And if there is a Spirit of God (mentioned in the Qur'an), it must have an undetectable mode of action; therefore, only depraved extremists, fanatic legitimist Shi'ites, and ascetic Sunnites, can claim that the Spirit of God infuses itself in their hearts; which can only be considered a blasphemy against the supreme authority of God, the Author of the oral revelation. Shafi'i was the first to deny the extremist Shi'ite Khattabiya the power to bear witness, because their interior inspiration imposed on them a mental reservation about the uninitiated. This spiritual rebellion is the worst crime in a religious society. Before the coming of Islam, the Sassanid capital, Ctesiphon, had discovered and condemned it among the Manichaeans under the name of *zandaqa*.

The Political Origin of Zandaqa (a Manichaean Heresy)

The word *zandaqa* is of Iranian origin: *zandiki*, from *zanda*, magic. According to Zoroastrian heresiography, *zandiki* is one of the thirty deadly sins: it is the belief that good can come from Ahrimam and from demons; and, consequently, it is the sin of the one who invokes demons.

When the Manichaeans (around 260 of our era) inverted the official Zoroastrian dualism of the Sassanid state (malefic stars), they were persecuted and massacred for *zandaqa*, because they were seeking inspiration, through prayer, from evil spirits. The 'Abbasid state would keep the epithet *zanadiqa* primarily for them, and the "ascetic (even vegetarian), spiritual" and initiatory nature of Manichaeanism would command the use—both judicial before the qadi and literary before public opinion—of the word *zandaqa*. Their patriarch, who was tolerated at Ctesiphon, the Sassanid capital (with the symbolic title of "Babel"), was watched closely by the Muslim police from the very beginning of the conquest; and ended up by being exiled to Sogdiana precisely in 296/908; he was sheltered there through the diplomatic intervention of a powerful neighbor, the Qaghan of the Uyghur Turks of Qocho (= Taqazgaz), bearing (second dynasty) the title of *Idiqut*: converted to Manichaeanism since 762 of our era. Let us recall that Hallaj, on his long journey to Turkestan, might have reached as far as Qocho.

The charge of *zandaqa*, usually reserved in the Muslim courts of Iraq for the strict Manichaeans in the large city of Mada'in (the Muslim name for Ctesiphon), was very easily expanded to include the newly converted townsmen whose Islamization concealed their secret initiation into rites of vegetarian asceticism and inspiration of the heart. Moderate Shi'ite heresiographers, like H. Nawbakhti, point to Mada'in as the center, at the beginning of the second century of the Hijra, of the extremist Shi'ite *zanadiqa*: professing the doctrine of *hulul al-Ruh* (infusion of the Spirit in the heart, transmitted from initiate to initiate, in a chain and through astronomical cycles); a doctrine of "liberation" from the Law of the Muslim State (at that time, Umayyad, anti-'Alid, and even anti-Muhammadian), thus a doctrine of political rebellion, because the divine Spirit invested the adepts with independence through a hidden leader who claims for himself the Supreme Power (*rububiya*), of theopathic speech, and speaks in the name of God in the first person singular, which a prophet may do only as a "transmitter" of the text of the revealed Law.

III. THE SOVEREIGN AUTHORITY AND ITS DELEGATION TO A COURT OF JUSTICE; THE COURT OF JUSTICE, ITS POWERS AND JURISDICTION

Exceptional Procedures and the Nazar al-Mazalim; *the Application of Divine Law to Hallaj's Case*

In Islam, the sovereign, the Imam, the "Caliph" of the Prophet of God, must first and foremost "prescribe what God commands, and prohibit what he forbids," to every member of the Community of believers. This is the *amr bi'l-ma'ruf wa'l-nahy 'an al-munkar*. [This power of the Caliph] is called *hisba*, the enforcing of [Islamic] morals, when it refers to the inspection of streets, markets, and schools; and *nazar al-mazalim* when it refers to the halting of unusually serious wrongs committed by government officials, exposed through appeal to the sovereign.

Usually the Muslim sovereign delegates his authority to various kinds of government officials. After the coming of the ʿAbbasids, he appoints a *mufawwid* vizir, invested with the power to make appointments in his name to public offices, the honorific posts of the sovereign's private entourage remaining more or less under his direct command. But according to doctrine, the religious disposition of certain offices issues from the Imam alone (the vizir is a layman in this respect; he and his secretaries wear the sword of the military and outrank them). The Imam is the foremost of the *imam salat*, of those in charge of the Friday public prayer; and he insists on performing this "liturgical" duty personally when he has the time to do so. Likewise the pilgrimage and the holy war. The mob cried out at Muqtadir: you have made a mockery of our canonical acts of prayer, pilgrimage and holy war, by your wrong behavior. Hence, his deposition in 317/929.

The sovereign delegates canonical proceedings to the qadi court. But this court of public officials can act only by appealing to two groups of believers whom the sovereign does not have to indicate, much less appoint: the professional witnesses (corresponding, from the "democratic" point of view, to our criminal court jurors) for the preliminary investigation of the trial, and the muftis, independent jurisconsults, for the correct interpretation of the Law. In fact, in the period in question, Qadi Abu ʿUmar, an unscrupulous politician, attempted to draw up a "professional" list of "trustworthy" witnesses, and, instead of asking another for the *fatwa* of conviction, he merged the two powers, the legislative of the mufti and the juridical of the qadi, by sanctioning his own *fatwa* himself.

The Members of the Special Court

THE CALIPH'S COUNCIL

The presiding judge of this complaints court is by law the Caliph, but in fact he no longer attends the sessions, and lets his *wali* conduct the proceedings. Nevertheless, his discretionary power always threatens the independence of a complaints court's jurisdiction, arising from his right of inspection of ordinary justice.

It appears that the emphasis among the members has shifted since the time of the *mihna* court of the Muʿtazilite caliphs, and that the makeup has evolved from regular qadis to politicians in Hallaj's time. The change has been so rapid for half a century that any *katib*, any state secretary, and any vizir now poses as a *faqih* and runs the preliminary investigation himself into the finest points of doctrine: he himself indicates what views are to be condemned, and resorts to the qadi only to ask him to prescribe the formula of the sentence. Whereas in the era of the Mu'tazilite caliphs, it seems that the qadis themselves had conducted the examination of defendants.

Immediately after that, with the weight shifting to the vizirs, the court increasingly takes on the appearance of a political High Court, in the hands of whichever party is in power.

Hallaj's drawn-out trial, with its interruptions and resumptions, shows that court proceedings reflect closely the political crises of the vizirate, or, to be more precise, the prevailing opinion in the Administrative Council: the trial is run there; the real judges are there.

In this era, the Administrative Council is normally composed of three legally authorized members: the *caliph*, the *vizir*, and the *hajib* or chamberlain: plus the *shaykh al-kuttab* as clerk of court. The following are a few brief accounts of the life and character of the Caliph and the titulars of the vizirate and the *hijaba*. The characters of the main actors in the drama seem very much alive to us even today.

Caliph Muqtadir

Abu'l-Fadl Ja'far, named "*al-Muqtadir bi'llah*," "he whom God makes powerful," when he became the eighteenth 'Abbasid Caliph, reigned for twenty-five years; second son of Mu'tadid, born of Shaghab on 22 *Ramadan* 282/November 14, 895, succeeded his elder brother Muktafi on 13 *Qa'da* 295/August 14, 908, when he was thirteen; killed on Tuesday, 28 *Shawwal* 320/October 31, 932, when he was thirty-seven. His ancestry: examination of his genealogy shows that Muqtadir had only 2/16 Hashimite blood (part Khwarizmian, Soghdian, Yemenite, and Berber) and 14/16 Greek blood (his mother Shaghab, his grandmother Dirar, and his grandmother Ashar were Greek).

Sovereign at thirteen, therefore before he could have been educated like his father (who was well-read in ethics and philosophy) by a private tutor (from the tutor of his sons, Zajjaj, he learned some poetry, however, for he used to quote lines of verse at the proper time), pensioning scholars and singers without having any special interest in their rival schools, patronizing grammarians, *qurra'*, and *muhaddith* rather than poets and philosophers, retaining a select group of *nudama'* (imperial house guests) among whom there was at least one eminent man, Ibn al-Munajjim, whose Mu'tazilism at times may have influenced him. Muqtadir, an extremely suspicious person, not trusting the loyalty of anyone, prodigal toward all, did not let any of his many concubines gain an upper hand; we know little more than the names Zalum (mother of Radi and Harun), Dimna (grandmother of Qadir, heard from in 319), Khalub (mother of Muttaqi) and Mash'ala (mother of Muti'), four *umm walad*, and Hurra (daughter of Commander-in-Chief Badr; who will remarry). Only the feminine influence of his mother reigned over his harem as well as over his Court. It was not a case of his being unable to free himself from the influence of his mother's advisers, of

Umm Musa in 310, of the faithful Nasr in 309 and 311; rather he continued to lean, for lack of something better, no doubt, on the family of his mother (particularly on a nephew, Harun-b-Gharib, a man of mediocre ability).

Carried to power by the loyalty of his father's high-ranking officers, more specifically by the small Greek group to which his mother's brother Gharib belonged, a group that fell apart over the years, he continued to provide for them generously even after their worst tirades against him; in point of fact, he was always able to regain the affection of élite corps (the Hujariya, 22,000, committed to Mu'nis, together with the Sajiya; the Masaffiya, 20,000, committed to Nasr, crushed by M-b-Yaqut in 318, with the other two corps being crushed in 325 and 324 respectively by Amir M-b-Rayiq, when he took away Caliph Radi's executive power); and though he was renounced in 320, it was only because he no longer had the wherewithal to pay them.

Supported in 296 by bankers affiliated with the Shi'ite party, Muqtadir will never be unmindful of the subtle importance of their interventions; this is why he will choose as his last vizir Fadl-b-Ja'far-b-Furat, but the latter, by dissuading him from going to Wasit, where he would have found money and reinforcements, and by deserting him during battle, seems to have made a pact with Mu'nis to betray him; and thereby to avenge the death of his uncle, Vizir 'Ali-b-Furat.

Muqtadir had a high regard for the state secretarial class and placed it, as he said very bluntly to the pious Vizir Ibn 'Isa, high above the jurisconsult and qadi class, which had questioned the validity of his enthronement at age thirteen. His policy in religious matters was decidedly secular; for many reasons: a lack of religious and moral order in his life, a weakness that he did not wish to overcome; certain doubts (of Shi'ite origin) about the legitimacy of his dynasty (Hallaj interested him, perhaps, because he was considered able to master the Shi'ite objections) prevented him from promoting, as his son Radi will promote, the *odium theologicum* through trials for heresy (people persuaded him to condemn Hallaj only by misrepresenting him as a sorcerer who was disturbing the social order).

Muqtadir was able to look beyond the frontiers with a certain grasp of the international balance of power. He knew, like his vizir, Ibn al-Furat, that the Islamic empire had two permanent enemies, the Byzantine empire to the northwest and the pagan Turkish (Uyghur) khanate to the northeast; added to these problems were two Shi'ite rebellions against his dynasty, the Zaydite and Daylamite to the north, which was backed up by an Iranian and anti-Arab democratic renaissance, and the Isma'ili [rebellion] in the Maghrib to the west and south, which was backed up by the Qarmathian social revolutionary conspiracy. Muqtadir appears to have had a clearly defined foreign policy: that of dividing the empire into two general areas, the west and the east (as will be the case under Rashid and Mu'tamid); and of moving directly with his army in the west against the Byzantines and Isma'ilis, and in the east against the Turks and

Daylamites with the army of his Samanid vassals, who had maintained a permanent ambassador (*sahib*) in Baghdad since 288. However, his Shi'ite vizir, Ibn al-Furat, who was hostile to the Sunnism of Samanid Khurasan, whose military effectiveness he minimized, wished to establish local military outposts on the eastern front, hoping to get a Hamdanid (Husayn in 305) or a Sajid (Yusuf in 296, 304, 311) to accomplish that. Muqtadir, on Nasr's advice, relied on the Samanid troups for the east front until the end of 309; the fall of Nishapur and Rayy, temporarily occupied by the Daylamites, made him doubt Nasr (at the very moment that he refused his request for Hallaj's free pardon) and entrusted the eastern front to the Sajid Yusuf (310–313; killed at the Qarmathian front in 315); this abandonment of the alliance with the Samanids against the Daylamites will finally deliver into the latter's (Shi'ite) hands the entire east and even the capital of the empire (cut off from contact with its original homeland, Khurasan).

In terms of domestic policy, Muqtadir had to reckon with his relatives' claims to power, the ambitions of his son's advisers, and the budgetary deficits incurred by the policy of holy war, by the religious and medical foundations that his mother persuaded him to build, and especially by the ostentatious celebrations of his Court, where leading titular but non-resident government officials (replaced even when military by incompetent representatives) resided all year long.

In the Court itself, though there was no serious 'Alid conspiracy during his reign, there were 'Abbasid princes prepared to oust him; without speaking of his brother Qahir, who succeeded in doing this the second time, Muqtadir was rather quickly rid of his most formidable rival, Ibn al-Mu'tazz; also, 'AA b-Mu'tamid died as early as 296, and the candidacy of Abu'l-'Abbas-b-M-b-Ishaq-b-Mutawakkil (d. 316) in 310 was not very serious; but that of his nephew Abu Ahmad-b-Muktafi (d. 321) was declared as early as 317 and 318; he was the candidate preferred by Commander-in-Chief Mu'nis, as was shown in 321. The latter also considered the eldest son of Muqtadir, Radi, as early as 319.

Muqtadir's numerous sons also gave him cause for concern. As early as 302, two of them, age five, were endowed with an appanage and a governor of their "House": Radi was given the west with Mu'nis as governor; 'Ali, soon disappearing and replaced by Harun, was given the east with Nasr, and afterwards Yaqut (316) as governor. In 307, two other sons were endowed with a "House" with a governor and a secretary: Ibrahim Muttaqi and 'Abbas, whose governor was Harun-b-Gharib. If Mu'nis and Nasr were in agreement, Harun-b-Gharib would use his position to try to oust Mu'nis. And two other sons ended up being officially installed, 'Abd al-Wahid and Ishaq.

Muqtadir had his secretaries, his physicians, and his *ghilman* to handle his personal affairs; no one exercised a privileged influence. Ibn al-Hawwari, who had served him for ten years, was dismissed in a back-handed way through the malice of Ibn al-Furat.

On whom could Muqtadir depend, apart from his mother? By dint of his taking advantage of the devotion of Commander-in-Chief Mu'nis, whom he paid generously but whose circle of associates he regarded with increasing suspicion for the possibility of a coup d'état, the Caliph succeeded in becoming finally estranged from this eunuch whom he called his father (317). As for Ibn al-Furat, whose fiscal talents mesmerized him, the Caliph knew full well that he was, deep down, convinced of the illegitimacy of the 'Abbasid dynasty. An advocate of the same fiscal policies as he, Muqtadir, as a Sunnite caliph, was obliged to dismiss him on three occasions in order to take on a Sunnite vizir from one of the three established vizirial families, the B. Khaqan, the B. Makhlad, and, after 317, the B. Wahb, or from among upstarts. However, in spite of the exceptional merit of a vizir such as Ibn 'Isa, which he fully recognized, Muqtadir never held the latter in the same esteem as Ibn al-Furat.

Muqtadir's personality remained that of a precocious and shrewd, temperamental and greedy child, lacking tenacity for work and resistance to pleasure; unusually concerned about questions of propriety and etiquette, (barely) capable even of making decisions, if he happened to be sober, involving important matters of state; whimsical and blasé, having no overriding purpose or extreme passion, using his absolute power for little experiments that were either ironic or nonsensical (he had a field of narcissus smoke-dried with perfume; he said his four pleasures of this world were "contemplating beautiful faces, ridiculing dull minds, slapping fleshy fat necks, and shaving long showy beards.").

It is only fair to say, however, that Muqtadir never took delight in the refined tortures that his father Mu'tamid, still the real chief of state, devised; and that he often intervened (in agreement with his mother) to check the cruelties of his vizirs. It was undoubtedly through sloth and indifference that he allowed Vizir Hamid to worsen the terms of Hallaj's execution.

There was a degree of metaphysical concern in the flighty and diversified mentality of this skeptical ruler; surrounded by increasingly partisan and officious untruths, he had doubts about the legitimacy of his dynasty; Hallaj did not succeed in curing him of these doubts; and on three occasions, in 305, 317, and 320, important statements by Muqtadir show him to us as disposed, out of need for spiritual comfort that required neither manly effort nor repentance, to believing not only in the sincerity but also in the divine inspiration of a profound and dangerous Shi'ite politician, the third *wakil* of the Mahdi, Husayn-b-Rawh Nawbakhti.

Queen Mother Shaghab and Thumal Dulafiya; Muflih

A Greek slave (d. 321), she was first named *Na'ima* ("gentle") by Umm Qasim, daughter of Amir M-b-'AA-b-Tahir and sister of Yahya, and given by her to Caliph Mu'tadid, who freed her and named her *Shaghab* ("turbulent") when she became *ummwalad* by giving him a son, Ja'far (= Muqtadir): in *Ramadan* 282.

Like most of the future imperial concubines, Shaghab must have received some training with Umm Qasim, particularly from the devotional standpoint: in an elementary but strict Sunnism (formulas of prayer; stressing the importance of their recitation, of the tithe and the hajj; based on hadiths of Hanbalite origin). The education of the harem, in the Court among the nobles (in this case, the Tahirids), had been Hanbalite since the time of Shuja', Queen Mother in the reign of Mutawakkil (she regulated the life of the concubines, selecting physicians and nurses) and especially Ashar, Queen Mother in the reign of Muwaffaq (guided by the Hanbalite Ibn Ghulam Khalil). The brother of Shaghab, Gharib-b-'AA, a professional military man, was also a *muhaddith* (*rawi* of the Malikite Firiyabi); Shaghab herself left the security of the palace in the hands of two Hanbalites: the chamberlain Nasr and the eunuch Muflih, for the external and internal security respectively; and as for the dynastic *waqfs* of the Holy Places, like Dar al-'Abbas (at first connected with the Zamzam well), she entrusted them, the latter at least, to a Shafi'ite *muhaddith*, Da'laj.

Shaghab immediately played a political role in the Court, with her brother Gharib belonging to a small group of converted officers of Greek origin, mamluks specially attached to Mu'tadid: including Mu'nis al-khadim ("the eunuch": the future commander-in-chief), Mu'nis *al-fahl* ("the male": the commander of the guard), Nasr, Yanis, Bunayy (who went for awhile to Byzantium and set himself up again as a Christian, after his rebellion in 317), and Qaysar. After the death of her rival, the Egyptian princess Qatr al-Nada (5 *Rabi'* II, 282 = 8 *Rajab* 287), the general anticipation was that the son of Shaghab would reign (his older brother, Muktafi, being scrofulous; as for his younger brother Harun, who died in 356, his mother must have been Dastanbuya, who was closely connected with Shaghab). One day, after a series of incidents, Mu'tadid threatened to cut off her son's nose. During the seven years of Muktafi's reign, in spite of various adverse schemes, the absolute loyalty of Mu'tadid's mamluks to the direct descendants of their master safeguarded Shaghab's son as the leading heir apparent.

Once she became regent, Shaghab had well-known mamluks attached to her personal service: such as Rayiq, Nihrir, Shafi', and Sabur, who betrayed her in 321: "*khuddam al-Sayyida.*" We also know the names of the managers of her landed estates, in Ahwaz (AY Baridi) and in Wasit (Qasim Jawhari), and certain agents within the Court, like the banker AB-b-Qaraba and Ibn Sayyar (perhaps the very same *wali* of Antioch, who was the father of a friend of the poet Mutanabbi, 'Ali-b-M-b-Sayyar); with whom she must have dealt directly, speaking to them from behind a curtain. For she was rather fearless: she even dared, in 306, to go out in public on horseback. But, following custom, she usually entrusted her dealings outside the harem to her *qaharmana*, Umm Musa, who went about dressed in black because of her dynastic nobility, and was the leading instigator of her policy for twenty years.

We have, in fact, pointed out the dominant notes in the internal policy of Muqtadir's reign, and they arose from the influence of his mother and her

Hashimite adviser: a policy of large expenditures for Court pomp and for pious works; and if Muqtadir assumed responsibility particularly for the ostentation of the Court, the works of piety were the personal predilection of the Queen Mother. "The Queen Mother is profoundly virtuous and pious," said Ibn 'Isa to the Caliph in 315, at a time when it was very urgent to try to save Baghdad. No 'Abbasid sovereign, not even Khayzuran, had so lavished her wealth *"fi sabil Allah"*; she will declaim it steadfastly in 320, when Qahir will persecute her for making him repeal her *waqf* constitutions: this would be illegal, since they are pious (*birr*) foundations built to please God (*qurb*) by sustaining the weak (*du'afa'* = the crippled and the sick) and the poor (*masakin*) in the places consecrated by hajj and jihad, Mecca, Medina, and the frontiers (*thughur*) of the holy war. In Baghdad, where she had found only one hospital, she left five, organized thanks to the consultations of Ibn 'Isa with eminent medical experts (Razi, Thabit). She expressed a generous gratitude to God at the time of the victory over the Qarmathians in *Qa'da* 315 (the unexpected release of 'Anbar) and in *Muharram* 316 (the raising of the siege of Hit): by having the huge alms assets distributed to the poor and touching the tithe of her private treasury (one half of which she had just spent for the enlistment of relief troops).

She was reproached for the ruinous prebends that she allowed the most useless of her protégés (her nephew Ahmad; the brother of Umm Musa) to monopolize; and it is certain that she was unable to prevent him, once he had become sovereign, from bleeding the public and private treasuries (the picture drawn by Ibn Sinan of 70 million dinars squandered during his reign seems a bit exaggerated): managing to be both lavish with jewels, objets d'art, and curiosities accumulated by his predecessors toward his most passing favorites, and childishly greedy, fooled by the lowest bid offered by a flatterer to win a commission. For all that, Shaghab had been able to put aside more than a million and a half dinars, a third of which was used to pay the relief army in 315; and it is not she, but rebellious praetorian guards who squandered, after having stolen in 317, the reserve of 600,000 dinars that she had hidden in her turba, and who, in concert with a wicked band of Shi'ite financiers who had been lying in wait for many years, compelled her some months later, her and her son, to sell the Crown lands at a low price. Unlike her son, she gradually understood only too well the dangers of the knowingly excessive taxation put in practice by Ibn al-Furat, and the need of equitable economic policies recommended by Ibn 'Isa: the one whom she had renounced in 304; she supported him more in 308–310, and she defended him until the end in 315–316.

Within the sumptuous luxury of her Court, Shaghab seems to have had a certain ideal of hieratic art (Greek influence), which one can unearth from the description of palace festivities (particularly in 305 for the Byzantine ambassador): the setting somewhat theatrical in its glittering sumptuousness: the tall silver tree of the Arbor Palace, having eighteen branches, with its fluttering leaves and its whistling mechanical birds; the shimmering solid tin pool with is

Jawsaq caïques, in the midst of an orchard of four hundred date palms whose trunks were inlaid with teak and encircled with flaming red and gold copper— such is the enchanted setting in which she had accustomed her son to amuse himself.

Muqtadir allowed her alone, together with her immediate friends, to attend to the embellishments of the Holy Places: the four cedar gates sent to the Sakhra from Jerusalem, Bab Ibrahim and the colonnade built at the Ka'ba, the aqueduct constructed for Mecca; the pomp of the annual Bagdadian pilgrimage, a caravan that was fitted previously with a kind of *mahmal*, or the *kiswa*, brocaded in Tustar, which was transported with jewels under an umbrella, *shamsa*; the profusion of alms for the poor in Mecca; and all kinds of things, which moreover aroused the cupidity of the Qarmathians and led to the pillage of Mecca in 317. It was also the Queen Mother who took an interest in the *Thughur*, the Byzantine "frontiers of the holy war" (Tarsus-Malatiya), ordering troops sent there and negotiating the exchange of prisoners.

No suspicion has been raised about Shaghab's private life; when the young regent, betrayed by the majority of Sunnite government officials at the end of the first year of her reign, was forced to choose a Shi'ite vizir, Ibn al-Furat, and she herself handed the infant sovereign into his arms "as if to a father," this gesture of feminine diplomacy deceived neither of them. Shaghab treated Ibn al-Furat with great caution, for she knew that his loyalty was neither unselfish nor sincere. She herself seems to have loved only her son, indulging him as a very spoiled child: not making him complete his classical education (Zajjaj is the one who must have taught him some poetry before becoming the tutor of his sons) and neglecting the literary education of her grandsons; allowing Muqtadir to be prodigal too early with the beauty of pretty slave girls and the wine of banquets.

That the feeling between mother and son was deep and lasting, history attests, having preserved the memory of supreme marks of affection that were shown by each other on the threshold of the final drama: the mother baring her breasts in order to dissuade him from going off to a hopeless battle; and the pained foreboding of the son standing before the famous silver tree of the Dar al-Shajara, from which his mother will be hung by one foot and be flogged by Qahir himself (reigned A.D. 932–934) at a time when her son will no longer be there to protect her. When he was approaching thirty, Muqtadir had taken over from his mother, on many occasions and increasingly, the supervision of the affairs of state, while leaving to her the management of the harem, where no favorite, not even Zalum (mother of Radi and Harun) and Dimna (grandmother of Qadir) challenged her authority. Their very human relationship does not seem to have rested on grounds of identical religious attitudes: Shaghab being a fervent Sunnite, probably a Hanbalite, and Muqtadir, on the contrary, doubting his dynastic legitimacy, leaning at critical times towards Shi'ism.

Which explains their contrasting and finally opposing attitudes about the

Hallaj case. Muqtadir seems to have had only a superficial outburst of feeling for him, out of curiosity for a genuine miracle worker (he sent him "to test" a dead parrot; in 303, probably); keeping that shade of reticent distrust that the blissfully indifferent maintain in the presence of mystics who preach and practice self-denial: he did not especially wish to jeopardize his comforts with that. Shaghab, on the other hand, through her benevolent works in the Holy Places and through her building of hospitals, had known of and appreciated the apostolic work of Hallaj, and afterwards, in prison, his charity toward his fellow prisoners. She had brought him to the bedside of her sick son, not only as a healer, but as a friend of God. And she realized by the half-superstitious, half-skeptical attitude of Muqtadir that she had thereby exposed him to the gravest danger, if, out of slothful cowardice, he failed to protect the threatened life of this innocent man who had been placed as a sacred trust in his sovereign hands. Through an ancestral calling to mind of the Christian idea of reversibility, Shaghab, like Nasr, saw that Muqtadir would be summoned before the Supreme Judge for having allowed an innocent man to be condemned; hence her continual entreaties. Muqtadir, for his part, anxious for a short time due to a bout of fever, calmed down after he had heard Vizir Hamid offer his own life as collateral for Hallaj's execution: "if you become ill over it afterwards, kill me." Later, when he was stricken with disease, he explained it to himself in terms of some Shiʿite reversibilities: in 317, it was his punishment for having allowed Husayn-b-Rawh to be persecuted; in 320, bidding farewell to his mother, he compared himself to Husayn at Karbala. But she who had remained a Sunnite remembered at that moment, perhaps, another Husayn, Hallaj, whose death warrant he had signed despite her efforts.

Shaghab was devotedly attached to memorials, and the religious *waqfs* that she had established in Baghdad survived her: a small chapel (*masjid*) on the east bank of the Tigris, her Turba (memorial tomb): built as early as 306, east bank, in Rusafa; her grandsons Mutiʿ (the Caliph, d. 363), Ishaq (father of Caliph Qadir, d. 377), and ʿA Wahhab (son of Caliph Taʾiʿ, d. 377), were buried there; and the tombs of prominent Caliphs in Rusafa were undoubtedly clustered around the Turba of Shaghab; finally, the Turba of her brother Gharib, west bank, which was adjacent to the *maslib al-Hallaj* (the gibbet or the pillory of Hallaj), a secret place of Hallajian pilgrimage of which Vizir Ibn al-Muslima will establish the identity in A.H. 437 during an official visit. And because this vizir, a confidant of Caliph Qayim, was authorized by him as the transmitter of an account of Muqtadir's Court in 305, thanks to Dimna, the daughter-in-law of Shaghab, one wonders if the vizir knew of the Hallajian *maslib* thanks to the tradition that was kept alive in the imperial harem after the time of Shaghab for the pious Friday *ziyarat* to the tombs of relatives and friends of the reigning family; *ziyarat* that were regulated by the director of the Baghdadian *waqfs* of the *Sayyida* Shaghab.

Shaghab, after being rescued from the punishment that Caliph Qahir inflicted upon her, died ten days later, on 6 *Jumada* II 321, received with honor by the chamberlain ʿAli-b-Yalbaq in the home of his mother (Qahir had him killed on 17 *Shaʿban* 321, together with his father and Mu'nis).

THE SULTANIAN COUNCIL: THE VIZIRS

ʿAli ibn ʿIsa-b-Jarrah

This important statesman has attracted the attention of scholars since Von Kremer and the important monograph by Harold Bowen.

Isn ʿIsa, like his cousins Vizir Hasan and Vizir Saʿid ibn Makhlad, belonged to a family of learned scribes who were originally Christians from the Nestorian intellectual center of Dayr Qunna; an allusion by the Nestorian patriarch Abraham, which was embarrassing to Ibn ʿIsa, infers that he had been baptized. However, he must have converted early to Islam and appeared throughout his life to be a convinced Muslim, supporting similar renegade Christians out of his own purse. Born in *Jumada* II 245/859, died *Hijja* I 334/946, he started out in 281 as a subordinate of ʿAli-b-Furat in the *Diwan al-Dar*, afterwards in 284 as fiscal *wali* of Nahrawan Awsat (chief city, Dayr al-ʿAqul), close to the fiscal *wali* Hy-b-A Madhara'i (probably the same Abu Zunbur who was to remain his main financial adviser until the end), in 284; promoted to state secretary in the *kharaj* (Maghrib branch), which position he held for ten years (286–296); implicated in the Ibn al-Muʿtazz affair, exiled to Wasit and afterwards to Mecca, where he led a life of prayer; recalled, on the advice of Mu'nis, in 301 to be named deputy vizir under Vizir Hamid (306–311); exiled to Mecca, then to Samʿa (311); inspector general of Egypt and Syria (312); vizir from 314 to 316; imprisoned briefly in the palace (in the custody of Zaydan); deputy of Vizir Sulayman-b-H-b-Makhlad (318–319), then of Vizir AQ ʿUA Kalwadhani (319); exiled to Safiya (near Dayr Qunna: 319-*Shawwal* 320); fiscal *wali* of Wasit (321); presided over the enthronement of Caliph Radi (322); became a deputy of his brother, Vizir ʿAR-b-ʿIsa (322); exiled to Safiya (323); deputy of Vizir ʿAR-b-ʿIsa (324: from 19 *Jumada* I to *Rajab*); presiding judge of the *Mazalim* (329); deputy of Vizir ʿAR-b-ʿIsa 3–12 *Shawwal* 329), after having enthroned Caliph Muttaqi.

The political position of Ibn ʿIsa can be defined as follows: continuation of the "Harithian" policy of the Islamo-Christian party of the B. Makhlad and the B. Wahb, which is to say, a policy of complete loyalty to the ʿAbbasid dynasty (contrary to the Shiʿite party), of consideration for the Nestorian minority, of moderate taxation, taking care of the interests of the fellah, with a marked personal emphasis on Sunnite orthodoxy. Profoundly aware of his duty as a civil servant of the Muslim state, confusing somewhat the posterity of the Caliph with that of God (Shibli twitted him for worshipping Muqtadir), Ibn ʿIsa fashioned for himself a doctrinal and juridical political ideal that he strove to realize. In government, he wanted to have the jurisconsults whom he weeded out of the courts (punishment of Ibn Khayran) participate even in the running of the vizirate, and in the selection of the sovereign (hence his support of Ibn al-Mu'tazz). In the provinces, he maintained a system of rotation among the main regional governors and charged the military commanders with full responsibility for their posts. His fiscal policy, which was very deliberate (we owe to him the splendid budgetary table for the year 306/918, studied by Von Kremer: based on the tax receipts of the year 303), derived from a great sense of fairness: docking the high officials, stopping the refunds to the state bankers (which drove them to the Shi'ite party) and the excessive taxation, trying to "redeem" the sin of non-Qur'anic indirect taxes by reinvesting a portion of it (the Baghdadian *mustaghallat*) in pious foundations in Mecca (*diwan al-birr*; a procedure previously employed in the reign of Mahdi for the *mustaghallat* of the Nahr al-Sila; and employed by Ibn 'Isa for his own income to soothe his conscience, for he was paid, and sheepishly let himself be paid, questionable little extras: a fiscal pirate, Baridi, one day reproached him for it to his face).

In dogmatics and canon law, Ibn 'Isa, who read and consulted in law, seems to have been a conciliatory Shafi'ite, though the state was Hanafite; he was well-read, exasperated by the narrow rigorism of the Hanbalites, perceiving the need of an orthodox Sunnite metaphysics to pit against that of the Mu'tazilites (among whom, moreover, he had friends), and against that of the Hellenistic philosophers (he was a patron of a translator of Greek authors, accepted the dedication of a work on the Sabaeans of Harran; his son 'Isa became a "philosopher"). He had his new orthodoxy defended by carefully selected associates (in hadith, by two Jaririties: Qadi A-b-Kamil and 'Ali-b-A 'Aziz Dawladi; in Shafi'ite law, by AB M-b-'AA Sayrafi [d. 330]; in Qur'anic exegesis, by the grammarian AH Khazzaz Wasiti and, especially, by the head of the Baghdadian *Qurra'*, Abu Bakr ibn Mujahid [d. 324] whom he allowed to assume more and more of the role of confessor [whence the contemporary satiric line: "say something to Ibn 'Isa that pleases Ibn Mujahid"]), at the time when, under the latter's influence, he finally renounced Hallaj.

Most of his regular associates were Nestorian Christians, as was the case with the other viziers of this period; except that many of his specialized scribes must have been connected with his family, notably the Qunna'i, of whom two were Hallajians. His fiscal secretary, Ibrahim-b-Ayyub, was a Nestorian.

He seems to have let his friends the amirs Mu'nis and Nasr handle the foreign policy of the empire, war, and diplomacy, retaining control of fiscal affairs (with the Madhara'iyun) and social affairs, hospitals, and pious foundations (the Holy Places, etc., with the Queen Mother). He negotiated with the Qarmathians in 301.

For thirty years, 'Ali ibn 'Isa was, for two-thirds of those years, in charge of the finances of the empire, which was going to collapse and which his patient fiscal reforms would fail to save.

The budgetary statement, according to his inventory for 306–307 (based on the results of the fiscal year 303–304), was as follows: the expenditures which, canonically speaking, were first those of the *sadaqa* (support of the *mujahidin*, pensions of the Hashimites, necessary assistance of the needy faithful) were in actual fact in 281 absorbed by a professional army (76 percent), a lavish Court (16 percent), the vizirial administration (3.3 percent), and the police (1.6 percent), with pensions and alms taking up only 2.1 percent. The receipts which, canonically speaking, should have only accrued from booty from the holy war, capitation tax on non-Muslim subjects, and tithe on flocks and crops, accrued in actual fact from the land tax (*kharaj*) on conquered lands, fictitiously regarded as still non-Muslim, and from noncanonical indirect taxes (customs, tolls).

The collection of taxes, reorganized after the crisis of 250–270 by the corps of eminent specialists trained by Vizir Khaqani, should have yielded, for the central budget (the plan for 281), 2,520,000 dinars per year (728,000 of which = two-days-per-week deduction from salaries, deposited at the bank for the support of Holy Places, jihad, and emergency expenses), and, for the total budget (comprising the provincial budgets), 16,919,082 dinars; but it yielded in 303–304 only 14,929,188 dinars (a deficit of 2,089,894 = 1/7). As much for making good the annual deficits as for securing, by means of staggered receipts, the guaranty of sums for deposit in cash each month, a real financial system was necessary, one that was conceived somewhat differently, according to their own doctrine, by the two parties that took turns running the vizirate, that of Ibn 'Isa (B. Makhlad) and that of the B. Furat.

The school of the B. Furat, based on commercial development, relied on credit, arbitrage (bills of exchange = *suftaja*), the agio; officializing and concentrating in Baghdad the dues for storage (*khazn*) of grain and the rates of exchange (the tax collectors fixing the dirham at 1/22 of the dinar, instead of the legal rate of 1/20 = *jahbadha*), at the time of the collection in kind of taxes; officializing even the selling of offices by deducting previously, in the budget of 305, from the commissions and free gifts (*marafiq*) obtained from newly promoted government officials, 540,000 dinars annually, which the vizir handed over, in twelve monthly installments, to a weak and conniving sovereign, for his pleasures. This school was monometallist—gold: it standardized the budgetary accounts in gold dinars after 281; it won over Egypt in 292, because of the market of gold mined in Beja, the Sudan, sought peace with Byzantium (because its gold bezant had primacy); it recommended the direct fiscal control of the provinces, the direct farming of taxes of certain provinces to state bankers, the combining of the *diya'* granted as fiefs with the regular *diya'* ('*amma* = taxed to the full), the draining of the reserve fund (Ibn al-Furat drained fourteen million dinars from this fund between 296 and 299 and Khaqani two million, 299–300).

The other school, that of the B. Makhlad (the school of Ibn 'Isa), was conservative and physiocratic: for decentralization (tribute-money paid by autonomous governors), reduction of indirect taxes (non-Qur'anic: one-half million dinars in 301) and suppression of usury (cf. Jahbadha), relief for certain categories of taxpayers, postponement of tax collection until after the time of harvest (*nayruz* moved back to June in 284), non-confiscation of the estates of government officials (*tarikat*, 282), observance of the weekly day of rest on Friday (281), careful recovery of resources by cutting down on numbers of salaries and pensions and by tracking down fraud (two million dinars in 304) instead of paying high bonuses to tax collectors, and establishment and maintenance of a reserve fund (ten million dinars in 289, fourteen million in 295, thanks to Egypt). This system had the disadvantage of weakening the authority in remote areas and of displeasing the privileged classes whose landed property it protected, but it put an end to immoral revenues by handing over to the provincial farmer-general, who was hired for a fixed annual fee (*muqataʿa*), the management of harvests (it was in his interest, being right there, to take better care of the interests of the peasantry and the artisan classes, by not taking too much advantage of the storage dues); it did not bankrupt the artisan or the laborer like the system of Ibn al-Furat, which arranged for the harvests to be drained by the bankers toward the *mustaghallat* of Baghdad.

The famous budgetary table for the year 306 was useful to Ibn ʿIsa and to his friend Abu'l-Mundhir Nuʿman in 307 for defending their physiocratic policy of protection of the laborer against the plan of fiscal exaction prepared by Hamid: an outrageous plan consisting of entrusting the vizir alone (and special agents) with the general farming of taxes (duly increased) for most of the empire; a plan of shocking monopolization that caused the riot of 24–26 Qaʿda 308, which the historian Hamza Isfahani, an eyewitness, rightly described as the collapse of the empire. Resumed in 324 and applied by the *amir al-ʿumara'*, this plan destroyed in a few years the last financial capacities of the state.

The moral sagacity of Ibn ʿIsa made him fearful of the social crisis which any excess of taxation was bound rapidly to bring on, and he patterned his diplomatic conduct on his financial system. Hence, his attempts at direct negotiation in the south with the Qarmathian rebels (to contain, not by a costly army, but by bedouin partisans, the B. Asad and B. Shayban), and his diplomatic recourse in the north to conservative Samanid princes (in agreement with Nasr and Mu'nis) defending against the threatening democratic army of the Daylamites (who had abolished feudalism). Fars, whose reconquest under Ibn al-Furat (297) provided with its plentiful yield in taxes an argument in favor of the opposing fiscal school, confronted Ibn ʿIsa with a double problem: of easing the excessive taxation and of not stopping the questionable bonuses taken there by his patron, Commander-in-Chief Mu'nis, who deducted through a middleman a share of the warehouse dues and agio banked on reserve by the farmers and state bankers in Fars-Kirman.

It is, in the final analysis, Mu'nis who must be held responsible for the defeat of Ibn ʿIsa's fiscal plans, much more than the Queen Mother. The selfish and unproductive hoarding that von Kremer believes must be blamed on the Queen Mother permitted him in 315 to raise the army that saved Baghdad, while her last 600,000 dinars, which Mu'nis had Amir Bunayy steal from her in 317, were not even distributed to the rebellious troops; and a few months later, the forced sale of the Queen Mother's landed estates benefited only the amirs who were friends of Mu'nis, who bought them at the lowest price. The increased aging in Mu'nis of this very military instinct for pillage, sustained in him by the Shi'ite B. Nawbakht gang of swindlers, led him to let Ibn 'Isa fall in 316; and this was, in 317, the final bankruptcy of the state.

The reform envisaged by Ibn 'Isa was certainly viable, and the shrewd agiotage of Ibn al-Furat certainly disastrous, since at the time of each of his departures from office, in 296, 304, 311, and 316, Ibn 'Isa left a restored budget, with reserves set aside, whereas at the time of his three falls from power, in 299, 306, and 312, Ibn al-Furat left an unbalanced budget and no reserves.

'Ali ibn al-Furat

He was certainly the leading statesman of his day: of noble extraction, boundless wealth, broad, even scientific education, an executive with all kinds of documents at his fingertips, a man of action commanding respect and knowing just when to act, his only shortcoming was his belonging to a secret sect of extremist Shi'ites, the Khattabiya 'Ayniya, the future Nusayris, which taught him hypocrisy and made him assume, by contrast, cynical and skeptical poses. His grandfather 'Umar (d. 203, killed by Ibrahim al-Mahdi), his father AJ Muhammad-b-Musa, his older brother Ahmad, all had held the highest positions in the sect. His father, grandson on his mother's side of a Persian dihqan of Baghdad, had been appointed wali of Masabadhan and Mihirjan Qadhaq by Vizir Hasan-b-Makhlad. His brother Ahmad, born around 225, started out in the Diya' close to Abu Nuh (d. 255), head secretary, afterwards was deputy to Vizir Ibn Bulbul and secretary of state for finances (Sawad: 274–278), followed by a time in prison (he asked then that people beseech the hidden Imam for his release: 278–281), secretary of state for finances (Mashriq, 281–286), demoted to the Sawad (286–288: Sabi, 119), reinstated in the Mashriq (beginning of 291; died at the end of 291).

His fiscal system is one of patronage based on salary scales, rebates and commissions; it guaranteed him loyal fiscal agents (Karkhiyun, etc.), and won for him finally the Jewish bankers of the Court (hence, his triumph in 296); he tried to spread into all domains: in the War Department, he counted on M-b-Sulayman, the former katib of Ibn Bulbul, on certain Arab amirs and even Turkish amirs, without succeeding in winning the support of the other high-ranking military leaders, who knew he was hostile to a military autocracy. In the area of diplomacy, Ibn al-Furat, an advocate of a long truce with Byzantium, worked to maintain the unity of the empire against the attempts at autonomy by the Samanids and Saffarids; and although he was accused of it, he surely did not act in collusion with the Shiʿite rebels such as the Zaydites, Qarmathians, and Fatimids. But was he truly loyal to the dynasty (he had chosen to support the infant Muqtadir only because the latter would have the throne under his regency); did his attachment to the B. Bistam and B. Nawbakht prove that Ibn al-Furat believed in the prompt return and the imminent reign of their hidden Imam? Did he work above all to prepare for this?

Regardless of whether he had taken part in the Shiʿite legitimist plot out of conviction, or had only lusted after power as a virtuoso in the art of politics, the persistent and deliberate hostility that Ibn al-Furat showed to Hallaj is significant; Hallaj represented a threat to the Shiʿites, a danger of infiltration by Sunnite mysticism into ruling circles and among the élite of the Baghdadian Court.

Hamid

Born in 223/[837], died in 311/924, Hamid is the typical tax farmer, wily, ruthless, greedy, and unscrupulous. At first an ordinary water bearer and pedlar of spoiled pomegranates, in the words of the satirist Ibn Bassam, he was one of Vizir Saʿid-b-Makhlad's (265–272) fiscal agents in the Sawad. He began his career with a master stroke in getting the regent Muwaffaq to finance the irrigation system (overhauling the elevating waterwheels) in the Khayzuran fief at Silh; which immediately doubled the tax returns in this devastated region that he had just recaptured from the Zanj rebels. Hamid captured the heart of the region by repairing the mosques destroyed by the Zanj and building a grand mosque in Wasit.

Although a Sunnite, he established contacts early with Shiʿite families of fiscal experts like the B. al-Furat; and when the new vizir, Ibn Bulbul, imprisoned him (in 272), Hamid was surprised that Ahmad-b-Furat, the deputy of the vizir (274), did not get him released. Recalled to the general tax farm of Wasit by Vizir Ibn Wahb in 278, he retained it for thirty years, in quadrennial periods (for 240,000 dinars and 2,400 *kurr* of barley each year); he received, besides, the financial supervision (*ishraf*) of Damascus, the general tax farm of Fars (287), and the general tax farm of Basra.

Having reached the highest rank when he was too old, Hamid was regarded by everyone as a sort of fiscal Trimalcion and a peasant Father Ubu, incapable of exercising power, surrounded by hundreds of more or less armed slaves whom he called by the names of those who annoyed him in the Court, his mouth full of obscenities which he considered witty, his mind fond of wily tricks. He displayed the ostentation of a newly-rich peasant, achieving popularity by investing in alms craftily lent to the lowly; Ibn ʿIsa considered him a tax collector who antedated the collection, a thieving farmer general who was irascible and ignorant. For an unscrupulously ambitious courtier like Qadi Abu ʿUmar, who was not ashamed to provide him with excuses for his habitual drunkenness, twenty others, more honest, like Ibn ʿIsa, the *Qaharmana*, Jihshyari, kept silent in his presence out of disgust. He was also vindictive and cruel, as he demonstrated with Muhassin-b-'Ali-b-Furat and with Ibn 'Ata', whose teeth he smashed back into his skull.

His hatred for Hallaj was one of long standing, seeing that he insisted on grilling him briefly at the time of his arrest in 301. Encouraged and intensified by his Shi'ite secretaries and especially by his fanatic confidential agent, Shalmaghani, it stemmed from the condemnations that fervent believers like Hallaj, Ibn 'Ata', and their friends pronounced in loud and clear voices against a policy of unlimited fiscal exactions that were forcing the people into hunger, poverty, and rebellion. It was certainly Hamid's stubborn and relentless hatred that led to Hallaj's being killed.

THE ARMY

The Commander-in-Chief: Mu'nis Qushuri

Abu'l-Hasan Mu'nis Qushuri, born in 231, died in 321, an officer at thirty (in 261), probably in Caliph Muwaffaq's forces, was of Greek origin; although a eunuch accepted for the harem, he had an exceptional military career, like the Narses at Byzantium and Kafur at Cairo. Devoted early to Mu'tadid himself and certainly very close to Badr. the Commander-in-Chief of that time, Mu'nis (nicknamed *al-khadim*, "the eunuch," in contrast to his colleague Mu'nis *al-fahl*, "the male," the commandant at that time of the stud farm) emerged in 287 as Badr's deputy in the *Shurta*: he was *"sahib shurtat al-'askar"* (which in this instance does not mean "chief of police of East Baghdad: 'Askar al-Mahdi; but "commander of the military field police"), and he accompanied Caliph Mu'tadid in this capacity to Amid, where he appeared at the head of the ranking officers at the funeral of the physician Ghalib, whose son-in-law, Danyal-b-'Abbas, was his secretary. In 288, when Commander-in-Chief Badr, on bad terms with the new vizir, Qasim-b-'UA-b-Wahb, was sent to reconquer Fars from the Saffarids, Mu'nis was sent in disfavor to Mecca: probably as amir (Amir 'Ajj-b-Hajj, d. 306, replaced him in 295, perhaps after having been his deputy). The historian, Dhahabi, notes that "Mu'tadid sent him in disfavor to Mecca, and it was Muqtadir who, upon his accession to the throne, recalled him." This semi-exile lasted for seven years. It is difficult to say what caused it. Vizir Qasim no doubt, before removing Badr, wanted to get his deputy out of the way. That the heir to the throne, Muktafi, was prejudiced against Mu'nis is evident from the fact that during his entire reign, even after the death of Vizir Qasim, Mu'nis remained in Mecca. Being a eunuch, he must have been involved in harem intrigues; and he surely must have sided with Shaghab's son, the future Muqtadir, at the time of the latter's succession. Shaghab brought him back to Baghdad. In Mecca, Mu'nus must have presided at the burial of Badr's remains and taken under his wing his son, Amir Hilal-b-Badr, who would remain henceforward on his general staff. After his return to Baghdad, Mu'nis was a member of a small group of loyal amirs who brought about the failure of Ibn al-Muʿtazz's coup d'état, in which Mu'nis's adopted son, Amir Hy-b-Hamdan, rather foolishly let himself become involved in 296 (in 303, Mu'nis would have to march against him again).

As early as 296, the Queen Mother, confident of Mu'nis's devotion to the young sovereign, entrusted all of the Hujariya to him (Nasr Abu Musaffiya), and trained him for the role of the commander-in-chief, which ran counter to the plans of Vizir Ibn al-Furat, who hastened to get Mu'nis out of the way by sending him on the holy war (Thughur, in 296), to Fars (297–298: Mu'nis negotiated independently there, which got him recalled). In *Jumada* I 300, Mu'nis was named Amir of the Haramaya and the Thughur, two regions to which the Queen Mother paid close attention. In *Muharram* 302, Mu'nis, as governor of the young prince Radi, in addition received the investiture as governor of the entire Maghrib, meaning Egypt and Syria, and, after a brief campaign in Mosul, left to repel the Fatimids, who were attacking Egypt. In 303 he put down the revolt by Hy-b-Hamdan at Mosul; from 304 to 307, he put down with difficulty the revolt of Ibn Abi Saj; in 308–309, he saved Egypt. Recalled to Baghdad (*Jumada* I 309), he was named *Muzaffar* (= the Victorious), became *nadim* (= imperial guest), and received confirmation as commander of Egypt and Syria. Mu'nis allowed himself to be tempted to try two coups d'état against Muqtadir: the first in *Muharram* 317, which proved abortive after three days but drained the public treasury; after a three-year truce, the second coup d'état, begun in *Muharram* 320, ended in *Shawwal* 320, with the defeat and death of the caliph. A little more than a year later, Mu'nis, as he had foretold would happen, was himself killed; by the new caliph, Qahir, whom he had previously enthroned in 317, and whom he wanted to keep in tutelage and afterwards to eliminate.

Since Mu'nis refused on 22 *Qaʿda* 309, to back his friend Nasr, who was calling upon the caliph to pardon Hallaj, it would be important to establish just when the Shiʿites put pressure on his immediate circle. The fact that at the trial of 301, Mu'nis, amir of the Haramayn, had not demanded the condemnation of Hallaj, proves that at that time, like his friend Vizir Ibn ʿIsa, he must have been favorably disposed towards him.

The Grand Chamberlain Nasr Qushuri

AQ Nasr, grand chamberlain (*hajib*) of Muqtadir for twenty years, was a career officer. A mamluk of Muʿtadid, thus one of twenty-five amirs in his general staff (*ghilman khassa*), and even the chief assistant to their *ustadh*, his friend Mu'nis Khadim, "the eunuch," his commander-in-chief. Both were of Christian and Melchite in origin, spoke Greek, and had the same *nisba*, "Qushuri" (an Arab or Greek soubriquet).

There were a number of Turks among the twenty-five amirs, but the leadership remained in the hands of a tightly-knit little group of Greeks following the splitting up of the Turkish group headed by Musa-b-Bugha; the Greeks were probably offspring of former Byzantine *cataphracti*, captured and converted to Islam when young at the Cilician front. Nasr, born around 250, made his first appearance at the side of the prince's favorite mamluk, Wasif Mushgir (d. 299), at the time of the Jazira campaign in 282, when he carried a very rude letter to Mu'tadid from a Kharijite rebel, Harun Shari, and took part, first in the submission of Hamdun-b-Hamdan Taghlabi, founder of the Hamdanid line, and afterwards in the submission of Harun, thanks to the support of an amir of exceptional military gifts whose friend he became, Husayn-b-Hamdan, Hamdun's own son. Sent afterwards to Jabal to combat, first of all, the Daylamite offensive and, secondly, the encroachments of a disobedient vassal, the Samanids, Nasr fought alongside Amirs Ukartmysh (or Kutarmysh), Abrun (brother of Kayghalagh), and Khaqan (father of *hajib* Ahmad 330–333, d. 364); he was captured and held prisoner for five years (from 286 to 290) by the Samanid amir Akh Su'luk, who made a friend of him by treating him honorably in Rayy, the residence of Prince Abu Salih Mansur-b-Ishaq, the patron of the physician Razi; Nasr, when freed in 290, would become the champion in Baghdad of the Samanid alliance for defending the eastern front against the Daylamite threat.

In 291, Nasr helped put down the Qarmathian uprising. In 296, he succeeded Sawsan as grand chamberlain, thanks to Mu'nis and Gharib, over the opposition of the Turk Takin, the candidate of the Shi'ite vizir, Ibn al-Furat. Guardian of the palace, the third highest ranking person in the Court and in the Council, he was also the deputy of the commander-in-chief in Baghdad; where the latter commanded the elite corps of the *Sittiniya* (or *Masaffiya*), the garrison's 20,000-man infantry (*rajjala*), while Nasr commanded the *Tis'iniya*, the 12,000 mounted archers, *fursan Hujariya*. Neither succeeded in bringing these unruly and greedy praetorians to heel (combined donativum of 3 million dinars in 295; respective allowances, 360,000 and 600,000 dinars for the period 303–306, 700,000 and 1,500,000 in 317; donativum of 2,256,000 in 317). Nasr also received in 301 in the form of a fief (after the Amirs Masrur, Balkhi, Ibn Mikal, and Rasibi) the two northern *kura* of Ahwaz.

Settled in the palace with his staff, the attentive and faithful adviser of the Queen Mother, he took part in all the affairs of state. As Mu'nis, when named guardian of the heir-apparent Prince Radi, had accordingly assumed the direction of the western part of the empire, so Nasr, upon becoming guardian of Prince Harun (Radi's brother born of the same mother), assumed responsibility for the eastern part. Consequently, it was Nasr who got his friend, the Samanid amir, Akh Su'luk, reinstated as *wali* of Rayy in 304 and in 308, being paid at this juncture a commission that von Kremer believed excessive, but which his position entitled him to. In 309, the defection of Akh Su'luk, who spent a little time in the Daylamite camp, caused Nasr's position at Court to be badly shaken; he lost control of the eastern empire; Yf ibn Abi'l-Saj, his old enemy and long-standing enemy also of the Samanids, was put in charge of Rayy and the entire eastern sector, on the advice even of Mu'nis, and given official priority over Nasr. Only the Queen Mother's urgent intervention saved Nasr's property from being confiscated and him from prison, at the end of 311 and the beginning of 312. Still *hajib*, Nasr had his brief but resounding revenge in 315. In command of the army mustered against the Qarmathians following the revolt of 15 *Rabi'* I 315 and the capture of Kufa (7 *Shawwal*), Nasr saved the capital and the dynasty: at Zubara, near Aqarquf (the dikes broken up on the advice of Abu'l-Hayja Hamdani); he was commanding this force again at the end of *Ramadan* 316/October 928, when he died of fever, near Hilla.

Nasr was the strongest supporter of Hallaj at the trial in 309. They must have known each other for a long time (perhaps as far back as his captivity by the Samanids), and Hallaj had dedicated his *Kitab al-durra* to him. Nasr was supposed to have had "debates with Ibn 'Isa and with Shibli" on the subject of Hallaj, prior to the latter's arrest (in 301?); he looked after him constantly in prison (301–309), and showed his grief publicly at his death (observing the *arba'in* on 4 *Muharram* 310; and intervening for the release of his family).

THE JURISCONSULTS

The Reopening of the Judicial Inquiry: the Denunciation by Awariji to the Head of the Qurra' *of Baghdad, Abu Bakr ibn Mujahid*

According to Zanji's account, the reopening of the trial during Hamid's tenure as vizir, which is to say, after 306, or, more precisely, at the end of 308/921, was due to Dabbas, an old man, a former disciple of Hallaj, supposedly knowledgable about the extent of his propaganda and his "deceits," who was anxious to do a good deed by denouncing him; and due also to Awariji, who joined Dabbas in this plan and who had previously written a book explaining the tricks Hallaj had used to make his deceptions work.

In fact, we have seen that it was not in 308, but between 298 and 301, that Dabbas, bribed and paid off by the police, had tracked Hallaj down; and, as for Awariji, his book could have been written well before 306.

The historian, Dhahabi, without giving his source, tells us that "Awariji, who held important posts in the fiscal administration (*kharaj*), had been a Sufi and had visited Hallaj; when he became aware of his doctrine, he made it public and denounced it to Abu Bakr ibn Mujahid and to Vizir 'Ali ibn 'Isa."

The initiative for the final onslaught, indeed, came from Awariji. He was thirty-one at the time; he had thrown off the hermit's garb; "to support his mother" he had moved to Hamadhan as fiscal *wali*; his sister was going to marry 'Ali Maghribi, founder of a famous vizirial family; he himself was for some fifteen years, together with the poet Mutanabbi, one of the regular visitors of the *amir al-umara'*, M-b-Rayiq, both in Baghdad and Syria; secretary to the financier Ibn Muqatil, secretary of state for finances with Ibn Bazyar under

Vizir Qarariti (329, 330), Awariji followed Ibn Muqatil to Cairo, where he died in 344. One has the impression that it was the Shi'ite bankers who encouraged Awariji to write against Hallaj and afterwards to denounce him. Isma'il Nawbakhti, being a Mu'tazilite in theology, denied the possibility of miracles, explaining them as ingenious tricks of legerdemain, which is precisely the theme of Awariji's anti-Hallajian pamphlet, fragments of which we reencounter in the anecdotes of Tanukhi and Baqillani on the inflated clothing, the disappearing fish, and the phony blind man; and something of this theme persisted in Sufi circles as a souvenir of Awariji's novitiate (Harawi).

Ibn Mujahid was not ignorant of mysticism; he meditated on the Qur'anic verses in a state of great collectedness; he had asked that the Qur'an be recited in his tomb, *post mortem*; and AH ibn Salim, head of the Salimiya, related that he had made a humble confession. But he did not understand the symbolic, personalizing, and anagogical exegesis of the Sufis; he tolerated its outbursts in Shibli (with respect to Qur'an 38:32; 5:21; 15:70, picked up by Abu 'Umar), for he found no basis for argument with them; but the systematic use that Hallaj made of it, as proof of a permanent state of inspiration (*ilham*), must have been intolerable to him; especially when the latter paraphrased certain verses in his own way; and when he affirmed, in commenting on himself, a plurality of lords (*arbab*) and gods (*aliha*).

In other respects, Ibn Mujahid was a man of the world, with different aspects to his character: cracking jokes with guests in a garden "which is no more fitting for scholarly discussion than a mosque is for lewdness"; remarking on the four types of people: the kind one who grumbles (which is bearable), the grumbler who growls (which is natural), the grumbler who puts on airs (which is odious), and the kind one who does kind things (which is beautiful). He invited his friend Qadi Ji'abi to a lavish banquet in order to surprise him by singing him forty-one profane songs (in the presence of the singer Hy-b-Gharib). "One has perfect style," he said, "if one recites the Qur'an according to Abu 'Amr, if one follows Shafi'i in law, if one sells fine materials (*bizz*), and if one quotes the poetry of Ibn al-Mu'tazz." Respected in the Court by amirs (Hilal-b-Badr) and by the sons of amirs, he had three hundred assistant masters supervised by eighty-four special representatives for his Qur'an courses. His son-in-law was Abu Talib, a Hashimite.

Ibn Mujahid appeared only for the reopening of the trial, but his role in it was decisive, because some time prior to it the deputy vizir, Ibn 'Isa, had chosen him as his spiritual director, consulting him every Friday, which amused the satiric poets. Now in 301, at the time of the first trial, Vizir Ibn 'Isa had been able to save Hallaj; but in 309 he dissociated himself rather quickly from its outcome: which shows the influence of Ibn Mujahid. It does not necessarily follow that Ibn Mujahid had accepted Awariji's opinion about Hallaj's charlatanism; perhaps he agreed with Shibli and the Salimiya in granting the sincerity of his mysticism and even the authenticity of his charisms, but he condemned his public activity on the grounds of its being bad for the security of the Muslim state and disrespectful toward the Book of God; the result being that, by his doctrine of the *shahidani*, he assigned to the Islamic Community a continuous series of spiritual leaders, of divinized *abdal*.

Ibn Mujahid sent Awariji to Ibn 'Isa; under which conditions? We must choose between two versions that are mutually exclusive. According to Zanji, who was already wrong in connecting Dabbas with Awariji in 309, the disclosures of these two men went as high as Muqtadir, who took the initiative of sending Hallaj (under escort) to Ibn 'Isa so that the latter might proceed with his investigation—which is unlikely, since Hallaj was still residing with Nasr at this particular time. The anonymous prologue (of Zanji's account) credits the entire initiative to Awariji, who went to tell Ibn 'Isa that the secretary of state M-b-'Ali Qunna'i worshipped Hallaj and was making (political) propaganda to get his authority (as supreme leader) recognized and indicates that it was only after the arrest of the aforesaid Qunna'i and the seizure of documents in his possession by Ibn 'Isa, that Hamid, who had already learned of the success of the Hallajian propaganda in the palace and with Nasr, induced Muqtadir, in spite of Nasr's efforts, to deliver Hallaj up to him, to dispossess Ibn 'Isa of him. Zanji, however, shows Ibn 'Isa withdrawing as early as the end of the preliminary investigation, and transfering the entire matter to Hamid, after which Hamid proceeded with the first arrests and seizures of documents, notably those in M-b-'Ali Qunna'i's possession.

To choose the anonymous prologue's version assumes, as indicated at the end of the prologue—which seems influenced by the similar trial of the Shi'ite Shalmaghani (thirteen years later)—that some secretaries of state worshipped the person of Hallaj, a charge that must have been held in reserve to use against them (as it was to be used against the worshippers of Shalmaghani, according to established procedure), since it did not arise; it also assumes that Ibn 'Isa, although a relative of the Qunna'is, took the initiative in the arrests, at the risk of jeopardizing the life of Hallaj, whom he had succeeded in saving in 301.

In the face of these improbabilities, it is preferable to follow Zanji's version by adding to it that, if Nasr complied with the caliphal order demanding he send Hallaj to Ibn 'Isa for investigation, it was because he still believed that Ibn 'Isa would save him; and that if Muqtadir took this initiative, it was because he had seen Awariji on behalf of Ibn Mujahid and Vizir Hamid, had considered the denunciation, and had sent Awariji back to Ibn 'Isa for investigation.

Unlike 301, when Ibn 'Isa had contrived to and was able to direct the proceedings, 309 saw him from the very beginning outclassed and outmaneuvered by Vizir Hamid, who took his revenge heavily on Ibn 'Isa through the only two men to whom he acquiesced, Ibn Mujahid and Muqtadir, his spiritual director and his sovereign.

The Qadis

Abu 'Umar Hammadi:

Abu 'Umar Muhammad-b-Yusuf-b-Ya'qub Hammadi, born in Basra on the first of *Rajab* 243/857, died in Baghdad on 27 *Ramadan* 320/932, came from an already famous family of Malikite qadis. We have many details about his role in the Court appropriate for bringing his character into focus.

His family's reputation had begun with his grandfather Ya'qub, who first was qadi of Medina, then, after a period in Samarra, qadi of Fars, where he died in 246.

Abu 'Umar's father, Yusuf (208, d. 297), by being appointed by Caliph Muwaffaq, qadi of Basra and Wasit following the death of his nephew M-b-Hammad (276), chosen by Mu'tadid as deputy qadi at the Court (280), named titular qadi of Mecca (281), and afterwards qadi of east Baghdad, prepared the way for his son.

When he was thirty, Qadi Abu 'Umar was already *hajib* to his uncle, Qadi Isma'il-b-Hammad, in Baghdad (before the former Sufi Ruwaym); named qadi of west Baghdad, 284–292, and afterwards both qadi of Karkh and assistant to his father in east Baghdad (292–296), he let himself be led into sanctioning the deposition of Muqtadir in 296; arrested as an accomplice of Ibn al-Mu'tazz (his hair turned white during a night spent in the dungeon), he recanted, and the Shi'ite vizir, Ibn al-Furat, foreseeing that he might make use of this versatile politician one day, granted him his life. Hit with a heavy fine, confined for two years in his house, Abu 'Umar resumed his work on hadith (as in his youth: at age four he had memorized the hadith, "during the fast, it is permitted to put on the kohl"). Back in favor, he was named qadi of east Baghdad, Karkh, and Kufa, *Jumada* I 301, titular qadi of Mecca and Medina, Damascus, and Yemen (305). Put forward for the position of vizir, end of 306; at the time of the 317 coup d'état, he at first advised Mu'nis to forcibly make Muqtadir abdicate; when Mu'nis refused, he himself persuaded Muqtadir to sign the act of abdication secretly which he returned to him two days later, once the coup d'état proved abortive. This ingenuity won Qadi Abu 'Umar the title of grand qadi of Baghdad and Mecca-Medina, which he had coveted all his life, ever since he was sixteen (305), and which he bequeathed to his son, A Hy 'Umar, who was officially his assistant.

Refined man of the world, skillful courtier, clever opportunist, Abu 'Umar, a century after his death, still stood in the eyes of Baghdad public opinion for all that was outwardly worthy of admiration in a high judge of Qur'anic law: alertness of mind, calmness under attack, loftiness in his bearing, impeccability in the cut of his clothes, exuding the air of dignified splendor. He loved fragrant flowers and transmitted (from his uncle to Qadi 'Ali-b-M-b-H Shafi'i) the hadith recommending that everyone inhale the scent of the narcissus at least once a month. His knowledge of Malikite law was poor, but he cleverly disguised his ignorance; he was anxious to prove himself as a *muhaddith* and undertook to read in *majlis* a bulky *musnad* that he had written: inviting some very old and highly respected traditionists for the occasion. He excelled in being able to analyze difficult situations and turn them unflinchingly to his advantage. He dismissed Qadi Saʿid, the son of Ibn Hanbal (d. 301) and his own representative to Kufa, from office, not because he believed he was guilty of anything, but on the grounds that anyone bearing such a name must not even be suspected. He dismissed a *shahid* for hypocrisy, because he had seen him holding his nose in front of an opened cask of wine; at a time when the canonical prohibition was not predisposed to find a pleasing fragrance offensive. He approved a false claim to which a beggar had forged his signature, in order to demonstrate that his name could not be used in vain. He agreed to judge mentally incompetent a vizir's son of whom he was the guardian (his colleague Ibn Buhlul predicted he would so agree), in order to help him elude his creditors.

The keen instinct that enabled Abu ʿUmar to guess men's fondest secrets, which he capitalized on, led him to go too far. Tabari, during his lifetime, in 302, had the courage to brand in writing, in his "history," the perfidiousness of Qadi Abu ʿUmar in *Ramadan* 289, when the latter agreed to take to Amir Badr a forged letter of safe-conduct in order to lure him into the trap that the Caliph set to assassinate him. At Vizir Ibn al-Furat's trial in 306, he conceived a plan by which, instead of simply returning the deposit of money he was keeping for this vizir, he would deliver the sealed bags on which he had inscribed the vizir's name, adding that he had kept the deposit for this period and that the money in the bags therefore really belonged to him, the qadi, and that he was yielding it only out of "generosity" to the ex-vizir. At Vizir Ibn ʿIsa's trial in 311, he aroused the caliph by his silences and even by his words (getting Ibn ʿIsa to testify as to the genuineness of the marginal corrections used in toning down a letter sent to Qarmathian rebels) to give his support to a charge of treason, which his courageous colleague Ibn Buhlul proved was absurd. To please Vizir Hamid, who had just been rebuffed by a disgusted Ibn ʿIsa, Abu ʿUmar improvised an imitation juridical "proof" of the licitness of wine, something not very proper for a qadi to do, of which Ibn Hamdun and Hariri have left us an account.

For a period of sixteen years (301–316), Abu ʿUmar suffered from being second in Baghdad, according to the protocol rating of qadis, behind Ibn Buhlul. It is possible that the real incentive behind all of his knavery was just for this nomination as grand qadi, which he won in 317. The contemporary sources have reported well on the moral crack beneath the distinguished exterior of Qadi Abu ʿUmar. Abu Khazim was whispering (prior to 292) that this qadi was not ʿafif (= disinterested: a quality required for his profession, for *tazkiya*). More harshly, with regard to the 306 trial, Ibn Buhlul said that Abu ʿUmar himself had "cast aspersions on his loyalty and his honor." Ibn Rawh Nawbakhti, the Imamite *wakil*, who was an expert in dissimulation, confessed that he had been exasperated by Abu ʿUmar in a debate (about the two types of fraud involving the tithe on livestock): "never have I seen a man, while knowing he must reverse his opinion, deny the evidence with such cynicism." After his death, his son had a dream in which he saw him saved thanks to the intercession of Ibrahim Harbi, whom he had revered. The father and son, who were both superstitious, became exploited by a prophesizer of futures, Daniyali.

The Sentence Reserved for a Zindiq

THE *TAWQIʿ* (BRIEF RESCRIPT FROM THE SOVEREIGN)

When the Imam appointed a representative to direct the proceedings of a special court, this representative did not have the power to begin the execution himself by summoning the police commissioner and the executioner, in accordance with the *res judicata* (cf. the execution of three Hallajians in 312/924). The sovereign himself had to pronounce the sentence; or rather, he had to dictate a rescript (*tawqiʿ*) and seal it with his seal. He acted "in the Name of God," on behalf of His written Law, for which he functioned as an "intermediary" (*yad ʿariya*; as when taking an oath). Official ʿAbbasid Sunnite doctrine had not yet achieved its proper formulation of the authoritative meaning of acts sealed by the sovereign; the Muʿtazilites (and Zahirites) leaned in the direction of giving the sovereign not only the preferential right of interpretive inherency recognized by the first four Caliphs (before the Umayyad usurpation), but also the right of initiative when deciding on matters of dogma; hence the intervention of pro-Muʿtazilite caliphs in A.H. 218 and A.H. 233. The Hanbalites, who were successful in getting these two edicts repealed, could not conceive of challenging the sovereign to issue edicts in the opposite direction; they were to become the avowed defenders of the dynasty only after they were outlawed in A.H. 323, when they would "cover" the Sunnite caliphate constantly against the Shiʿite pressure of the Buwayhids; at which time they let the moderate Shafiʿites work to get the caliphal dogmatic edicts of 4[09] and 4[33] issued. In Hallaj's lifetime, the Sunnite jurisconsults remained rather guarded about the authoritative value of the sovereign's rescripts (the conspiracy of 296/908 shows this; a conspiracy by "the orthodox"). Only Sahl (and the Salimiya school) taught that the ʿAbbasid caliph is indeed the Imam chosen by God; if he acts justly, he is the "Pole" (*qutb*; cf. the *mustakhlif* of the Hanbalites, having similar spiritual rank; acting for the salvation of the Community devolving upon a private individual, not the Caliph), and, quite uniquely, absolved in advance as a guarantee of public order. This formula, which was to be used again by Ghazali, seems to have been the one used by Hallaj, according to the interview that he was supposed to have had with Muqtadir, in which he stated that the caliph is the *wasita*, the intermediary instrument of transmission of God's command. This was the position taken much earlier by Hasan Basri against the Kharijites.

It is interesting that the *tawqi*' that Muqtadir issued against Hallaj had been preceded by another *tawqi*' condemning Hallaj, namely, the one that the third *wakil* of the Imamites, Ibn Rawh Nawbakhti, had presented publicly as having been issued by the "hidden" Mahdi and sealed by him as the authorized representative of a mysterious "absent one." The sentence of exile, which was not materially practicable, was a decree of damnation without appeal.

In the case of *zandaqa*, the Sunnites generally accepted the procedure of calling for resipiscence (*istitaba*) prior to the sovereign's confirmation of the sentence.

The death sentence implied the following for the *zindiq*: *ibahat al-mal wa safk al-dam*, confiscation of all possessions and the shedding of blood, and *hukm al-khulud fi'l-nar*, presumption of eternal damnation. Some added to these the selling into slavery of the condemned man's wives and children.

THE CORPORAL AND IGNOMINIOUS PUNISHMENT

The Qur'anic text usually applied in the case of the criminal convicted of *zandaqa* was the following (Qur'an 5:33):

"Verily, the reward of those who make war against God and His messenger and create corruption in this world will be that they will be killed or crucified or have their hands and feet cut off, or will be banished from Muslim lands. Such will be their degradation in the world, and in the Hereafter theirs will be an awful punishment." Of the three types of death prescribed here, we find the same "serial combination" in the punishment prescribed by the ungodly Pharoah for his magicians who had been converted by Moses (Qur'an 20:71; 26:49): "Now surely I shall cut off your hands and your feet alternately and I shall crucify you."

The word *taslib* meant exposure on a pedestal in which the condemned man was fastened to a "scaffold," either by ropes or by nails (*masamir*). *Taslib* usually took place *post mortem*. The wooden pillory (made of palm trees in Iraq: *judhu' al-nakhl*) was either a high post (*sari*) or a small movable cross (*niqniq*). The arms were extended; the head up, or down (in the case of Hallaj; according to Iskaf) or even hung over between the legs (Ibn Fusanjus in 448/1056), the trunk hanging or seated (*rakib*; Ibn Abi'l-Qaws in 287/900), perhaps impaled (the burning stake for the *sahib al-khal* in 291/903).

Two centuries after Hallaj's execution, *taslib* no longer meant "crucifixion," but "hanging"; this is why the Persian and Turkish miniatures depicting the martyrdom of Mansur Hallaj show him being hanged.

For the intercision and decapitation the condemned man was stretched out on a square leather mat (*nat*') on which his blood was spilled; stretched either on his back or face down. We shall give further details in Chapter VII.

The burning of the victim's remains was a common practice. Also the displaying of the head, followed by its preservation in the "museum of heads," in the palace.

ITS THEOLOGICAL MEANING

A solemn condemnation carried out by order of the Imam implied, for most people, the presumption of eternal damnation for the one condemned (a damnation stated in the caliphal *tawqi'*). In the particular case of Hallaj, his strange desire to be put to death anathematized for Muslims helped contribute to a certain Hallajian theory concerning Hallaj as "the disciple of Satan up to and including damnation," "the saint in Hell."

But the case of Ahmad-b-Nasr, the martyr of the Mu'tazilite inquisition whom Caliph Wathiq's (reign A.D. 842–847) brief had sentenced not only to death but also to Hell, was a precedent, one that led Hallajians to regard Hallaj as having died a martyr. Which is what several of his friends, led by Grand Chamberlain Nasr, were to claim without any qualms.

The Shi'ite minority, resting its case on Mahdi's brief (sealed by Ibn Rawh, "damning" Hallaj), seems to have regarded Hallaj as a satanic madman and even interfered to have the punishment made worse.

The theologians held debates over the physical effect of crucifixion. In terms of the body, the amount of suffering needed for purification is up to the discretion of God, Whose mercy is fathomless. To those who believed in the substantiality of the soul, like Sahl Khuza'i, the executed criminal, if he deserved it, felt the punishment in his soul.

Hallaj's punishment was inflicted on him in this world for his having encroached upon the "rights of God" (*huquq Allah*, whose *hudud* are set by the Qur'an) with respect to the matter of pilgrimage (Kilani would one day say that, as a blazer of new trails, [Hallaj] had his hands cut off for having stolen the Divine Pearl). In a later period, some mystics wondered if he had not been condemned *post mortem* by being deprived of the vision of the Prophet, for having minimized and thus insulted his intercession ("the rights of man," *huquq al-adami*).

TASLIB: CRUCIFIXION FOLLOWED BY HANGING:
SYMBOLISM AND ICONOGRAPHY

Hallaj, who had been put on the pillory in 301 when alive, died in 309 *maslub*. We have examined previously the various traditional interpretations of punishment clearly defined as *taslib* by the Qur'an.

In 309, his sentence of death called for flagellation followed by decapitation; to which the vizir was led by his hatred or by his adherence to the literal interpretation of the Malikite *fatwa*, to add the cutting off of the four extremities and the burning of the trunk.

Taslib was thus suspension on a gibbet with the trunk bound to a post: first, for the flagellation on his bare back, with his hands tied in front of him; then, after the intercision, for the crowd to see him in living agony (cf. in 291). This second *taslib* was done by impalement on a stake head down, as Iskaf affirms, and as was done in the case of Ibn Fusanjus in 448 (his head between his legs). The Sufi sources have this second *taslib* lasting one whole night before the decapitation; to them this is the central image of the martyr connected explicitly with the crucifixion of Jesus.

No earlier source claims that Hallaj was strangled prior to being decapitated. How does it happen, therefore, that, from that time onwards, the old *Dar-e Mansur* initiation rite, preserved by the Bektashis, requires the novice to bow down in the center of the cell, called "the gibbet of Mansur," with the *tighbend* rope around his neck, symbolizing that he is prepared to hang out of love of God, like Hallaj?

And why do the Persian and Turkish miniatures almost always depict the *taslib* of Hallaj as a hanging? A hanging in which the victim is still able to speak (in the Yesewiyan *Qisse*, he begs that the cord not be tied too tight), which is paradoxical. 'Izz Maqdisi himself even attributes to Hallaj *maslub* long discourses called *bihabli tukhtanaq*.

It seems there was also a reaction similar to the one to Jesus, "who was not himself on the cross" (Jami). Because Islam increasingly believed that there had been a substitution; the Christian icon as a replica of a man not really crucified was to be avoided. On the other hand, hanging appears to have been the punishment inflicted later on two pro-Hallajian mystics, 'AQ Hamadhani and Suhrawardi of Aleppo; this punishment was less Qur'anic in the strict sense, but more expeditious and increasingly in use.

So much so that even outside mystic circles, in worldly society, Hallaj symbolized those sentenced to hanging. At Malaga around 550, Abu Ja'far A ibn 'Ammar 'Ansi, an Andalusian poet-conspirator, before being hanged evoked the *mihnat al-Hallaj*. At Tabriz in 803, Muhammad Quhistani, a Persian satiric poet, before being hanged on Timur's order, made a final pun on *pay-e-dar:*

"Like Mansur, if they drag you off to the base of the gibbet, bear yourself bravely; this base world is unbearable." In India, Sermed in 1660 and Iqbal in 1932 referred classically to "the gibbet and the rope" in connection with Mansur.

CHAPTER SIX

The Trials

I. A CRITICAL NOTE ABOUT THE HISTORICAL SOURCES FOR THE TRIALS*

Hallaj was indeed a *cause célèbre*. But it was because of the prominence of Baghdad at that time as the setting for the case of divine love to be pleaded by its protagonist, that the secular historians deigned to mention the name of this mystic among the celebrities of the period. It also appears that, as in the case of Joan of Arc, the canonists had made it a point of honor to be punctilious about the proceedings and to choose the grounds for the final verdict only after lengthy investigations.

We no longer have the official record of the trial, and therefore, in order to reconstruct it, we must resort to three kinds of sources: the *caliphal chronicles,* recorded on a day-to-day basis; the *vizirial biographies,* posthumous collections of more or less biased praises (or criticisms), employed again in excerpts a generation later by the chroniclers; and the *biographical dictionary-lists,* compiled from the two preceding sources many years later: arranged according to period, country, and profession; sometimes including private documents.

The authentic documents of the "Hallaj" record were certainly grouped together and preserved among the *watha'iq* [written documents] of which the head of the "upright witnesses" (*wajh al-shuhud*) in the east Baghdad district was in charge. This record was no longer extant in Yaqut's time (at the beginning of the thirteenth century of our era), when he was in a position to consult the records of two other contemporary Baghadadian religious trials, that of Shalmaghani (a chancellery document rediscovered in Marw), and that of Ibn Shannabudh (*mahdar* copied by AY Qazwini, *afwaj al-qurra'*). It must have contained the following: first, the autographed transcript of the verdict of condemnation (copies of which were sent out to be read in the mosques); next, if not the transcript of the court sessions (kept by the vizir), at least the authenticated deeds of the incriminating documents read during the examinations, countersigned by the *shuhud* and by the defendant; among these documents there must have been either a "testament of faith" (*'aqida*) signed by the accused, or, in the absence of that, a list of propositions that were considered heterodox (cf. the trial of 'Ayn al-Qudat Hamadhani) found in excerpts from his works. This *canonical record* must have disappeared fairly early; but cer-

*From *The Passion of al-Hallaj,* vol. 1, pp. 454–58, 465–73, 475–978, 500–59

tain remarks by Baqillani (d. 403/1012) seem to suggest that he consulted it (at the home of the head of the *shuhud,* Talha).

Another record must have been drawn up by the vizir's secretary; with the documents being copied by his clerk Zanji, in session, it is strange not to find any extract of it in the aforementioned Zanji's "account"; this record must have been kept by the vizir's secretary, Ibn Muqla, who filed it away or destroyed it after the fall of Vizir Hamid.

A third record existed in the chancellery, containing the diplomatic dispatches giving, in a florid style, the official version of trials for heresy (cf. for Shalmaghani's trial): in the custody of A B ibn Thawaba.

A fourth record, different perhaps from the third for those years, was preserved for the director of the caliphal postal service (*barid*), Shafiʿ Luʾluʾ by an old *katib*, Abu Marwan Kharaʾiti; containing the dispatches sent to the governors, especially to the Hijaz (hajj), concerning arrests (Sus 301; Khurasan, "about twenty," in 309).

Almost nothing survives of it in our chronicle, biography, and dictionary sources. In that period, the thing that held sway was the prejudice of the *muhaddith,* for whom true history was the hearing of testimonies by word of mouth. This is the way that Zanji, Suli, and, before them, Tabari present to us their own recollections of the trial.

Because Islamic legal procedure does not provide a defense lawyer for the accused, one rarely finds in the transcripts testimony favorable to the defense. The pro-Hallajian tradition has handed down to us only one such, that of Ibn ʿAta'; and his arrest freed the clerk from having to record it, while obliging him to countersign it. It is surprising that Sufi tradition yields only two texts (by Ibn Mumshadh and Ibn Ghalib) dealing with the trial.

Lacking authentic official documents, we should be reduced to entirely subjective personal impressions left us, for the most part, by hostile witnesses, were it not for the fact that in the period in question there were three authors who were concerned with objective inquiry and technical information: an Ashʿarite theologian, Baqillani (around 355–360); a historian of the Sabaean religion, Ibn Sinan (around 355–360); and a Muslim philosopher, Abu Zayd Balkhi (d. 340). Baqillani states precisely the stages of the second trial, and even quotes a sentence from the "letter to Shakir"; Ibn Sinan brings to light the "account by Zanji" and analyzes it *in extenso,* adding to it a discerning and somewhat ironic observation about the Hallajian idea of the votive replacement of the five Muslim ritual obligations; Z Balkhi publishes the *hululi* formulation of the heresy attributed to Hallaj, a formulation borrowed, perhaps, from Karramiya theologians (Ibn Yazdanyar? Ibn Mumshadh?), and which Ashʿarite heresiography was to deal with again.

One of the recensions of the incriminating proposal about the hajj perhaps supplied the text withheld at the trial by the prosecution.

Tabari's text, which we translate later on, is strictly contemporary; the distinguished character of its author gives this subtly shaded testimony a very special value. Tabari, who died at 86 in *Shawwal* 310, completed his great Chronicle on 28 *Hijja* 302 (expressly forbidding anything to be added to it after *"yawmina hadha"*); twenty months earlier he made a point of mentioning the first appearance in court, in 301, "of a man who, it was said, used to call himself Hallaj, and whose given name was Abu Muhammad *Mash'udh" (sic*; I believe that one should read "aw Aba Mas'ud" = "or Abu Mas'ud"). One notes the tone of detached ignorance affected by Tabari. Then, before investigating the pillory episode (18–21 *Rabi'* II 301 = November 15–18, 913), Tabari, suddenly assuming the professorial tone of a *muhaddith*, moves into the first person (*sami'tu*): "I myself heard a group of people affirm that Hallaj claimed divine power (= for performing miracles)." Why doesn't he name these witnesses for the prosecution, when he was the personal friend of one of them, Awariji, who was beginning to draft a pamphlet filled with skepticism of a very Mu'tazilite sort about the "miracles of Hallaj"? Tabari does not hesitate, *sub anno* 289, to blast the conduct of a powerful figure, Qadi Abu 'Umar; why does he hesitate here to give his personal opinion on a matter that he was certainly acquainted with thoroughly and for many years; having taken a position, as a dissident Shafi'ite, against the leading Shafi'ite mufti, Ibn Surayj, his "junior in rank," as he says, who twice had saved Hallaj from conviction, once prior to 289 and again in 301?

Manuscript B (= Berlin 9422) of his chronicle concludes at this point. But the Köprülü manuscript 1047 includes an addition, of which we have no reason to question the authenticity, but which constitutes an author's interpolation that is very unusual, one that is revealing of the interest taken by the aging historian in Hallaj's death sentence in 309, less than eleven months before his own death, when he was already forced by the Hanbalite demonstration (on Hallaj's behalf) to remain in his house. This addition occurs in the chronicle under the year 301, immediately after the pillory incident: "And he was imprisoned a long time; finally, a group of people, including Nasr Qushuri and others, became outraged on his behalf, to the extent that a popular demonstration occurred during which people began to utter prayers against those who wished him harm. Which only made matters worse for him. Taken from his dungeon, his hands and feet and head were cut off; then his body was burned in the fire."

Tabari does not analyze the trial; he doesn't say a word about either the theological grounds for complaint (the deification charge) or the canonical pretext (the replacement of the hajj) for the condemnation, and attributes the sudden execution to a misguided *pietistic* demonstration by his followers. His excuse is that this demonstration, staged by Hanbalites, in *Qa'da* 309 (during which Ibn 'Ata' had the audacity to invoke God against Vizir Hamid, and Ibn Abi Dawud had the gall to turn over to the *hajib* Nasr, a Hanbalite and instigator of the demonstration to save Hallaj, a list of heretical propositions attributed to Tabari) confined him in his house until his death (on 26 *Shawwal* 310/923)— he, Tabari—preventing the vice vizir, Ibn 'Isa, who had ceased to support Hallaj, from entering into any negotiations with Tabari, who was forced to recant in writing.

Viewed as a *muhaddith*, Tabari was a great scholar, a critic who was honest and scrupulous to the letter, but a soul insusceptible to fervor and piety. His hostility toward the piety of Ibn Hanbal led him to write the "*radd 'ala'l-Hurqusiya,*" a violent and unjust pamphlet, opposing him; which was the reason for the Hanbalites' hatred of him in Baghdad. He had shocked Ibn Abi Dawud with a cynical remark about the saliva of the Prophet.

As a canonist, Tabari had broken away from the Shafi'ite school and from Ibn Surayj. Ambitious to start his own school, he did not understand the originality, high moral and spiritual purity of its positions, particularly that of the Surayjiya (which Tabari opposed with a very shabby formalistic guile); and probably also its *fatwa* pardoning Hallaj.

After the death of Ibn Surayj, Ibn 'Isa, who had become conservative and formalistic under Ibn Mujahid's influence, had become on close terms again with Tabari; he wanted to reconcile him with the Hanbalites in order to organize a united front of Sunnites opposed to the return of the Rafidite Shi'ites to the vizirate. It was a limited front; through cowardice Ibn 'Isa excluded from it Hallaj, whose mystical dynamism and keen apologetics had given new life to the dull and narrow pietism of the Hanbalites. But Tabari, who wanted to depend only on Sunnite tacticians with a sprinkling of sober Mu'tazilites, foresaw sadly that the division among Sunnites caused by this Hanbalite manifestation, which accused him stupidly of being a Rafidite, would bring a Rafidite vizirate back to power; and in 310, as in 296, he guessed right.

II. THE FIRST TRIAL (298/910 TO 301/913)

The Pursuits

"In the period of his first vizirate, Ibn al-Furat had ordered (the home of) Hallaj (*kabasahu*) surrounded, putting Musa-b-Khalaf in charge of arresting him. He escaped, however, with one of his disciples, an office-holding Karnaba'i" (Suli).

AH Musa-b-Khalaf (born in 217, died in 306, executed by Hamid) was an elder secretary to whom the vizir confided his personal secrets; it appears that Hallaj had become a celebrity in the capital.

This incident of the escape must be dated, as we shall see, at the latest in *Sha'ban* 298, the time of the arrest of four Hallajians. From the very beginning of his vizirate, on 21 *Rabi'* I 296, Ibn al-Furat had to be on his guard, as a good Shi'ite, against those Sunnite, Hanbalite preaching pietists, like Barbahari, to whom the defeated Ibn al-Mu'tazz had directed a final appeal: "O people of the Sunnite masses, come to the rescue of your Caliph, the Sunnite, the Barbahari." But, since they had not been involved in the orthodox elite's conspiracy, we do not find Hallaj, any more than Barbahari, on the lists of those executed, sent into exile, imprisoned, granted amnesty, or considered fugitive. However, the fact that Hallaj had known ties with the Qunna'iya family (Hamd, Ibn 'Isa) and with Amir Hy-b-Hamdan (who escaped), leads us to believe that they put off imprisoning him only in the hope of intercepting through him some plot on the part of this defeated vizirial party.

The new vizir, a Shi'ite (and, secretly, even an extremist, a Mukhammisi), was anxious to appear to defend orthodoxy; by reviving the edicts of 192, 235, and 249 against the *kitabiyun* (= the people of the Book), excluding them from all professions except banking (*jahbadhi*) and medicine (*tabib*), and forcing them to wear the strip (*ghiyar* = "the crow foot") of the mediaeval ghettoes: a strip of cloth worn on the turban and on the shoulder, yellow (for Jews) or blue (for Christians), and on a waistband (*zunnar*). The Sunnite Tabari declared in the period that the government must remove the *kitabiyun* specialists as soon as replacements could be found for them. But since the vizir retained the two bankers of the Court, two Jews who had helped him defeat the conspiracy by refusing any credit to Ibn al-Mu'tazz, and took on five Christian government secretaries, this edict seems to have been merely a fiscal weapon to use against the pro-Qunna'iya Christian scribes. This edict still permitted the apprehending of the *zanadiqa*, whether they were Islamized Manichaeans or not, who were finally "chased out of Baghdad during the reign of Muqtadir" and "took refuge in Khurasan" without waiting for a *mihna* court to be set up to deal with them. After which two *zanadiqa* Muslim philosophers were pursued, the celebrated Ibn al-Rawandi (ex-Mu'tazilite, editor of the *Muqtadab* of Mubarrad [210, d. 285], who died in hiding in the home of a Jew, Abu 'Isa-b-Levi, in Ahwaz, in 298, probably together with his master, Abu 'Isa Warraq, author of the *Kitab al-gharib al-mashraqi*). Was Hallaj, as early as the year in question, put on the list of *zanadiqa* to be arrested? This is quite possible, but he was not declared officially a *zindiq* before the second *fatwa* of Qadi Abu 'Umar in 309.

Hallaj does not appear to have been involved, prior to his escape, in the attempted coup of Ibn 'Abdun's Sunnite vizirate plotted by the chamberlain Sawsan; and it was even a friend of Hallaj, Nasr, who succeeded the assassinated Sawsan (296). Perhaps also the personal secretary of Musa-b-Khalaf, A-b-Hammad, who would be arrested in 309 as a Hallajian, helped him arrange his escape.

Two incidents, which occurred in 298, seem to coincide with this escape. First, the arrest of a Qunna'i government secretary, Sulayman-b-H-b-Makhlad, who kept his post, a nephew of the Hallajian Hamd Qunna'i: for having approved the setting up of a Sunnite vizirate entrusted to the Sayyida's secretary, A-b-M-ibn ʿAbd al-Hamid, a pious and upright Sunnite, who was probably pro-Hanbalite and possibly pro-Hallajian.

Next, in Shaʿban 298/April 911, the arrest, in the Baghdad suburb of Bab-Muhawwil, of four Hallajians (not designated as such): "In this year, according to ʿAyni, they arrested a man from the Bab-Muhawwil district named Abu Kathir (Malik?), another named Abu Shakir (sic: for Shakir), another named Abu Muslim, and another named al-Samarri. It was said that they were disciples of a certain Muhammad ibn Bishr, who claimed divine authority for himself (yuddaʿiʾl-rububiya).

The charge is identical to that which Rasibi brought again against Hallaj in 301; Ibn Bishr and Shakir became his lieutenants in Khurasan in 309; Samarri seems to be the only one to be kept in prison from 298 to 309, when he must have been released.

This expression, "daʿwa ilaʾl-rububiya," claiming, on the part of one of the ordinary faithful, the sovereign authority reserved to the ʿAlid Imams alone, and only by the extremist Shiʿites, shows the intervention against Hallaj of the Mukhammisa government secretaries (such as the Karkhiyun and the B. Bistam), and not merely of moderate Shiʿites like the people of Qumm or the B. Nawbakht. It is interesting to note that the home of Sulayman-b-H-b-Makhlad, like that of the Hanbalite leader Barbahari, was in Bab Muhawwil. If Ibn Bishr and Shakir had preached Hallajism in Khurasan earlier, when the Samanid government was allied with Vizir Ibn al-Furat against the Saffarids of Fars, it might have delivered them up; but in 309, it refused to do so.

With Hallaj in flight, there could be no trial in 298. But his confederates were kept in prison for some time; in particular, Dabbas:

"A disciple of Hallaj, a certain Dabbas (probably Abu ʿAA A-b-ʿUA Dabbas Baghdadi, a muhaddith and also a Sufi, a disciple of Junayd and of Rudhbari), had been captured; he languished in prison and grew sick of his confinement; so much so that he was released, after he had raised bail and promised to spy on Hallaj. They provided him with money, and he set about following his trail from country to country." Zanji will introduce this later to us as the disinterested "conversion" of Dabbas.

Only the maʿuna (municipal police) and the barid (official postal and general investigation service) would be involved in these arrests, and not the shurta (district militia) nor the haras (caliphal guard), which we shall see entering the scene in 309.

From his secret residence, Hallaj attracted public opinion: "in the year 299," states the Sabaean historian Ibn Sinan, "Hallaj's fame spread." Which means that on the eve of the year 300, a prophetic date in Muslim eschatology, the Hallajian propaganda troubled many souls.

The Arrest in Sus

Hallaj had gone into hiding in the heart of Ahwaz with Karnaba'i, his disciple, the maternal uncle of his son Hamd. The Karnaba'iya were a family that enjoyed a prominent position among the notables both of Basra and the rest of Ahwaz; they were *mawali* daring to keep up with the Hashimites, like the Al Sulayman of Basra; they were probably *shuhud*, and were envied by the tax collectors, who were usually extremist Shi'ites. Karnaba'i hid his brother-in-law in Sus, near the tomb of the prophet Daniel.

The town of Sus itself was intensely Sunnite, Hanbalite, and *hasbiya* pietist in coloration: which is the way I interpret "practicing the litany taught in the religious community of 'Abbadan" for the *tawakkul*: "*Hasbi Allah*," a litany condemned by Nazzam and the Mu'tazilites. A Sufi from Basra, Subayhi, who had been persecuted by the jurisconsult A 'AA Zubayri (like Tustari), had also just sought refuge there (his tomb is located there, Sulami notes). Over and above the outpourings of popular feeling (aroused by him under an assumed name), Hallaj must have been privately supported by important persons who knew his real identity: perhaps by Rasibi himself.

A small group of Shi'ites had wangled their way into positions of authority: Amir 'AA ibn Mikal (*wali* from 295 to 298) was sympathetic toward this group, particularly toward the estremist Shi'ite financier, Ibn Bistam, son-in-law of the Sunnite financier Hamid, toward the fiscal *wali* Qasim Karkhi (d. 298), who was succeeded by his son Ja'far (298–300), both of them Mukhammisa, toward their *wakil* Ibn Abi 'Allan, a Mu'tazilite pupil of Jubba'i, the maternal uncle of Qadi 'Ali Tanukhi, source for the anti-Hallajian documentation in the Nishwar; and toward Abu Yf Baridi, who was from a banking family of Jewish origin, the manager of the Sayyida's lands in Ahwaz, who was given the promise of a great political future.

Among Sunnite functionaries, Nu'man (who in 301 succeeded 'UA-b-H-b-Yusuf, 300–301, as fiscal *wali*) was the only one sympathetic to Sufism, therefore to Hallaj (a close friend of Ibn 'Isa, a protector of the poor, Nu'man, who had converted around 304, was executed, very likely as a Hallajian, by Shalmaghani by order of Muhassin, in 311). The Sunnite *wali* of Wasit, Hamid, had a Shi'ite son-in-law, Ibn Bistam, and plotted with Abu 'Adnan, the son-in-law of Rasibi, a former high-ranking official of the Court, endowed with a huge fortune, the size of which we know. The *muhtasib* of Ahwaz was a Hashimite nobleman, Ahmad Zaynabi, a favorite of the Sayyida and probably already pro-Hallajian.

In *Ramadan* 300, Ahmad Zaynabi, being dissatisfied with the incumbent vizir, Khaqani, went to visit, in the custody of the fiscal *wali* Karkhi, a candidate for the vizirate who was interned by him, named Ibn Abi'l-Baghl, a true scholar, bold critic in the field of Qur'an exegesis, and an old friend of Ibn 'Isa; was he trying to get Hallaj, among other prisoners, released? The scheme failed, and must have hastened the denouement.

The director of the postal service (*barid*) for the town of Sus spent a day in one of its districts called "Rabd wa Qattaʿa"; there he heard a woman in one of its alleyways saying "stop it or I'll talk." He told his Arabs (= policemen, it being an Arabized Persian town): "seize her," after which he questioned her: "What's wrong with you?" "Nothing," she said. He then had her led away to his headquarters for grilling, after which she talked: "All right, a man is living in the house next to mine, a certain Hallaj, and he has a great number of acquaintances who come to see him night and day, in secret, and they talk together about forbidden things (*munkar*)."

He immediately called into service a group of local people and some government (*sultan*) police to help him, and had them surround the place. They did as ordered, and captured a man whose hair and beard were white, and seized him and all of his possessions, consisting of gold pieces (*ʿayn*), musk, clothing, safflower (of red dye), ambergris and saffron colored. He said, "What do you want with me?" They said, "You are Hallaj." "No, I am not," he said, "and I don't even know this man." They brought him to the residence of the postal service director, ʿAli-b-Husayn, who locked him up in a room under heavy guard. Then they confiscated notebooks, letters, and materials belonging to him. The news of this capture spread through the town; everyone came to look at him. ʿAli-b-Husayn asked him, "Are you Hallaj?" "No," he said. Then a resident of Sus said, "I would recognize him easily by a mark from a blow on the head." They examined him and found it. Now, it so happened that Dabbas (the investigator for the Baghdad police) arrived in Sus at that same moment. Upon learning the news, he hurried off (in order to collect the reward) to tell it to the authorities (*sultan*) in Baghdad, who acknowledged (and rewarded him for) the news.

This account by Ibn Sinan calls for some observations: the informer knows Hallaj only by his real name, even though at the trial the pseudonym "M-b-A Farisi" (thus out of Fars) will be bestowed on him, and even though Baqillani, going one better, will complete the name as follows: "M-b-A Farisi, of the family of Husayn, son of ʿAli-b-Abi Talib." What does *munkar* mean? Probably "seditious remarks," for this old woman may not have appreciated theological discussions. As for the precious objects that were seized, they were gifts from his admirers, not a collection of some charlatan's tricks.

Handed over to the *khalifa* of Rasibi in Sus, ʿAbd al-Rahman-b-X (lacuna), Hallaj was transferred by him to the residence of his master, Dur al-Rasibi; without any interference from the Sunnite Qadi of Sus, AH-b-ʿAli Sarraj, the *wakil* of the titular qadi of Ahwaz (the qadi of west Baghdad, Ibn Abi'l-Shawarib). It was a political affair at first. And, acording to Suli, Rasibi, who was to die a few months later, on 29 *Rabiʿ* II 301, after his questioning of the prisoner and a hasty examination of the confiscated papers (written in a coded language: *marmuz*), was supposed to have formulated in writing the charge of "usurping the sovereign authority (of God)" and of "preaching *hulul* (= the coming down of the Spirit of God into hearts)," and to have drawn up the report sent back with the escort that was to lead the accused, reputed to be an extremist Shi'ite conspirator (of the Qarmathian variety), to Baghdad.

If Suli, himself an extremist Shi'ite in secret (but really a Mukhammisi) is telling the truth, it was Rasibi who was the first to define Hallaj's *hululi* heresy, a definition that all of the heresiographers were to repeat; clearly influenced in this by his fiscal collaborators like the Karkhiyun, who were themselves Mukhammisa.

But we know from the trial of 309, and from Hamid himself, that the minute Hallaj's capture was known, this fiscal *wali* of Wasit did not wait (which would have been customary) for the escort to pass through his territory, but hastened to Dur al-Rasibi, to be with his friend, Rasibi's son-in-law, Abu 'Adnan, who like him was associated with Hamid's superior in Baghdad, Akh Abi Sakhra, a state secretary in the Sawad (of finance) from 299 to 304, when he interrogated Hallaj, who would himself be declared "the Mahdi." And Rasibi, then old and sick, may have let Hamid draft the aforementioned report. In every way possible Hamid, through his haste, expressed a hatred against Hallaj that his extremist Shi'ite advisers would consciously revive in 309, but which had profound roots in the mentality of the old farmer general, of the "famine pact" expert, which Hamid [at heart] was.

Hamid took over the supervision of the escort, and during a stopover in Wasit interrogated Hallaj for the second time. Hallaj answered him, saying "I am (merely) a pious man." Then they set out again for Baghdad, with their grand arrival occurring on 6 *Rabi'* I 301/October 10, 913.

With the entire journey from Sus to Wasit and then to Baghdad taking three weeks, plus the stopovers in Dur al-Rasibi and Wasit, for perhaps at least a week, and the imprisonment in Sus amounting to another week, Hallaj's actual arrest can be dated around 25 *Muharram* 301/September 1, 913 at the earliest. Because Vizir Ibn 'Isa had assumed power on 11 *Muharram*/August 16, Sus had not yet received official confirmation of this fact on the day of Hallaj's arrest; and far from Vizir Ibn 'Isa's having instigated it, we shall see that it annoyed him. And that Hamid had not arranged it for Ibn 'Isa.

On 6 Rabi' I, Hallaj made his entry into Baghdad, under escort, hoisted onto a camel, followed by his disciple and brother-in-law (*khal waladihi*, says Miskawayh = *akh imra'atihi* by Ibn Dihya; that is, Karnaba'i, about whom we know nothing more), also astride a camel, while a crier shouted out: "Here is the apostle of the Qarmathians, come and identify him!" A production clearly staged by Hamid. Ibn Dihya has some people cry out: "Here is the sorcerer Hallaj, the charlatan"; adding "humiliated and ashamed, the two men had their heads covered with one *burnus*" (exact detail). "They were paraded through Baghdad."

"He was charged in Ahwaz and in Madinat al-Salam (Baghdad) with having called himself God, the divine nature (*lahut*), coming down to infuse Itself in noble men (*ashraf min al-nas* = Hashimites, or only 'Alids; or superior men); that this was found revealed in his letters, and that he used tricks" (Ibn Sinan). Tabari records and credits to hearsay only the first charge (*rububiya*).

The Interrogations in Baghdad

Strictly speaking, there was no trial; and Vizir 'Ali ibn 'Isa, of the Qunna'i party, favorable to Hallaj on account of his secretary of state and cousin, Hamd (successor to Akh Abi Sakhra in the Sawad), and a supporter of the *fatwa* of incompetency by Ibn Surayj, succeeded in hushing up the whole affair, as Harold Bowen has noted; collecting the materials of both the preliminary investigation (examination of documents) and the interrogation [of the accused]. Without taking into account the terms of the warrant, at least three years old, which the Shi'ite vizir Ibn al-Furat had issued, and which the dynamism gained from the administrative changeover had managed to keep unchanged, under the Sunnite vizirate of Khaqani, through the zeal of such fiscal *walis* as the Karkhiyun and Hamid.

Tabari writes, prior to 26 *Rabi'* II 303, and even prior to 28 *Hijja* 302 (the colophon of his *Chronicles*), that the vizir "summoned a man who, it was said, was called Hallaj; to his house." He refers to the first indictment, but says nothing about the interrogation. The common source (Mutawwaq?) summarized by Ibn Abi Tahir and Suli, states the following:

> He examined him and found that (Suli adds: in the presence of *fuqaha'*, stammering) he knew nothing in the sciences of the Qur'an (reading, commentary), of law and of hadith, nothing in history (*akhbar al-nas*), nor in poetry, grammar, and other Arabic sciences. The vizir concluded with this reproach: "You should set about to learn how to purify yourself (*tuhur*) and how to carry out the five prescribed duties (*furud*; var. *fara'id*, inheritance duties?). What good does it do you to write tracts that prove your ignorance of things that you discuss in them? How many times do you write to people, Woe unto you (*waylak* = perhaps: you say to them 'Woe unto you'): 'He is going to come down (from Heaven), the Master with the sparkling Light, who is going to glisten (*yalma'*) after having sparkled'; oh, how much you need to be educated (*adab*). . . ."

This reference to the "*Nur sha'sha'ani*" is not found again among the Hallajian fragments; it is a technical term belonging to extremist Shi'ism, commonly used at that time by the Mukhammisa and the Qarmathians; to the Qarmathians, it is the first emanation of the *Nur'ulwi*, therefore the *kuni*, the *Mim*; to the Nusayris, it is the emanation at the Last Judgment of the '*Ayn al-shams* (the sun will rise in the west: Qur'an 18:84), which is Fatir (the pre-eternal name of Fatima and of Maryam: *Umm al-kitab* of the Khattabiya); Khasibi compares it to the *Nur tasini*, which dazzled Moses on Mt. Sinai.

Hallaj introduced this term into Sufism; Ibn 'Arabi, in his *Tajalliyat* identified it with the red light (*ahmar*), the spiritual emanation corresponding to 'Ali
(ecstasy with Ibrahim Khawwas) before the white (Abu Bakr), followed by the
green ('Umar).

In the authentic Hallajian texts "*yatasha'sha*' " is told of the irradiation of
annunciatory lights of divine union for the soul. But the term has a dynamic and
eschatological meaning, as the reference noted by the vizir in 301 proves; the
gradual interior lights of ecstatic souls announce to them the coming full light,
and before everyone, of the Witness, whether Messiah or Mahdi (and, according to the hadith of Hasan Basri and of Shafi'i, "there is no mahdi but Jesus");
in whom God will judge, on the day of the final meetings.

Who were the vizir's assessors during this abortive trial, which lasted only
forty days? Usually the assessors represent the Muslim Community at large,
but their role in 301 did not involve them as responsibly as the *shuhud* in 309,
for they were obliged neither to sign the official records of the proceedings
verifying the genuineness of the texts or of the heretical responses to questioning, nor to approve a conviction in the name of God, since the vizir's decision
to put him in the pillory fell within his full powers of *ta'zir* (correction).

Hallajians had been in prison since 298, but the vizir did not bring them to
trial; if he did not release them, perhaps it was because of the police commissioner, Mu'nis Fahl, the inventor of the additional staging of the "Qarmathian"
scene on both occasions of the entry into Baghdad and the exposure on the
pillory. The vizir dismissed the witnesses for the prosecution, didn't submit the
confiscated documents to any qadi, and limited himself to making an abstract
of them (*supra*). Taking his inspiration from the *fatwa* of Ibn Surayj, he resorted in his dismissal of Hallaj's case not to the convenient device of irrespon-
sibility for reasons of insanity (*fasad al-'aql*), but to that of the establishment
of crass ignorance (*jahl*), deserving at most exposure in the pillory or a flogging.

The Exposure in the Pillory

And by way of conclusion to the case, Hallaj was simply sentenced to a degrad-
ing punishment; the vizir mocked him, slapped his face, had his beard shaved
off, and beat him with the flat edge of his sword; then he was hung up (alive,
on the gibbet), along with his *khadim*, not for six months (Ibn Dihya, who adds
"children were cursing, slapping, and mocking him"), but for four consecutive
days, on Wednesday, 14 *Rabi'* II and Thursday 15 on the east bank, in front of
the east-bank police headquarters, and Friday 16 and Saturday 17 on the west
bank (Tabari: three days, "from morning to evening").

The public onlookers included not only revilers but also disciples. One of the
latter, remembering his Nehavend prophesy, that he would find the joy of the
Nayruz (the New Year) only on the day when, hung on a gibbet, he would be

brought nearer (to God: Qur'an 96:19): "Ahmad, our *Nayruz* has come," Hallaj incurred this quasi-ironic retort: "Have you now received, O master, your New Year's gifts?" "Completely," Hallaj responded; "I have received them: revelation and certitude so long as I am ashamed of rejoicing in them too soon (before seeing God)."

The two prisoners, exhibited, were clothed in a *jubba ʿudiya* (aloes-wood color = dark gray); and the public crier proclaimed: "Behold the apostle of the Qarmathians; come and recognize him." This statement was probably invented by the police commissioner as an underhanded slap at the vizir, who was pursuing a policy of rallying the Qarmathians to orthodoxy, misunderstood by the public.

III. THE EIGHT YEARS OF WAITING

After this pillory exposure, Hallaj was returned to prison. He [remained] there for eight years, seven months, and eight days, (15 *Rabiʿ* II 301/November 19, 913 to 23 *Qaʿda* 309/March 25, 922). This calculation comes from an unknown pro-Hallajian, but antiquated, source; Sufi tradition is unaware of it. Why didn't the vizir set him free? Perhaps to protect him against his Shiʿite enemies. Perhaps because the police commissioner refused to allow it.

The Transfers from One Prison to Another; His Influence, His Writings

Hallaj was at first returned to the prison of the Dar al-Sultan (Sultan, in this instance stands for the vizirial part, not the caliphal part, of the east-bank palace). The dungeons of Matamir being abolished, it must have been near the palatial gateway Bab al-ʿAmma, where a fragment of the Black Stone had been inlaid, which must have been greeted by foreign ambassadors on the way into the city, ambassadors like the two Byzantine ambassadors, John Radecues and Michael Toxaras, sent by Constantine VII in 305/917; it was in the dungeon of the Dar al-ʿAmma that, according to Wakiʿ, Constantine Dukas was supposed to have been kept prisoner before his coronation of a day. Hallajian legend preserves an echo of this news item, in the account that shows Hallaj compelling the son of the Byzantine emperor by the power of his prayer to come forthwith and wait (at table, cf. the Christian *ghilman* cup-bearers of the faithful in Paradise) on his Sufi disciples, and finding himself the next morning in Constantinople with a piece of Arab lupine in his hand. During his execution, Hallaj perceived in the distance the taking of Istanbul by Islam.

We have only two anecdotes about his treatment in prison, both of a secular literary nature, and one isolated testimony, indirect, coming from the Hallajian Faris Dinawari.

ʿAW-b-ʿAli Sayyari (d. 375), according to Faris: "at the beginning of his imprisonment, he was chained from his neck down to his heels with thirteen chains, and he prayed, despite that, a thousand *rakʿa* each twenty-four hours." ʿAttar reproduces this anecdote and adds the following: "someone asked him: "since you claim to be God, why do you pray in this way?" (He answered:) "Because we know what we are worthy of."

Both secular documents make certain references, one to the old Matbaq prison (west bank), the other to the palace, indicating he was able to meet people; but we don't know if he was allowed to see his former disciple, Amir Hy ibn Hamdan, again; the latter died in the palace prison in 306.

Ibn Hayyawayh, according to the *katib* A ʿAA M-b-ʿUA ibn Hirrith: "Abu Mansur A-b-M ibn Matar said: Hy-b-Mansur Hallaj recited to me the following lines of poetry, composed by him, when we were imprisoned together in the Matbaq:

> Your toyings, friend? the season is past for toyings with old brows.
> You conquered and broke the silence of a heart you played with;
>   though a peaceful sojourn has consoled it.
> No more eyes in which desire grows again, and no more heart
>   in which love's memories may clash.
> There you are, reduced to the ranks of the foes, solitary,
>   no longer visits from you, and therefore none from me.
> This is the way the donkey went along, bearing Umm ʿAmr;
>   neither the donkey nor she came back again.

This poem, which uses a profane system of symbolism to represent divine love, cannot possibly be by Hallaj, whose *diwan* is free of any concession to this genre. However, he could have borrowed it from a profane poet, like *Nadimi* from Abu Nuwas and (*Ma li jafayta*), in order to extract some mystical symbols from it, much as Rudhbari was to do from a poem by Ibn Dawud.

M ibn al-Munajjim said:

I often used to visit my brother when he was in prison in Baghdad; one time, in the dead of night, I heard a very moving prayer; I listened closely; it was the voice of a heart that was keeping watch, of a tongue that was witnessing, saying: "my Friend, You have hidden me (here) according to Your will, and revealed according to Your will; by Your glory, if they were to torture me with every kind of suffering, I would consider that the most beautiful of Your graces, by Your glory; for the lightning flashes shining forth in consciences have already destroyed the external appearances of their conditions." Then I heard him utter this *duʿaʾ*: "My God, I fear You, me a sinner, and I trust in You, me a believer; I rely on Your favor in asking Your pardon, and I trust in Your generosity in asking Your forgiveness; I rejoice when I speak with You, for I have the highest respect for You." I asked who had spoken in this way (he added then), and I was told "it is Husayn-b-Mansur Hallaj."

One of Hallaj's poems, which is undoubtedly authentic, appears to have been written by him during his long stay in prison: (*al-hubba ma dama maktuma*, . . . cf. *Diwan*, no. 24):

Love, as long as it is hidden, feels it is in great danger,
  and you gain confidence only by going out to brush with danger
  (variant: and it gains confidence only if it leaves prudence in abeyance);
And love is no longer sweetly scented when the breath of calumny permeates it,
  like fire which no longer serves any purpose when it smoulders in the stone;
And now that the jailor (*sajjan*) has come and the police have assembled their
  forces, and the informer (*sahib al-khabar*) has "given" them my name,
I am at the point of wishing to free myself of Your love;
  but then I would have to be freed from hearing and seeing.

The four previously cited texts form a very slender complement to the two historical summaries of this eight-year period of waiting; the first is preserved in the Prologue of Zanji's account, the second in Hamd's account, published by Ibn Bakuya. The first puts together a few references to facts not dated, the second omits the trial and the pillory episode in 301, which is strange.

To make up for this meagerness, the caliphal chronicles give us in detail the political intrigues surrounding Muqtadir; these enable us to make conjectures with a reasonable assurance of accuracy, and even to determine the intrigues' consequences in relation to Hallaj and his family.

From 301 to 308 we see that Hallaj was still able, from the depths of his prison, to reach out, to have a wide correspondence, to write his later works, to read them to his visitors. Those opponents who had accused him prior to 301 of presenting himself to the Shi'ites as a deified mahdi, reported that after 301 he changed his strategy and, appealing to the Sunnites, became himself a candidate for the Caliphate—a ridiculous charge, which no one raised at the trial in 309.

The support that he gained while in prison came about in actuality from the dissemination of his mystical writings by his disciples, whose leader was a Hashimite from Ahwaz, Abu Bakr, whom he called Abu'l-Mughith. We believe that the portions saved from his later writings are those that form the miscellaneous collection of the *Tawasin*.

These portions give us the last position of his dogmatic thought as he approached the threshold of his sacrifice for the Law. Since 306, an extremist Shi'ite, a gloomy and bitter soul, Shalmaghani, was disseminating in the Court (by taking advantage of the confidence of the Shi'ite *wakil* Ibn Rawh and of the Sunnite vizir Hamid) a doctrine that combined the Law and rebellion, virtue and crime, election and damnation, forming antithetical pairs of equally important terms as being holy and pleasing to an ineffable God. It was the hypocritical malice of a madman, the angelic source of which Hallaj examined in his *Ta' Sin al-Azal*, an astonishing treatise whose complete title is "the pre-eternal purity and legitimacy of sermons (on divine Unity) when their real meaning is inverted."

Two beings, it is said, have been predestined to bear witness to the fact that the One essence of God is inaccessible (by law and in actual fact): Satan (= Iblis) before the Angels in Heaven, and Muhammad before Men on earth; they are heralds, the first of pure angelic nature, commanded to rule an "inferior" material world, the second of pure human nature, committed to a superhuman witnessing of the heart (over and beyond the intellect: *amana*). And this being accomplished, both stopped midway; they reversed the thrust of their zealous love of God's glory, their fondness for the pure idea of a simple Deity. Their proclamation of the *shahada* remained external, they did not assimilate it by uniting with the unifying will of God. At the first Covenant, Iblis refused to consider the idea of a divine Presence's wrapping itself in the lowly and material form of Adam (a prefigure, thus, of the Judgment). At the time of the Nocturnal Ascent, Muhammad, being too virile, stopped at the threshold of the divine fire, without passively "becoming" Moses' Burning Bush; and Hallaj, who served as a substitute for him after his third *waqfa* at ʿArafat, urges him to go further, beyond the *Qab Qawsayn*, to enter the divine Will's fire even to the point of dying, like the mystical butterfly, and "to fulfill himself in the Object of his love. Muhammad, on his last pilgrimage, at ʿArafat, restored the ʿUmra in the hajj," renewed and eased the prohibiting Law; though he took pity on men, not daring to impose on them the heroism of self-sacrifice, which fulfills the Law and Islam, he nevertheless decreed the abolition of the *diya* (and *riba*), and he knew (and said) that the symbolic Sacrifice of Abraham, which he reestablished, gains forgiveness for the multitude only through the intercession of self-sacrificing souls (from 9 *Hijja*, prior to the ritual sacrifice of 10 *Hijja*), who are the apotropaic pillars (*abdal*) of his community. These souls, daring to take issue with the Merciful One (Who offers them for the admiration of His angels), would in the end bring about the unification of men's different forms of worship, not only in spirit, but in actual practice (Hallaj adhered to the material pillar of the rituals, the resurrection of the body), the fulfillment of Islam in a complete gathering together of forgiven humanity. By stopping to return, Iblis brought on the sins of men, and he presides over the disintegration of the material universe; and Muhammad delayed the hour of the destruction and Judgment of men that he was sent to announce.

And yet Iblis, by suffering the unpardonable damnation of his angelic legalism, arouses humanity to go beyond this threshold of supreme diselection to find Love (Hallaj understands that it is the Law of nature itself that stopped him; he admires its true beauty, which comes from God: that terrible ambiguity of grace, that divine temptation which the heart (not the intellect) must enter in order to find [Love]).

Muhammad, by his momentary delay in surrendering himself, determines the time needed for the molding of hidden saints whom he waits to pass beyond him. Both stand like two cornerstones of pure created nature, marking the threshold that the divine Spirit makes those sanctified beings fly over, whom he introduces to the One through an unforeseeable and transnatural trick of love, which is the secret of divine glory and justice.

Hallaj does not compare the final destiny of Iblis with that of the Prophet, as Shalmaghani and the Druzes do; rather he, who must have gone to Medina to venerate, like the Hanbalites, the Prophet's dormition in his tomb (*Rawda*), does not regard this delay on earth as a punishment, but as the anticipation of the ecstasy of ultimate union (*ma'ad*) that is promised him (Qur'an 28:85). The initial exclusion of the herald of angelic nature (unknown, of course, in mystical union) must contrast with the final election of the herald of human nature (elevated into union thus by the saints). Hallaj, in a famous poem, defines the obstinacy of Iblis shown in the quietism of his self-enclosed contemplation, refusing what the Deity stoops to doing:

> I refused (to worship the form of Adam, at the Covenant),
>   because I wanted to proclaim You Holy;
> But here Adam is You; and the only one who separates each of you is Iblis.

By inciting men to sin, by forewarning humanity to remain "separate" from God, and by dualizing being, not wanting to be himself the third, Iblis labored in vain: the ecstasy of the One shines with the Judgment; and it sparkles already in the sanctity of hearts.

But isn't Hallaj, by desiring to die as a sacrificial victim, as an anathema, a damned creature like Iblis? This was the question that his excommunicate's execution for a long time raised for the mystics who read his *Sin al-Azal*. No, his commentator Baqli was to answer: Hallaj, who remained bound to religious observance and morality, by dying accursed was surrendering his heart to the sanctifying counsel of the Spirit of Union; whereas Iblis deceived himself, draped in the romantic pose of a scorned lover, through a lack of synthetic and unlimited acceptance of the divine example.

Hallaj's Situation vis-à-vis the 'Abbasid Caliphate; His Favor at Court

The final decision belonged to the Caliph concerning Hallaj's fate. We have sketched briefly (*supra*) the character of Muqtadir, his personal position, and his intermittent doubts about the legitimacy of the 'Abbasid dynasty revived by his cunning Shi'ite vizir, Ibn al-Furat, who had rescued him at age fourteen (in 296), and who tactically played the role of his tutor to the very end. Muqtadir, on the other hand, owed his enthronement to the Mu'tadidya *ghilman*, a small group of officers faithful to their oath of allegiance to the son of Mu'tadid. The latter were recent converts to Islam, but avowed Sunnites, Greek turncoats (Mu'nis, Nasr, Bunayy) closely allied to three sovereigns who were of Greek origin like them: Ashar (mother of Muwaffaq), Dirar (wife of Mu'tadid), and

Shaghab, who had been raised as Hanbalites, like most of the Turkish women of the imperial harem, and were Turkish converts from Ushrusana. These two elements of Sunnite dynastic continuity—Turkish and Greek officers, Arab and Arabicized "Yemenite" adminstrators—counterbalanced, in the service of Muqtadir, the corrosive influence (that is, for the dynasty) of the Persian Shi'ite financiers and their Arab allies.

They kept him mindful of the 'Abbasids' basic historical function in Islam: the safeguarding of the hajj and the maintenance of the Holy Places of the Hijaz.

Hallaj's singular devotion for the hajj led to his being protected in the Hijaz by the 'Abbasid officials, the Hashimite nobles, and the Mu'tadidiyan officers. He was known at Court very early in his career by them (and by Shibli) and by the Harithiya administration secretaries. We have, from a Sufi source, a short speech delivered by Hallaj to Muqtadir on the latter's duties as a sovereign by divine right.

Hallaj thus recognized Muqtadir as legitimate, and this is what must have won him the heart of the Queen Mother. Hallaj's matrimonial alliance with the Karnaba'iya of Basra, who were Zaydites sympathetic toward the Zanj rebellion, and the Diri incident (examined earlier) do not prove that he had been pro-'Alid in his youth.

Hallaj, trained in the Sunnite milieu of the *people of hadith*, had accepted the legitimacy of the 'Abbasid power from his masters, such as Sahl. The traditionists, who at first had been anti-'Abbasid, threw their lot in with the 'Abbasids as being answerable to the Prophet and his Community for the care of the Holy Places. This was increasingly the position of the Hanbalites.

Furthermore, Hallaj had settled Ahwazian notables from Tustar in Baghdad at the time of the transfer of the *Dar al-tiraz* (official Harithi expensive fabrics; provider of the veils for the Ka'ba) from Tustar to Baghdad; and these two transfers came about through the initiative of 'Abbasid officials. But these caliphs did not push the "mobilization" of the hajj and the extension of the *ta'rif* outside the Hijaz to the point of embracing the Hallajian idea of transferring the sacrifice of the hajj for the Community to one of its members as ransom for the sins of all, at each hajj. And this is why Muqtadir renounced Hallaj, over the entreaties of his mother, when it was explained to him that Hallaj's basic intent was to destroy the Temple, that he was really a Qarmathian anxious to destroy the hajj, in accordance with the secret doctrine of the budding Fatimid dynasty, which the Druzes will bring to light.

Awariji's Pamphlet

According to Zanji, it was when Nasr had gotten Hallaj's prison sentence lessened that a former Sufi, Awariji, who had become a functionary in the Department of Finances, wrote a pamphlet entitled *Makhariq al-Hallaj wa'l-hila fiha*, "the Miracles of Hallaj and their trick." The Prologue to "Zanji's account," in a slightly different way, reported that, in opposition to the credulousness of Nasr's civil servants who believed that Hallaj could revive the dead and was waited on by the *jinn*, who brought him whatever he wished ("and he had brought birds back to life"), Awariji was supposed to have informed against another fiscal functionary to the vice vizir Ibn 'Isa as a worshipper of Hallaj, perhaps his rival, M-b-'A Qunna'i, in order to get him arrested. However, Ibn Dihya's account shows that this arrest occurred only after Ibn Mujahid approached the vice vizir, and Dhahabi states precisely that it was Awariji who urged Ibn Mujahid to take action by reporting to him, not the tricks of Hallaj, but the heresies that he had heard him teach; thereby joining, as Zanji says, another ex-Sufi informer, Dabbas.

Zanji, by remark, appears to have been misinformed, for it was between 298 and 301, and not in 308, that Dabbas betrayed his former master. Whereas Awariji, as we have seen previously, born in 278 and a hermit in Lukkam before renouncing the Sufi life, can hardly have been associated with Hallaj anywhere but in Baghdad, and during the period of his long imprisonment (with undoubtedly the ulterior motive of betraying him, like Dabbas); after the first vizirate of Ibn 'Isa, thus after 305.

His pamphlet, intended to derail the workings of Hallaj's "tricks," must have employed the Mu'tazilite method for explaining the "miracles of saints," of accepting neither the hypothesis of a divine charism nor the idea of a magical pact with the *jinn*; it was a rationalistic tract, as befitted a close friend of a historian as antipietistic and anti-Hanbalite as Tabari.

Mhs Tanukhi preserved for us two long and labored anecdotes about Hallaj's tricks (the fake blind man, the zoological garden for the credulous), which, like the texts of Baqillani (the apparatus for inflating the pleats and skirts of his robes), must have originated in Awariji's pamphlet; and thus must have derived from an already old and indirect documentation collected in Ahwaz around 280 by AS Nawbakhti based on Jubba'i—in an industrialized region where the technical advance in machinery was astonishing.

The Political Crisis and the Social Disturbances of 308

A shrewd observer, convinced Shi'ite, and passionately nationalistic Persian, Hamza-b-H Isfahani (d. circa 355), whose *ta'rikh* and *tanbih* are very intelligently written, and who had just arrived in Baghdad, begins his Chapter 8 of Book X in the following way: "for 177 years the empire of the 'Abbasids had remained standing, . . . until the thirteenth year of the reign of Muqtadir . . . this was at the end of the year 308; when fighting and riots broke out in the capital; both the army and the subjects lost all respect for their rulers, the treasury was exhausted, the valuable collections of their forefathers were plundered; and these disorders continued for twenty-five years in the capital of their empire" ("until God saved what was left of them," thanks to A Hy Buya, he adds as a good Shi'ite a little later on).

Then Hamza examines one by one the riots in Baghdad: 14–17 *Qaʿda* 308 (over the high cost of bread); 24 *Rabiʿ* I 311 (the Qarmathians in Basra, the fall of Vizir Hamid, the atrocities committed by Ibn al-Furat); 20 *Muharram* 312 (the Qarmathains massacre the hajj caravan at Habir); 21 *Qaʿda* 313 (the Qarmathians capture Kufa, after having destroyed the hajj caravan); 15 *Rabiʿ* I 315 (mutiny by the army; the Qarmathians at Kufa, 7 *Shawwal*); 9 *Ramadan* 316 (the capture of Qasr-b-Hubayra; the Baghdad mob burns the granary opposite the vizirate [*majlis al-sultan*], burns the fiscal registers of Baduraya and the archives of the caliphal accountancy department); 14 *Muharram* 317 (the army deposes Muqtadir for three days); 7 *Hijja*–18 *Hijja* 317: the Qarmathians occupy Mecca, they bury 3,000 bodies around Kaʿba, throw the rest in the Zamzam well, abduct seven hundred virgins, make off with the gates of the Kaʿba (given by the Queen Mother), the Black Stone (*hajar al-taqbil*), the jewels and relics of the prophets (the Pearl weighing fourteen *mithqal*, the earrings of Mariya (the Copt), the ram's horns of Abraham, Moses' rod embellished with precious stones, seventeen silver candlesticks, three silver *mihrab*) and the Veil (*kiswa*) covering the Kaʿba. . . ."

The economic and social crisis appears to have been threefold: inside Baghdad and other cities, precipitated by the sudden increase in the cost of bread, a riot by the small crafts workers against the wholesalers and the Court; in the eastern sector, in the Persian mountains, a nationalist uprising of serfs, peasants, against the old and the new imperial feudalism; in the western sector, in the Arabian desert, the old instinct for pillage stirs up the bedouins against the villagers of Iraq and the rich cities, with the full support of the revolutionary propagandism of the Qarmathian conspirators, who unleashed the Arab nomads as an assault division to destroy official Islam and to create a new, universalist City.

Riots for food supplies, and above all for bread, in Mecca (in 262) and later in Mosul (in 307), served as a prelude to the revolutionary events in Baghdad lasting from Friday, 14 *Qaʿda* to Monday, 17 *Qaʿda* 308. Since 306 Vizir Hamid, former farmer general and tax expert, had clashed with the sober "physiocratic" doctrine of his vice vizir, Ibn ʿIsa, who had studied the budget for the year 303 in depth in order to draw up his estimates for 306. An honest physiocrat, Ibn ʿIsa looked out for the fellah and curbed the monopolists, which brought about an easing of fiscal pressures; Hamid, in his counterattack, had baited the Caliph with a heinous speculation on the monopolized wheat stocks (stored in Baghdad in the government warehouses, the *mustaghallat*; burned down in the riot of 316); the price inflation was such that the small crafts workers, all Hanbalites, staged a systematic revolt (they were grouped in trade guilds, *hiraf, ashab al-taʿam, asakifa*); they attacked the wholesalers and the warehousemen, who were Hamid's accomplices in the "famine pact." A good many of the soldiers and the crowd were killed. The attitude of Chamberlain Nasr, a Hanbalite, and Vice Vizir Ibn ʿIsa, both openly sympathetic to the insurgents, reveals the more than just moral support of these high officials, who no longer believed at all in the right of the state to act this way; a prerevolutionary state of mind.

Threatened, Hamid got himself sent to Wasit, from which he returned with supplies of grain, which calmed the people of Baghdad, at the same time as Commander-in-Chief Mu'nis, who had just saved the empire, in Egypt, from the Fatimids' western attack, reentered the capital.

At that point Mu'nis was called upon to face another danger for the empire, this time to the east; the Daylamites, Persian nationalists, were dividing up the feudal lands among the peasantry and had just entered Rayy, at the crossroads between the Caspian and the Lut desert: owing to the desertion of the *wali*, Akh Su'luk, Mu'nis's former assistant, a Samanid amir, ever the favorite of Nasr and Ibn 'Isa. To save the situation it was necessary to equip an army, to find a commander for it (Devdadh, commander of Hamid's guards, must have at that time suggested his uncle, Ibn Abi'l-Saj, to Mu'nis), then to break with the Samanid state, whose sovereign was an ally, and also the "honorary" police commissioner of the capital (there was an ambassador there, AH ibn Marzubani 'Imran, and lastly, to adopt a tougher fiscal policy. But all of this could be done only by ruining Ibn 'Isa's and Nasr's reputations with the Caliph.

It was then that Hamid's long-standing hatred of Hallaj brought him to realize that he could destroy both Ibn 'Isa (who saved Hallaj in 301) and Nasr (who had saved Hallaj in 308) if he were to succeed in reopening Hallaj's trial. The break with the Samanid state and its vizir, Bal'ami, a pro-Hallajian Shafi'ite (who was to refuse, in 309, to extradite the Hallajians, and to enforce the excommunication fulminated in Baghdad), had this one advantage of cutting Hallaj off from his friends in Khurasan (the Shafi'ite mufti of Nishapur, M-b-'Abd al-Wahhab Thaqafi, a friend of Shibli, enforced the *fatwa* of Ibn Surayj). Hallaj, moreover, must have been sympathetic toward the rioters in 308 who opened up the prisons; Hallajian legend has him freeing his fellow prisoners through a miracle (*markab al-najat*), then returning voluntarily to his cell.

IV. THE SECOND TRIAL (308/921 TO 309/922)

The Initiative of Ibn Mujahid, Head of the Qur'an Reciters; He Delivers a Mystical Tafsir by Hallaj to the Vice Vizir, Ibn 'Isa; the Arrests

One sentence in Ibn Bakuya dates Nasr's parting (with the custody of Hallaj) at the end of *Rabi'* II 308. Now, Hamid had returned from Wasit on the first of *Rabi'* II, and Mu'nis from Egypt a few days later. It was certainly not by accident that Ibn Mujahid, urged on by Awariji, went and denounced Hallaj to the vice vizir, Ibn 'Isa. Bowen believes that this took place prior to Hamid's return. Nasr was closely associated with Ibn 'Isa, and in order to take away the custody of Hallaj from Nasr, it was necessary first to prevent the vice vizir from saving Hallaj, as he had done in 301 in accordance with the *fatwa* of Ibn Surayj. Since the death of Ibn Surayj, Ibn 'Isa had chosen Ibn Mujahid as his spiritual director, and all that was needed in order to reopen the trial was to persuade Ibn Mujahid to bring his influence to bear on the vice vizir. But Ibn Mujahid, a Shafi'ite and friend of such pro-Hallaj Sufis as Shibli and Ibn Salim, undoubtedly did not decide to denounce Hallaj on a basis of "tricks" whose fakery Awariji may have come forward to reveal to him. Ibn Mujahid, head of the corporation of *Qurra'*, could have been aroused only if confronted by some sort of offence against the text of the Qur'an, by a shocking *tafsir* accredited to Hallaj, and I believe that Awariji, a former Sufi, was the one who got it for him.

Ibn Dihya's text states the following:

> In 309, a book signed by Hallaj was brought forward containing his *tafsir*, which described the multiplicity of Lords (*arbab*) and the plurality of Gods (*aliha*); the head of the *Qurra'*, AB-b-A-b-Musa ibn Mujahid handed it over (to the authorities); the (vice) vizir AH (ibn 'Isa) examined it, and when he had grasped what it was, denounced it as scandalous and ordered a search of the house of his *khadim*, M-b-'A (Qunna'i); he was arrested, and his books were confiscated.

What was this *tafsir* by Hallaj, which is not included in the exhaustive catalogue of his writings published by Ibn al-Nadim? The plural words "Lords" and "Gods" are found in a suspect document referred to both by Ibn 'Ayyash and by the heresiographers (Baghdadi, Biruni); but this is a letter, not a *tafsir*. This accusation is aimed beyond any doubt at the *qawl bi'l-shahid*, the "theory of the inspired apotropaic Witness," who possesses "divine knowledge," *'ilm ladunni:* like the Seven Sleepers and Khadir (in Qur'an 18:64). It may also be aimed at the chains (*isnad*) of more or less hierarchically deified Witnesses who are supposed to transmit to Hallaj his 27 *Riwayat*, which are actual *hadith qudsi*, in which God speaks through him in the first person; but this work is not at all a *tafsir*; and the 243 snatches of Hallajian *tafsir* compiled by Sulami and Baqli give the impression of having been collected at random.

Ibn Mujahid may have initiated in 309 the interventionist policy of instituting proceedings against authors who use abnormal, noncanonical (*shadhdha*) Qur'anic readings, which enabled him, after the condemnations of Ibn Shannabudh and Ibn Muqsim (322–323), to get every other Mushaf but that of 'Uthman, and the choice of any other vocalization of the sacred text but that of the traditional Seven Readings, forbidden. Upon close examination, I find in Hallaj only two abnormal Qur'anic readings, *anzala* (for *farada*: Qur'an 28:85), and *taqul* (for *qala'l-insan*: Qur'an 99:3); his exegesis of Qur'an 2:141, contrasting *ya'rafuna* with *ya'lamuna*, repeated by Ash'ari, shocked Ibn Hazm; but these are peccadillos. More serious is the question of *qira'a 'ala'l-hikaya*, of reciting the Qur'an "as if" (*ka'annahu*) it were God who is speaking (cf. Shibli, for Qur'an 15:70: *nanhaka*: at the time of the execution). Especially since, according to Hallaj, the transforming union does away with the "as if" and puts the saint in the immediate grasp of divine elocution. We note, in any case, that Ibn Mujahid stood aside and does not appear to have taken a seat in the court. It was Awariji who had pushed him to speak, since he took advantage of Ibn 'Isa's agitation to get him to arrest his colleague M-b-'A Qunna'i.

M-b-'A Qunna'i appears to have been the first of the implicated government secretaries to be involved; although, later, Zanji reports that it was Hamid and not Ibn 'Isa who had him arrested: together with three others—and later, after Hamid's interrogation of Samarri's daughter, which seems anachronistic.

M-b-'A Qunna'i, a recent convert (like his relative, Ibn 'Isa), the son and brother of Christians employed in the Department of Finances, was a scholar with wide and varied political connections, who seems to have written a compendium of astronomy highly regarded by Battani; his Shi'ite connections make one doubt that he was a convinced Halajian; he was a casual admirer, a lover of art who had arranged to have his collection of Hallaj's works transcribed in deluxe manuscripts; for aesthetic, not liturgical, reasons. Here, again, is the text of the "Prologue," followed by Zanji's text: (Prologue): (denounced by Awariji as an ardent admirer of Hallaj, enlisting political supporters for him (by his sovereign authority: ta'a), M-b-'A Qunna'i's house was surrounded by order of Ibn 'Isa and he was arrested. Ibn 'Isa got him to admit that he was a supporter of Hallaj; notebooks and letters written by Hallaj were turned up in his house.

> (Zanji): When Hallaj was handed over to Hamid, the latter hounded his disciples relentlessly, with the help of spies; he captured Haydara (executed in 312), Samarri (arrested in 298), M-b-'A Qunna'i, and the one that they called Abu'l Mughith Hashimi. The appointed Ibn Hammad (= A Mawsili) escaped, but they surrounded his house and in it they found, as in the case of M-b-'A Qunna'i, several notebooks of rice paper, some written in gold ink, lined with brocade and silk, bound in expensive parchment.

The Seizure of a Text on "Deification" Leads to Hallaj's Being Handed over to Vizir Hamid

Ibn Dihya tells us that "when AH (Ibn 'Isa) examined the captured manuscripts, he found among them a book on "the secret of the Deity" (*sirr al-ilah*) containing more blasphemy, anthropomorphism, and heresy than all the tongues of believers put together could utter. He then administered eighty slaps on the face, and afterwards had him put in prison." The Caliph then ordered that he be turned over, together with his writings, to Vizir Hamid-b-'Abbas, whom he put in charge of everything involving Hallaj and his party of followers.

The "Prologue" says that "Hamid-b-'Abbas requested of Muqtadir bi'llah that Hallaj and his (arrested) agents be turned over to him. Chamberlain Nasr was opposed to this; he was considered sympathetic toward Hallaj; but Hamid persisted (Hallaj was confined in the palace) and Muqtadir bi'llah ordered that he be turned over to him; Hamid took him away and locked him up."

Zanji says (skipping the incident of the book) that "Muqtadir bi'llah had dispatched Hallaj (at the time of the disclosures by Dabbas (*sic*) and Awariji) to AH Ibn 'Isa for cross examination; he made him appear before his council; but after he had spoken sternly to him, it was recounted at the time that Hallaj had walked up to him and said 'shut up, don't say anything more, or I'll unearth secrets about you,' or something like that. Ibn 'Isa then refused to continue his examination and took himself off the case. It was then that it was given to Hamid."

Suli says the following: "they found some writings by him filled with silly things and words misused. To make a long story short, he became so ridiculous that the chamberlain, Nasr, had to come to his defense, for someone had said to him: 'Hallaj is a Sunnite, and there are *Rafidites* among the government scribes who are after his head.' But others said to him then: 'but Vizir Hamid-b-'Abbas is surely a Sunnite, isn't he?' 'True,' answered Nasr, and he turned Hallaj over to Hamid."

This text by Suli is true to type, with its secretly extremist Shi'ite mental reservations. He speaks with irony and detachment of an affair in which he undoubtedly played a direct role. In point of fact, Suli, fully devoted to his patrons, the Banu'l-Furat, was particularly attached to the former secretary of state, Muhassin-b-'Ali, an extremist (Nusayri) Shi'ite like his relatives, and closely connected with the famous Shalmaghani, head of the 'Azaqiriya sect, whom Vizir Hamid had brought back from Wasit, and whom he consulted, he, a Sunnite vizir, on every ticklish matter. Hamid, preoccupied with getting Hallaj delivered up to him, got Shalmaghani to work on Suli, whom Nasr had appointed private tutor to the heir apparent prince, in order to convince Nasr of his, Hamid's, Sunnite loyalty: an incontestable loyalty, but one that was superbly exploited, under the circumstances, by the Shi'ites.

One will note the discrepancies between the four preceding accounts concerning the role of Vice Vizir Ibn 'Isa and the cause of his resignation. Suli dimisses him as a minor walk-on; Zanji depicts him as being scared to death by a charlatan's threats (he was writing that as the vizirate was about to fall); the theological source by Ibn Dihya credits Ibn 'Isa, who had pretensions of being a canonist, with having straightened out a terrible heretic with his own hands, an act of violence probably transposed from Hamid, who was not as concerned about this theology; the "Prologue," like Suli, passes over Ibn 'Isa.

This first phase of the trial appears to have lasted a few weeks, according to Khattabi: "a group of his disciples were informed on to the vizirate (*sultan*); they were arrested and writings were seized in their homes confirming what had been said against him; several confessed; rumor spread about it; people began to talk in public about his being put to death; and the Commander of the Faithful ordered Hallaj to be turned over to Hamid-b-'Abbas."

What was this book by Hallaj on "the secret of the Deity," which is missing in the *Fihrist* list of his works? Was it from this book that Suli took the quotation *"Inni Mughriq qawm Nuh, wa muhlik 'Ad wa Thamud,"* "I am the One Who sent the flood to Noah's people, Who destroyed '*Ad* and *Thamud*"? Suli conceals from us the fact that this sentence, which is revered by the Nusayris, is a verse from the liturgical litany enumerating the *divine* names of 'Ali, and hides from us the fact that he hated Hallaj for having committed this sacrilegious usurpation of the role of either *'Ayn* or *Sin*. But what Ibn Dihya says about this book points us instead toward a dogmatic treatise in which Hallaj, discussing the *shahid* (the "inspired witness") thesis, established testimonial monism (*wahdat al-shuhud*, not *wahdat al-wujud*, existential monism) in the transforming union, the *'ayn al-jam'*, the mystical state in which the uncreated divine Word modulates itself directly through the articulated speech (*nutq*) of the saint: beyond prophetic revelation. This is what chapters V and IX-X of the *Tawasin* set forth, as does the *Bustan al-ma'rifa*, the account by Ibn Mumshadh of the letter seized in Dinawar, the final *salam* to his readers in some form of writing.

The Composition of the Court in the Judgment Hall

We have already indicated the authorized members of this special vizirial court of the *"nazar al-mazalim"* type, which we meet again in the Shalmaghani trial and especially in another trial involving heresy initiated by the head of the Qur'an reciters, Ibn Mujahid, that of Ibn Shannabudh.

The hearings were definitely not held in the mosque (near the *mihrab*) nor in the residence of the principal qadi, but, at the request of the vizir, either in his residence or in a special *dar al-'adl* in the palace (*Dar al-'Amma*). We can prove this by the presence of a Jewish banker of the Court and by the vizir's ushers' (*a'wan*) ill-treatment of the accused during the session. Furthermore, Zanji affirms it is so.

According to Maqrizi, the magistrates were seated on high mattresses backed by cusions in two rows facing each other: the one to the right of the vizir holding a high-ranking military offical; to the left, a high-ranking fiscal bureaucrat and the Caliph's scribal clerk. The row presided over by the principal qadi including, on either side of him, two *shahids* ("upright witnesses"), at least; and facing him a writing desk with inkstand.

At the back of the hall, on two sides, sat the authorized assistants, laymen and jurisconsults (mainly the *qadis* and the *shuhud*).

The vizir (Hamid) must have had to his right neither Mu'nis nor Nasr (in this place during the trial of Khaqani) nor the commissioner of the *shurta*, but the commander of his guard (*haras*), Dawdadh; and, to his left, Ibn al-Hawwari and the *katib* AB ibn Thawaba (or the vizir's *katib*, Ibn Muqla), and next to him the clerk of court, Zanji.

The principal qadi (Abu ʿUmar: neither Ibn Buhlul nor Muhamili wanted to sit in this trial, nor, *a fortiori*, did the son of Ibn Surayj) must have had to his right Qadi Ibn al-Ushnani, accompanied by his two Malikite advisers, the qadis AF Laythi and Ibrahim-b-Hammad; and, to his left, his head of the *shuhud*, Qadi Ibn Mukram, his *katib*, Ibn Abi Khumaysa, next to him.

During the less important sessions, these eminent figures were represented by deputies (Ibn Abi'l-Hawwari by Ibn Bazyar); Qadi Abu ʿUmar by his son and *na'ib* ʿUmar.

The Shuhud, "Upright Witnesses" of the Community, Signatories Authenticating the Written Documents of the Canonical Court

The essential role played by the *shuhud* in Muslim canonical court procedure stems from a basic principle in Islam: (witnesses') evidence is oral, not written. This is why the historical legacy of the Community consists of chains of testimonies received in "audition" (*samaʿ*) transmitted from generation to generation in "cities of learning." Similarly, responsibility for the protection of family and inheritance rights was in a practical sense given to a particular social group, the *shuhud*; according to the hadith of Ibn ʿAbbas: "honor the *shuhud*, for it is through them that God restores one's rights and protects one from injustices."

For almost three centuries, the class of "upright witnesses" included all adults, and the Hanafite qadis (the official qadis of the dynasty) kept this rule: in Baghdad until 256, in Basra until 272. It was the Malikite qadis, from the Azdite family of the B. Hammad, who, faced with the numerous and varied duties incumbent on the *shuhud*, required them to undergo a special technical training, restricted by an entrance examination (*tazkiya* = "purification," "purging [of morals]") subject to renewal. In Baghdad, Qadi Ismaʿil Hammadi reduced their number to 1800; later, after 301, Qadi Abu ʿUmar Hammadi, in making the examination more demanding, reduced their number further, but their social influence and their fees increased; in 383, under Caliph Qadir, there were no more than 303 enrolled; and, in order to guard against the secular influence and venalities of the military commanders and the Buwayhid sultans, the caliphs kept control of the nomination and supervision of the *shuhud* beginning with Caliph Mustakfi (in 333). In 309, there must have been around five hundred *shuhud* in Baghdad; and tradition states that Hallaj's condemnation was countersigned by eighty-four *shuhud*, which is a very reasonable percentage, given the fact that the qadi in charge had complete control over the list of *shuhud* to be summoned for the trial. Unanimity among those *shuhud* who were present was needed for the validation (countersignature) of the theoretical judgments of *ijmaʿ*, in the name of the Community, before the Caliphs' confirmation was given. In 255, the abdication of Muʿtazz was validated by nine *shuhud* for the good of the Community (*salah al-muslimin*); in 279, two *shuhud* attested to the death of Mu'tamid; in 317, four *shuhud* recorded the abdication (countermanded two days later) of Muqtadir.

The qadi leaned increasingly on this class of witness-assistants chosen and deputized by him alone. Authenticating the handwriting, signature, and seal of the qadi, bringing forward in court the three legal proofs (external proof, confession, refusal to swear an oath), validated at the end of session by their countersignature—all of that resulted in their being put in charge of rogatory commission, interrogation of noble women who had to take off their veil in front of them at home (Shaghag in 321 in the presence of AQ Jawhari and Ibn 'Ayyash), and the administrative supervision of *waqfs*.

At Hallaj's trial, Qadi Abu 'Umar Hammadi summoned three categories of *shuhud* to sit in pairs, to his right and to his left (opposite the vizir, who was flanked by high officials): first, a certain number of qadis, in preference Malikites, working together with him as experts, but countersigning the documents as special *shuhud*; next, the professional *shuhud*, *shuhud mu'addala* ('*udul*), responsible for the drafting and preservation of documents, hence their present-day comparison with Western "notaries public"; next, some theoreticians of the law (*fuqaha'*), most likely Malikites, and reciters of the Qur'an (*qurra'*), surely referred to the qadi by the head of their corporation, Ibn Mujahid, the initiator of the proceedings (perhaps he did not seat them, but was content to have them countersign certain documents plus the sentence by proxy on certified copies); and lastly, certain *ashraf*, Hashimite nobles.

The quasi unanimity of the *shuhud* who tried and condemned Hallaj came about because of the fact that most of them belonged to the Malikite school of law, and because of Qadi Abu 'Umar; the support of Qadi Ibn al-Ushnani, whose reputation for being unprincipled was well known, did not involve the majority of the Hanafite school's members, who adhered to the restraint of their leader, Ibn Buhlul.

The *shuhud* of the two other Sunnite schools abstained on a large scale. The Hanbalite school, immediately after the public protest over Ibn 'Ata' (which cost him his life). The Shafi'ite school, because of the *fatwa* of Ibn Surayj, refrained from participating in the judgment, except for a few who had personal reasons for defecting, like Ibn Zabr and 'Utba (and possibly Istakhri). The most prominent among the Shafi'ite *shuhud* abstentionists was, without a doubt, the famous patron AM Da'laj-b-A Sijzi (262, d. 351); the heir of a shipowner, a writer on traditionists (Ibn Khuzayma), he assigned his immense fortune to Shafi'ite *waqfs* for programs of public welfare and canonical instruction; at first in Mecca, where he directed the dynastic *waqf* of the Dar 'Abbas; afterwards in Baghdad, where he settled after 290 near Karkh, on Saluli Street (cf. Saluli, the Hallajian), Darb Abi Khalaf (the name of a monkey that belonged to Zubayda); he built a *masjid* there. After 306, Da'laj created, near his own home, in Qati'at al-Rabi', around the tomb of Ibn Surayj, a Shafi'ite *waqf* (modeled after the Khaffaf *waqf* that he had been acquainted with in Nishapur, and that exchanged professors with his), a center for the teaching of Surayjian Shafi'ism, which lasted until 469 (the time of the founding of the Nizamiya). It was from the very beginning a pro-Hallajian center, since the head of the Cairo *shuhud*, the Surayjian Shafi'ite Ibn al-Haddad, collected there, as early as 310, the text of Hallaj's last prayer; and it must have remained so, for the transmission of the *fatwa* of Ibn Surayj in his favor. It was also the direction center in Baghdad for the 'Abbasid (as opposed to the Buwayhid) dynastic *waqfs*, with Da'laj being in charge of the one in Mecca. The leading defender of Sunnism in Baghdad in the period of Shi'ite rule, Da'laj, left at his death a *tarika* of 300,000 dinars, which was confiscated by Mu'izz al-Dawla (in 351), after a lively struggle with the Hashimites. He had written a *Musnad al-muqillin* and some *nawadir*.

The Position of Prisoners

What was Hallaj's position in prison in 308 and 309?

In *Jumada* I 308, Nasr, won over by Hallaj, got permission from the Caliph to transfer him to the palace in his custody, thus close to his own residence (*dar al-hijaba*), "in a room belonging to him, one in which Hallaj was able to receive visitors." Hamd's account states the following: "Nasr Qushuri got permission from the Caliph to build him a separate cell in the prison; the outside door of this house was walled up and the house itself was surrounded by a wall; one entered it through a door within the prison. Hallaj received visitors there for a period of one year (*Jumada* I 309). . . ."

Nasr, who brought Hallaj to the Caliph and to his mother, the Sayyida Shaghab, "told everybody that, when Muqtadir was stricken with a bowel ailment, he understood its symptoms, consulted Hallaj, and asked permission to bring him to the Caliph; thus authorized, Hallaj had come and, while reciting some verses [of the Qur'an?], touched the place where he was suffering with his hands; after which the malady disappeared. Afterwards, this same malady gripped the mother of Muqtadir and Hallaj cured it in the same way." This is the basis, Zanji adds, of Hallaj's influence in the palace, especially among Chamberlain Nasr's staff.

Which would date the incident in 308; but Muqtadir's only recorded bowel ailment was in *Hijja* 303 (*ishal* [diarrhea] for thirteen days, "cured by bloodletting").

People also said that [Hallaj] could revive the dead, for he had brought birds back to life. The following two texts deal with this subject:

Harawi (summarized by Jami, 173): "Someone brought him a dead parrot. 'You wish me to bring it back to life?' Hallaj asked. 'Yes,' was the answer. [Hallaj] then raised his finger, and the bird sprang up, alive."

Kitab al-ʿuyun:

Muqtadir had a servant bring a dead bird to Hallaj and had him say to him the following: "This parrot belongs to my son Abuʾl-ʿAbbas (= Radi, Caliph in 322), he loved it, and now it is dead; if what you preach is true, bring this parrot back to life." Hallaj got up and went to urinate against the wall of his room (cf. Thomas More), and said: "a mere man, subject to such needs as this, hasn't the power to revive the dead; go back to the Caliph and tell him what you have seen and heard." The servant agreed. "However," Hallaj said, "I have a *jinn* who serves me, and at my instant call, the bird can live again as before." The slave went back to tell Muqtadir what he had seen and heard. Muqtadir said, "Return to him and tell him the following from me: 'What I wish is that this bird may live again; call on whomever you wish to accomplish that.' " Then he had the dead bird brought back and laid before Hallaj. Hallaj set it upright on its feet, covered it with his sleeve, uttered some words, then lifted his sleeve, and the bird was alive. The slave returned to Muqtadir to tell him what he had seen. Muqtadir went to tell (Vizir) Hamid: "Hallaj did this and that." Hamid responded: "O Commander of the Faithful, my advice is that he be put to death; otherwise there will be a revolt."

This miracle supposedly dated from 308; but it must involve the parrot that the black *shahid* Filfil brought back to Radi from Oman in 305. Ever since Ibn Sinan (d. 366), Hallaj was presented as having restored birds to life and as being served by *jinn* who could bring him whatever he asked for and desired. But also, during Hallaj's lifetime, Ibn ʿAtaʾ admitted to having contributed to the spreading of this report in order to conceal the fact that, in reality, it was God Who directly performed such miracles through Hallaj by his living spirit; like Jesus making the clay birds come to life (Qurʾan 3:43).

Mufid, a little later, notes that the Hallajians recount miracles by their founder similar to those that the Christians say are performed by their monks.

One government secretary (director of the Department of Finances for the west, between 301–304), Hamd-b-M Qunnaʾi, claimed to have been "cured of a sickness by drinking some of Hallaj's urine" (Ibn Sinan). This account presented as factual in 308–309 dates back further, for Hamd Qunnaʾi, a candidate for the vizirate in 306, must have died in extreme old age soon after, since he was not arrested in 309.

Some phials of urine were actually found during the investigations, along with dry dung. This "coprophagy" is not sadistic in origin, as in the case of the tax farmer for the granaries of Samarra, Abuʾl-Khattab referred to by Tawhidi (*Basaʾir*); Malati (d. 377) undoubtedly is thinking of these Hallajians when he explains that, for Qarmathian initiates, everything becomes pure, even excrement: "so much so that some of them eat the excrement (*rajiʿ*) of others, convinced that it is pure unadulterated food (cf. Marguerite-Marie and Mélanie, in which instance it was an act of heroic mortification). Harawi regretted the presence of "filthy things" in these miracles.

One other miraculous account is more felicitous:
Hamadhani:

> One of Nasr's sons was suffering; one day the doctor (Razi? at that time associated with the Queen Mother's hospital) prescribed for him an apple. But it was not possible to find one (in that season). Hallaj raised his hand up in the air and produced an apple. Those present, astonished, asked: "Where did he get it from?" "From Paradise," he said. Someone remarked: "A fruit that comes from Paradise shouldn't be spoilt: there is a worm in this one." Hallaj said, "Since it had to leave the perdurable world to enter this perishable one, a little of the corruption (of this world) crept into it." They were even more impressed by his reply than they had been by the miracle.

The concluding remark is that of an amused skeptic, probably the Mu'tazilite AY Qazwini (in connection with a similar explanantion that one encounters again in the life of Anna Catherine Emmerich.

The sign of fruit being found out of season is, in Islam, a Marial sign shown in connection with Hallaj, from the Ahwaz period onward. One finds it again in Christian hagiography (Agnes of Langeac).

These accounts are not introduced as conclusive evidence. But we do have two incidents, whose preternatural character is indisputable, in the hostile acount by Zanji, written before 311, and endorsed by his son as a cowitness:

> One day I was seated with my father in Hamid's tribunal; and, after the session ended, we left to go out and sit in the courtyard (*riwaq*) of the *Dar al-'amma*. Harun-b-'Imran, the banker of the Court, came over to be near my father, without speaking to him; we were together like this, when we saw one of Hamid's servants coming, the official in charge of guarding Hallaj; he beckoned to Harun to come forward, and Harun left us abruptly, without our knowing why. After a brief absence, he returned, his face very drawn looking. My father, being amazed (at his appearance), questioned him about it. And he answered him as follows: "Hamid's servant, the one in charge of guarding Hallaj, called to me and I went. He told me that he had gone into Hallaj's cell with the tray that he was instructed to bring him every day, and he found him inside filling the entire room (with his person, all by himself) from ceiling to floor, from wall to wall. The sight terrified him; he let the tray fall from his hands, and ran out of the room." In fact, this same servant was trembling and deathly pale, and had a fever. Harun was still mystified by it all. Now, while we were sitting there sharing his amazement, one of Hamid's court ushers came and notified us to return to his presence. We returned, and we spoke with this same servant; Hamid bid him step forward and made him repeat his story: and, all in a dither, he repeated it. Hamid then called him a liar and insulted him, saying to him: "Were you afraid of the charlatanism (*niranj*) of Hallaj, God curse you! Get out of my sight!" And the servant left; but he remained for a long time in a feverish state.

Hallaj exhibited the preceding phenomenon several times. The Ashʿarite theologian Razi's *Makhariq al-anbiya'* explained it in the Muʿtazilite manner as a fake system of pipes in the walls and a cellar with vents for the air to pass through from outside which he made to open before an audience in such a way as to inflate his silk robe until it filled the whole "hall of Majesty" (*bayt al-ʿazama*, in Basra). Sufi legend deals with this "hall of Majesty". It is even embellished by a dramatic contrast that Hallaj exhibits, either before his arrest or when confined in his prison tower, when at one moment he fills the tower entirely (making it disappear, filling the oratory), and another moment he shrinks to the size of a three-year-old child or even to that of a rat.

We must call attention to the role played by the Court banker, Harun (Aaron-ben-Amran), the official arbitragist connected with the firm of Joseph Pinehas and Company, which, from 260 until around 329, held the tax-farm of Ahwaz, in payment for its monthly advances to the treasury, which paid the salary of the praetorians. I even think that the vizir's reliance on him went so far as to include entrusting him with the guarding, not only of the Crown jewels (which Zaydan the *qaharmana* will let be stolen), but also of important prisoners like Hallaj, a Jewish banker being more ransomable than a Muslim jailor should they escape.

> Hamid was informed that a disciple of Hallaj told of having gotten into his dungeon, and of having spoken with him, without any difficulty. Hamid issued a formal denial, and proceeded straight off to interrogate the guards and gatekeepers of the prison, for the order was to let no one enter to see him. Several gate-keepers were whipped, and swore on their eternal salvation that they had let no disciple of Hallaj in to see him, and that they had seen none pass through. Hamid then had the terraces and walls inspected, but the entire inspection turned up nary a footprint nor a breach (in the wall). Finally Hallaj, questioned as to the means by which this man had gotten in to see him, disclosed that "it was divine power (*qudra*) which sent him down to me, and it was through its opening in me that he went out again" (= outside of the three dimensions).

This account by Ibn Zanji is cross-checked by Hamd's account of his father's time in prison: "for one year he received visitors. Then that privilege was forbidden him (on orders from Vizir Hamid), and he went five months (*Jumada* I to *Shawwal*, 309) without any visitors; except for one time, when I saw Abu'l-ʿAbbas ibn ʿAta' enter secretly (*bi'l-hila*), and one other time AʿAA ibn Khafif (entered)." After that, there followed two months of increased secrecy (*Shawwal* and *Qa'da*, 309) (Hamd).

Ibn Zanji reports this deed to us about the very daring Ibn ʿAta'. Harawi seems to be unaware of it, for he shows Ibn ʿAta' merely asking Hallaj in prison: "Is all that you have uttered of your own accord?" "No, God forbid! [Hallaj answered], like the sword or the arrow, I have been only a passive instrument." Ibn ʿAta' must have come to bid him farewell, before organizing the Hanbalite riot that brought on his appearance before the court and his death.

Ibn Khafif's Visit

The historical importance of this visit must not be underestimated, for Ibn Khafif is an independent witness, who, without having belonged to a Hallajian group, and without letting up in his fight against the Salimiya in the name of Ash'arism, did not waver for the remainder of his life in his defense of Hallaj's orthodoxy and especially of his union with God; he called him "al-'alim al-rabbani," "the inspired scholar."

In 309, Ibn Khafif was forty-one years old. Born in Shiraz of an aristocratic Persian family (his mother, an Arab, Dabbiya, from Nishapur), he made the hajj between 290 and 295, returned via Baghdad, where he was converted to Sufism, received the habit from Ruwaym, and visited Junayd. One account by Ahmad-b-Yunus (Akhbar) shows him holding his own in public with Junayd, who was criticizing Hallaj's preaching in Baghdad: "O Shaykh, you are going too far. Having his prayers answered and reading into hearts implies neither occultism, nor magic, nor sorcery." This rather improbable account suggests moreover that Ibn Khafif did not at that time try to go and see the one whom he, in a youthful burst of enthusiasm, was supposed to have defended. And that must be correct. From 296 to 301, the exiled presence in Shiraz of Qadi Ibn Surayj led Ibn Khafif to study Shafi'ite law in a milieu sympathetic toward Hallaj. A second hajj led Ibn Khafif to visit Cairo, the ribat at Ramlah, Jerusalem (where he was treated badly), and Sur, and to pass again through Baghdad, where he saw Ibn 'Ata' again and some Shafi'ites, and dared to make his way into Hallaj's prison (a little more than two months before his death; and not fifteen days before, as legend has it). Was it before or after Baghdad that he came to Basra to join in the theological teaching of Ash'ari, who had recently renounced Mu'tazilism? If it is true, as Firuzabadi believed, that Ibn Khafif influenced Ash'ari's renunciation, he would have had to have been an Ash'arite already when he visited Hallaj.

He was well acquainted with the bitter objections [to Hallaj] of Sufis whom, in other respects, he counted among his masters: 'Amr Makki, AB Fuwati, Awariji. He left the prison again very moved, convinced, and he remained so right up to his death, at ninety-one, in 371/982.

A Tayfurian Sufi, 'Isa-b-Yazul Qazwini questioned him as follows: "What do you think of the orthodoxy of Husayn-b-Mansur?" "This man was a Muslim purely and simply." "But the Sufi shaykhs and most Muslims have excommunicated him." "Ah, if only those who have excommunicated him had seen what I have seen of him, first hand, myself, in his prison; if that is not [evidence of] tawhid, then there is no tawhid at all in this world here below." (Ibn Bakuya, no. 18. To which an anonymous source adds the following): "But Bundar-b-Hy Shirazi excommunicated him." "For what [offense]?" "For these two lines of verses. . . ." "Which two?" "Praise be to the One Whose Humanity has shown forth (to the angels) the mystery of the Glory of His radiant Divinity—and

Who, ever since, has manifested Himself to His creature, openly, in the form of someone 'who eats and who drinks.' "

The later Shafi'ite historian, Dhahabi (d. 748/1348), tried in vain to weaken the thrust of this resounding protest by objecting in the following terms: "This statement of Ibn Khafif proves nothing. The basis for God's rejection of a human being's works does not have to be the fact that their author has never acted in accordance with the truth. On the contrary, it is possible for all of his acts to have been [rooted in] truth, and on behalf of truth, and for him to still be rejected for a single action, a mere word even, which renders everything he has done null and void."

What did Ibn Khafif see in the prison? Legend has embellished accounts with pomegranates, visions through walls, [and so forth]; but here follows the original account by Ibn Khafif, according to the *lectio plenior* published by Ibn Bakuya, compared with the shorter or older text by Daylami (of which we only have two Persian translations, by Baqli, and by Ibn Junayd:

I heard Abu Ahmad Saghir (= H-b-'Ali Shirazi, 315, d. 385; *ummi* servant of Ibn Khafif for thirty-five years); he said: I heard A 'AA ibn Khafif say: "On my return (from Mecca) via Baghdad, I desired to meet Hy-b-Mansur Hallaj; however Nasr Qushuri, who revered him highly, had built for him a little house at his own expense where he was confined), no one could visit him; (wondering how I could see him) I went straight to someone I knew in the army (*jund*); (I told him what I wanted to do), he told me he could arrange it; he took me to meet Hallaj's jail-keeper; the jailkeeper greeted him and said, 'What is your wish?' 'To see Hallaj.' 'What do you want to ask him?' 'This Sufi explained to me when he came that his one goal was to see him.' 'Very well; be off, I will take him there.' And the jailer, through a clever trick, made it possible for me to slip in after he opened the gate to a group of high government officials who were on horseback. Once inside the prison, the jailer guided me along to a door recently made in the prison wall, and said to me 'go in here' ('Hallaj is here'). I went in; I found a comfortable little house, which had been built at the expense of a wealthy man, one of Hallaj's initi-ates, named Nasr Qushuri. I saw a comfortable room, fitted out with a carpet (*dest*) made of gold brocades (*zerbaf*); I had never seen anything more beautiful; and, within reach of my hand, linen had been spread out. And I saw only a young man in the room (*ghulam hadath*)

"He stood up, greeted me, invited me to sit down, and said to me, 'No one has visited us for some time, except the jailer' . I said, 'Where is the shaykh?' 'He is busy (going to the bathroom)' And I said 'how long have you served him? (and this man was Ahmad ibn Fatik.)' 'Not long (eighteen months; var.: two weeks).' 'What does the shaykh do here?' (Interpolation by Jami: each day he does one thousand *rak'a* [bearing] iron chains weighing thirteen *mann*). 'You see those doors, they lead to a prison where there are bandits (*'ayyarin*), robbers (*lusus*), and bums off the street (*sa'alik*); he goes in to see them, he makes them mindful of

God; they do penance (under his guidance); after that, he clips their moustaches and trims their hair, then he returns.' 'What does he eat?' 'Every day a table is set for him with various dishes of food; he looks at each dish for a moment, touches them with his finger (mutters some words), and they are cleared away without his having taken a bite.'

"We had gotten that far in our conversation when Husayn-b-Mansur came to- wards us. I saw him: handsome face, dressed neatly in a white woolen (*suf*) sur- plice (his head encircled with a *futa* from Ramlah), wearing babouches (*taq*) from Yemen on his feet; with great dignity of bearing. He greeted me, sat down on the edge of the bench (*suffa*) and said to me: 'Where is the *fata* from?' 'From Shiraz.' He asked me for news of the shaykhs; I gave him some. 'Where have you come from just now?' 'From Mecca.' And he asked me some questions about the shaykhs in Mecca, and I answered him. Then he said to me: 'Have you seen the shaykhs of Baghdad?' 'Yes.' And he asked me about Abu'l-ʿAbbas ibn ʿAta'. 'He is in good health,' [I said]. 'If you meet him (greet him for me), tell him: 'keep a close watch over these writings (*riqaʿ*).'' Then [he asked me]: 'How did you get in to see me?' 'Through the help of a military officer whom I had known in Shiraz.' We were at that point in our conversation when the prison director (*amir al-habs* = Abu'l-Fath M-b-A Qalanswa, until 315) came in, shaking all over, and threw himself down before him. 'What is the matter?' [Hallaj asked.] 'Someone had done me a disservice with the Caliph, saying that I had taken a bribe (of 10,000 dinars), released one of the amirs, and substituted a man of common extraction for him; they àre going to take me out and chop my head off.' 'Go, fear nothing (hold yourself erect).' And the man left. Then Husayn-b-Mansur stood up, came to the middle of the room, knelt down, raised his hands, his index finger (*sabbaba*) or the rosary (*masbaha*) upward toward Heaven, saying '*ya Rabb* (Lord).' Then he leaned his head over until his cheek touched the ground, and he wept so much that the ground was soaked with his tears. Then he remained lying down, as if he had fainted (his cheek against the ground). Until the prison director returned, and he sat up. 'What happened?' 'They pardoned me (O Shaykh, it was through the *ba- raka* of your spiritual fervor (*himma*) that God saved me).' Then he rose to his feet, returned to his seat, and said: 'What did the Caliph say to you?' 'He told me: (why did you do that? Someone has slandered me.) "I had you brought here only to behead you, but now you are pardoned; don't do it again."—"Someone has slan- dered me." He presented me with a robe of honour, a gift in kind, a bonus in cash.'

"At this particular moment, Hallaj was sitting at one end of the bench, and, at the other end there was a little hand towel. The bench was about fifteen cubits long. He extended his hand toward this linen, and took it; and I don't know whether his hand grew longer or if the linen came to him. He wiped his face with it. (And I said to myself: 'this is where that comes from' = from this 'power' (of which he is accused?).

"After I left him, I went to deliver the message to Abu'l-ʿAbbas ibn ʿAta'. When he heard me mention the name [of Hallaj], he sent those present outside, and told me 'Now then, how did you get in to meet him?' I told him how I did it, then I came to the message: 'He told me to tell you: keep a close watch over those writings.' Then he [Ibn 'Ata'] responded: 'Tell him if you see him: yes, I will. (var.: if I survive him).' Even if they put me through what he has been through, I will not stray from his words."

Ibn Khafif left for Shiraz before the condemnation, and no early source shows him among those present at the execution, contrary to what Ibn al-Qassas and 'Attar were to write later. As indication of the genuineness of the above account, one should note the emphasis put on the fervor of the prayer, and the deliberate toning down of the insignificant charism.

Zayd Qasri's Position

We have only one account of the position of the imprisoned Hallajians, by Ibn al-Azraq:

When I learned that Husayn-b-Mansur Hallaj had fasted, a complete fast, under supervision, for about a month, I was very moved; since I was a friend of the Sufi Abu'l-Faraj ibn Ruhan, a pious and zealous *muhaddith*, whose sister a disciple of Hallaj, Qasri, had married, I questioned him about it. "As regards Hallaj, I do not understand how he was able to fast up to the very end. In the case of my son-in-law, his disciple Qasri, he had forced himself for years to cut down gradually on food, to the point where he could go without it for about two weeks, more or less; and he managed it with the help of a trick which he had concealed from me. When he was imprisoned with the other Hallajians, he revealed it to me, saying: 'when the close watch kept on a man is prolonged, and nothing suspicious shows up, it slackens off, and more and more there is nothing at all to look for; so much so that, finally, it stops altogether , and he is able then to do as he pleases. During the fifteen days that I was watched closely, no one saw me eat anything; but this is as long as I can go at a time in fasting, and if I don't eat on the sixteenth day, I will die. So, take a *ratl* of Khurasan dried grapes, and a *ratl* of almonds, mash them up fine like sesame seeds, make them into a thin wafer. And, when you come tomorrow, slip this wafer between two leaves of a notebook, hold the notebook tightly in your hand, for all to see, rolled up, not folded, in your palm, to hide what it contains. Then, when you are alone with me, without any of my guards seeing you, place it under the skirt of my robe, and leave. I will eat on the sly, and I will drink water when I rinse my mouth out for the mid-day prayers. That will last me for two weeks, until you bring me another such wafer. And with their surveillance during this third two-week period seeing me in actual fact eating nothing until you return with this vegetable sustenance, I will have baffled them as to how I am keeping alive.' And I did that during his entire term of imprisonment."

The Preliminary Investigation and the Interrogations

It is difficult to distinguish Ibn 'Isa's part from that of Hamid in the early house searches and arrests. But it was Hamid, beyond a doubt, who investigated the case systematically, including the examination of confiscated papers and the interrogation of the accused.

The confiscation of papers disclosed other names: those of Ibn Bishr and Shakir. From those accused already arrested, Hamid learned that they were both Hallaj's agents in Khurasan. He "made us write," said Ibn Zanji (his father was responsible for the correspondence with the eastern provinces) "more than twenty letters written to get them to come to Baghdad; but most of the letters went unanswered, and in the responses that we got, we were told: that they were being sought, that if they were arrested, they might be traced to us; but no one has traced them to us up to now (ila hadhihi'l-ghaya)." The final clause shows that Zanji's account was written before 311, for that was when Shakir returned fearlessly to preach in Baghdad, and was executed; he must have been in Talaqan then, under the protection of the amir of Marrudh.

The Samanid central government paid very little attention to the letters sent repeatedly by Hamid, because its vizir, Bal'ami, a Shafi'ite, protected the Hallajians (he did not enforce the ruling of 309 that banned his books and out-lawed his disciples, who reestablished their propaganda little by little under the guidance of Faris Dinawari).

"One finds among the confiscated documents some astonishing things," adds Ibn Zanji. "In the letters to disciples sent forth to preach in the provinces, he indicates to them how to attract listeners to him and what instructions to give them for bringing them, step by step, to the ultimate point (ghaya quswa) of his doctrine, so that each might pursue, according to his own intelligence and un-derstanding, his own degree of devotion and involvement. And the letters from his correspondents used code words (marmuza), comprehensible only to the sender and the recipient. There were also some notebooks (madarij, catechet-ics) written in the same way; some contained miniatures on which the name 'Allah Ta'ala' was inscribed ornamentally in a circle, with "'Ali, 'alayhi'l-salam' written on the inside, with a stroke of the pen that one had to examine very closely in order to decipher."

The catechesis of these texts, adapted for use by various sects, is mentioned in the source (Mutawwaq) used by both Ibn Abi Tahir and Suli. This could refer to authentic Sufi documents (a gradation of the maqamat wa ahwal). But the description of the miniature deifying 'Ali, which is the very opposite of the Hallajians' devotion for Abu Bakr, shows us that this set of documents (proba-bly seized at the home of M-b-'Ali Qunna'i, whose Hallajism was not very trustworthy, and who was an old friend of the Shi'ite vizirial family of Ibn al-Furat) was inserted among the papers of the preliminary invstigation to in-flame Vizir Hamid, a Sunnite, against Hallaj, "that apostle of the Qarmathians," diverting against him the action that Hamid had initiated against the third *wakil* of the Imamites, Ibn Rawh Nawbakhti; Hamid was to remain to the very end on good terms with AS Nawbakhti, an Imamite agent among Mu'tazilite Sunnites and a relentless enemy of Hallaj.

The letters referred to here have been preserved for us as follows:

1. A standard model of a letter from Hallaj to his missionaries, an encyclical written for different regions (AM-b-II ibn 'Ayyash, a *shahid* at the trial, via AH ibn 'Ayyash; he goes too far in saying "confiscated from Hallaj's house" (*sic*): "We introduce you herewith in all regions according to the pure name that he acknowledges (a reference to the Qarmathian *ard zakiya*); thus some believe you to be the Bab, the name which they give to the *Imam* (*sic*: Bab, "Gate," stands for the *Sin*, Salman, among the Mukhammisa), others believe you to be the *Sahib al-zaman* ("the Master of the Age"), the name which they give to the *Imam Muntazar* ("the awaited one" = the mahdi) whom the Imamiya (*Ithna'ashariya*) await; others the *Sahib al-namus al-akbar* (= "the supreme Master of Justice), meaning the Prophet, all blessings be upon him (*Mimiya*); and still others say to you *'Huwa huwa'* (= 'he is He'), meaning God, be He praised and exalted"; far from God are these sacrilegious words, concludes Ibn 'Ayyash. It is a poor forgery.

2. Another circular from Hallaj, read to Ibn 'Ayyash by an (ex)-Hallajian *katib:* "Now your Hour has come to proclaim the glorious glittering Fatimid dynasty, the dynasty longed for by the people of heaven and earth; go forth, so that the pure body (of partisan supporters), strengthened in its weakness, may rise up in revolt in Khurasan, that Truth may lift its veil and Justice reach out its arms." This again is a poor forgery aimed at "Qarmathianizing" Hallaj.

3. Titles from the letters of Hallaj: "from the *Huwa huwa*, the Pre-eternal, the dawning and flashing Light, the original Beginning, the Proof of proofs, the Master of masters, the Gatherer of heavenly clouds, the Recess of light, the Lord of Sinai. He who has assumed a form in every appearance, to his slave So and so, etc. . . ."

4. Titles from his disciples' replies: "Praise be to you, the Essence of essence, the Object of supreme desires, O Strong One, O Great One. I bear witness to the fact that You are the Creator, the Eternal, the Illuminant, that You have assumed a form in every era, and in every moment, and in our time it is the form of Husayn-b-Mansur. Your lowly slave, Your beggar and Your poor, who is beseeching You and repentent to You, hoping in Your mercy, O Thou Who knows all mysteries, says (this and that). . . ."

Documents 3 and 4 are more peculiar; the tone of flattering adoration is exactly that found in the letters of the *'Azaqira* Shi'ite heretics distributed at the 322 trial; let us point out, in this connection, that Hallaj, unlike Shalmaghani, was not convicted of having caused others to worship him (a vague sentence in Awariji was not taken seriously), nor of having taught and practiced immoral sexual relations with his disciples (the insinuation [probably obtained by force] by Samarri's daughter came to nothing in session). These two documents show a distorting plagiarism (of authentic Hallajism, in which "*Huwa huwa*" is not God, *Stf*, no. 205) relative to two kinds of witnesses of the "*wahdat al-shuhud*" taught by Hallaj: those whom Baqli calls "the witnesses of the Kingdom" (*shawahid al-Malakut*), with its hierarchy of blessed beings already transfigured in the next life, referred to in the preambles of the twenty-seven *Riwayat*; and the series of *Shawahid Aniya*, "the contemporary witnesses" (apotropeans, *abdal*), whom we shall see actually discussed along with other Sufis at the trial.

Suli gives us briefly two extracts; first, of a circular letter: "I am the One Who drowned Noah's people, Who destroyed 'Ad and Thamud" (a perfidious attribution to Hallaj of a verse from a Nusayri Shi'ite litany honoring 'Ali); and secondly, of an address to his disciples: "you are Noah, you are Moses, you are Muhammad . . . their spirits have returned in your bodies" (a perfidious attribution [to Hallaj] of the teaching of the extremist 'Azaqira; motivated by the title of *Sayyid* conferred by Hallaj on his representative, elevating this AB Hashimi, and his rank of *Siddiq* [a word used by Nasrabadhi and AT Makki], to the high position of the first Caliph of Islam, Abu Bakr).

All of these forgeries, giving a Shalmaghanian extremist Shi'ite flavor to the messianic mysticism of Hallaj, are to be attributed to the subtle influence behind the scenes of one of Hamid's secretaries, an accomplice of the B. Nawbakht and of Ibn Rawh, who shared their hatred of Hallaj and Shalmaghani; this syndrome points to Ibn Muqla, Hamid's first secretary (and not to such cohorts as Suli and Zanji).

This brings us back again to the method followed in the preliminary investigation of the trial. This method was not worked out by Ibn Mujahid, Ibn 'Isa, nor even by Qadi Abu 'Umar, whose main objective was to make clear that the Hallajian mystical tendency, by its very interpretation of Sunnite rituals, was destructive of the religious practices of Islam. On the other hand, the suspect documents, of Shi'ite coloration, which we have just seen inserted into the preliminary investigation, were designed only for one immediate effect, that of exploiting the confidence of the hate-filled and aged Vizir [Hamid] to get rid of envied rivals. They were the creations thus of his personal entourage, which made use of this old Sunnite vizir to promote the accession to power of the B. Nawbakht's political Shi'ism, that "wicked gang" of skeptical and greedy intellectuals, as they were clearly recognized by contemporaries. Hamid's friends and Shi'ite secretaries did not agree on everything, but they did not let him know this fact. Shalmaghani had not yet broken with the *wakil*, Ibn Rawh (322), but Ibn Muqla already distrusted him; he was to succeed, thirteen years later, in getting him executed. And already, in 309, he put him in a class with Hallaj; which his friend Ibn Rawh was to bear out in 312 in his excommunication brief on Shalmaghani (perhaps even the alleged excommunication of Hallaj by Ibn Rawh boils down to this example from 312).

As regards the interrogations, Zanji has preserved for us only those of

Samarri and his daughter, saying nothing about all of the lengthy arguments of theologians with Hallaj and with the Sufi witnesses summoned before the court (Jurayri, Shibli, Ibn ʿAta').

Even regarding Hallaj, Zanji informs us of little more than the following:

> At the first session, as soon as Hallaj was introduced, spectators slapped his face and yanked his beard; and Hamid said to him: "Don't you remember that I am the one who arrested you in Dur Rasibi, and who brought you to Wasit; that you said to me then, on one occasion 'I am Mahdi,' and on another, 'I am a pious man enjoining men to worship God and to perform the works commanded [by Him].' How is it said that, after that, and in front of others, you have laid claim to divinity?" [Hallaj replied], "Far be it for me to claim the rank of God or of Prophet. I am just a man who worships God, fasts and prays frequently, and knows nothing else."

"At most of the court session," Zanji records, "Hallaj was seated next to me, and I heard him repeating constantly: 'Praise be to You. There is no god but You. I have done wrong, have misused myself; and so, forgive me, for no one forgives us our sins but You (Qur'an 3:129)'; and he was dressed in a black woolen robe (*midraʿa*)." This formulaic act of contrition, which Hanbalites say before mounting their camels to set out on the holy war, is taken from the Qur'an (*Adam*, 7:23; *Jonas*, Q: 21:87; *Moses*, Q: 28:16; *Bilqis*, Q: 27:44).

The interrogation of Samarri's daughter:

> The daughter of Samarri, a disciple of Hallaj, was imprisoned near him for a time in the Dar al-Sultan (no doubt deliberately). Hamid summoned her to report to him what she had observed of Hallaj's behavior. One cold winter's day [Zanji tells us], I went to see Hamid and found this woman there. Seated near Hamid was Abu ʿAli A-b-Nasr-b-Hy Bazyar (Raqqam Samarri, d. 352, in Aleppo), a representative of (his uncle) AQ ibn al-Hawwari (secretary of the Caliph, and friend of the *qaharmana*, Umm Musa), who had come to hear her account. She expressed herself well, using choice phrases, and her face (unveiled) was pleasing to behold. She told us that when her father, Samarri, took her to meet Hallaj (before the year 298), [the latter] gave him various gifts; among those that she described was a green head veil (as dowry?), and he added that "I gave you in marriage to my son Sulayman, my favorite son (who was living in Nishapur, in a section which she named but whose name I have forgotten, Zanji says). Misunderstandings may arise between husband and wife, you may not know about him as much as you would like; I told him to think of you. Therefore, whenever you are anxious about him, fast on that same day, and when evening comes, go up on the roof; take some ashes [with you] there, eat them with coarse salt; then, lift your veil in front of me, and tell me what you would like to know about your husband; for, I am clairaudient and clairvoyant." (She did not say whether or not she tried this divinatory procedure, which can be compared with the corporate *tamlih* and with the *nar al-*

tahwil of the Shu'ubiya secret oaths. "One night, I was sleeping on the roof; Hallaj's daughter was there with me; it was in the Dar al-Sultan, and he was with us. When night was almost over, I sensed suddenly that he was reaching out to me (in order to rape her, Kutabi remarks), and I woke up shaking all over, thinking he was making an illicit gesture; but he said to me: 'I have come to wake you for prayers.' When prayers (of *fajr* [dawn]) were over, we went back down into the house, his daughter and I, and also he; when he stopped at a point on the stairs where we saw him and from where he saw us, his daughter said to me: 'Worship him.' 'Can one worship anyone but God? [I said].' He heard my statement and said: 'Yes indeed! There is a God (*ilah*) in Heaven, and a God on earth.'

"One day he called me over to him, and, putting his hand in his sleeve, he took out a handful of musk. After repeating this gesture several times, he said to me: 'Keep it together with your perfumes, for a woman, when she goes to her man, needs to be perfumed." She continued: "Later he called me over; he was seated in the matted room, and said to me: 'lift the edge of this mat and take out from underneath it whatever you like,' pointing to the corner of the room. I went [to the corner], raised the mat, and found that the underlining of the mats was covered, all across the room, with dinars (gold); and this (imaginary?) vision dumbfounded me" (she does not say if she took any of them, nor if they grew "out of dung," to use Hamid's expression, *infra*); Zanji adds: "and this woman was kept prisoner (shackled?) in Hamid's house until the execution of Hallaj."

Her testimony was hardly usable.

The interrogation of Samarri (AH—AH 'Ali-b-M Samarri Misri, d. 338). Zanji:

I was present in Hamid's court; [he] had summoned Samarri, Hallaj's friend, to appear and asked him for some details about Hallaj: "tell me what you have seen him do." "If the vizir expects me to pardon him, yes, but I forewarn him that he will not pardon me if I do." The vizir repeated the question, "What have you seen?" and he repeated his excuse [for not answering]. Under Hamid's persistent questioning during the colloquy , Samarri confessed: "I know that if I tell you, you will contradict me, and I am afraid of the beatings that will follow." [Hamid] gave his word that this would not happen after which Samarri said: "We were together in Fars en route to Istakhr in winter; on the way, I confided to him that I had a craving for a cucumber. 'Here, in this season?' [Hallaj responded]. 'I just thought of it by chance.' Several hours later, Hallaj said: 'Do you still want it?' 'Yes,' [I said]. We were on the slope of a snow-covered mountain [when] he thrust his hand [into the snow] and pulled out a green cucumber and gave it to me.'—"Did you eat it?" Hamid interrupted him.—"Yes." [Hamid then said:] "You are a liar, son of a hundred thousand adulterous couples. Bash him in the jaw." The guards rushed up and inflicted the ordered punishment upon him, as he bawled out "isn't that just what I feared?" Then, on Hamid's orders, they threw him out. After that Hamid proceeded to tell us that certain performers of wonders went about producing figs and other such fruit, but that this fruit, once it was in the hand of the one who craved it, changed into camel dung.

Suli: another interrogation of Samarri: Hamid said: "Weren't you claiming that your master (Hallaj) went away from you and afterwards returned [flying] through the air, you blockhead?" "Yes." "Then why doesn't he escape at will, now that I have let him go out into the courtyard of my house alone and without chains?"

Ibn Zanji: I was present in Hamid's court, where a beautiful cucumber basket (made of reeds) had just been brought in, confiscated, I believe, from the house of M-b-ʿAli Qunnaʾi. Hamid ordered it opened and, when it was opened, we saw that it contained some dry green dung, some bottles containing a liquid the color of linseed oil, and a piece of dry bread. Samarri was present at this session, seated near my father; and my father was amazed to see that dung, those bottles, and that piece of bread, put this way in a sealed basket. My father, inquiring of Samarri, asked him what all of this was; [the latter] at first refused to answer, giving some excuse or other. When my father persisted, he told him that the dung was some of Hallaj's excrement, which was used as medicine, and that the bottles contained some of his urine. Hamid, informed of this admission, was astonished at it, as were the others present, who were unanimous in condemning Hallaj.

My father returned to the charge, on the subject of the piece of bread, surprised to find it there preserved in such a way. He handled it so well that Samarri grew angry, and said to him: "Look here, I understand you well enough! I can see that you really want this piece of bread; there it is, take what you want of it, and then, afterwards, you will find out how your heart inclines toward Hallaj, once you have eaten a mouthful of it." But my father refused to taste it, afraid that it was poisoned. Hamid summoned Hallaj to appear and asked him what was in the basket and why his disciples kept some of his excrement and urine. Hallaj said in reply that this was something he knew nothing about and that no one had told him about it.

The "piece of bread" is none other than the famous *luqma*, or "mouthful of bread" found in the *hadith al-luqma* specifically transmitted from Hasan Basri to Shibli and Husayn ibn Mansur Hallaj: "I entered the house of my shaykh who gave me a mouthful, saying I entered the house of Y, who gave me a mouthful, saying . . ." (and so forth, back to Hasan Basri). This hadith is the basis of the communal meal celebrated in the crafts guilds, and it is very interesting to find this ritual practiced by Hallajians. The Qarmathians' "food of Paradise" seals might be connected with this. Number 1 in the *isnad* of the *hadith al-luqma* adds: "eat this which we give you for your well-being, for we may have partaken of the meal of the holy people (*qawm salihin*), the custodians of graces; we have therefore shared in their blessing; you share too, therefore, in their blessing." This also refers to the sign of the *Ma'ida* (the list of Apostles, Qur'an 5: [112–114]).

The Hallajian Testament of Faith

In the accounts, official and unofficial, of the secular historians, the only interrogations reported contain, as we have seen, no discussion of a theological or
philosophical nature. Nevertheless, there were such discussions at the trial, and
the testimonial monism professed by Hallaj was clearly defined at it as a heresy, from the standpoint of both dogmatics and philosophy (AZ Balkhi says
hulul, and Ibn Dihya *tajsim*). Though their directly experimental asceticism
shies away from involving itself, of imprisoning itself, in systems of "external"
definitions, the Sufi historians have nevertheless passed on to us three documents that throw light on that aspect of the trial. However, they are anecdotal
in form, at the very time when the influence of the period's scholasticism was
forcing (cf. Ibn Hanbal earlier) an accused person like Hallaj to present a "testament of faith" dealing at least with theodicy (*tawhid*, the main basis of
Mu'tazilite *kalam*): this same *i'tiqad* which, according to Sulami, Hamid
forced him to draft and presented to the jurisconsults of Baghdad. This is the
"*nutq bi'l-shahadatayn*," the doctrinal confession of Islamic orthodoxy that
one acknowledges before a court, which the first *fatwa* by the two qadis of
Baghdad recorded.

Offically, the theological orthodoxy of an author was judged on a basis of
the strictness of his terms used to affirm the transcendance of the Unique God.
And these terms had to give a clear rendering always by a *via negativa* (*tanzih*),
to be "univocized" through a grammatical nominalism of "common sense," of
the insights revealed by the Qur'an into the Mystery of the One (*ghayb al-
Huwa*, Hallaj says), reducing this essential mystery to a sterile and vacant arithmetical unity, devoid of life and thought; following a bare outline of the
Mu'tazilite model (adopted by the Kharijites, Zaydites, and Zahirites), which
still prevailed, reducing revealed monotheistic dogmatics to a natural and rational theology based on a purely formal and abstract deism: in spite of
Mutawakkil's edict, which grew out of Ibn Hanbal's fervent protest in support
of the uncreated reality of the revealed divine Word, and out of the earlier protest by Shafi'i against the nominalistic "univocization" of religious terms. Because these two protests were founded upon the living faith of men of sacrifice
and prayer, it fell to the *sulaha'*, to the mystics alive to an "interiorization" of
the rituals of worship and to the transfiguring meditation of the divine attributes, to revitalize the fossilized *tawhid* of the schoolmen, to demonstrate without skepticism and without illogicality, that the faculty of reasoning (*fahm*:
'*aql*; in opposition to the Imamites) can only locate the divine Object outside
ourselves and that only the experimental Wisdom of the heart (*ma'rifa*) con-
summates the subject in his Object. Hallaj, with his intellectual power and by
his life of self-renunciation, attempted to meet this challenge, in a dogmatic
synthesis, only fragments of which remain; an undertaking that was resumed
imperfectly by the Salimiya, more profoundly by the Hanbalites (Ibn Qayim

al-Jawziya more than Ibn Taymiya), too formalistically by the Ash'arites, and too mathematically by the *hukama'*.

Let us now examine this *'aqida kalamiya* (the complete, annotated translation belonging to the second part); from the standpoint of theodicy, it affirms that: God is not a body. [He] has neither the material composition, nor attributes, nor dimensions (time, space) [of a body], [He] is subject neither to contact, nor to penetration, nor to limitation: vis-à-vis either the senses or analogies, [He is] different from everything we imagine about Him; can the intellect assign to Him distinct attributes: living, just, good? Is He a Being, a personal Being?

The following are the answers found in the two Hallajian *'aqidas* (sigils: K, Q), paragraph by paragraph:

1. "He has connected totality to contingency, for the Absolute is His"; a negation of corporeity by excluding in God not only the grammatical particles of equivocation, but also the logical categories (and the four causes) (N.B.: in opposition to the rationalism of the Mu'tazilites and Imamites).

2. "If you name Him *HuWa* (= He), the letters *H* and *W* are His creation"; "the letters are His signs" (according to Q); Q: "if you ask who is this *HuWa* (= He), it is His Ipseity (= *Huwiya*) [co-essentiality, His essence] that is separated from things: (cf. "He is beyond all 'He' ") (N.B.: against the "uncreated" Qur'anic letters argued by certain Hanbalites. An affirmation of the personal God, hyperpersonal).

3. "Visible, Hidden, First, Last, Near, Far" (Q). K: "Hidden in His visibility, Apparent in His very disappearance, Visible, Hidden, Near, Far, preventing creatures in this way from comparing themselves to Him. He is all-embracing without meeting, He guides without a wink." Q: "His nearness is His generosity; His absence is His disdain" (N.B.: against the literalism of certain Hanbalites; however, this use of metaphor is not nominalistic like that of the Mu'tazilites).

4. K: "His essence has no likeness (*takyif*), His act is without stipulation (*taklif*); thinkers do not get to know Him well." Q: "His act is without cause (*'illa*), and does not improve" (N.B.: in opposition to the divine justice of the Mu'tazilites, which compels God).

5. Q: "His being (*wujud*) is His essence (ideal: *thubut*), and His wisdom (*ma'rifa*) is His Uniqueness (*tawhid*)" (N.B.: which establishes, inversely, a differentiation between these notions, with respect to us, against the nominalists.

6. Q: "*kayf yahill bihima minhu bada*" = "how can this (the accidental) which He created (outside [Himself] enter Him?" (N.B.: in opposition to the *ihdath* of the Karramiya, which is presented as being natural for creatures); "*aw (kayf) ya'ud ilayh ma Huwa 'ansha'hu*" = "or how can that (the form) which He created reenter Him?" (N.B.: a sentence by Imam Rida' condemning Isma'ili and Nusayri emanationism, presented as being natural for God; Hallaj in this instance is putting in the interrogative form the ingenuous pietistic affir-

mation by the Hanbalite ʿAli-b-ʿUthman Nufayli [d. 272] of the divine *hulul al-lafz* in the recitation of the Qurʾan, whatever the consciousness of the reciter may be). Hallaj, deliberately and boldly, we believe, in an interrogative (and non-negative) way presents these two affirmations of a transnatural possiblity of this deifying transfiguration. But he did not dare say any more here, and the Salimiya are the ones who first introduced improperly into theology and into their *ʿaqida* the notion of *tajalli* (transfigurative explication) which falls within the domain of the supernatural, that of the *wahdat al-shuhud* (= testimonial monism), and concerns the *shawahid* (the witnesses of God suprapersonalized by the Spirit); Hallaj teaches the realization (through grace, not through nature) of the *tajalli* and of the *shahid*, through the direct act of God "Who has no likeness (*takyif*)": "in love there is no longer either 'why (*lima*)' or 'how (*kayf*).' "

The Qawl biʾl-Shahid, *the Thesis of Testimonial Monism*

It appears that a special session was held at the trial to discuss this "theory of the Witness," which is at the heart of Hallaj's theology of (mystical) grace, and which is inadequately conveyed by the term "*hulul.*"

Ibn Ghalib, a pupil of Ibn Khafif and, like him, an Ashʿarite, said the following:

One of our friends (= Khafif?) told me: when it was decided to put Hallaj to death, jurisconsults and *ulama'* were assembled for the decision, and he was ordered taken (from prison) to appear before the Sultan (= the vizir). "We have a question to pose" [the vizir said]. "Ask it" [Hallaj said]. "What is the demonstrative proof (*burhan*) of the existence of God?" [Hallaj answered:] "What proves (God) are the *shawahid* (= graces) that God (*Haqq*) bestows on the sincere believers (*ahl al-ikhlas*), drawing souls to them by [these graces]: by persuasion." And everyone unanimously said: "That is the language of the ungodly (*ahl al-zandaqa*)": advising the Sultan (= vizir) to put him to death.

Khatib, who was pro-Ashʿarite, criticizes this account (1) for attributing "gratuitously to the jurisconsults the judgment that such language is ungodly"; (2) for having an unknown (*majhul* = "one of our friends") as *rawi*; (3) for not knowing that the jurisconsults considered his death necessary for another reason (= [his teaching on] the hajj). To us, however, this account seems interesting, for it contains an Ashʿarite dogmatic attenuation of the Hallajian idea of the *shahid*, the "witness," reduced to the impersonal meaning of "divine witnessing, grace, charism" (the Imamites reduced it even further, to its early meaning of a "conclusive example in grammar," which is usually a line of poetry convincing to reason; and, accordingly, they deny that the *shawahid*, or the *ʿaql* [the faculty of reason], can "grasp" [= *tudrick*] God).

This is the same skillful alteration that Ibn Bakuya, an Ashʿarite on this point, made at the beginning of Hallaj's famous prayer uttered during his last vigil: "*nahnu bishawahidika naludh*" = "we seek refuge in Your graces"; instead of the initial text of Ibn al-Haddad: "we are Your witnesses, and we take refuge in the pre-eternity of Your glory . . ." In order to accept "*shawahid*" in the strong sense of "deified Witnesses," one has to accept the uncreated nature of the Spirit Who transfigures (*tajalli*) these Witnesses through their profession of faith in the One God, of the Spirit Who utters (*natiqa*) their testimony (which, even though charismatic, can only be created). Now, apart from the mystics Hallaj and AB Wasiti, the only ones to use the expression "*ruh natiqa*" are the Isma'ilis and the Khattabiya; and the uncreated *Ruh* "appears only in Nuri" and in some Hanbalites (A-b-Thabit Tarqi, d. 520; Ibn Hanbal wavers; the Hallajian Nasrabadhi abandons it upon becoming an Ash'arite; Harawi accepts it but calls it *La'ih*). In an independent way Nusayri Shi'ites and Salimiya Sunnites, who accept the notion of a transfiguration (*tajalli*), conceive of *Ruh* as an emanation (*Sin*) or a hyperangelical creature, a "Former" (*Musawwir*); hence the theological retouching, Salimiyan this time, in the famous prayer: "*al-sura hya'l-Ruh . . .*," "the Adamic form, which is the Spirit": instead of *fiha*, "in whom is. . . ."

This Hallajian thesis of testimonial monism about God's "instrumentary Witness," which is to say, the accountable Witness, whose life in union with god is committed to witnessing, arose in connection with a series of other contemporary theses that were condemned by the scholasticism of that time, which was Mu'tazilite and bent on safeguarding divine transcendence against them: theses about God's descent (*nuzul*: to hearken to us), God's movement (*haraka*), God's desire (*'ishq*), and renewal (*tajaddud*) through God. The "living Witness" of God claimed for itself an investiture, an anointing, a sovereign power, considering its act to be God's act and thus a pure, uncreated act. The Salimiyan solution of emanation (uncreated *taf'il*) was only a compromise and would be condemned when official Sunnite scholasticism became Ash'arite with Baqillani (after the efforts of Ibn Kullab, Muhasibi, Qalanisi) and Al Isfara'ini, and would force the Hallajian Nasrabadhi to abandon the thesis of the uncreated Spirit (underlying the *qawl bi'l-shahid*). The manuals of heresiography were to decree, therefore, that this thesis falls under the heading of *zandaqa*, a heresy subject to the secular arm, in the same way that the Mu'tazilite Sunnite theologians had denounced it to Qadi Abu 'Umar. The qadi thus had to arouse the vizir with this charge of *zandaqa*.

The First Consultation with the Two Qadis

Hamid then covened the qadis, including Ibn Buhlul and Abu 'Umar, *fuqaha'*, *shuhud*, and *ashraf*, and entered into consultation with them by *istifta'* (request for a *fatwa* [a formal legal opinion] from the "*muftis*," not yet distinguished in the period from the qadis): "What do you say about it? Suppose he were executed? But he has pronounced the two *shahada*" (N.B.: "there is no god but God," commented upon by his *'aqida kalamiya*; "and Muhammad is the Messenger of God"). The Zahirite Ibn Dawud, in 288, had denounced Hallaj on the grounds of his having denied this second *shahada* by his doctrine of sainthood accomplishing the mission of Muhammad; and in 309, the judges still show proof both of the limitations placed by Hallaj on and his praise of the Prophet as precursor of the awaited Judge; this praise, which resembled the pietism of the Hanbalites, seeking at that time to define the "*maqam mahmud*" ["the praised estate"] of the Prophet (Qur'an 17:79) either as "enthronement at the right hand of God" or as "intercession on behalf of the great sinners of his Community." Hallaj himself extolled the predestination of the Prophet to an ultimate ecstasy as supreme Annunciator (without making him out to be a divine emanation, as the Mimiya Shi'ites did). This very unusual praise of the Prophet had to be considered valid (for the second *shahada*).

The qadis' response to Hamid was as follows: "Because he has pronounced them, it is no longer possible to put him to death (as a turncoat), unless one were to show us cause as to why he should die. It is unlawful to concur with the opinion of those who accuse him of what we know, even though this opinion is plausible, without some proof (*dalil*) and his confession (*iqrar*)."

This deferral, this pause, in the workings of the trial underscores the logical force of Ibn Surayj's argument in his *fatwa* concerning one's incompetence to judge, according to the precepts of the Law, in matters of mystical inspiration, *ilham*, intuitive knowledge (*'ilm laduni* = knowledge imparted directly by god through mystic intuition]), which falls within the competence and sphere of inspiration and the grace of the spiritual world.

It seems that certain judges, Mu'tazilite grammarians influenced by Hellenistic philosophy, had detected this difficulty. The objectivity with which AZ Balkhi defined theopathic utterance, the *hulul* criticized in Hallaj, and which Hallaj recognized as being an experimental verification of mystical psychology, a decentering of the subject speaking in opposition to the strict Law, *Akhbar* [no. 74], the insertion of this definition in the manuals of heresiography—all confirm this impression. The *qawl bi'l-shahid* refers, in psychology, to a special modality of *hulul*, and it is the concern of the metaphysician to reconcile correctly this experimental datum with the first monotheistic theology. Independently of intellect (like the grammarians, who had previously accepted the idea of the influx of the accident of inflexion infusing a word with its syntactical value, its "vocalic Life" in *i'rab: hulul al-na't*); they were inclined to accept as normal the infusion of divine nature into human nature of heroes; such was the reconsideration (the minimum sense), going back to AS Sijzi Mantiqi and AH Tawhidi, in the name of spiritualism, of Hallaj's thesis of the union of essence with essence (*'ayn al-jam'*: the expression of AS Kharraz, Ibn 'Ata', Shibli, and Harawi) between the two natures, divine and human (*lahut wa nasut*).

The Threat of the Hanbalite Riot

During the last forty days of the trial (*Shawwal* to *Qaʿda* 309), there was agitation in Baghdad in support of Hallaj. Tabari confirms it: "... a group of people, including Nasr Qushuri and others, became impassioned on behalf of Hallaj; so much so that there was a public riot during which people began to utter prayers against those who wished him harm. All of which damaged his case. ...."

There are [other] indications [of this unrest]: the violent death of Ibn ʿAta', the besieging of Tabari's house by the Hanbalites, Vizir Hamid's admitted fears.

This idea of forming processions to pray loudly in the streets and *suqs* against injustices committed by the powerful originated with the Hanbalites; it was an extension of the duty of *amr bi'l-maʿruf* (setting to rights what God commands); the not unlawful character of which was contested by the Malikites (*duʿa' 'ala'l-zalim*). In actual fact, people formed in procession, crying out for divine rescue, on Friday, at a nonofficial mosque, a "schismatic" mosque, as Ibn ʿIsa notes indignantly: *masjid al-dirar*; either at Bab-Muhawwal, in the *masjid* of Barbahari, or in Harbiyah, near the tomb of Ibn Hanbal; to close the prayer of obligation with some supererogatory curses. This was the manner in which Barbahari, the head of the Hanbalites, was entreated to act (in 296, he refused; in 308, he agreed).

It was Ibn ʿAta', a traditionist recognized by the Hanbalites, who, at the end of *Shawwal*, decided to resort to this device of the Hanbalite processional demonstration in order to try to save his friend; aided probably by Chamberlain Nasr, himself a Hanbalite. It very quickly turned into a riot, which focused anger on the aging historian Tabari, who had attacked the Hanbalites in 293 (over the "*maqam mahmud*" issue), and with whom the deputy vizir requested them to hold a meeting for reconciliation (in *Qaʿda* 309). [The Hanbalites] refused to meet; the great traditionist Ibn Abi Dawud denounced Tabari to Nasr for committing three heresies; and in spite of help from the regular police, dispatched by the deputy vizir along with their chief, Nazuk, Tabari remained blockaded until his death and his secret burial (26 *Shawwal* 310/February 16, 923: i.e., for one year) in his house (Rahbat Yaʿqub, in Qantara Baradan).

The Interrogation of Ibn ʿAta'; His Protest and His Death

Ibn ʿAta', among the mystic leaders of the *ahl al-hadith*, seems to have been the only one to defend Hallaj openly. It was he who found a way to go and join him, so long as it was in secret, perhaps to urge him to save his life. It was he to whom Ibn Khafif conveyed a final message from Hallaj. When the vizir wanted to determine how many Sufi masters adhered to Hallaj's teaching, there was only one (like Nuri, not long before, at the so-called trial of Ghulam Khalil) who dared to speak up at the risk of his life; and this was Ibn ʿAta'.

We have a major text for this stage of the trial, which Khatib published based on a very interesting *isnad*. He got it from the *hafiz* and *muhaddith* M-b-AH Sahili (d. 441), one of his principal masters in hadith, who had found it in the *Tabaqat al-Sufiya* of A-b-M-b-Zakariya Nasawi (d. 396); which had taken it from Sulami's *Ta'rikh* ; Sulami took it from the *wa'iz* Ibrahim-b-M, meaning Nasrabadhi (d. 369), and, through him, from AQ Ja'far-b-A Razi (d. 378), who, probably through the agency of Husayn-b-A Razi, had received it from the author: Abu Bakr ibn Mamshadh Dinawari.

A man came to our house (*'indana* = to my father's *khanqah*, which was a Karrami *ribat*) in Dinawar, carrying a case that he did not let out of his sight day and night. The box was seized and inside it a letter was found from Hallaj, the heading of which read: "From the Merciful, the Compassionate, to X son of X." The letter was forwarded to Baghdad. At the tribunal, Hallaj, to whom it was shown, responded as follows: "it is indeed my handwriting; yes, I wrote it." "So, you used to claim to a Prophet's mission, and now you come along claiming to divine omnipotence?" "No" [Hallaj said], "I do not claim divine omnipotence (*rububiya*); that is what we call, between ourselves, *"ayn al-jam'*' ('the essential union'), the mystical state in which [we ask]: who is it but God who writes, since I am no more than the hand that serves Him as an instrument?" "Are there any others who think like you?" "Most certainly: Ibn 'Ata', AM Jurayri, AB Shibli." Jurayri and Shibli were to escape, but not Ibn 'Ata'. In fact, Jurayri, when summoned to appear and be interrogated, responded as follows: "this man is an infidel, he must be killed along with all those who speak as he does." Shibli responded under interrogation as follows: "If someone speaks in this way, he must be forbidden to do so." And Ibn 'Ata', when questioned about Hallaj's thesis (*maqala*), embraced it as his own: which cost him his life.

This text is of major importance, in the sense that it connects the precise charge made by Hallaj's Shi'ite enemies of *"da'wa'l-rububiya"* (a claim to divine omnipotence) with the claim admitted by Hallaj to a state of " *'ayn al-jam'* " (essential union with God). This expression, standard since the *Luma'* of Sarraj (d. 377) and used prior to 337 by Su'luki in the presence of Nasrabadhi, may have been adopted by Hallaj to transcend the alternative *jam' tafriqa* put forward by Kharraz. However, it could not have been the subject for a formal condemnation by the court, which did not intend at all to go into the question of Sufi terminology. Let us grant merely that the incident, which led to a clash between the vizir and Ibn 'Ata' that later had a fatal consequence for the latter and caused the vizir to speed up the scenerio (prepared at his convenience) for the session at which Hallaj was to be condemned.

We have five accounts of Ibn 'Ata's appearance before Vizir Hamid, which can be divided into two groups, according to the type of punishment inflicted on Ibn 'Ata'. In the first group, which represents a Khurasanian tradition (Abu 'Amr-b-Hamdan Hiri, Harawi), his teeth are pulled out; in the other, his skull is beaten with his own sandals until he died (Ibn Shadan, Sarraj, Qushayri, ʿAttar). The first is more legendary in character.

According to Abu ʿAmr Hiri, the vizir said to Ibn ʿAta': "What does Hallaj say?" [Ibn ʿAta' responded:] "Why are you concerned with him? Rather, worry about the piracies and murder that you have committed." And the vizir ordered his teeth pulled out, which was done while he was exclaiming: "May God cut off your hands and feet"; then he died, fourteen days later. In the course of time, the vizir's four limbs (*sic*) were (in fact) cut off.

Harawi, who puts the incident in the reign of Qahir (*sic*), in 311, gives the following dialogue: the vizir: "What do you think about Hallaj?" [Ibn ʿAta' answered:] "What about yourself, what do you do with all of the money you have taken, so much that you don't even know what to do with it; return people's money to them." "You defy me? [the vizir said]. Let his teeth be pulled out one by one, and let them be hammered into his skull"; which was done, and he died as a result.

AN Sarraj depicts Ibn ʿAta' appearing before the vizir, who brutally admonished him. "Speak softly," Ibn ʿAta' countered. Then the vizir had his skull beaten in with his own sandals until he died.

The reference found in the account published by Sulami taken from "M-b-ʿAA Razi" meaning Ibn Shadan (d. 376) alias Bajali, reads as follows:

> At the time of the trial in which Husayn-b-Mansur was condemned to death, the incumbent vizir was Hamid-b-ʿAbbas and he ordered [Hallaj] to put his testament of faith in writing (monotheistic faith: *iʿtiqad* = *ʿaqida*), which he did; the vizir then submitted it for scrutiny to the canonists of Baghdad, who condemned it. Someone then informed the vizir that Abu'l-ʿAbbas ibn ʿAta' approved it, and so [the vizir] directed it to be submitted to him. It was submitted [to Ibn ʿAta'], and he asserted: "that is a good testament of faith; I profess it also, and anyone who does not profess it is simply a man without faith." Then the vizir ordered him to appear. Brought to the tribunal and introduced, Ibn ʿAta' came forward and took a place in the front row. Irritated by that, the vizir held up to him his signed declaration [and said:] "is this really your writing?" "Yes." "You endorse this testament of faith therefore?" "Why are you concerned with him? Look rather into the evil that you have gone about committing, the seizure of properties, the unjust taxes, the murders. What business of yours are the statements of these respected men?" "What impudence!" shouted the vizir; and they struck him in the mouth. "O my God," Ibn ʿAta' cried out then [to God], "if You surrender me to these injuries, it is to punish me for having become involved with such a man." "[Take] his sandals, Guard" [the vizir ordered], and the guard pulled off his sandals. "Now, [bash] his skull," exclaimed the vizir; and they continued to beat his head with his sandals until blood flowed from his nostrils. "Put him in prison," the vizir added. But someone urged him not to do this, saying : "O Vizir, that is going to incite a riot among the (Sunnite) people." And so, Ibn ʿAta' was taken back to his house,

where he uttered this curse: "O my God, give Hamid the worst of deaths, have his hands and feet cut off." Ibn 'Ata' died seven days later. As for Hamid, he died the most hideous and cruel death, after his hands and feet were cut off and his house was burned. And it was said of him: "he was stricken with the curse of Ibn 'Ata'."

This account, which focuses its attention in its beginning on the account by Abu 'Amr, retains the curse and its alleged fulfillment—when, in actuality, as Amedroz pointed out, Hamid did not die from this form of punishment (though he did die a rather wretched death). More curious is the fact that Hallaj, the friend of Ibn 'Ata', is the one on whom Hamid inflicted this additional punishment of intercision; he may have conceived of the idea immediately after the curse, if indeed it is genuine. Unless, of course, this curse was a copy of the actual curse made by Ibn Shannabudh against Vizir Ibn Muqla and fulfilled in reality between 323 and 326.

'Attar, who, like Sarraj, confused Ibn 'Isa with Hamid, depicts the vizir interrogating Ibn 'Ata' in a contemptuous manner, with the latter responding to him violently. "Take off his sandals!" exclaims the vizir in anger, "and beat him on the head until he dies." And Ibn 'Ata' shouts, "O my God, make his hands and feet be cut off!" to which 'Attar adds an interesting comment on this curse. When a believer (like Ibn 'Ata') is able to have his prayers for good (*salah*) answered, is he permitted when praying, to ask for something other than good (for others)? Yes, in the case of Hamid, since he was mistreating Muslims. Or was Ibn 'Ata', in fact, in that instance acting simply out of *farasa* (divination), with God foretelling, through his voice, Hamid's destiny? Perhaps Ibn 'Ata' was, in fact, expressing in this way, on behalf of Hamid, a wish for eternal happiness, forewarning him that he would die through martyrdom, brought low on earth; and that would be noble, he concluded.

With the death of Ibn 'Ata' dating from *Dhu'l-Qa'da,* a few days earlier than that of Hallaj, his appearance before the vizir was, of course, prior not only to the visit that he paid to Hallaj in prison, but also to the one he received from Ibn Khafif.

V. THE DENOUEMENT AND THE JUDGMENT
OF CONDEMNATION

The Final Week and the Political Alignment: Commander-in-Chief Mu'nis for Ibn Abi'l-Saj and against Nasr

The final week of *Qa'da* 309 (March 922), eight years after the high-sounding promises of Ibn 'Isa's first vizirate, that peaceful beginning when Hallaj was saved by his act of toleration; eight years before the looting of Mecca by the Qarmathians. and the looting of the treasury by the praetorian guards, in

Baghdad into which grieving refugees flowed; marks a critical point in the Muslim Community's life curve.

The balance of the empire had been upset by the accomplished and Machiavellian policy of Vizir Ibn al-Furat, a statesman of the first order, whose background and connections with an extremist Shi'ite sect freed him from any moral scruple vis-à-vis the Sunnite state he was commissioned to support. A fiscal policy of credit and speculation based on investment returns to the banks, on "squeezes" in the tax system, on secret hoarding of wheat and precious metals (gold mines in the Nubian West 'Alaqi, silver mines in Isfahan and Afghan Penjhir), all resulted in the state's being bled for the benefit of a "gang" of Shi'ite functionaries monopolizing the big estates of land. And administrative policy of centralization, exploiting the provinces for the capital; a diplomatic policy of suspension of holy war; a religious policy of "playing down" the hajj (a subconscious Shi'ite reaction); and of repression of popular preachers, all Sunnites (Hanbalites).

Since 301, Ibn 'Isa had returned to the opposite Harithian policy of the Islamo-Christian Qunna'iya party (the B. Makhlad and B. Wahb viziers), a policy of loyal support for the dynasty, of moderate taxation, providing for and improving the condition of the fellah and the worker, administrative decentralization, arranging for Khurasan (Samanids) and Fars (Saffarids) to confront the Daylamite agrarian danger, even arranging for the Qarmathian bedouins to halt the peril in the west of the nascent Fatimid state, a religious policy of reinforcement of frontiers bordering on the infidels, of transfer of 85,000 dinars a month to the Hijaz for the hajj pilgrims, and of pedagogical readaptation to the canonical sciences (Ibn al-Furat having promised the Hellenistic sciences, mathematics and logic).

After 306, in his position as second in command to the Sunnite vizir Hamid, Ibn 'Isa saw his policy undermined by the Shi'ite speculators and stock manipulators by whom Hamid allowed himself to be surrounded. The social crisis smouldered, one of the ôdînès, eschatological "birth pangs," in the whole Muslim empire, threatened with the loss of Egypt following that of the Maghrib (an independent khutba in Cordova), and with being hard pressed by the young anti-Caliphate of the Fatimids.

The sovereign and the Court, squandering the dynastic wealth, were losing all faith in the Islamic vocation of the descendants of 'Abbas, and were leaning toward allegiance to the Twelfth Imam of conservative Shi'ites, the "hidden" and, in fact, vanished Imam, whose investiture two crafty policemen were wrangling over "like dogs fighting over a cadaver."

Monotheistic Islam, lying in the shahada, was slipping into three forms of idolatry that "cry out to heaven for vengeance": a spread of abnormal behavior that prevents people from loving each other in God; a bloody [Zanj] war, aimed at procuring slave labor; withholding of the wages of workers and peasants, resulting in the stocking of bread and gold. A contemporary poet, Kisrawi, described all of this perfectly.

For twenty years an ascetic, who claimed to be, during the hajj at ʿArafat, the "*shahid ani li'l-tawhid*," the supreme "witness of *Tawhid* at this moment" for the community, of the "two doves that are thirsty for the rest of the year" (= two *rakʿa*), and who said also that they could not satisfy divine justice "until their preliminary ablution is performed in blood,"—this same ascetic had preached in vain that God must be loved first and foremost, that the holy war of the Law against idolatries must be waged against our own consciences, making us abandon all of our riches, and he, Hallaj, ended up by having his own life taken from him. The number of hearts he converted was not great, but it was about one out of seventy thousand, he told us himself, per day; considering the fact that the yearly average number of pilgrims each day at ʿArafat was seventy thousand (on *hajj sarura*), representing the same number of homes, the figure may be three hundred fifty thousand souls. The Muslim empire, after three centuries, had reached a population figure then of fifty million, and the average life expectancy was thirty years; perhaps around one hundred seventy-five million Muslim souls (of the living and the dead represented by proxy) for whom during these three centuries around three hundred thousand pilgrims had prayed, among whom the one annual apotropaic intercessor (al-Ghawth) had, in any case, on three hundred nine occasions, reached four million nine hundred thousand souls, bringing them closer to God (i.e., 5/175 of the whole of Islam reached by the *shafaʿa* of these three hundred nine intercessors substituted for Abraham to validate the [ritual] sacrifice of Abraham restored and transferred to Mecca, the first of whom, Hilal, a slave belonging to Mughira, had been designated by the Prophet before Uways Qarani).

He [Hallaj], in any case, was shortly going to die. A whole musicality of intersigns, marked by his destiny to serve as the victim of hatreds, was going to become clearer, with the reminder of their archetypal marks, in an explosion of his ultimate finality. *Lan yujirani min Allah ahad* (= "no one can save me from God"; Qur'an 72:22).

The Islamic Community of Baghdad, the populace of this great metropolis where he had preached, had had a final burst of affection for him; it had prayed in the streets "against those who wished him harm," and his courageous interpreter, Ibn ʿAta', had gotten himself killed by the vizir for rebuking him [the vizir]. But out of the depths of pietism of its literalistic traditionists, especially its *Qurra'*, "Qur'an reciters," a muffled cry of vengeance rose, coming from hardened hearts: attacking him again with the denunciation of "outlaw" uttered by his former Sufi masters who were traitors to their vow of poverty (like ʿAmr Makki and Ruwaym), affronted in their sacerdotal monopoly of the sacred text by his inspired fervor. As for the canonist and theologian elite, the death of Ibn Surayj (the only opposing member) had freed it to attack his affirmation of the superiority of love over legalistic arguments. All that was left was for the executive authority, which was indeed already wavering, to let itself be convinced, by Vizir Hamid, of the imminent danger of revolution that the state was incurring as long as Hallaj remained alive.

Caliph Muqtadir, who harbored mixed feelings toward Hamid, both admiration for his cynical acts of brutality, and contempt for his administrative incompetence, delivered his victim up to him in a backhanded way, on *Nayruz* day, 309, in the magnificent setting of the al-Rayyan garden; where the vizir received him amid the flower beds under the felt tapestries from Khurasan and the Maghrib, laying out one hundred fifty thousand dinars. Yes, if the *Nayruz* (= New Year's Day) given in this report stands for *Nayruz al-Sultan* (= the astronomical vernal equinox, falling at that time on Friday, March 15, 922 = 13 *Qa'da* 309 = first of *Hamal*; the Nusayri calendar, which dates from this period, celebrates *Nayruz* on 17 *Adhar* = March 17, two days later); however, there is also *Nayruz al-Majus* to consider, celebrated particularly by the Zoroastrians, shifted to 4 *Nisan* = April 4 = first of *Farwardin*, with the calendar of Yazdagard; shifted later to 17 *Nisan* = April 15; and, lastly, *Nayruz al-Dahaqin*, the start of the fiscal year, which Hamza Isfahani's table places in 309 in the fifth month, on 20 *Nisan* = April 20, 922, the more likely day for a floral setting (= 19 *Hijja*).

In any event, it was around March 15 that Muqtadir must have authorized the vizir to arrange the scenario for the condemnation session with the qadi, overruling Ibn Buhlul's objections, which occupied the five days prior to this session, which occurred on Thursday, 19 *Qa'da* (= March 21).

Every Thursday since 306, Muqtadir was in the habit of visiting around noon (*idhasama*; this was the day for the women's *hammam*) his old childhood vizir [Ibn al-Furat], who was kept under house arrest in the palace in the custody of the *qaharmana* Zaydan, the one in charge of the jewel collection. In spite of all his betrayals, the Caliph still had a spoiled child's attachment to this crafty old man; a kind of understanding existed between them tying him to the fiscal magic of Ibn al-Furat, the only vizir who had made money flow for his pleasures without stinting. As a result, he had saved him, in 299 and 304, keeping him in captivity near him, in order to consult him. Ibn al-Furat took advantage of all of this to hatch the plot for his third vizirate, for which his son Muhassin, left free, was paving the way, using the influence of Qadi Ibn Sayyar Ji'abi on the Queen Mother, of Shalmaghani, his friend, on Vizir Hamid, and of Muflih on the harem. On two Thursdays, 14 and 21 March (12 and 19 *Qa'da*), Muqtadir could not possibly have concealed from Ibn al-Furat the fact that Hallaj would be condemned; and Ibn al-Furat could not have failed to urge him to free himself from the tutelage of his enemy Nasr, Hallaj's sole protector, while also attacking Nasr through his ally Akh Su'luk, by freeing Ibn Abi'l-Saj; Nasr lost by the latter action Ibn 'Abd al-Samad, and Ibn al-Wawari, another enemy of Ibn al-Furat, lost his son-in-law, Niramani—both entering the service of Ibn Abi'l-Saj.

To pardon and promote Ibn Abi'l-Saj to Rayy was to divide the empire in two, as it had been divided under Rashid (cf. Theodosius), in both military and fiscal terms: East and West. As early as 301, Muqtadir had assigned the West to his son Radi, flanked by Mu'nis, and the East to ʿAli; whom instead of flanking with an amir of Rayy as military commander (Wasif Buktamiri, followed by Akh Suʿluk), Nasr had merely unofficially advised, granting his friend Mu'nis, the commander-in-chief, the honor of keeping vacant in the East the post corresponding to his own. Ibn al-Furat, who had seen through the rising military ambitions of Mu'nis, and who wanted to preserve the primacy of civilian over military authority (Mu'nis was to end it over [his opposition], in 312, for 125 years), anticipated that Ibn Abi'l-Saj would like to be, in the East, on a level with his rival, Mu'nis, and that he might play off one against the other. In actual fact, from the time of his return to the vizirate, Ibn al-Furat treated Ibn Abi'l-Saj as the equal of Nasr, and in 314, Vizir Khasibi treated him as the equal of Mu'nis: the East versus the West. With Ibn Abi'l-Saj killed in 315, starting in 316 a new rival to Mu'nis was created in the person of the Queen Mother's nephew, Harun-b-Gharib, guardian of Prince ʿAbbas, provided with a secretary of the first order (the future vizir, Ibn Shirzad), inspector general of the army promoted to commander of the entire East in 316 and, later, in 320–321.

Only Ibn al-Furat had the stature to free the sovereign from Mu'nis's tutelage in this way, while benefiting to the detriment of Mu'nis from his rash proposal of pardoning Ibn Abi'l-Saj, [in order] to appoint him to Rayy. This idea had come to Mu'nis, because he was in need of a second in command in the army of the East who would also oppose Akh Suʿluk, the Samanid *wali* of Rayy, who, caught unprepared by the Daylamite attack led by Layli, prince of Ishkawet, had for a brief period (*Hijja* 308 to *Rabiʿ* I 309) surrendered Nishapur and Rayy to him, which caused great fright in all of Baghdad. Because Akh Suʿluk was Nasr's friend (a friendship born during Nasr's imprisonment at his home), Mu'nis held Nasr personally accountable for this serious military and political defeat, which had just shown the direction, as foreseen by Muʿtadid, from which the destruction of the universal Caliphate, and the captivity of the dynasty for a century, would come. To be sure, the Samanids had soon defeated and killed Layli (*Rabiʿ* I 309), but Ibn Abi'l-Saj was maintaining over there, as he described it in writing, "a front more important than the Byzantine front, opposite a rampart more fortified than that of Gog and Magog, whose penetration will prove to be more dangerous than the Qarmathian rebellion" (to which he was sent off to get killed in 314–315). Mu'nis had recommended Ibn Abi'l-Saj only because he was unable to recommend one of his B. Hamdan charges (Husayn, his favorite, who was far too wild a character and died in 306, had been sounded out for this post, against Mu'nis, by Ibn al-Furat, and the second, Abu'l-Hayja, who was to have command for three days, in 317, of the army of the East, was content, in 309, with Dinawar and with Tariq

Makka); in another connection, Mu'nis retained toward Ibn Abi'l-Saj the same feeling of gratitude that Nasr felt toward Akh Su'luk, that of a prisoner who had been well treated and released with honor (in 305; Mu'nis, in his turn, had captured Ibn Abi'l-Saj in *Muharram* 307, taking him prisoner to Baghdad, and was anxious to restore his freedom and honor).

Mu'nis realized immediately the mistake he had committed; Muqtadir did indeed promote him to *nadim* (imperial confidant), but not to Amir of amirs.

The appointment of Ibn Abi'l-Saj to Rayy, officialized in *Muharram* 310, represented a diplomatic break with the Samanids, which was to cut off once and for all the ['Abbasid] dynasty from the support of Khurasan, its original homeland. Only the Samanids could have carried out the task, too great for Ibn Abi'l-Saj, of preventing the apocalyptic storming of the rampart of "Gog and Magog," which was battered down after 315 by the Daylamites (the *da'i* Hasan, Asfar, Makan, Mardawij), cutting Baghdad off from the region that took the lead in the great pilgrimages to Mecca, in the levying of volunteers for the holy war on all of the empire's frontiers, and in industrial, artistic, and cultural advance. The Samanids responded immediately to Mu'nis's move by pardoning, at the same time as Ibn Abi'l-Saj, three Saffarid amirs (members of the dynasty supplanted by the Samanids in 287); to flank Ibn Abi'l-Saj's offensive on the right side, in Sijistan, Simjur, after 310 with a Saffarid amir who had been won over.

It was also to cut off the Hallajians from one region where their propaganda had actually proved successful and where the governmental elite, notably the Samanid vizir, Bal'ami, and the mufti of Nishapur, Thaqafi, supported them.

Finally, at the center of the empire, in the Court, the condemnation of Hallaj, while weakening the attachment of Chamberlain Nasr, the soldier loyal to the dynasty, affected the Queen Mother doubly: henceforth, Mu'nis would be increasingly on his guard against her and would pilfer the spoils of war that she had accumulated; and Muqtadir, whom Hallaj had exhorted to examine himself with "constant circumspection" (*shahid al-hadhar*) as the "intermediary agent" (*sabab, wasita*) of divine commands, could no longer honor the policy of support for the Holy Places that Ibn 'Isa had established thanks to her, would only consult Ibn 'Isa when it was too late, and would fall again under the influence of the third Imamite *wakil*, Ibn Rawh Nawbakhti, who, after three years, had gone into an eclipse lasting from 308 to 313, owing to proofs furnished to Muqtadir of his phony underhanded fiscal schemes. He was to set him free, after eight years in prison, in 317, convinced that his own deposition for three days, in this same year, was his punishment [for having imprisoned him]. His last vizir, who was to be his undoing, would be a Shi'ite, one Ibn al-Furat; and he would regain control of himself only when going to meet death, after a touching word for his mother, on horseback, a Qur'an in his hand, in an 'Uthmanian posture of fatalistic resignation.

The Choice of the Incriminating Proposal:
the "Letter to Shakir" about the "Destruction of the Temple," and the Proposal about the Votive Replacement of the Hajj (Based on Ikhlas)

From peripeteia to peripeteia, the trial was drawing near its denouement. Confronted by mystical writings employing an objectionable and farfetched vocabulary, by letters spreading the teaching of the transforming union [with God], by the Hanbalite pietistic riot coupled with Ibn ʿAtaʾ's protest introduced at the court at the cost of his life, by the external Daylamite danger and the stiffening of the fiscal policy that was destroying the policy of Nasr and Ibn ʿIsa, it became urgently necessary to come up with the fortuitous and conclusive evidence making it possible to condemn Hallaj.

It came from the party of the "pious ones," the *sulaha*ʾ, which is to say, from the moderate Sufis. Realizing that the Caliph had turned the matter over to Vizir Hamid to bring it to a close, the *sulaha*ʾ (their leader, Jurayri, was the one who must have acted) produced and turned over to the court the letter that Hallaj had written to Shakir-b-Ahmad: urging him to "destroy the Kaʿba (of his body) in order to rebuild it in Wisdom; so that it might actually take part in the *sajda* and *rakʿa* of the true worshippers (Qurʾan 3:43, like Mary in the *qunut* of the Angels)." Followed by another letter to one of his disciples: "if you want to make the hajj, choose an appropriate room in your house, stand erect outside its door, similar to *wuquf* at the Kaʿba gate, and enter dressed as a *muhrim*; go out again, go into another part of your house, pray two *rakʿa* there, and this will be as if you had prayed in the *maqam* (of Abraham); run from this place to the door of the room which you had previously entered, and this will be as if you had run between Safaʾ and Marwa."

So goes the account by Ibn Dihya. In fact, some delay must have occurred between deliveries of the two letters. The first urged Shakir to die accursed; meaning, to fulfill the hadith of Suraqa concerning the farewell pilgrimage of the Prophet, to "insert the *ʿumra* in the hajj," to leave the Kaʿba to offer oneself up at ʿArafat with the sacrificial victims (sacrificed at Mina), to fulfill the ritual of the *taʿrif*, outside the Holy Places (*hill*), as a martyr. The elliptical style of this symbolic text makes it barely usable for the charge [against Hallaj]. And so, the second letter was then discovered.

Later we shall compare the four extant recensions of this second letter (Ibn Dihya, *supra* Zanji; Ibn ʿAyyash; Ibn Sinan); all limit themselves to authorizing the transfer, outside Mecca, of the *ʿUmra* rituals, and do not even suggest the transfer of the hajj rituals (at first the *waqfa*, at ʿArafat; afterwards the *Nahr*, at Mina). This is because in actual fact, Islam, from the very beginning, practiced the *taʿrif* in its worship outside the Hijaz, in union with pilgrims who represented those who were absent, on the holy places at ʿArafat (9 *Hijja*): by offering everywhere the sacrifice of the lamb on 10 *Hijja* (simultaneously with the liturgical sacrifice at Mina). And because, to legalize the transfer (*already* practiced in this way) of the *taʿrif* (in *hill*), Hallaj only had to transfer its prologue, which is to say, the *ʿumra* rituals (in *hurm*).

Although the *yawm al-Nahr* has always been celebrated everywhere (this is the Great Feast Day, the *ʿid al-Qurban*), the yawm *ʿArafat* (its vigil is the time when prayer achieves collective pardon, without waiting for the Feast), a purely spiritual ceremony, has been celebrated outside ʿArafat by a *taʿrif, sensu stricto*, only in certain regions and in certain periods (the Basra school, in opposition to the Medina school; in Shiraz in the ninth century, in Khurasan and in Dj. ʿAlam [Morocco] in the nineteenth century). And yet Hasan Basri, Jabir, Anas-b-Malik, Muslim, and Ibn Abiʾl-Dunya place ʿArafat day above the Great Feast (opposing Ibn Hanbal, Abu Dawud, and Nasaʾi; ʿUmar is undecided); its superiority over Friday was challenged by Malik.

It was an ʿAbbasid, the *wali* of Basra, ʿAbdallah-b-ʿAbbas (who had been *amiruʾl-hajj* in Mecca in 35 and 36), who instituted the *taʿrif* in Basra, as far back as the years 37–40 (when Syrian rebels occupied the Hijaz): which is to say, the celebration, following the *ʿasr* in the mosque, of the *waqfa* at ʿArafat: in spiritual union with the pilgrims celebrating it down there on 9 *Hijja*. The *taʿrif* was adopted by the Basra school, ʿAmr-b-Hirrith (d. 485), Hasan Basri, Bakr Muzani, Thabit Bunani, and Yahya-b-Muʿin; allowed by Ibn Hanbal. Condemned by the Medina school, Nafiʿ (*mawla ʿAmr*), Ibrahim Nakhaʾi, Hakam, Hammad, and Malik; in line with it Malikism characterized it as "*bidʿa munkara*" (Turtushi), but Ibn al-Hajj called it *mustahabb* [recommendable as pleasing to God]. The majority of Hanafites (Qadikhan) dismiss it as "useless innovation" inappropriate for obtaining grace (Mulla Miskin approves it on the condition that one's head be shaved to distinguish one from the true pilgrim). Shafiʿites, Hanbalites (Qudama is favorably disposed), and Zahirites, more cautiously, permit one, in any case, to perform the *taʿrif* outside ʿArafat (on Abu Qubays or in the Kaʿba).

Another ʿAbbasid, Caliph Muʿtasim (d. 228), living in Samarra at the time of the installation of his Turkish mercenaries (amir: AJ Ashinas, d. 231, having directed the hajj in 226; *katib*: Sulayman-b-Wahb, 226), had built for them at Karkh Firuz (221) a square kaʿba surrounded by a courtyard for the *tawaf* and other sites patterned after Mina and ʿArafat; so that these Shibliya Turks, fervent neophytes, could make the hajj without leaving the posts (the Queen Mother Shajaʿ, their kin, made the hajj in 236).

Another ʿAbbasid, Caliph Muʿtadid, had a portion of the Black Stone brought to Baghdad and set in gate of the palace; it was seen there as late as 533. In Cairo, his fiscal *wali*, Madharaʾi, had a kiosk built, around A.H. 300, in the form of the Kaʿba, in which to celebrate the fifteenth of *Shaʿban*. Hallaj may have known about this [earlier] transfer of the hajj to Samarra through his friend Shibli, a member of the Turkish tribe of Ashinas; and he must have known that the Hanafite grand qadi of the period, Ibn Abi Duʾad (218–233,

d. 240), had canonically endorsed the project carried out by Muʿtasim. He was one of those Hanafites who gave the most unequivocal approach to this kind of indirect taʿrif or "pilgrimage by proxy."

These various transfers of the hajj's liturgical effectiveness away from its physical site testify to the ancientness of the symbolization of its rituals and even to its mystical symbolization; to touch the Black Stone is to swear an oath directly to God, for it is His Right Hand on earth (yamin; Rabiʿ even called it His "idol," sanam; which the Qarmathians wanted to destroy, as "the magical magnet of hearts"). The muhrim's vow of chastity is perhaps the source of the Sufi hermit's vow of chastity, and the futa worn by Hallaj on the third hajj is that of the muhrim.

The hajj is above all taʿrif, for it is an expatriation (ghurba), outside the hurm; especially for women, for whom it is the jihad.

Hasan Basri was supposed already to have broadened the taʿrif to the point of teaching that "it is more meritorious to honor one's mother than to go on the hajj" (as stated by Abu Hazim Madani); Bishr Hafi had his fortune, which he had amassed with a view to the hajj, given away in alms; Dhu'l-Nun Misri claims that it was the giving up of his hajj by a single Damascene who had been staying behind in order to help some starving people, which won from God the general pardon for pilgrims on ʿArafat day of that particular year (a typical Tolstoian interpretation). Finally, Ibn ʿAtaʾ, commenting on a gloss by Jaʿfar on Qurʾan 3:101 notes that "to the one who has denied himself everything for God, the route of the hajj opens before him, very wide, for this is the basis (qiwam) of the call summoning (every Muslim) to the hajj."

Hallaj, by this slow effort of interior spiritualization of ritual, adduced his dogmatic formulation and extracted its whole theological meaning in two striking texts:

> "God prescribed two kinds of religious duties (taklif): one concerning intermediate things (wasaʾit = rituals), and the other concerning realities (haqaʾiq). Now, duties to realities involve knowledge that flows from God and returns to Him. Whereas duties to intermediate things involve knowledge that, flowing from objects below Him, is able to rejoin Him only by transcending them and destroying them. Now, one must include the building of the sacred enclosure and of the Kaʾba among duties to 'intermediate things,' just as it is said: 'the first sacred enclosure established for the people was that at Bakka (= Mecca), a blessed enclosure . . .' (Qurʾan 3:96). As long as you remain attached to this enclosure, you will remain separated from God. But when you have really detached yourself from it, then you will reach the One who built and established it; then, meditating on the temple (destroyed) in yourself, you will possess the real presence of its Founder." This is the notion of isqat al-wasaʾit (Baqli, Tafsir, no. 24, on Qurʾan 48:10), apropos of the oath of fealty made to God through the "intermediary agency" of the Prophet: "the perishableness of intermediaries."

(Kalabadhi, *Ta'arruf,* no. 60): "A 'AA M ibn Sa'dan told me:

I heard one of the great masters (= Abu'l-Mughith = Hallaj) say to me: one day I was sitting near the sacred enclosure when I heard a moan coming from the temple: "O wall, depart from the route followed by these beloved ones. The One Who visits you in yourself does the *tawaf* only around you, whereas the one who visits *Me* in *My*self does the *tawaf* in *Me*"; a tercet collected by Muzaffar Ghulam Jamil: Shaykh Husayn-b-Mansur Hallaj, may God be merciful to him, recited the following to me:

O you who censure me for loving Him, how much you crush me,
If you could only see the One I mean, you would no longer censure me.
People make the pilgrimage; I am going on a (spiritual) pilgrimage to my Host;
While they offer animals in sacrifice, I offer my heart and my blood.
Some of them walk in procession around the Temple, without their bodies,
For they walk in procession in God, and He has exempted them from the *Haram.*

Outside of Sufi circles, Hallaj's contemporaries realized that his proposal concerning the votive replacement of the hajj was the application of a general principle to the four other religious duties of fasting, prayer, alms, and worship. One non-Muslim historian, whom we believe to be Ibn Sinan, recopied by A Yf Qazwini, Ibn al-Jawzi, and Kutubi (who inserted this text, in the account of the condemnation taken from Zanji by Khatib, instead of and in place of the proposal given by Zanji), judged this text to be more incriminating; it is even too much so to be authentic, and if, indeed, it was a Sabaean like Ibn Sinan who accepted it, it was because of the well-known hatred of Sabaeans for Sufis.

In the works of Hallaj seized by Vizir Hamid-b-'Abbas, one read the following: "The man who fasts for three days, both day and night (cf. Qur'an 5:89: according to the *qira'a* of Ibn Mas'ud, followed by Abu Hanifa: *mutatabi'at*), totally, and on the fourth day, eats some endive leaves, will be exempted from fasting in Ramadan. If he prays for one single night a prayer of two *rak'a* that lasts from dusk to dawn, he is freed henceforth from the obligatory prayer. If he distributes his entire wealth in alms in one day, he is exempted from the tithe. If he builds an enclosure, fasts, and then walks around it completely naked (*'uryanan*) several times, he is exempted from the hajj. If he goes to the Qubur al-Shuhada', to the Quraysh cemeteries, and stays there for ten days to pray and invoke the aid of God, breaking the fast only with a little barley bread and raw salt, he is freed from every act of worship (*'ibada = shahada*) for the rest of his life." Further, in the presence of the canonists and qadis convened by Hamid he was asked: "do you know this book?" "Yes" [he replied], "it is the Book of Traditions (*Kitab al-sunan*) by Hasan Basri." "Don't you regard this book as the guide of your worship?" Hamid continued. "Yes" [Hallaj said], "this is the book that regulates my worship of God." "This book," exclaimed Qadi Abu 'Umar, "is destroying the canons of Islam," and he continued his sentence until he said to him, "O you whose blood may be spilled without sin." Then he signed the formula "his blood may be spilled"; and the canonists signed the statement after him making it lawful to spill his blood.

This tendentious text is confirmed by the contemporary Shi'ite attacks against the Hallajiya:

—(Ibn Babuya, d. 381, *I'tiqadat*): ". . . their form of worship does away with the legal prayer and other religious duties."

—(Mufid, d. 413, *Sharh 'Aqa'id Ibn Babawayh*,". . . they profess the *ibaha* (= repeal of religious duties). . . ."

One can see the tendentious way in which Shi'ite tradition set forth the Hallajian theory of the "perishableness of intermediate rituals."

The Second Consultation with the Two Qadis

Qadi Abu 'Umar seems to have weighed very carefully in his conscience his choice of grounds [for condemnation]—the proposal concerning the votive replacement of the hajj—to affix (*ta'liq*) to the sentence that the vizir wanted to get from the canonists. Previously under indictment before Abu 'Umar, in the period between 288 and 296, Hallaj had been prosecuted as a popular preacher, a *qass*, for breach of Mu'tadid's edict (of 284) [against public preaching], despite the fact that his topics as an itinerant preacher, when reporting the trances of joy and sorrow into which divine love had thrown him, could not have been used against him as grounds for a specific charge: two *fatwas* had clashed with one another, that of the Zahirite Ibn Dawud, which declared that the Sunna of the Prophet condemned this kind of behavior, and that of the Shafi'ite Ibn Surayj, which denied the canonists any competence for examining hearts and passing judgment on mysticism. Which had prevented the reopening of the trial in 301.

In 309, Hallaj was no longer a simple street preacher, nor a country miracle worker. As a fugitive or prisoner for thirteen years, no longer allowed to speak in public, he had turned to writing; he had become an unseen but revered scholar whose doctrinal treatises, disseminated by authorized and zealous spokesmen, were expressed with an authority that was disquieting for both the scholars of the Law and the state. They had to prove that he was daring to alter the legal rituals, a right which, according to the Shi'ites, belonged only to the Mahdi, and which, according to Hallaj himself, will be exercised only by Jesus, upon his return. With respect to the hajj, particularly, a Shi'ite hadith said: "no (true) hajj before the coming of the Mahdi and the return of Jesus" (Ja'far, according to Malati. This change had an unsettling eschatological effect, taken as the warning of an apocalyptic catastrophe, which the Qarmathians fermented (cf. 317; and the "stab" of 413 against the Black Stone). It provided the grounds sought by the vizir.

Armed with this text, Hamid consulted, *istifta'*, Ibn 'Ayyash tells us, the two qadis then officiating for Baghdad, Abu Ja'far A-b-Ishaq Buhlul Tanukhi Anbari, and Abu 'Umar M-b-Yf (Hammadi Azdi Basri). The *fatwa* by Abu 'Umar was as follows: "The proposal represents a diabolical rebellion (*zandaqa*), which calls for the mandatory death sentence, for we do not have to invite the *zindiq* to show repentance" (Malik's and Thawri's solution). That of Abu Ja'far was as follows: "There is no [legal] obligation to put him to death as long as he has not acknowledged (by *iqrar*) that he believes in this proposal; for we know that traditionists relate acts of impiety without this implying any belief attached to them on their part. Therefore, if he declares that it is an opinion that he has related but that he personally disavows, no charge will stand against him; if, on the other hand, he declares that he believes in it, he must be invited to repent on this point; if he complies, no charge will stand against him; but if he refuses, and only then, there is an obligation to put him to death" (the Hanafite solution). They decided on a basis of Abu 'Umar's *fatwa*, and in accordance with what had been circulated and divulged about him, what was evident in terms of his heresy and impiety, and his ways of deceiving people and debasing their religious practices.

The *fatwa* of Abu 'Umar, according to the logic of both its system and political career, was accepted beforehand by the vizir. That of Ibn Buhlul was a fine recall of the integrity of his school, the official legal school of the state; a Platonic recall; for, regardless of what Hamadhani and Ibn al-Wardi say about him, Hallaj was not a man to seize the opportunity of a retraction in order to save his life; Ibn 'Aqil was to do so in 465, but in his case it was not a question of the testimony of his whole life; and it is a tribute paid by the qadi to Hallaj's character, that he could have had him only by the snare of a denial made *in extremis*.

The Condemnation Session

When a wicked judge holds the pen, a Mansur (= Hallaj) will die on the gibbet.
When authority passes into insane hands, surely Prophets are bound to be slain
(Qur'an 5:70). —Rumi, *Mathnavi*, 2, 23:13–14.

The following are three separate major accounts of it:

1. The account given by the vizir's assistant clerk, Zanji, presented by his son Isma'il ibn Zanji (the version summarized for external use).

Each day Hamid was brought a few of the notebooks found in the homes of Hallaj's disciples; they were put before him, and he handed them to my father to read to him. And this was the procedure he always used. Now it so happened that, on one of those days, my father read to him, in the presence of qadis Abu 'Umar and A Hy ibn al-Ushnani, from one of Hallaj's writings in which it was reported (*hukiya*) that "when a man wants to carry out the legally required pilgrimage and has no way of doing it, he must set aside a room in his home (variant: a square building) that no impurity touches, where no one goes, and which no one may pass through; then, at the time of the pilgrimage, he must walk around in a circle, as one does at the *Bayt al-Haram* (add.: seven times); once that is done, he must perform the rituals (*manasik*) at Mecca. After that, he will gather together thirty orphans, prepare them the best possible meal, invite them into this [special] place, and serve them this meal himself; when they have finished their meal and washed their hands, he will dress each of them in a [new] shirt and give each seven drachmas (or three: I am not quite sure which); and all of that, when it is carried out, will take the place of the hajj for him."

When my father had finished reading this passage, Qadi Abu 'Umar turned to Hallaj [and asked]: "What have you taken that from?" [Hallaj replied:] "from the *Kitab al-ikhlas* of Hasan Basri." "You have lied about it, O you whose blood may be shed without sin (*ya halal al-damm*); for we have heard the *Kitab al-ikhlas* of Hasan Basri read in Mecca, and it does not contain a word of what you have related."

As soon as Abu 'Umar had uttered the words "you have lied about it, O you whose blood may be shed without sin," Hamid said to him, "write that" (variant: with your hand, sign it); while Abu 'Umar was himself busy speaking to Hallaj. But Hamid asked him again to put in writing what he had said; the qadi refused to do it, and instead busied himself with something of his own; so much so that Hamid offered Abu 'Umar the ink-pot already provided him, had a piece of paper handed to him, and he passed it back to [the vizir]. But Hamid pressed him to write with such authority that he could not stand up to him; and he signed [the formula] "lawful to shed his blood," and the members of the court who were present signed [it] after him.

Realizing then what had happened, Hallaj cried out "my back is forbidden (to your whips), my blood inviolable (*haram*); you are not allowed to use this interpretation [formula] to render shedding it lawful; my religion is Islam, my rule of conduct is tradition (*sunna*), founded on the acknowledged superiority of Abu Bakr, 'Umar, 'Uthman, 'Ali, Talha, Zubayr, Sa'd, Sa'id, 'AR ibn 'Awf, and Abu 'Ubayda ibn al-Jarrah. I have written books, Sunnite books, which are available in bookshops. God, God will answer for my blood." And he went on repeating this sentence (add.: that he was allowed the courtesy of commenting on), while the signature continued to be given, thereby completing the formalities necessary for concluding the session.

2. The account by Qadi AH ibn 'Ayyash, taken from his paternal uncle Abu Muhammad (allied to Qadi Abu 'Umar), taken from Ibn al-Azraq, taken from an eyewitness (= this uncle) seated near Hamid-b-'Abbas.

(Confiscated) notebooks were brought forth in which Hallaj related (*ahdatha*) the following: "When a man wishes to carry out the legally required pilgrimage, he may make up for it by deciding to set aside a room in his house in which to make a *mihrab* [prayer niche] (of some sort), to purify himself, to put on the *ihram* [garments of the Mecca pilgrim], to say this, to do that, to pray such and such a prayer, to recite such and such a verse [of Qur'anic scripture], to walk around (in such and such a way [as at the Ka'ba]), to recite the *tasbih* [rosary] (in such and such a way), and to perform certain (pious) works which he listed in detail, saying that he was the author of these directives; to make a long story short, when all of that was carried out, this man was freed (from the legal obligation) of making the pilgrimage to the *Bayt al-Haram*."

Now, that is a well-known proposal among the Hallajiya; one of their members, who claims to be a master, admitted it in my presence, pointing out, however, that Hallaj had issued it as a tradition derived from the *Ahl al-Bayt*, may divine prayers be upon them; and adding: "it is not true, in our cases, that that makes up for the hajj: [rather] that replaces it in the case of one who is prevented from going on it because of interdiction, poverty, or sickness;" this [man] accepted the gist of it to me while arguing with me about its form. AH (ibn al-Azraq) told me further: "when we asked Hallaj about that (at the condemnation session?), he thought that this proposal did not make him liable to any punishment, assumed full responsiblity for it (by *iqrar*), and declared, 'it is a tradition that I produced just as I received it (by *sama'*)'" (Ibn al-Azraq includes here the *istifta'* of the two qadis, Abu 'Umar and Ibn Buhlul).

3. The account published by Ibn Dihya (theological source):

The vizir received (from the *sulaha'*) this (second) letter (concerning the replacement of the hajj) and turned it over to Qadi Abu 'Umar (Hammadi), a Malikite. He read it and found it erroneous, but Hallaj defended it before him. The qadi said to him: "I see that you still approve it?" "Yes," [Hallaj said] "that is what I have written and what I know [to be true]." When Hallaj had assumed full responsibility for it before him (by *iqrar*), and given the *isnad* going back, through "so and so" ('Abd al-Wahid-b-Zayd? Ja'far Sadiq?), to Hasan Basri, the qadi exclaimed: "you have misrepresented it, O enemy of God, O *kafir*, O *fajir*, O you whose blood can be shed without sin," I do not speak like this to a Muslim. The vizir then took this judgment by the qadi and submitted Hallaj's case to the canonists, who authorized his execution.

Comparison of the three accounts reveals:

1. *The malice aforethought.* Zanji shows us the qadi being "cleverly manipulated" in session by the vizir; even though Ibn Sinan and Ibn Dihya agree in affirming that the litigious proposal was examined on two occasions, submitted to expert opinion in the interval; therefore Abu 'Umar was play acting during

the session, having intended beforehand to let himself be forced to consent. This lacuna makes us suspicious of Zanji's account, whose ingenuous tone brushes aside the *iqrar* of the accused (cf. ʿAyyash and Ibn Dihya) with the greatest ease.

2. *The revolutionary implication of this approach to the hajj.* Hallaj, while affirming his belief in the incriminatory proposal, maintains that he received it, by *isnad*, from Hasan Basri. Hallaj was schooled in Basra, where the influence of the ʿAbbadan *ribat* had for a century drawn the disciples of Hasan Basri together; however, it is not necessary to imagine that he had gotten this proposal (*ikhlas al-hajj*) in his native Harithite milieu of Bayda just because Hasan Basri had resided there (between A.H. 50 and 55) with the *wali*, Rabiʿ-b-Ziyad Harithi, the conqueror of Sijistan, as his *katib*. In Basra, the traditions of Hasan Basri were preserved, on the one hand, by the Bakriya theologians, and, on the other hand, by the mystic disciples of Abd al-Wahid-b-Zayd. We have several indications of an alliance of Hallajian religious devotion with this latter group (*hasbi; takhalluq*) and with the *Riwayat* (*marasil*) that it was transmitting in Hasan Basri's name: in terms of *hadith qudsi*, of the maxim communicated directly by God (through *ilham*, inspiration; not through [the intermediary agency of] the Prophet or the Angel) to the heart of the mystic. One of them specifically, the *hadith al-ikhlas*, defines this Qurʾanic word (Sura 112) as the secret of hearts predestined for perfect worship, which consists of "drawing nearer to God through supererogatory works (*hadith al-taqarrub bi'l-nawafil*)," by means of a purificative method of ritual practice; in which it is no longer even the content of the ritual duty (*fard*), but the spirit in which one practices it (*sunna*), that constitutes actual membership in the Muslim Community and unites the believers with the prophets. This conception of *ikhlas* is connected with the practice of retreats and forty-day fasts (*hadith al-arbaʿiniyat (cf. Taw.* III, 1) and with the notion of union with God achieved by the *abdal*. ʿAbd al-Wahid-b-Zayd was *siddiqi*; he pictured Abu Bakr to himself as the first in this traditon. And Muhasibi, his disciple, through Mudar, made *ikhlas* the very basis of the true *sunna*'s spiritual continuity.

There is no doubt therefore but that Hallaj rightly connected the "replacement of the hajj" with the spirit of Hasan Basri, who practiced the *taʿrif* in Basra, on ʿArafat day. But we have not succeeded as yet in rediscovering the text in his juridical style to which he referred; Ibn Abi'l-Dunya (d. 281) and AB Warraq from Tirmidh (d. 294) both wrote a *Kitab al-ikhlas* before Hallaj wrote his *Kitab al-sidq wa'l-ikhlas* (cf. also the one by Ibn al-Jawzi). Did they include it in theirs? An Andalusian Malikite, Mufarrij (d. 380), compiled the various *fatwa* of Hasan Basri in six large volumes; it would be necessary to look through these in this respect.

Abu ʿUmar, according to Zanji, was supposed to have denied that this text was in the *Kitab al-ikhlas* of Hasan Basri. But according to the account (given by Ibn Sinan) preferred by Ibn al-Jawzi and Kutubi, the Malikite qadi, on the contrary, was supposed to have declared that the *Sunan* (in general) of Hasan Basri were "destroyers" of the Laws of Islam; and was supposed to have condemned this text as being by Hasan Basri. The Malikite school of Medina was very hostile to Hasan, to be sure; but a Hammadite from Basra, such as Qadi Abu 'Umar, had "to accommodate" himself to the influence of the works of Hasan Basri in his native city. Undoubtedly he preferred to use bowdlerized editions of Hasan, from which this text was missing: such as the "concordance between Malik and Hasan" compiled by his cousin and assessor at the trial, Ibrahim-b-Hammad.

3. *The seriousness of this innovation.* Did this proposal concerning the hajj call for capital punishment? Mahdi Naraqi Kashani (d. 1209/1794), an Imamite, comments in his *Mushkilat* that "to legalize the fulfillment of the hajj in one's house or in the desert, as Hy-b-Mansur reportedly did, is a *bid'a* [innovation] that alters the quiddity of the ritual." As if the quiddity of a ritual was first the site where it was to be performed, then the prescribed deeds, and lastly the pure intent behind it, the *ikhlas.* Such is, indeed, the order of importance generally allowed by the literalism of the canonists. One independent Ibadite had upheld the priority of the prescribed deeds over their localization, like Hallaj. Everyone knows that, chronologically, the hajj rituals include, first, a pure intention, followed by at least eight physical deeds to be carried out in two places, the Meccan *Haram* (*'Umra*) and 'Arafat (hajj *sensu stricto*): *ihram, wuquf, tawaf,* which are *fard* (the contravener becomes *kafir*), and five *wajib* (the contravener becomes *fasiq*), and fifteen others, which are *sunna.* Added to these ritual acts performed for God (*manasik*) are acts of almsgiving to the poor (*masakin*), expiatory acts for breaches of regulations (for having hunted animals, or shaved off one's hair).

The Hallajian proposal is conservative as far as ritual deeds are concerned (at a time when a contemporary Mu'tazilite, Abu Hashim, was proposing, without being prosecuted, that *wuquf* and *tawaf* be omitted from the *fard* and *sa'y* from the *wajib*); it even incorporates, by tripling it, the expiatory alms for the poor. But it has a revolutionary spiritual effect of transforming a canonical duty decreed for once in a person's lifetime (*sarura*), if possible, into a vow of an annual visit to God, the prescribed physical setting for which evaporates into abstract contemplation (Ibrahim-b-Adham previously called the hajj the *muraqaba*); the immense press of the pilgrims at the *waqfa* becomes a solitary elevation of the soul, a *mi'raj* leaving the Ka'ba for the *Aqsa* and the *Aqsa* for the *Durah* (*Bayt Ma'mur,* the fourth heaven) and the Throne. To be sure, the emphasis put by the Prophet on the *waqfa* at 'Arafat, in *hill*, outside the Meccan *Haram*, at the time of his farewell pilgrimage, hence on the "descent of forgiveness" preceding the sacrifice (physical, of the victims at Mina), responding to the heart's sacrifice (free *du'a*), and putting a stop to the *talbiya* (which is the main mark of the *muhrim*), steers devotion rather toward an ascension consecrating the election. Hasan Basri placed 'Arafat day above *yawm al-Nahr,* above Friday; it is the day of the "*shahid al-tawhid,*" the "Prophet's desired apotropaic witness who will testify to divine unity," when God rejoices with His angels at the holy souls (*abdal*) for the love of whom He grants annual plenary indulgence to all, present and absent (whose names are at that time called out to Him). For Hallaj, the *ta'rif* is just that, the condensing of the entire Hijazian ritual on 9 *Hijja*: into a spiritual sacrifice transcending the physical sacrifice of the lamb, which common devotion shifted everywhere (in union with the pilgrims at Mina) to the next day, the day of the *'Id al-Qurban*.

But even though this physical transfer to 10 *Hijja* had never been contested, Abu 'Umar assails the *spiritual* transfer conceived by Hallaj for 9 *Hijja* as bringing about the incorporation of the *'Umra* in the hajj. He saw in it an eschatological sign, the suspension of the legal sacrifices, something that Shi'ites reserved for their mahdi, the expectation of the *Hajj Akbar*, which, according to Hallaj, Jesus must institute.

He declares that Shi'ite revolutionaries, the Qarmathians, are trying to destroy the pilgrimage to Mecca; for twenty-two years (317–339), they will bring it to a halt, carrying off the Black Stone, whose *istilam* is a *wajib* ritual according to Malikism (and Hanafism). He believes that "the spiritual destruction of the Ka'ba" called for by Hallaj in his letter to Shakir puts him in a class with the Qarmathian, as worthy of being destroyed in the name of the *maslaha mursala*, for the "common good."

The Khatt al-Mahdar

The *khatt al-mahdar*, the official wording of the death sentence signed by the qadis and witnesses, was, taking that of 7 *Rabi'* II 323 (against Ibn Shannabudh as a model, as follows:

> *nuskhat al-mahdar al-ma'mul 'ala* (al-Hallaj) *bikhatt* (Ibn Zanji): . . . *fa Amir al-mu'minin atala' Llah baqa'ahu fi was'at min damihi . . . wa dhalika fi yawm (al-khamis baqiyin min dhi'l-qa'da sana 309); fi majlis al-wazir* (Abi M Hamid-b-al-'Abbas) *adama' Llah tawfiqahu wahasbi Allah wahdahu.—khatt* (Abi 'Umar); *shahida bima fi hadhihi ruq'a wa kataba* (Ibn al-Ushnani) *biyadihi wa dhakar'l-ta'rikh.—shahida bidhalika* (Ibn Mukram) *wa kataba biyadihi.—shahida* (followed by the names of the other *shuhud*).

> A transcript of the authentic act carried out against (Hallaj), in the hand of (Ibn Zanji, court clerk): . . . and the Commander of the Faithful, May God grant him long life, is permitted to put him to death . . . and that [to be done] on Thursday, 19 *Dhu'l-Qa'da* 309; in the court of the vizir (AM Hamid-b-'Abbas). May God prosper him a long time. Let God alone be my reward.—Here follows the signature of (Qadi Abu 'Umar); the attestation of the contents of this missive, written in the hand (of Qadi Ibn al-Ushnani), and dated. Signed attestation of that by (the head of the *shuhud*, Ibn Mukram). Attestation (followed by the names of the other witnesses).

The Andalusian Malikite procedure followed in the next century (Cordova, in 464 and 465: against *zindiq*) provides us with two variants for the clause "*fa Amir al-mu'minin . . . fi was'at min damihi*": "*nara, wa'Llah al-muwaffiq li'l-sawab, annabu mulhid kafir wajaba qatlahu bila i'dhar*" = "we consider, and God will obtain the just solution, that this [man] is a heretic and an infidel who deserves to be executed without invitation to [show] repentance."

The Meaning of Hallaj's Last Two Statements at the Trial

No confirmation or echo of these two declarations has come down to us from a Hallajian source; which would suggest the absence of any counsel for the defense among the *shuhud* convened for this "ready-made" session. As there is no reason to question Zanji's account in this instance, it is fitting to allocate a place to them, without trying to connect them directly, in relation to his oral and written preaching.

1. "My religion is Islam. . . ." Which harks back to: "I am not, as people said (and wrote in 301), one of those rebels against the Law, extremist Shi'ites (Siniya, Isma'iliya, Qarmathians), who reject the sunna, who accept no other true *sahaba* than the five (Salman, Miqdad, Abu Dharr, Ibn Maz'un, and 'Ammar), and who want to destroy the Ka'ba and replace the hajj with a visit to the Imam. No, I am very simply a Sunnite, and *siddiqi*: a believer in the superiority of Abu Bakr over and above, and even separate from the nine others."

This declaration is authentic; regardless of what the Shi'ite heresiographers say, the Hallajiya are pure Sunnites, from those in Ahwaz (Mansur, d. 326; AB Hashimi) down to Vizir Ibn al-Muslima.

2. "My blood is inviolable . . . God answers for my blood (*Allah fi dami*)." This latter is a formula commonly used: it is the cry of innocence in the face of the threat of legal death: the call to God Who will not allow a Muslim to be slaughtered by his brethren. In this instance, the formula was immediately understood by those present themselves (before the ironic reflection of a Sabaean, Ibn Sinan) to be an insolent *mubahala*, a curse assigned the vizir to an ordeal, to a judgment of God. This curse is allowable only between private individuals; one may not use it against the Imam (cf. Shalmaghani's contempt of court in 322). The oldest account of the condemnation (by Mutawwaq? known from Ibn 'Ayyash, recopied by Ibn Abi Tahir, according to Ibn al-Qarih:) paraphrases: "*ana ubahilukum*" (from Qur'an 3:54) = "I pledge my life against yours so that the true Judgment of God may shine forth," said Hallaj; to which Hamid responded: "this is the very charge against you, proven" (= "you believe you are "inspired" and entitled to dispute the Law; you are no longer a Muslim"). And indeed if one attaches this *mubahala* to Hallaj's words, consid-

ered blasphemous, "*'ala din al-salib yakun mawti*" = "I will die nailed (in heart and in body) to the cross," the vizir's answer means: do you intend to revive the *mubahala* of the Christians of Najran vis-à-vis the Prophet and the Law? Which could have led Hamid at the time of the execution to make the declaration (preserved by Tuzari) deflecting the effect of this curse onto the eighty-four *shuhud*.

"*Allah fi dami*," "God is in my blood" (= He is its guarantor) is the "first dram" of the popular legend of Hallaj's *tazkiya*, the physical attestation of his innocence by his blood which, [it is said] writes *Allah* on the ground, at the time of his dismemberment, eighty-four times, standing for the eighty-four *shuhud* who sanctioned his sentence. *Hululi* legend (like that concerning the effect of his ashes on the flooding of the Tigris); the Pure Name was indeed "in his blood," since this blood wrote it on the ground (Ibn 'Arabi, Ibn 'Alawan). This Hallajian belief blossomed forth independently of Zanji's account, which was unknown among the Sufis, through collective meditation on martyrdom; its similarity with this account is therefore all the more significant.

One may object that this kind of concordance has merit only with respect to the *Akhbar* of Shakir and the teaching therein of Hallaj as the victim who died accursed for the Muslim Community, to which he had cried out (*Akhbar*, no. 50): "*Abaha lakum dami*" = "God permits you to shed my blood; sacrifice me therefore (as a victim)." And that this cry, which is authenticated by the letter to Shakir and which is equivalent to "*dami halal*" ("my blood is licit"), contradicts, at the very least in its form, the statement uttered before the court "*dami haram*" ("my blood is inviolable"). Isn't this statement a kind of retraction of his teaching about victimal sacrifice made at the moment when his sentence made him visualize the punishment? Like Joan of Arc in the Saint-Ouen cemetery.

He is suddenly terror stricken, in fact, in the face of the reality before him; he feels compassion for his body, for the blood of that heart in which he claims God lives. Hallaj has not yet realized, or accepted, the full horror of sacrifice for which he yearned so much. He no longer has the strength to thank those who, by wanting to kill him, accomplish his sacrificial offering (his "faithful friends," *thiqati*, from *Akhbar*, no. 1; his *ma'jurun*, repaid, from *Akhbar*, no. 7). He still believes that the divine presence, which he feels within him, will protect his body; he no longer grants the Law dispensation (cf. the statement by Suhrawardi) from executing him. This is also a recall of the suspensive *fatwa* of Ibn Surayj.

This was Thursday, 19 Qa'da. Four days later, when praying his last vigil, after having had doubts (*makr*; Qur'an 3:54–57) about the painful reality of his coming execution, Hallaj grasped completely the symbolism of his "Letter to Shakir"; the "Temple" (of his body) will indeed be destroyed; "God, the guarantee of his blood," yes, He will be his guarantee—of his immortal life, for blood (in the whole Semitic tradition) is the spirit: which cannot be killed;

which God will preserve, this pure unpolluted witness, among the souls of the martyrs; as assurance of the glorious resurrection of the temple (*hakul = ka'ba*) of his body. He affirms his faith in the victory of his cause, since he accepts being really sacrificed and burned, in laudatory incense, *yanjuj*, for Him, the next day.

The Delayed Confirmation

The session over, "Hamid handed the minutes over to my father," says Ibn Zanji; "he instructed him to send Muqtadir the official report of the session in relating what had happened, and to attach to this letter the various *fatwa* in requesting him to authorize the execution; after that, to write another letter, this one to Chamberlain Nasr, asking him to send the first to Muqtadir, and to pass on the imperial response that would be given to it. My father wrote the two letters, inserted the *fatwa* in the envelope intended for Muqtadir; but two days went by without his getting any answer.

What had happened? Nasr had definitely sent the letter, but, adds Ibn 'Ayyash, "he had frightened the Sayyida, the Queen Mother of Muqtadir, about the [possible] consequences of Hallaj's execution. I am convinced that the punishment of this holy man (*shaykh salih*) would fall upon your son (= Muqtadir)." She wanted to prevent Muqtadir from ordering the execution (N.B.: through her *katib*, Ibn al-Khasib 307–314, a friend of Nasr; or through Ibn al-Hawari); but he did not yield, and ordered Hamid to proceed with the execution. He came down with a fever the next day, and Nasr and the Sayyida redoubled their appeals to him. He countermanded the order, and sent a messenger back to Hamid (N.B.: his regular emissary, Nasim Sharabi, the head cup-bearer): to notify him that the execution was called off. The affair dragged on for several days (N.B.: three days); then the sickness that had frightened Muqtadir briefly, left him.

Let us resume Ibn Zanji's account:

> such a delay upset Hamid; regret for having written this letter, fear that it had been intercepted, frustration at being unable to do anything more to carry out the sentence that he had gotten passed. And, on the third day, he dictated a second letter to my father addressed to Muqtadir, who reproduced the terms of the first and added: "what has taken place at the tribunal has been officially recorded (N.B.: *tanfir?*) and made public. Seeing that the execution of Hallaj does not ensue, everyone is going to revolt on his behalf; there are not two persons who disagree with me on this"; he also asked again that the execution be sanctioned; he had this missive delivered to Muflih (= Abu Salih Muflih Aswad, head of the black eunuchs), whose mission it was to forward it, to get a reply, and report back to him.
>
> Put more pointedly, according to Qadi Ibn 'Ayyash: (Hamid declared): "O

Commander of the Faithful, if he is not put to death, he will change the canonical
Law, and everyone will apostasize [from the faith] under his influence: which will
destroy the state; allow me to have him killed, and, if some unfortunate consequence befalls you because of it, have me put to death."

Lastly, Ibn Sinan (according to Abu Yf Qazwini):

the reply being slow in coming, Hamid was afraid that Muqtadir had reversed his
decision, being influenced by his friends and by the life of renunciation, asceticism, mortification, and piety led by Hallaj in prison. He wrote to him as follows:
"the *fuqaha'* have agreed by *fatwa* on his execution. His heresy, his blasphemy,
his sorcery, and his claims to divine power have been revealed and made public. If
the Commander of the Faithful does not carry out what the *fuqaha'* have ruled on,
there will be people who will rise up and be emboldened to rebel against God and
His prophets." And Hamid did his utmost to win acceptance for his position, fearing lest the whole affair should turn against him.

Muqtadir examined his vizir's letter in the early morning of Sunday, 22
Qa'da, during a great banquet that he had arranged (the historian Hamadhani
states precisely that it took place on that date) in honor of Mu'nis and Nasr:
Mu'nis Qushuri and Nasr Qushuri, two comrades in arms, the staunchest supporters of the throne, now enemies. Following the custom with heads of state,
he called for a show of reconciliation, in which his chamberlain, Nasr, defeated
by his commander-in-chief, Mu'nis, all along the line, had to do all the talking.
Muqtadir on this occasion officially declared a pardon for Ibn Abi'l-Saj (and
for three Saffarids) requested by Mu'nis, the impending appointment of same
to the command of the eastern front, in the war against Akh Su'luk, Nasr's
friend, whose head he was to send (A.S. was defeated and killed on 8 *Hijja*
311) to Muqtadir via Muflih as go-between "in order not to sadden Nasr" (*sic*),
two of whose associates Ibn Abu'l-Saj was taking from him: M-b-'Abd al-
Samad (who gave up the post of police commissioner of Baghdad to Nazuk,
Mu'nis's trusted agent) and Niramani, whom his father-in-law, Ibn al-Hawari,
allowed to go to Rayy as fiscal *wali.* After which, when leaving the banquet
with his regular table companions (*nudama'*), the B. al-Munajjim, the B. Hamdun, the poet 'Allaf, etc., Muqtadir agreed in writing to Hamid's request; in the
presence of Nasr, who was already demoralized by the promotion of Ibn Abi'l-
Saj, the weak sovereign gladly granted the vizir the head of Hallaj, Nasr's
friend.

This is how, on 22 *Qa'da,* at the end of the morning, the tawqi' (sealed order
of execution, bearing the seal of Muqtadir, who returned to the Harem), so
recorded in the office of the Seal (directed by Khara'iti), reached Hamid by
way of Muflih (from the hand of his Christian secretary, the eunuch Bishr-b-
'AA ibn Bishr) as go-between.

The order read as follows: "In view of the fact that the qadis have concurred, by *fatwa*, in his execution, and that they have declared it lawful to shed his blood, you must summon Muhammad ibn 'Abd al-Samad, the Police Commissioner (who was going to tender his resignation): to notify him of the order to take custody of Hallaj and to have him administered a thousand lashes of the whip, even though he were to die from it (500 lashes constituted the "*darbat al-mawt*"); and if he were not to die from it, to have his head chopped off. "Hamid was overjoyed at this reply, and the anxiety which had bothered him went away," writes Zanji.

This *tawqi'* text, probably drafted by the secretary of the caliphal council, AB ibn Thawaba (pro-Shi'ite), seems incomplete here; a similar, Andalusian *tawqi'* dating from 464/1071, adds to the wording of the kind of punishment:

> Decreed by the Sovereign, in his indignant (*ghadba*) zeal, for service to God, His Book and His Messenger: as punishment for whosoever should profess the same opinions and should be convinced by the same machinations, proof of which has been established against X, may God's curse be upon him.

Immediately upon the signing of the *tawqi'*, Ibn Sahl tells us, the palace guard (N.B.: *Haras*, commanded by Sa'd Nubi, eponym of Bab al-Nubi) ordered the *tanfir* sounded, as was done for every declaration of holy war. With the mob ever watchful, waiting to release its joy and its expression of loyalty. Incited to that by the vizir who had a copy of the *tawqi'* sent to (each of the three) cathedral mosques (N.B.: J. al-Qasr: M-b-Ishaq-b-'Abd-al-Malik; J. Madinat al-Mansur: 'AA-b-M ibn Burya; J. 'Ask. Mahdi: Ahmad Zaynabi): through the good offices of the *muhtasib* (Ibrahim-b-Batha); after having read it to the staff of the vizirate. In the mosques the text was recopied from group to group on into the evening amidst acclamations praising the Commander of the Faithful for the influence of God acting upon him and for his zeal in submitting to God.

In the case of Hallaj, this kind of ritual demonstration, if it took place, could not have been very spontaneous, for the vizir feared a violent reaction by Hanbalite rioters, incited secretly by Nasr, as in 308.

Hamid, says Ibn Zanji, then summoned M-b-'Abd al-Samad, and read him the Caliph's order himself notifying him thereby to take custody of Hallaj; but the other refused to do so, fearing, he said, that people (= the mob? Nasr?) might snatch him right out of his hands. Then Hamid notified him that he would send Hallaj to him escorted by his personal guards (commanded by Dawdadh, the nephew of Ibn Abi'l-Saj) as far as the police headquarters on the west bank (at Bab Khurasan: where the commissioner had moved after the rebellion in *Qa'da* 308); and it was agreed that the condemned man would be led out on the following evening (= the 23rd), after the hour for the *'isha* [evening prayer] (= the first stars), encircled by a contingent of Hamid's guards, surrounded by other policemen leading pack mules and running beside them like grooms, so effectively that by setting the condemned on one of these mules, they could make their way with him through the crowd. He instructed him to "give him a thousand lashes; if he dies from them, chop off his head, and preserve it when you order his body burned; if not, stop the flagellation (after the thousandth blow), cut off one of his hands, then a foot, then the other hand and the other foot; and, once the trunk is burned, display his head on the bridge." Then he adds: "And even if he says to you: I am going to make the Euphrates flow with gold and silver for you, don't listen to him, don't answer him, don't interrupt his punishment."

Did the vizir's instructions augment the standard punishment called for by the Caliph (decapitation after flagellation)? According to Ibn Dihya, the caliphal *tawqi'*, which he dates as coming on the 23rd, was longer than Ibn Zanji reported it: "if the case (of Hallaj) is indeed just as Muhammad-b-Yusuf (= Abu 'Umar) and other canonists state it, and if in your judgment clear proof has been established against him, go to M-b-'Abd al-Samad, the head of the Criminal Investigation Department (*ma'una;* not *shurta*; *sic*) a *mawla* of the Commander of the Faithful, [see that he:] gives him a thousand lashes, cuts off his hands and feet alternately, chops off his head, burns his body, and scatters his ashes into the water of the Tigris."

This intensification [of the punishment] does not appear to be the achievement of the vizir (unless his Shi'ite adviser, Shalmaghani, had goaded him to ask for it from the Caliph as a posthumous precaution to be taken against a sorcerer capable of complete metamorphosis). In any case, it assigns to Hallaj's execution the character of damnation, in the name of the Qur'an. Intercision (*with* public display, which Zanji and Ibn Dihya omit from their accounts, and which the Sufi sources attest to) is the Qur'anic punishment for sorcerers (Qur'an 20:74; 5:33; 26:49) whom the Pharoah wants to damn for having listened to Moses. Cremation followed by "the scattering of ashes into the deep" is scripturally speaking the destruction of a diabolical idol, that of the golden calf of the Israelites who disobeyed Moses (Qur'an 20:97). Hallaj is likened to the golden calf, because he claimed to be God, and because he made people worship the idol of his body, which must be completely destroyed (God alone may burn punitively; Abu Bakr regretted having had a pervert burned, and it is not certain that 'Ali had burned the Zutt Sabi'iya alive). It is curious that in A.H. 125 the Umayyad Caliph Walid II had the body of the 'Alid Zayd cremated and [his ashes] scattered in the Kunasa of Kufa as an application of Qur'an 20:97; and that the Shi'ite rebel Basasiri in 450/1058 had put on the head of the Hallajian vizir Ibn al-Muslima, to execute him, a pair of cattle horns, [dressing him] like the Golden Calf or the reddish-brown Cow (Qur'an 2:68–71) according to Mu'ayyad Shirazi: *baqara,* corresponding to *thawr* in Hamadhani. To cover Hallaj's head, they had merely to put on the usual tiara worn by those condemned to death, a kind of "san-benito" bearing an ignominious inscription. This *qurmus,* this *kulah,* a high pointed cap, which Baqli, in a dream, saw Hallaj wearing when coming to thank him for his commentary on the *Tawasin.*

Despite the vizir's instructions, the site (and manner) of exposition of the condemned man's remains was changed. The established custom was to display them in the middle of the Bridge of Boats, between the two police headquarters; as was done in the cases of the Qarmathian Ibn Abi'l-Fawaris in 287/899, the eunuch Wasif in 289/901, Layli Daylami in 309, and the Police Commissioner Nazuk in 317/929. A change had to be made at the last moment because of the cremation; it was decided rather to scatter the ashes from the top of a minaret and not from the middle of a bridge into the Tigris. As for the head and the four extremities, we shall see that the sources are not entirely in agreement about the site of their exposition.

CHAPTER SEVEN

The Martyrdom

THE PERIPETEIAS OF THE EXECUTION*

In the eager crowd of onlookers, contained by a strong peace-keeping force that did not make it easy for him to notice, Hallaj did not have only exultant enemies. There were spectators, sympathizers also, and the rather fanatic followers, expecting some rescuing miracle to give them the courage to overthrow a hated government. There were even friends, who could not be deterred from their love of him by the sickening carnage of an ignominious execution.

The Official Testimony of the Clerk of Court, Zanji: Its Lacunae

The next evening, at nightfall, Muhammad-b-ʿAbd al-Samad made his way to Hamid's convocation with foot policemen and pack mules. At that time the vizir notified his guard to escort the commissioner on horseback right to the police headquarters (west bank); and he issued the order to the official in charge of Hallaj's guard to take him out of his dungeon and turn him over to M-b-ʿAbd al-Samad's escort. And this man told how, when he opened the gate for him and ordered him to leave, at a time when it was unusual for the gate to open, Hallaj asked him: "Who then is with the vizir?" "M-b-ʿAbd al-Samad" [was the reply. Hallaj said:] "O God, we are done for." Taken from prison, put on one of the pack mules, Hallaj was led away, jostled by grooms who ran alongside them (Ibn Dihya: "On the way the crowd formed into a mob; the commissioner, afraid of being killed [or: lest someone kill Hallaj] said: "this is not he, Hallaj; Hallaj is still in the *Dar al-Wazir*"); while the men of Hamid's (mounted) guard escorted him [the commissioner] on horseback as far as the bridge; then they went away. And Muhammad-b-ʿAbd al-Samad spent the night there, with his men stationed around the police headquarters.

And when morning came, on Tuesday, 24 *Dhu'l-Qaʿda* (309/922), the commissioner had Hallaj led out on the very esplanade of the police headquarters on the western end of the bridge of boats (fastened on the east bank opposite Bab al-Taq),

*From *Passion of al-Hallaj,* vol. 1, pp. 560, 569–73, 598–600, 605–7, 609–13, 628–31, and vol. 3, pp. 218–19

and ordered the executioner to scourge him. A large crowd formed whose numbers were considerable, countless. (Ibn Dihya: at the four hundredth lash from the whip, Hallaj cried out: "now Constantinople is taken," without anyone hearing him; at the six hundredth lash, he murmured: "here are two men in the Sultanian service with 200,000 dinars" without anyone paying attention to it; but it was feared he might die without undergoing the full prescribed punishment; and so the commissioner ordered the executioners to stop the flagellation, and the remainder of the thousand lashes were cancelled).—(N.B.: probable version: five hundred lashes = *darb al-mawt*; which is the figure used by Ibn Bakuya. But Zanji says: he was beaten a thousand times all told without crying out "enough"—or "ah." He said only, after the six hundredth blow, to M-b-'Abd al-Samad: "let me give you a piece of advice which is worth as much as the capture of Constantinople." But Muhammad answered him as follows: "I have already been warned that you would say that and much more, but there is no way to stop the blows you still have coming to you.")

Once the thousand lashes had been administered, they cut off one of his hands, then a foot; then the other hand, followed by the other foot (N.B.: he then had to be hoisted in full view, on a stake.) His head was cut off. (Ibn Farhun: then his body, in which there was still a trace of life, was hurled to the ground from the flagellation platform). And the trunk was burned (Watwat, *Ghurar* : wrapped in his mantle.—N.B.: or in a mat, which was customary and in accordance with Shibli's account.—"In oil—The cost of this cremation: nine dirhams.")

I was there, that very moment, motionless, on the back of my mule; the trunk twisted on the embers and the flames blazed forth (cf. 'Attar, *Mantiq*: "Then a foolish love-smitten man came forward, stick in hand; squatting near this handful of live coals, he began to speak glowing words to them while stirring them [with his stick]: tell the Truth . . ."). When there were only ashes left, they were thrown into the Tigris. The head was on display in Baghdad for two days, on the bridge, afterwards it was taken to Khurasan, where it was shown around from district to district.

This detailed account by an eyewitness directly involved in the incidents has some more or less unintentional omissions and even some deliberate misrepresentations. Why does Zanji insist that the thousand lashes were indeed administered, when two other independent sources deny it? Why does he say nothing about the time, perhaps two hours, perhaps twelve hours, elapsed between the intercision and the decapitation, when the punished victim had to be hoisted, in full view of everyone, according to the Qur'anic rule, onto a gibbet, which was more or less in the form of a cross? Why, since he admitted that he was present at the cremation to the very end, in his capacity as vizirial secretary, doesn't he say that he was there next to Vizir Hamid: who came in person to verify the execution of the condemned man, bearing witness with the "upright witnesses" scattered through the crowd to the lawfulness of this execution? It is not only the Sufi source of Tuzari that is explicit about it, but also the theological source of Ibn Dihya: "they cut off his hands, his feet, his head; they burned the body, they scattered it in the water (of the river); then they hoisted his head (on the end of a pike, before hanging it on a post), and the Muslims shouted 'Allah akbar' ('God is the greatest'), and recalled the warning of the Prophet of the Lord of the Worlds against antichrists and imposters; they acknowledged it to be true, according to his word: 'God will show that this word is true.' " Zanji specifies neither the place from which the ashes were thrown nor, above all, where the head was displayed. Now, the place where the ashes were thrown was still a pilgrimage site in the time of Ma'arri in 399/1008: "his disciples still waited there, on the banks of the Tigris, in the hope that he would arise from it," ghufran; one of them saw him there (Baqli) and later, according to the legend of the shaykhs of the Bata'ih (Rifa'i), of the holy Ahmad Kabir cited by the Mongol vizir, Rashid al-Din, and of his sister, who became pregnant there by swallowing his ashes (Yazidis).

It was customary to have next to the displayed head, pinned to its ear, a placard identifying it and bearing the following inscription: "This is the head of the blasphemous conniver and deceiver N-b-X, one of those whom God has put to death at the hands of Imam Y (= the Caliph), after proof was produced showing that he claimed the sovereignty of divine law; glory be to God, Who hastened him to shed his blood and to curse him."

Let us resume the account by Zanji:

> His disciples began to make preparations for his return after forty days. It just so happened that, in this particular year, the flooding of the Tigris (measured by the Miqyas, built in 293, copied from the Nilometer of Roda) was high (fadl: it measured eighteen cubits, according to Hamadhani) at the end of Hijja (end of April): his disciples claimed that this was due to him, because his ashes had mixed with the water.
>
> And one of Hallaj's disciples maintained that the one who had been executed was an enemy of Hallaj, changed to look like him (Ibn Sinan: just as in the case of Jesus, son of Mary). Some of them claimed that they had seen him the very next day (Ibn Sinan: on the same day) where they had seen him meet his end and his punishment, mounted on a donkey, going along the Nahrawan route; and, as they were welcoming him, he said to them: "Can it be that you are like those people who delude themselves into thinking that I am the one they scourged and put to death?" And one of them maintained that it was a mule that had been changed into his image.
>
> After the execution, Chamberlain Nasr went into mourning (taraththi) publicly, declaring that this man had been wronged (mazlum), that he was a true servant of God.
>
> And they (Ibn Sinan: Hamid) summoned the booksellers (warraqin) to appear in a group; and they promised neither to sell nor to buy any of Hallaj's books.

Can we ascertain the number of spectators at the execution? A "countless" number (Zanji). "This was a solemn day" (yawman 'aziman; cf. Qur'an 83:5), says Mas'udi, "on account of the ideas that were attributed to him concerning religion, *diyana*." "It was told that no one was present at this event who was not overtaken by some misfortune, *usiba*," says Ibn Fadlallah. "There was no one in Baghdad at that time who was not present at his execution" (*Manaqib*, quoted by AY Qazwini).

The Testimony of Ibn al-Haddad, Head of the Shuhud of Cairo, Concerning Hallaj's Last Vigil and "Spiritual Testament"

Isnad of AB ibn al-Haddad; Ibrahim ibn Fatik, according to Shakir:

When night fell on the place where he was to be taken, at dawn, from his cell, Hallaj stood up for the prayer and performed one that consisted of two *rak'a*. Then, when this prayer was finished, he continued to repeat himself, saying "illusion, illusion": until the night was almost over. Then, he was silent for a long time; and then he cried out "truth, truth." And he stood up again, put on his head veil and wrapped himself in his coat, stretched out his hands toward the *qibla* (= in the direction of Mecca) and entered into ecstatic prayer (*munaja*):

"We are here, we, Your witnesses (*shawahid*). We are seeking refuge in the (pre-eternal) splendor of Your glory, in order that You show (finally) what You wanted to fashion and achieve, O You who are God in heaven and God on earth.

"It is You Who shine forth when You desire; just as You shone forth (in the pre-eternal heaven, before the Angels and Satan) Your decree under "the most beautiful form" (= the human form, in Adam): the form in which the enunciating Spirit resides, present in it through knowledge and speech, free will and evidence [of being].

"You then bestowed on this present witness (= myself, Hallaj) Your "I," Your essential Ipseity.

"How is it that You, . . . You Who were present in self, after they had stripped me, Who used me "to proclaim Myself to me," revealing the truth of my knowledge and my miracles, going back in My ascensions to the Thrones of My pre-eternities to utter there the Word itself which creates me.

"(You now wish) me to be seized, imprisoned, judged, executed, hung on the gibbet, my ashes to be thrown to the sand storms which will scatter them, to the waves which will play with them.

"If only because their smallest particle (of my ashes), a grain of aloes (burned in this way to Your glory), assures to the glorious body (literally: "temple") of my transfigurations a more imposing foundation than that of immovable mountains."

Then he recited the following verses:

I weep to You for the Souls whose (present) witness (= I myself) now goes
—beyond the "where" to meet the very Witness of Eternity.
I cry to You for hearts so long refreshed (in vain)—by clouds of revelation,
which once filled up with seas of Wisdom;

I cry to You for the Word of God, which since it perished,—has faded into
  nothing in our memory;
I cry to You for the (inspired) Discourse before which ceases—all speaking by
  the eloquent and wise orator.
I cry to You for Signs that have been gathered up by intellects;—nothing at all
  remains of them (in books) except debris.
I cry to You, I swear it by Your love,—for the self-controls of those whose
  mastered mount was the discipline of silence;
All have crossed (the desert), leaving neither well nor trace behind;—vanished
  like the ʿAdites and their lost city of Iram;
And after them the abandoned crowd is muddled on their trails,—blinder than
  beasts, blinder even than she-camels.

The Waqfa *of the Offering and Forgiveness ("Kill Me . . .")*

Ibrahim-b-Fatik said:

When they brought Hallaj out to crucify him, and when he saw the gibbet and
the nails (*masamir*), he laughed so much that his eyes were weeping. Then he
turned to the crowd and recognized Shibli in it: "Abu Bakr, do you have your
prayer rug with you?" [Shibli said:] "Yes." [Hallaj said:] O Shaykh, spread it out
for me."

Shibli spread out his prayer rug: then Hallaj prayed two *rakʿa*: and I was near
him. In the first *rakʿa*, he recited the *Fatiha* and the verses (Qurʾan 2:155–157):
"Surely We will afflict you, when the occasion arises, with fear and hunger, and
losses of goods, of lives and of fruits. Give good tidings to the patient, who, when
they are struck with a misfortune, say: we belong to God and to Him we shall
return. It is upon them that blessings and mercy from their Lord descend, and
those—they are Rightly Guided."

In the second *rakʿa*, he recited the *Fatiha* and the verse (Qurʾan 3:182): "Every
soul shall taste of death, and you shall be paid your wages on the Day of Resurrection; whosoever is saved from Hell and admitted to Paradise shall be blissfully
happy: for what is the present life but the precarious enjoyment of vanities?" And
after he finished this *rakʿa*, his final *salam* and his *rukhsa*, he uttered a prayer
(*duʿaʾ*): I do not recall all of his words, but only some of them, among them these:
"O our God, it is You Who radiate on every side without being located on any
side: through the right of Your attestation (*bihaqqi qiyamika*) that affirms me;
through the right of my attestation that affirms You (and my attestation that affirms You is subordinate to Your attestation that affirms me, for mine comes from
nasut [human nature] and Yours comes from *lahut* [divine nature]; and yet, this is
what I have of *nasut*, which is lost in Your part of *lahut* without mingling with it,
and what Your *lahut* has possessed of my *nasut* without having touched it);—

through the right of Your Eternity ruling over my temporality: through the right of my temporality: clothed in the disguise of Your Eternity: I beseech You, O my Master, to grant me the grace to thank You (*an turziqani shukran*) for this joy that You have given me, to the point of concealing from everyone else's sight what You have revealed to me of the flames of Your countenance (which has no form), and of forbidding to any other the look that You have permitted me to cast on the hidden things of Your (personal) mystery.—See these people, Your worshippers: they have assembled to kill me, out of zeal for You, in order to draw nearer to You .... Forgive them (*irhamhum*).—If You had revealed to them what You have revealed to me, they would not do what they are doing, and if You had concealed from me what You have concealed from them, I would not be able to undergo the ordeal that I am enduring. Praise be to You in whatsoever You do, praise be to You in whatsoever You will." And he recited:

Kill me, O my faithful friends (*Uqtuluni, ya thiqati*),
for to kill me is to make me live;
My life is in my death, and my death is in my life.

Then he was silent and conversed with the Lord in silence. Then the executioner, Abu'l-Harith, approached and hit him in the face so hard that his nose was broken and blood flowed from it over his clothing (variant: his white hair).

And Shibli let out a cry, tore at his robe, and fainted, just as did Abu'l-Husayn Wasiti (= Qannad) and the group of well-known (*madhkurin*) *fuqara'* who were there. A riot failed to materialize, for many of his disciples set fire to houses while his execution was being carried out.

The Crucifixion, the Last Utterances, and the Coup de Grâce

IBN BAKUYA

The official sources (Zanji, Ibn Dihya) say nothing about the interval, during the execution, between the intercision and the decapitation, when, in accordance with Qur'anic law, the condemned man, maimed in his four limbs, but still alive, must be hoisted up, according to the formal rule of the Qur'an (Qur'an 26:49: confirming Qur'an 5:33) on a form of gibbet, not necessarily a raised post (*sari*), but a pillory (*niqniq*) overlooking the esplanade, fixed on a base (*mastaba*) with steps, so that the crowd and the official witnesses could see that justice was carried out. Before the *coup de grâce*.

The old Sufi sources are unanimous in affirming that "crucifixion" in which the condemned man was allowed even to utter some *ultima verba*; it is difficult, however, to distinguish which are authentic among those that have been handed down to us. Many are the fruit of a *post eventum* meditation, having undeniable "liturgical" value for anyone who reflects on them.

The synthetic account of Ibn Bakuya attributes to Hallaj, on the cross, two Qur'anic quotations, one "response," and two ecstatic sentences, and blocks together under a single *isnad* (that of Hamd) these five utterances that Sulami had previously collected with independent *isnads*: "my God, here I am now in the dwelling place of my desires . . ."; Qur'an 15:70: "have we not forbidden you from receiving any Guest . . ." (Shibli reprimands Hallaj, who is silent, for this verse is "his"); "what is *Sufism* (asks Shibli)?"—"Its lowest degree you are seeing now, . . . and tomorrow you will see . . ."; "everything for the ecstatic is to be alone with his Only One, in Himself; Qur'an 42:18: "Those who do not believe in the final Hour seek to hasten it; but those who believe in it await it. . . ."

The Last Utterances

1. Here I am now in the dwelling place of my desires . . ." (Sulami)

Abu Ishaq Ibrahim-b-M Qalanisi Razi said to M-b-Husayn Warraq: "when Husayn-b-Mansur was crucified, I was standing before the post, and he cried out 'O my God, here I am now in the dwelling place of my desires (*Ragha'ib*), and my gaze is surprised by Your marvels. My God, I see You show Your love specifically to those who wrong You (*yudhika*); how therefore does it happen that You do not show Your love to the one (this one = myself) to whom injustice is done in You (*yudha fika*)?'"

2. "What is Sufism?—Its lowest degree you are seeing now . . . ," taken from Khargushi.

Hallaj was asked on the cross: "What is Sufism?" [He answered:] "Its lowest degree you are seeing now."

This independent testimony by a great, good, and widely cultivated man, shows that, seventy years after the event, people characterized him just as in this response. Directed to Shibli, according to the synthetic account, studied above, and used again, by Ibn Bakuya. We have seen that [the latter account] is somewhat longer and adds this: "(Shibli asks further:) and its highest degree?" [Hallaj responds] "You cannot (yet) reach it; however, tomorrow you will see (what will happen). For I witness it in divine mystery (*Ghayb*), where it exists; and where it remains hidden to you."

We have here a case of a "response" that was probably not actually given, but which expresses what Shibli must have felt, assuming it is true that he remained "until evening" before the gibbet of his friend, and what he communicated very quietly to his closest disciples as an initiation: the goal of mysticism is to be beheaded and burned "tomorrow" by the Law out of love of God.

This is what 'Abd al-Malik Iskaf in Balkh and the Turkish Qastamunian *Hikaya* were to repeat.

One Sufi tradition which was later, but which was already known by the historian Hamadhani (d. [513/1119]), reproduced by Baqli and Jildaki, gives to the question "what is Sufism?" a different answer, preceded, which is strange, by lines of verse from Khali' (the author of the *Nadimi* quatrain, also put in the mouth of Hallaj):

Then Shibli arrived, in the midst of a group: someone had put his sash around his neck and was pulling him toward Husayn-b-Mansur Hallaj for him to curse him also. He said to them: "let me go." [They said:] "We shall not release you until you curse him (on the cross) or send a messenger with your curse." He looked both right and left, and saw Fatima Naysaburiya: "come here to me." She approached him, and he said to her: "Go find Husayn-b-Mansur: tell him: 'God gave you access to one of His secrets, but because you made it public, He has made you taste the blade.' Remember what he says to you in response, then ask him, *what is Sufism?*" he said, and she went to him and said: "I am the messenger of Abu Bakr Shibli." [He said:] "Give me your message." [She said:] "He tells you: God gave you access to one of His secrets, but because you have made it public, He has made you taste the blade." But he recited: (*Tajasartu . . .*):

I was rash, I revealed Your Name, yes, when my patience was exhausted;
What is more beautiful in regard to the likes of You than to remove [Your] veils?
If I am criticized for doing it, my excuse is in Your face, for the full moon is poor next to Your face, O full Moon.

Then he said: "go and find Shibli and tell him: by God, I did not divulge His secret; and if it had happened as he said, then the best thing would be to speak of the tribulations (*mihan*) of the prophets, that they were designed to punish them." Then she said: "O master, what is Sufism?" [He answered:] "That in which I am (*ma ana fihi*); by God, I have never been able to dissociate for a moment its good fortune from its bad (*ma faraqtu bayna ni'matihi wa bala'ihi sa'atan qatt*)."

Another Sufi tradition puts the question "What is Sufism?" in the mouth of another of Shibli's messengers, his disciple Bundar-b-Husayn Shirazi, which is strange: for Bundar, one of the early Ash'arite theologians, was later obliged to force Ibn Khafif, who had also become an Ash'arite, to repudiate Hallaj. This is the text, abridged:

Ibn Khafif (*sic*), after a fortnight, was present, calm and collected, at the intercision of Hallaj; afterwards, on the gibbet, when questioned by Bundar, Hallaj, looking at him sternly, answered: "the beginning (*ibtida'ahu*) (of Sufism) you are seeing here; its end you will see tomorrow." Of which Shibli commented: "Husayn-b-Mansur is right: Sufism is spiritual sacrifice; pay no attention to the 'follies' of mystics."

Another Sufi account, after giving Hallaj's statements to Caliph Muqtadir, the condemnation by the canonists, the flagellation (with a thorny *sidra*), the prayer for deliverance *"Ya Mu'in,"* presents Shibli sending a woman (*jariya*: not named) to ask the question, "what is Sufism?" and also to ask Hallaj why he revealed the arcanum; after a long dialogue, Shibli comes and repeats the question himself: Hallaj responds, "its exterior (*zahiruhu*) is what you see; its interior remains hidden to men; its beginning is today (*awwaluhu*), its end will be tomorrow."

Abu Bakr (M-b-M) ibn Thawaba said: "I saw my brother Zayd al-Qasri writing down verses uttered by Hy-b-Mansur Hallaj on the gibbet:

> Through the sacred holiness of this Love which the world
> cannot lust after to corrupt
> I have felt no harm since suffering came upon me, nor
> has it caused me any injury;
> No limb, no joint of mine has been cut off which has not
> made you remember (God).

3. "Have we not forbidden you from receiving any Guest . . . ?" (AH 'Ali-b-Ibrahim Basri Husri) said:

> Shibli came and stood before the gibbet from which Husayn-b-Mansur (looked at him) and cried out to him: "Have we not forbidden you from receiving any Guest, whether man or angel?" (Qur'an 15:70). About which the qadi (= Abu 'Umar), who had arranged this crucifixion to be carried out, declared (to Shibli, who was brought before him): "That one had pretended to be a prophet, and now this one pretends to be God?" Shibli retorted: "I said the same thing he did, but my madness was certified, and his sanity killed him."

(Sulami):

> Mansur 'Abdallah (Sadusi Harawi) said: "I heard one of our friends say: 'Shibli came and stood before the crucified Hallaj, looked at him and said: "Have we not forbidden you from receiving any Guest, whether man or angel?"'

This is the famous verse in which the people of Sodom accuse Lot of treason against the Perfect City, in which human nature is self-sufficient with respect to the racist secret of its original identity: how dare you transgress the order of the arcanum by giving, you our host, hospitality to Angels, messengers from a threatening foreigner?

Shibli's application of it to Hallaj is ambivalent: did he really betray his Sufi brothers by giving himself over to a public apostolate of mysticism, in opposition to the rule, held to by Islam, of not throwing pearls to swine? One piece from Hallaj's *Diwan*, revealing a truly sarcastic irony with regard to the discipline of the Sufis' arcanum, shows that in this he was following the advice of Hasan Basri, prophesizing to those who do not want to be delivered of what they have conceived to be good, that their womb will burst open. Shibli, who was living the Qur'an profoundly, utters this verse as a challenge. Has the time for divulging the secret come, since you may dare transgress the Law, so that it may execute you for having sworn that you received God Himself as your Guest? Do you intend to save Sodom this way, and, with it all those human societies that wish to abuse the Angels of God, your guests?

One will note that Hallaj is silent: for "at sunrise, the 'Clamor for Justice (*al-Sayha*) surprised them';" his cry, uttered by the Angels, overthrew, says the Qur'an (15:73), the accursed City.

Indeed, Shibli knows in his conscience that Qur'an 15:73 answers Qur'an 15:70. But insofar as the Hour has not yet come to pass, he approves of the Law's forbidding (*yumna'*, he says at the trial = here, *nanhaka*) any premature apocalyptic divulgence.

Our interpretation is confirmed by Shibli's legendary gesture of throwing a rose at Hallaj, whom the crowd was stoning; to throw a rose is an act of challenge.

4. "All that matters to the ecstatic is the increasing solitude of his Only One, in Himself."

'Isa Qassar Dinawari said: "I was present when they took Husayn-b-Mansur from prison to kill him; his last words were: 'All that matters to the ecstatic is the increasing solitude of his Only One, in Himself.' " He added among the shaykhs of Baghdad at that time there was not one who did not admire these words uttered by him.

5. Qur'an 42:18: "Those who do not believe in the Hour seek to hasten it; but those who believe await it with a reverential fear, for they know that is the Truth." (Sulami: "he said nothing more after that.")

The Public Grief of Grand Chamberlain Nasr and Its Effect

It was Zanji, a member of the vizir's secretariat, who noted the public mourning (*azhara'l-taraththi*) for Hallaj, "unjustly put to death" (*mazluman*). He did not add *talafan*, unavenged. Nasr, by this show of grief, worked out in accordance with the Queen Mother, at least on behalf of the military House of Nasr, merely asserted his Belief that Hallaj had died a Muslim and not a turncoat.

This public mourning led to several events:

—*public recitation of the Qur'an* at the home of Nasr for the repose of the soul of Hallaj, given by renowned *Qurra'* (such as AB M-b-J-Adami, b. 250/864, d. 348/959) with the authorization and attendance of Hanbalite jurisconsults (from Nasr's school), with visits of condolence, on the first three days, the first Friday (27 *Qa'da* or rather 5 *Hijja*), and the fortieth day (= 3 *Muharram* 310/923);

—*distribution of alms* in the prison shelter that Nasr had prepared for Hallaj, particularly to the prisoners, repentant bandits *'Ayyarin Tawwabin*, whom Nasr had placed at that time in Hallaj's spiritual care;

—*recovery of relics*, in the absence of burned parts (the trunk and clothes?)

or preserved parts (the head, kept for a year in the Museum of Heads) of the body, hands, and feet (?); for the purpose of burying them secretly in the fixed site referred to as "*maslib al-Hallaj*" and revealed publicly by the Court in 437/1045 (near the *waqf*-supported tomb of Gharib, the brother of the Queen Mother; a *waqf* supervised, I believe, by the *shahid* Da'laj). In fact, legend tells of a mantle (*khirqa*) belonging to Hallaj which was "entrusted by" Nasr to ward off floods. And that implies that he was already venerated as a martyr;

—the *release from prison* of Hallaj's son and daughter, his *khadim*, and most of his imprisoned disciples (a release authorized for M-b-A Qunna'i, AB Hashimi: for the daughter, who was to marry a Sunnite, the son of Shaykh Ibn Shaluya [= Salbin?]; for his widow and his sister, who were permitted to go into mourning [dark blue clothes, bare feet, as the story goes]). Nasr thus managed to get the vizir to exempt the Hallajiya from the statute on "turncoats," which would involve the death sentence: a statute that was to be issued only around 361/971 (Baqillani; Al Isfara'ini; particularly against Faris, and the Hululiya). It appears that Vizir Hamid made this concession to Nasr out of fear (cf. his shifting of his responsibility onto the *shuhud*; hence the delay in the *coup de grâce?*), or out of remorse for having yielded to his Shi'ite adviser Shalmaghani, who was soon to let him be persecuted and killed by Muhassin.

The simultaneous participation of the officers of Nasr's military House and the repentant bandits of the prison in this mourning demonstration against the legal execution of an excommunicate got Nasr more involved in organizing an anti-Shi'ite clandestine resistance movement made up of militant Turks and Kurds on whom Caliph Qadir, and especially Caliph Qayim, would count for shaking off the political and financial tutelage of the Buwayhids; in cooperation with the Hanbalites, whose demonstrations Nasr had encouraged as far back as 309/921. It was at Nasr's home that his son Ahmad was to shelter and to arrange the burial of Barbahari, the leader of the Hanbalites who was ostracized and banished, and to assemble the Barbahariya Hanbalite traditionists who would supervise, after the pro-Hallajian Murta'ish, the Sufi convents of Shuniz, defending them against the Buwayhid Shi'ite sultanate.

It was as a result of Nasr's gesture of mourning that the devotion of the 'Ayyarin Tawwabin (and of the Hanbalite women) for Hallaj resumed.

The Intersigns, Dreams, and Apparitions

Hallaj, perhaps more than any of his predecessors, had been deeply involved during the course of his travels in the life of the Muslim Community. Though Islam was intensely "stirred up" already by the dynamic, centralizing, and unifying ritual of the hajj to Mecca, Hallaj, the eternal pilgrim, committed himself intimately to that stirring.

While taking part in the elitist intellectual quest for technical terms enabling him to formulate a spiritual orthodoxy, he had kept "in touch" with the passerby, *ibn al-sabil*, among craftsmen or workers daily crossing the frontier, with the man in the street and on the highway, with nomad and soldier, shopkeeper and peasant. It was particularly there, in dialectal folklore and popular melodies, that his memory persisted; whereas the scholiasts of classicism and scholasticism increasingly were to pass over him in silence, as was the usual way of treating an excommunicate.

We recall a man after his death, first of all, by intersigns. Which is to say, by unusual and unforeseen events of his life whose imprint we rediscover in ourselves through "correspondence." These "correspondences" are not rational normalizations that reduce individual existences to fortuitous series of analogous and impersonal components: they are shared anomalies. And instead of depicting individual lives as an infinity of segments of parallel straight lines, of commonplace probabilities computable by statistics, the philosophy of history must arrange them inwardly in curves, marking the nodes of realization, the "points of osculation": through which they "communicate" where souls recognize each other outside the dimensions of time. At first psychological analysis had a difficult time establishing the authenticity of social "communication" through such intersigns. The infrarational musicality of signs begins, in Hallaj's life, with coincidences in vocabulary, valueless as long as the scope of his spiritual life, his "consonance" with the traditional archetypal themes of Islam, did not arouse the instinctive sympathy of the humble and of the "enlightened" sarcasm of the learned. On his part, the imagination "works" in its way and *dreams* loom into view, suggesting a finalistic explanation of observed *intersigns*. The right to dream exists in Islam; and oneirocriticism is practiced with regard to it by experts, sometimes Hanbalite and sometimes Shi'ite, to determine the validity of the "responses" obtained by dreams that are "guided" during sleep.

Islam forbids one to dream about the Prophet when one is *awake*; but other ordinary *apparitions*, of those absent or dead, are allowed. And it is not impossible for the shapes momentarily assumed by these apparitions to embody authentic significations related personally (and even exclusively) to us: be they imaginary projections or preternatural "opalizations" of the surrounding atmosphere.

The torrent of signs, dreams, and apparitions observed at the time of Hallaj's death gives the impression that the working of the Muslims' collective imagination had come to a halt on his person; it fixed a "time-origin," an *epochè* permitting a recapitulative remembrance by introversion and consideration of the interdependence of the destinies of other Muslims with his own.

One could quote various passages by 'Izz al-Din Maqdisi and Jalal al-Din Rumi. We will merely give here, *in extenso*, a very beautiful chapter of the *Mirsad al-'ibad* by Najm al-Din Razi (d. 654/1256), where Hallaj's voluntary sacrifice is examined with penetration: Book III, chapter XX:

To unite with the divine presence, without becoming absorbed in it or separated from it:

The being of the sincere lover produces a scent of fire, so that the entire human tree, outwardly flesh, but (spiritual) kingdom of God inside, burns and blazes. Then the fire makes all the parts of the being of this tree luminous, the entire being of the tree becomes an incandescent fire, so that all that was tree is now a fire of live coals. It is here that the true mystical union is accomplished.

Along with the green wood, Satan also becomes the prey of the essential fire, which draws fire from green wood for you;—God, who "gives you fire from green wood" (Qur'an 36:80), who cries, "it is I who am the fire, not the tree, without the tree's knowing it." The cry went up from the banks of the right hand wadi, in the blessed valley, from the tree "Oh Moses, it is I, God . . ." (Qur'an 28:30).

Poor Husayn Mansur! While the divine fire smouldered under the tree of his being, without yet consuming his members, "I am the Truth!" sparks flew out of it. As other men (immoral men, his enemies) were standing nearby, Husayn, who was ablaze with the very clemency of the All-Powerful, asked for their salvation by means of these "I am the Truth!" sparks, and thus made himself their intercessor. For you must know that this fire is such that both he who is in it and he who is near to it are equally blessed by it. "Blessed is the man who is in the fire and he who is in the vicinity of it" (Qur'an 27:8). Oh Husayn! this fire in you is blessed! As for those who are near to you, it does not need to burn them, it will be a benediction for them as well:

For my friend, I am benediction, and for my enemy also.

. . . In fact, not only did Husayn Mansur sacrifice himself, but putting himself ahead of malicious men, he attempted to obtain their pardon and placed his physical being in the fire, between them and the fire, saying, "Oh my God! Since You have consumed my humanity in Your divinity, by the right of my humanity over Your divinity, I ask You to have mercy on these men who have conspired to have me killed."

Certainly it is not in every tree of the human condition that the fire of sacrifice comes to set ablaze such aloes, which rise into the air in this way, perfumed with mercy, asking to be a benediction for those men also.

Oh, Husayn! when this fire of Our love was ignited in your human tree and when "I am the Truth!" sparks flew forth from it, since your personality was not consumed, these sparks diffused some of its smoke. But when you became the prey of the fire in the entire tree of your being, and when the form of your mold, the smoke of your self rose up from it and disappeared, when the ashes of your body were burned by the fire of Our grief,—We commanded that they be thrown into the waters of the Tigris, and We then raised the pierced veil that hid the beauty of your perfection. Upon the surface of the water the smokeless fire of your being wrote for all to see "God! God!". . .

MYTHOS: The Princeton/Bollingen Series in World Mythology

J. J. Bachofen / MYTH, RELIGION, AND MOTHER RIGHT

George Boas, trans. / THE HIEROGLYPHICS OF HORAPOLLO

Anthony Bonner, ed. / DOCTOR ILLUMINATUS: A RAMON LLULL READER

Jan Bremmer / THE EARLY GREEK CONCEPT OF THE SOUL

Joseph Campbell / THE HERO WITH A THOUSAND FACES

Henry Corbin / AVICENNA AND THE VISIONARY RECITAL

F. M. Cornford / FROM RELIGION TO PHILOSOPHY

Marcel Detienne / THE GARDENS OF ADONIS: SPICES IN GREEK MYTHOLOGY

Mircea Eliade / IMAGES AND SYMBOLS

Mircea Eliade / THE MYTH OF THE ETERNAL RETURN

Mircea Eliade / SHAMANISM: ARCHAIC TECHNIQUES OF ECSTASY

Mircea Eliade / YOGA: IMMORTALITY AND FREEDOM

Garth Fowden / THE EGYPTIAN HERMES

Erwin R. Goodenough (Jacob Neusner, ed.) / JEWISH SYMBOLS IN THE
    GRECO-ROMAN PERIOD

W.K.C. Guthrie / ORPHEUS AND GREEK RELIGION

Jane Ellen Harrison / PROLEGOMENA TO THE STUDY OF GREEK RELIGION

Joseph Henderson & Maud Oakes / THE WISDOM OF THE SERPENT

Erik Iversen / THE MYTH OF EGYPT AND ITS HIEROGLYPHS IN EUROPEAN
    TRADITION

C. G. Jung & Carl Kerényi / ESSAYS ON A SCIENCE OF MYTHOLOGY

Carl Kerényi / ELEUSIS: ARCHETYPAL IMAGE OF MOTHER AND DAUGHTER

Stella Kramrisch / THE PRESENCE OF ŚIVA

Roger S. Loomis / THE GRAIL: FROM CELTIC MYTH TO CHRISTIAN SYMBOL

Bronislaw Malinowski (Ivan Strenski, ed.) / MALINOWSKI AND THE WORK OF MYTH

Louis Massignon (Herbert Mason, ed.) / THE PASSION OF AL-HALLAJ: MYSTIC AND
    MARTYR OF ISLAM

Erich Neumann/ AMOR AND PSYCHE

Erich Neumann / THE GREAT MOTHER

Richard Noll, ed. / MYSTERIA: JUNG AND THE ANCIENT MYSTERIES

Maud Oakes with Joseph Campbell /WHERE THE TWO CAME TO THEIR FATHER

Dora & Erwin Panofsky / PANDORA'S BOX

Paul Radin / THE ROAD OF LIFE AND DEATH

Otto Rank, Lord Raglan, Alan Dundes / IN QUEST OF THE HERO

Gladys Reichard / NAVAHO RELIGION

Géza Róheim (Alan Dundes, ed.) / FIRE IN THE DRAGON

Robert A. Segal, ed. / THE GNOSTIC JUNG

Philip E. Slater / THE GLORY OF HERA

Jean-Pierre Vernant (Froma I. Zeitlin, ed.) / MORTALS AND IMMORTALS

Jessie L. Weston / FROM RITUAL TO ROMANCE

Heinrich Zimmer (Joseph Campbell, ed.) / THE KING AND THE CORPSE: TALES OF THE
SOUL'S CONQUEST OF EVIL

Heinrich Zimmer (Joseph Campbell, ed.) / MYTHS AND SYMBOLS IN INDIAN ART
AND CIVILIZATION